An Introduction to Tivoli's TME 10

ROLF LENDENMANN ■ JENNIFER NELSON ■ CARLOS P. LARA ■ JANET SELBY

PRENTICE HALL PTR, UPPER SADDLE RIVER, NEW JERSEY 07458

Published by

Prentice Hall PTR
Prentice-Hall, Inc.
A Simon & Schuster Company
Upper Saddle River, NJ 07458

Editorial/Production Supervision: James D. Gwyn

Acquisitions Editor: Michael M. Meehan

Editorial Assistant: Barbara Alfieri

Manufacturing Manager: Alexis R. Heydt

Marketing Manager: Stephen Solomon

Cover Design Director: Jayne Conte

Cover Designer: Anthony Gemmellaro

Prentice Hall books are widely used by corporations and government agencies for training, marketing, and resale.

The publisher offers discounts on this book when ordered in bulk quantities. For more information, contact: Corporate Sales Department, Phone: 800-382-3419; FAX: 201-236-7141; E-mail (Internet): corpsales@prenhall.com; or write: Prentice Hall PTR, Corp. Sales Dept., One Lake Street, Upper Saddle River, NJ 07458.

Printed in the United States of America

10 9 8 7 6 5 4 3 2

ISBN 0-13-889717-9

Prentice-Hall International (UK) Limited, *London*

Prentice-Hall of Australia Pty. Limited, *Sydney*

Prentice-Hall Canada Inc., *Toronto*

Prentice-Hall Hispanoamericana, S.A., *Mexico*

Prentice-Hall of India Private Limited, *New Delhi*

Prentice-Hall of Japan, Inc., *Tokyo*

Simon & Schuster Asia Pte. Ltd., *Singapore*

Editora Prentice-Hall do Brasil, Ltda., *Rio de Janeiro*

Contents

Figures

Tables

Foreword

In 1989, when "client/server" was a still a new buzzword, Tivoli's founders looked far into the future. They correctly foresaw that the typical large organization would want to combine all its computers, databases, and business applications into a single, integrated environment—a network computing environment.

They also foresaw that the cost and complexity of systems and network management would be a major barrier to network computing. Existing management solutions couldn't be integrated to support network computing because each of these solutions was developed to solve one kind of problem on one computing platform. Customers would have to use multiple management solutions and employ multiple teams with multiple skills. This fragmented approach would create costly islands of management.

To overcome cost and complexity, customers would require a single network computing management solution—an integrated solution that could manage all the systems, databases, and applications in a network as well as the network itself. But it was unlikely that any single vendor could provide such a comprehensive solution.

So Tivoli saw a tremendous opportunity: Create an open, object-oriented, flexible, scalable management framework and build an entirely new industry around it—an industry based on standards and cooperation.

During the next eight years, Tivoli relentlessly pursued this opportunity. Working closely with our partners, we developed and refined TME 10—the first and only software specifically designed for seamlessly managing an entire enterprise from desktop to data center. TME 10 truly is the network computing management solution.

TME 10 can manage an entire network computing environment, regardless of its mix of platforms: MVS, UNIX, Solaris, AIX, OS/2, Microsoft Windows NT, Windows 95, Lotus Notes, and Internet and intranet platforms. TME 10 can do all this because it's based on a scalable, open, cross-platform architecture:

- Scalable: As your enterprise grows, you can manage any number of systems—even tens of thousands of systems—from a single, logical view. The object-oriented TME 10 Framework makes Tivoli solutions massively scalable.

- Open: You can choose best-of-breed solutions from more than 350 Tivoli partners. Our close collaboration with our partners creates an unprecedented level of integration, enabling partners' solutions to plug into TME 10. You can deploy these third-party solutions with confidence.
- Cross-platform: You can manage your mission-critical, cross-platform applications from a single, logical view. The TME 10 Framework hides the cross-platform differences. You don't need multiple teams with multiple skills.

These unique capabilities of TME 10's architecture deliver substantial benefits. In terms of the benefits most often mentioned by customers, TME 10 enables you to:

- Substantially improve the availability, reliability, security, integrity, and scalability of your network computing environment.
- Automate all your systems management activities: deployment, availability, security, and operations and administration.
- Drastically reduce the time required to bring new network computing solutions on-line.

Today, hundreds of organizations are enjoying these benefits. Tivoli customers are some of the world's leading companies in financial services, telecommunications, transportation, manufacturing, electronics and computers, healthcare, retail, the service industries, and the utilities business.

You're in good company. On behalf of Tivoli and our partners, I welcome you to TME 10, the first true network computing management solution.

Best regards,

Frank Moss

President and Chief Executive Officer
Tivoli Systems Inc.

Preface

Consistent and centralized management of distributed systems of different brands and architectures is crucial to large customer environments. Tivoli's TME 10, which stands for Tivoli Management Environment, is a suite of distributed systems management (DSM) products that has been gaining a lot of attention within International Business Machines (IBM®) and among customers since the merger between IBM and Tivoli.

If you are an IS manager, a system administrator, or anyone who wonders what Tivoli's TME 10 is and does, read this book to quickly get an understanding of its concepts, functions, and features. As a system administrator, you will get invaluable help to get started quickly when you follow the hands-on tutorial in Part 2 of the book.

The first part of this book presents a high-level technical overview of the concepts and architecture of the TME 10 core components, notably:

- TME 10 Framework (object oriented, CORBA-based framework)
- TME 10 User Administration (user and UNIX® host management)
- TME 10 Software Distribution (software distribution)
- TME 10 Inventory (inventory management)
- TME 10 Distributed Monitoring (monitoring of computing resources)
- TME 10 Enterprise Console (monitoring and managing resources)

Part 2 walks step-by-step through the installation for all of the above products on different platforms, such as UNIX, Windows NT, Windows 95, Windows 3.1, and OS/2®. Some practical hands-on examples are added to familiarize readers with the way the basic functions work and to deepen their understanding of the concepts explained in Part 1.

How This Redbook Is Organized

This redbook is divided into two major parts. The first discusses concepts and features of one of the TME 10 core components, and the second provides hands-on examples.

Part 1

Each chapter in Part 1 describes, in a high-level, technical manner, the concepts and architecture of the TME 10 core components. It is organized as follows:

- Chapter 1, "TME 10 Environment" on page 3

  This introductory chapter talks about the Tivoli/IBM merger and the roadmap for their streamlined common product set. It also describes some common concepts of operation for the TME 10 products covered in this book.

- Chapter 2, "TME 10 Framework" on page 15

  The TME 10 Framework is the distributed, object-oriented framework providing some core TME 10 capabilities and services that are needed by other TME 10 applications. This chapter also provides the GUI, which lets the administrator view the environment.

- Chapter 3, "TME 10 User Administration" on page 47

  TME 10 User Administration allows you to manage user accounts on the UNIX, Windows NT, and NetWare platforms from a single location. It also provides UNIX host management functions.

- Chapter 4, "TME 10 Software Distribution" on page 85

  TME 10 Software Distribution provides a simple, centralized point of control for software distribution across distributed and heterogenous environments.

- Chapter 5, "TME 10 Inventory" on page 111

  TME 10 Inventory keeps track of the hardware and software installed on each machine. It provides a means to centrally gather the information from each system in the environment.

- Chapter 6, "TME 10 Distributed Monitoring" on page 129

  TME 10 Distributed Monitoring is an application that allows you to monitor the status of a wide range of geographically dispersed hardware from different vendors running different operating systems, including resources that are not part of your TME 10 Framework.

- Chapter 7, "TME 10 Enterprise Console" on page 163

  TME 10 Enterprise Console is a management system for the enterprise that provides a simple, centralized point of control and a homogeneous approach to managing complex, distributed and heterogeneous environments.

Part 2

Step-by-step installation instructions and practical examples are given in each chapter of Part 2. It is organized as follows:

- Chapter 8, "Installing and Using the TME 10 Framework" on page 203

  After installation instructions for a TME 10 Management Region server, managed nodes and PC managed nodes, this chapter discusses creating policy regions, administrators, and profile managers, as well as using the bulletin board and creating automated tasks.

- Chapter 9, "Installing and Using TME 10 User Administration" on page 247

  This chapter describes how to create, populate, edit and distribute user, group and namespace profiles. It also shows the usage of the UNIX host management functions.

- Chapter 10, "Installing and Using TME 10 Software Distribution" on page 269

  This chapter walks you through a simple software distribution scenario.

- Chapter 11, "Installing and Using TME 10 Inventory" on page 283

  Besides installation instructions for TME 10 Inventory and the Oracle database, this chapter shows you how to run inventory scans and how to use queries to select subscribers for profile distribution.

- Chapter 12, "Installing and Using TME 10 Distributed Monitoring" on page 303

  This chapter discusses how to create monitors that keep track of the state of some system resources and report problems in various forms. Indicator collections are created to provide the administrator with visual evidence of the presence of problems.

- Chapter 13, "Installing and Using TME 10 Enterprise Console" on page 323

  After showing how an enterprise console is created for an administrator, we generate some events and discuss how the administrator can take care of the problems that are reported in the form of events. We also walk through the creation of rules that are used to automate event processing.

The Team That Wrote This Redbook

This redbook was produced by a team of specialists from around the world working at the International Technical Support Organization (ITSO), Austin Center.

Rolf Lendenmann is an Advisory Systems Engineer at the International Technical Support Organization, Austin Center. He writes extensively on Distributed Computing Environment (DCE) and the Tivoli system management products. Before joining the ITSO three years ago, Rolf worked for nine years in the AIX Technical Support Center in Zurich, Switzerland, as a product specialist and consultant supporting all areas of AIX systems management, networking (TCP/IP, SNA), and middleware (DCE).

Jennifer Nelson has six years of industry experience in the areas of UNIX and networking. She holds a Bachelor of Science degree from the University of Illinois at Urbana-Champaign. She is currently working for IBM's AIX Support Family as a software analyst with the NetView for AIX customer support team in Roanoke, Texas.

Carlos Patino Lara is a Systems Engineer in charge of the Systems Management area in Grupo PISSA (Profesionales en Informatica y Soluciones S.A. de C.V). Grupo PISSA is a business partner of IBM Mexico. Carlos has six years of experience in the open systems field. His areas of expertise include UNIX system administration on different platforms (AIX, HP-UX, Solaris, and UNICOS) and performance evaluation.

Janet Selby is an Advisory Systems Engineer with IBM in Toronto, Canada. She has 10 years of experience in the systems and network management arena. She has worked with IBM for six years. Her expertise has been in network and systems management on the MVS platform. She is currently involved in providing Tivoli services to her Canadian customers.

Thanks to the following people for their invaluable contributions:

Guy Oliver	Tivoli Systems
Sally Derrick	Tivoli Systems
Billy Gee	Tivoli Systems
Walt Giroir	Tivoli Systems
Karla Griffin	Tivoli Systems
Amy Heaslip	Tivoli Systems
Dan Martillotti	Tivoli Systems
Bill Smith	Tivoli Systems
Marcus Brewer	IBM ITSO, Austin Center
Rebeca Rodriguez	IBM ITSO, Austin Center

Comments Welcome

We want our redbooks to be as helpful as possible. Should you have any comments about this or other redbooks, please send us a note at the following address:

redbook@vnet.ibm.com

Your comments are important to us!

Part 1

Concepts and Architecture

CHAPTER 1

- 1.1 TME 10 Product Architecture
- 1.2 The Tivoli-IBM Merger and Product Roadmap
- 1.3 TME 10 Disciplines and Products
- 1.4 TME 10 Components Covered in This Book
- 1.5 Layout of the TME 10 Environment
- 1.6 Common Concepts of Operation

TME 10 Environment

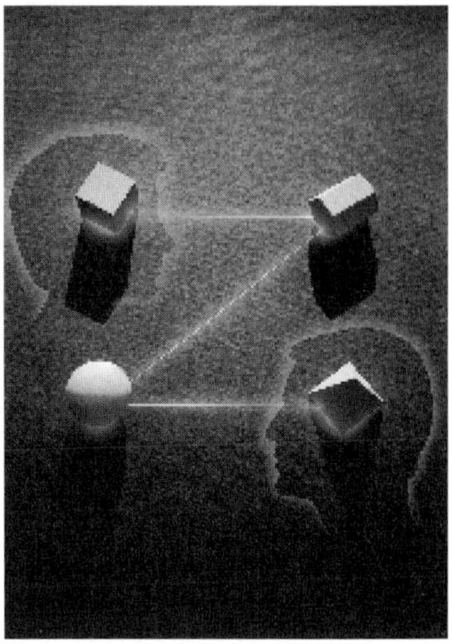

Today's computing environment relies more and more on distributed client/server setups for information system needs, where users at the client workstations perceive the network as one big server or service provider. Distributed computing or network computing ties people, information, and resources more closely together, but brings a challenge when considering the management of these systems. Managers face the complex problem of maintaining many different types of hardware and operating systems.

Tivoli Systems' answer to managing a network computing environment is a set of management applications known collectively as TME 10, where TME stands for Tivoli Management Environment. TME 10 provides a way to manage network computing resources of many different types from a single point. TME 10 products provide a consistent interface to different operating systems and services. TME 10 allows administrators to control users, systems, and applications from one desktop and provides a streamlined way to automate and delegate routine, time-consuming tasks.

1.1 TME 10 Product Architecture

The TME 10 applications all share a common framework, called the TME 10 Framework. The TME 10 Framework is open and object-oriented and includes a set of managers, brokers, and agents that conform with the Common Object Request Broker Architecture (CORBA) specifications produced by the Object Management Group (OMG). This technology allows major differences between computer operating systems to be hidden from the TME 10 user and allows the encapsulation of key services in objects that can be used by multiple management applications. Basically, it allows for platform-independence, a unifying architecture, and the ability of third-party vendors to easily adapt to the TME 10 Framework.

1.2 The Tivoli-IBM Merger and Product Roadmap

Tivoli Systems, Inc. was founded in Austin, Texas in 1989. The TME 10 product line was developed and had become a leader in distributed systems management when the company was merged with IBM in March of 1996. The Tivoli Systems name has remained, and it has become an independent business unit of IBM.

Before the merger, IBM had its own systems management product line known as SystemView. Tivoli's products were known collectively as TME 3.0. The merger allows the best of both product lines to be combined into one offering called TME 10. Many products were or will be merged and supported as a single application. The combined offering keeps the TME name due to the fact that the products will continue to be built around the object-oriented TME 10 Framework.

1.2.1 TME 10 Roll-Out Plans

The change from the independent product lines of TME 3.0 and SystemView to TME 10 is happening in three phases. A brief description follows:

- Phase One: Product Consolidation – Involves the repackaging of products from TME and SystemView. For example, the former Tivoli/Courier and IBM NetView®/Distribution Manager products both perform software distribution functions. An orderable product called TME 10 Software Distribution contains both of these individual products. This step was taken to help eliminate confusion on which products customers should order.
- Phase Two: Application Integration – Involves integrating the applications for each functional area. To continue our example above, Tivoli/Courier provides the core functions for TME 10 Software Distribution that will be extended with a module to allow functions that NetView/DM possesses but Courier does not, like Multiple Virtual Storage (MVS) support.
- Phase Three: Framework Integration – Involves migrating all of the services to the TME 10 Framework. For our example, this would involve releasing a new interface that includes MVS capabilities built into the TME 10 Framework.

IBM SystemView® products that are specific to certain machines or operating systems will be treated as third-party products. Their functions will remain, and modules will be added to incorporate them into the TME 10 desktop.

For detailed information about plans for each of the products and product areas, consult the *TME 10 Product Roadmap*. This document was written after the merger to lay out details of the products that will be merged and time frames associated with these plans. It can be accessed from Tivoli's Web site at `http://www.tivoli.com`.

1.2.2 Current Status of TME 10

At the time of this publication, Phase One of the TME 10 roll-out is complete, with Phases Two and Three in progress. Developments and enhancements are also being made to the original Tivoli product line.

1.3 TME 10 Disciplines and Products

The TME 10 products, which allow you to manage your entire computing environment including applications, fall into four distinct categories:

1. **Deployment management**
   Configuration and change management activities. Example: Distributing new software and maintaining an enterprise-wide hardware and software inventory repository. The products that cover this category of management disciplines are:
   - TME 10 Software Distribution
   - TME 10 Inventory
2. **Availability management**
   Maintaining mission-critical service levels through proactive analysis of the entire computing environment, including centralized system and network monitoring, automated actions, and performance management. The products that cover this category of management disciplines are:
   - TME 10 Enterprise Console
   - TME 10 Distributed Monitoring
   - TME 10 NetView
   - TME 10 Performance Management
3. **Security management**
   Protecting information and controlling access to resources. The products that cover this category of management disciplines are:
   - TME 10 User Administration
   - TME 10 Security Management

4. **Operations and Administration**
   Enabling day-to-day operation of managing thousands of applications through automated facilities for job scheduling, help desk, backup/restore, and output management. The products that cover this category of management disciplines are:
   - TME 10 Job Scheduler
   - TME 10 Remote Control
   - TME 10 ADSM (ADSTAR® Distributed Storage Manager)
   - TME 10 Plus Modules for integration of third-party products

The TME 10 Framework builds the foundation for all of the above products. In addition to the products that cover specific disciplines, there are several so-called multi-discipline products:

- TME 10 Framework
- TME 10 Global Enterprise Manager (GEM)

  Unifies network computing management processes across mainframe datacenters and distributed environments. An S/390 system becomes an element of the network computing environment – as a point of centralized management, as a peer manager or as a managed endpoint. The bi-directional Management Integration Services are GEM's centerpiece and provide

  - an exchange and update of management data between the management products on both environments,
  - a common view and collection of events from both environments with the possibility of performing a single action that executes a function on all platforms,
  - the ability to issue common commands from the S/390 interface or from the TME 10 interface.
- TME 10 Net.Commander

  Manages Web servers, mail servers, new servers, and proxy servers.
- Tivoli Manager for PowerBuilder applications and a Tivoli Developer Kit for PowerBuilder applications
- TME 10 Module for SAP R/3
- TME 10 Module for Lotus Domino/Notes

1.4 TME 10 Components Covered in This Book

The chapters in this book cover the TME 10 products that originated in Tivoli's pre-merger core products. At the time of this publication, the TME 10 product suite is at version level 3.0. A discussion of new products that will become available in the next few months, or that originated in pre-merger IBM products, is planned for inclusion in future volumes.

Figure 1 on page 7 depicts the layout of the TME 10 product structure as discussed in this book together with the various integration and programming toolkits.

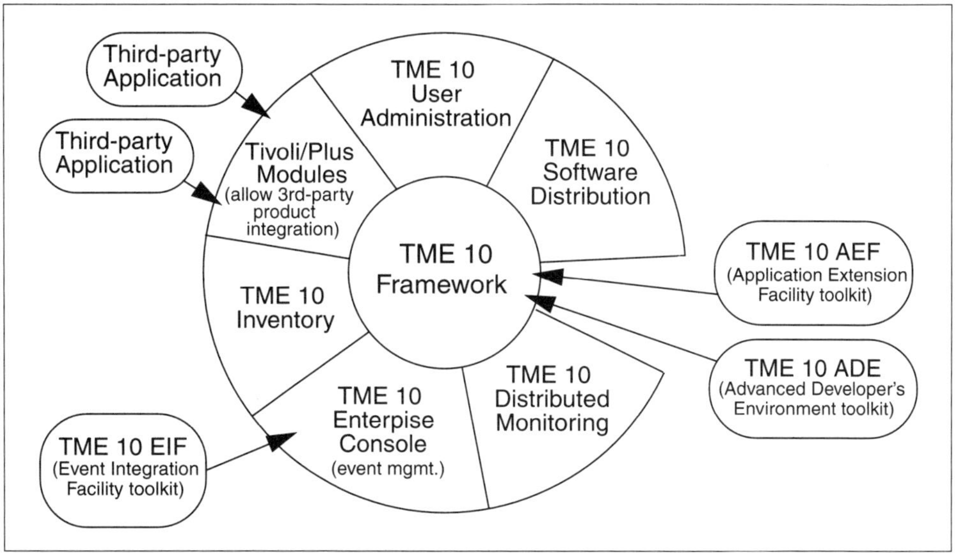

Figure 1. TME 10 Environment Software Components

Here is a short description of what each of these components do:

- ***TME 10 Framework*** – The foundation for other TME 10 and third-party management products. Provides a graphical desktop, object-oriented databases, and base services used by the other products. The TME 10 Framework is discussed in detail in Chapter 2, "TME 10 Framework" on page 15.
- TME 10 management applications – TME 10 applications installed "on top" of the TME 10 Framework that perform specific functions as listed briefly below. Many of these products are discussed in detail in later chapters.

    - ***TME 10 User Administration*** – Performs user, group, and host management.
    - ***TME 10 Software Distribution*** – Performs software distribution.
    - ***TME 10 Inventory*** – Views and records software products installed on remote systems.
    - ***TME 10 Distributed Monitoring*** – Monitors system resources and services.
    - ***TME 10 Enterprise Console*** – Collects management messages and alarms and performs automatic responses.
    - ***Tivoli/Plus*** modules – Modules designed for specific third-party applications that allow them to be integrated into the TME 10 environment. An example of one of these modules is Tivoli/Plus for NetWorker. NetWorker is a product from Legato Systems, Inc., a third-party company, that performs backups and restores of different systems. If the Tivoli/Plus for NetWorker module is installed with the actual NetWorker software, you can then perform NetWorker functions from the TME 10 desktop.
- TME 10 Toolkits - Allow extension of TME 10 applications or development of new applications using standard APIs. There are three:
    - ***TME 10 Application Extension Facility (TME 10 AEF)*** – Allows dynamic customization of TME 10 applications by adding site-specific behavior or values to standard applications. A typical AEF extension would be to create customized icons for your TME 10 desktop.
    - ***TME 10 Event Integration Facility (TME 10 EIF)*** – Allows adaptation of events from other applications into the TME 10 Enterprise Console. An example of using the EIF would be to take events generated by Hewlett-Packard OpenView and integrate them into the TME 10 event console.
    - ***TME 10 Advanced Developer's Environment (TME 10 ADE)*** – Has programming tools to create new applications on top of the TME 10 Framework.

Figure 2 shows in which pre-merger Tivoli products the TME 10 products are rooted. In some cases, the new TME 10 product name also includes a former IBM product with matching functions until the two are merged into one. For example, TME 10 Distributed Monitoring corresponds to the former Tivoli/Sentry product but also includes the IBM product, *Systems Monitor.*

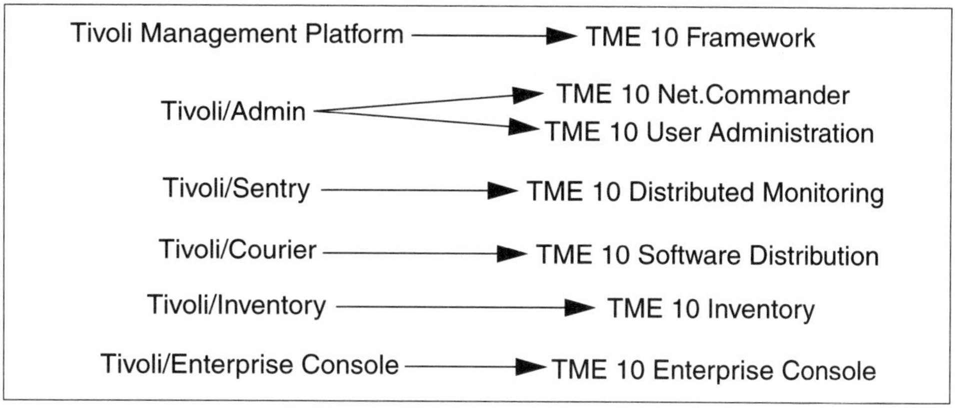

Figure 2. Summary of Product Name Changes

This list is not inclusive of all TME 10 products. For more information on TME 10, see the Tivoli Web site at `www.tivoli.com`.

1.5 Layout of the TME 10 Environment

The TME 10 Environment refers in general to the set of TME 10 management applications, but can also refer specifically to the set of TME 10 products functioning at a particular site. TME 10 products are used in environments where businesses have many machines that must be managed, so it will be helpful to look at the layout of the TME 10 products in these situations.

1.5.1 TME 10 Servers and TME 10 Clients

The TME 10 environment consists of machines designated as either a TME 10 server or a TME 10 client. A *TME 10 server* runs software and a database that allows it to manage TME 10 clients. The *TME 10 clients* run software that allows them to interact with the server and with each other. A TME 10 client can only be configured to interact with one server.

1.5.2 The TME 10 Management Region

The basic unit of TME 10 functionality is the TME 10 Management Region (TMR). It consists of one TME 10 server and the clients that server is managing. The server for a TME 10 Management Region is normally referred to as the TMR server for a particular TMR and will hold the database for that TMR.

Depending on the size and requirements of an environment, there may be more than one TMR defined. If multiple TMRs are present, they can either stand on their own or be linked together. Linking TMRs allows management functions to be exchanged between the regions. These connections can be of a one-way or two-way nature in terms of access permissions and exchanging information between TMRs.

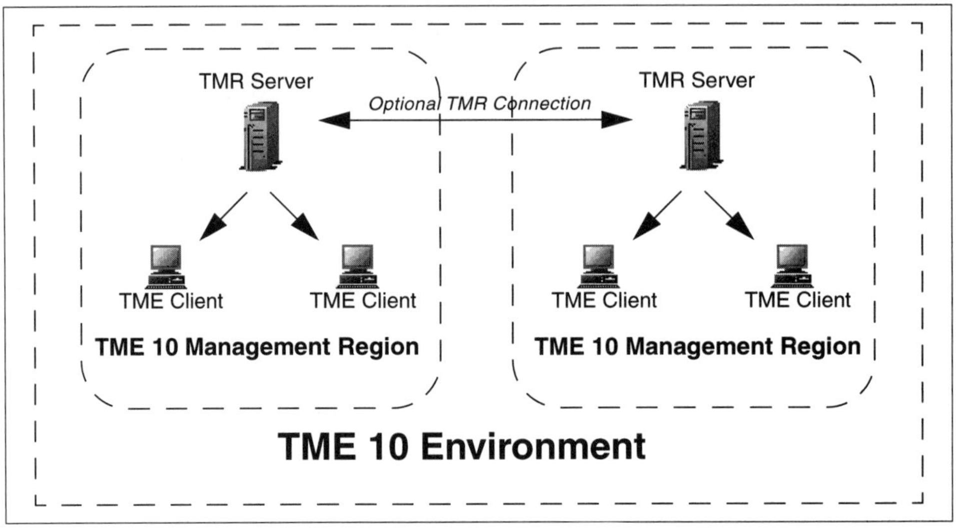

Figure 3. TME 10 Management Region Layout

1.5.3 TMR Configuration

There are many criteria that should be considered when deciding how to divide an enterprise into one or more TME 10 Management Regions and then how to connect these TMRs.

1.5.3.1 Server Load

The performance of TMR servers will affect whether or not multiple servers are needed. Load will be caused by the processes used to contact client machines, by network traffic processing, and by the CPU and memory used by the server. If the load on a server becomes too high, it may be necessary to create multiple TMRs to aid performance.

1.5.3.2 Number of Clients

It is recommended that a single TMR server support no more than 200 clients. A client in this scenario does not include any PC clients running the PC agent software. For descriptions of these terms, please see Chapter 2, "TME 10 Framework" on page 15. With a future extension of the TME 10 Framework architecture, the number of TME 10 clients in a TMR is drastically increased. This further detailed in Secion 2.11, "Light Client Framework: A Glimpse Into the Future" on page 42.

1.5.3.3 Network Topology and Limitations

TME 10 uses TCP/IP, for the most part, for its communications. All direct traffic between clients and the server is TCP/IP. This should be taken into account during the planning of the TME 10 environment to assure that good connectivity and bandwidth is available for the operation of the TME 10 environment. A feature of the TME 10 that may be helpful in planning the network portion of the environment is the Multiplexed Distribution (MDist) service, which allows a distribution hierarchy. MDist is discussed in Section 4.4, "TME 10 Software Distribution Topology and Scalability" on page 102.

1.5.3.4 Location of Administrators

The location of administrators is another consideration. If a company's administrators all work from one central location, one TMR may be sufficient. However, if there are three geographic locations, each having separate administrators responsible for their site's servers, multiple TMRs may make more sense.

1.5.3.5 Security

There are two issues to be concerned with for security: encryption levels and limited access.

At the time of the TME 10 installation, you must choose the level of encryption to be used for this TMR. The encryption level you choose will determine the security of the sensitive data stored by TME 10. Only one encryption level can be chosen per TMR; so if different levels of encryption are necessary, it may be necessary to have multiple TMRs.

Multiple TMRs will also allow you to limit administrator access to sets of machines.

1.5.3.6 Reliability

Multiple TMRs can provide some forms of reliability. If one TMR server goes down, other TMR servers can still function properly. Note that this will not provide redundancy for management of the clients located in the TMR of the down TMR server.

1.6 Common Concepts of Operation

Most of the TME 10 products operate under the same set of concepts. These concepts are described briefly below and in more detail in the chapters that follow.

- The communication within the TME 10 environment is performed by the oserv daemon, which runs on the TMR server and all of the managed nodes.
- The information relating to all objects in the TME 10 environment, along with the application-specific information, is stored in a distributed, object-oriented database.
- One graphical user interface, called the TME 10 desktop, provides a window into the TME 10 environment and access to all of the TME 10 applications.
- Most TME 10 functions are performed in the context of *profiles*. A profile is a collection of specific information that can be manipulated and distributed to machines in the TME 10 environment. The general concepts of creating and distributing a profile are common to all of the TME 10 applications.
- The operations in the TME 10 environment are all subject to *policies*, or rules for operation.

CHAPTER 2

TME 10 Framework

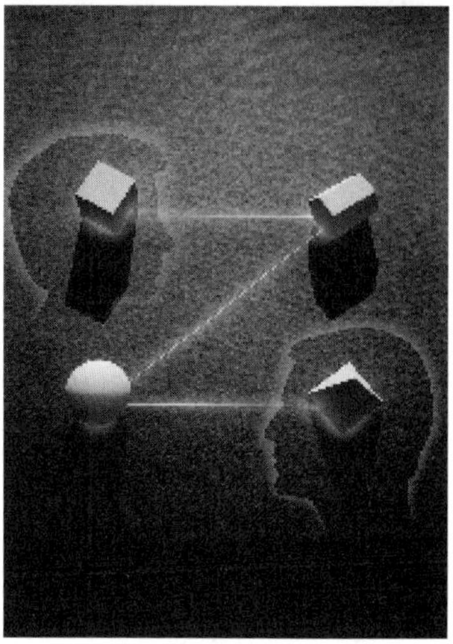

The foundation of TME 10 is the TME 10 Framework. This base software is required to run any of the other TME 10 management applications, as shown in Figure 4 on page 15. It provides some core TME 10 capabilities and services that are needed by other TME 10 applications as well as the graphical user interface (GUI), which lets the administrator view the environment.

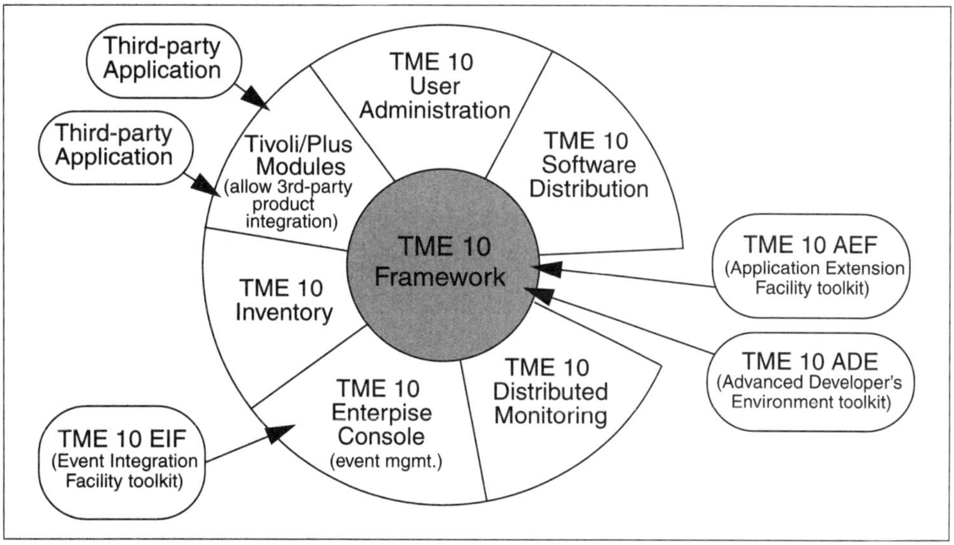

Figure 4. TME 10 Software Components

In this chapter, we discuss the TME 10 Framework's components and features. Chapter 8, "Installing and Using the TME 10 Framework" on page 203, provides step-by-step instructions on how to install the platform and use some of its management functions.

2.1 Overview and Product Information

This book covers the TME 10 Framework at version level 3.0, or more precisely, it describes the functions and features of the Tivoli Mangement Platform Version 3.0 using the new TME 10 terminology. The majority of the information provided in this chapter is common to the TME 10 Framework 3.1 product.

2.1.1 Overview of Components

The TME 10 Framework consists of the following features:

- ***Graphical User Interface (GUI)*** – The TME 10 desktop that allows administrators to view and control the TME 10 graphically. It provides standard logical layout of the TME 10 environment and keeps this standard throughout the addition of other TME 10 products.
- ***Command Line Interface (CLI)*** – Used to run commands to view and control the TME 10 environment.
- ***oserv daemon*** – The service that runs continuously and coordinates communication within the TME 10 environment.
- ***Databases*** – The storage for information about objects in the TME 10 environment. TME 10 uses one database that is distributed among all of the machines running TME 10 Framework within a management region.
- ***Application Services*** – The core TME 10 capabilities and services that are needed by other TME 10 applications, such as profile managers and *MDist* for distribution. It also provides the task library, the scheduler and the bulletin board for notifications.
- ***Installation*** – The component used to install all TME 10 applications locally and remotely.

2.1.2 TME 10 Framework Software

The TME 10 Framework is first installed on a machine designated as a TME 10 Management Region (TMR) server. Installing the TMR server installs each of the components listed above. Once the server is installed, you can create TME 10 clients by installing the TME 10 Framework on UNIX or Windows NT systems. You can perform this installation either remotely from the TMR server or locally on the TME 10 client machine. Following installation, the TMR server and each TME 10 client has an oserv daemon running locally. It is through these oserv daemons that the TMR server and its clients communicate and perform TME 10 management operations.

The TME 10 Framework also includes PC agents that allow the TME to manage PCs as well as UNIX and Windows NT systems. The PC agent is installed locally on these machines, either directly from the TME 10 Framework CD-ROM or from diskettes made from the CD-ROM. See 8.1.3, "Installing and Configuring Clients Running the Framework" on page 212, for instructions on installing TME clients. The supported operating systems are listed in Section 2.1.3, "Supported Platforms" on page 17.

Also included with the TME 10 Framework software package are two programming toolkits (TME 10 ADE and TME 10 AEF), the UserLink/DHCP service, which provides support for TME 10 UserLink and PCs running the DHCP (Dynamic Host Configuration Protocol), and PostScript documentation for these products. These products must be installed separately after the TME 10 Framework is installed.

2.1.3 Supported Platforms

The TME 10 Framework runs on the following operating systems:

- AIX
- HP-UX
- Solaris
- SunOS
- Windows NT

The TME 10 PC agent software runs on the following operating systems:

- DOS
- NetWare
- OS/2®
- Windows 3.x
- Windows 95
- Windows NT

For specific information regarding operating system and maintenance level compatibilities and requirements, consult the latest release notes and installation manuals for the TME 10 Framework.

2.2 TME 10 Machine Roles

As explained in Section 1.5.2, "The TME 10 Management Region" on page 9, each TME 10 Management Region has one TMR server. The TME 10 Framework is first installed on this TMR server. Then TME 10 client software can be installed on remote machines. There are basically two kinds of TME 10 clients: those that can run the TME 10 Framework software and those that run the PC agent software.

The client/server relationships between the server and the two types of clients is shown in Figure 5 along with the supported operating systems. These relationships are discussed in the subsections immediately following.

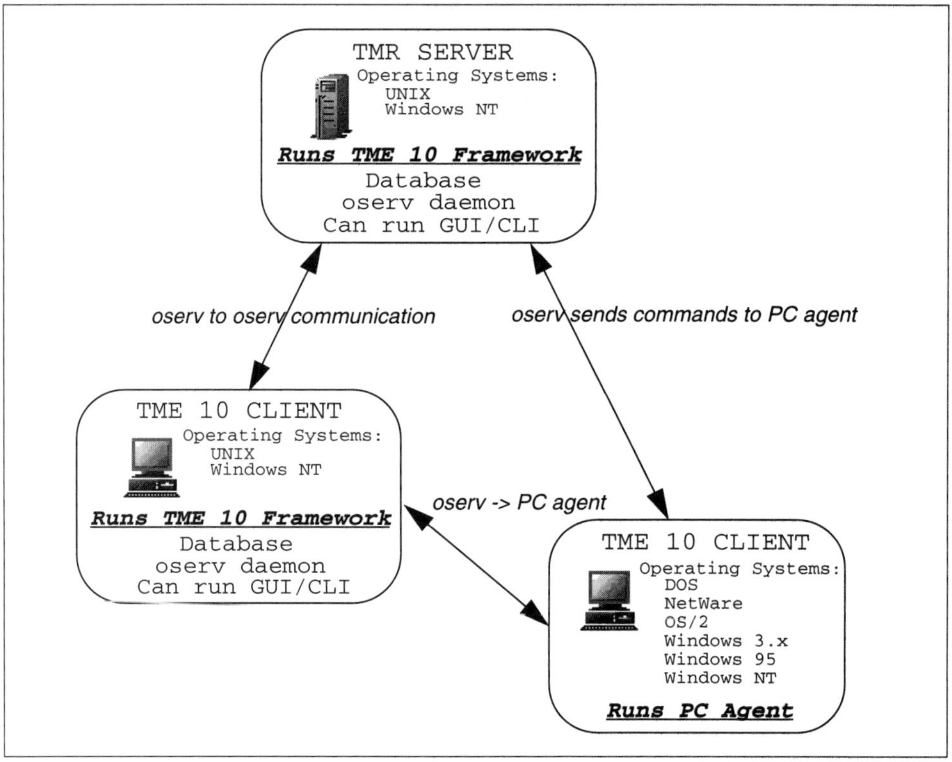

Figure 5. TMR Server and Clients with Software Requirements

2.2.1 TME 10 Clients Running the TME 10 Framework

UNIX or Windows NT clients are able to run the TME 10 Framework. For a list of supported UNIX platforms, see Section 2.1.3, "Supported Platforms" on page 17. These clients run an oserv daemon and have a local database that is integrated with the server's database. You can run the TME 10 desktop from these systems, in which case the device is called a ***TME 10 management station***. Management stations have slightly greater system requirements than clients that do not require the TME 10 desktop. Guidelines for sizing these and the other TME 10 machines can be found in the *TME 10 Framework Planning and Installation Guide*.

In some cases it may be beneficial to cascade the flow of information from the TMR server to its clients instead of having the default, flat distribution. *Multiplexed Distribution (MDist)* provides the functionality to do this by allowing TME 10 clients running the TME 10 Framework to be designated as repeaters which can resend information they receive from the server to other clients. This concept is discussed further in Section 4.4, "TME 10 Software Distribution Topology and Scalability" on page 102.

2.2.2 TME 10 Clients Running PC Agents

PCs can be managed without having to run a full TME 10 Framework. These "limited-function" TME 10 clients are called ***PC agents***. They run the TME 10 PC agent software and are only used with the TME 10 Software Distribution and TME 10 Inventory products. A list of supported operating systems can be found in Section 2.1.3, "Supported Platforms" on page 17.

The PC agent software is available through the TME 10 Framework software package in two versions, one to communicate via TCP/IP and the other via the Internet Packet eXchange/Sequenced Packet eXchange (IPX/SPX), the latter being used only between a NetWare server and clients. When PC agents are defined to the TME 10 environment, they must meet one of two criteria:

- Have a TME 10 client or server running the TME 10 Framework to sponsor them and communicate with the TMR server on their behalf.
- Be a client of a NetWare server running TME 10 NetWare repeater software.

  The NetWare repeater software allows a NetWare server to distribute software to its clients and is discussed further in Section 4.5, "NetWare Configuration" on page 104.

In order to support Windows machines that connect using the Dynamic Host Control Protocol (DHCP) addressing environment, you install a product on the TMR server called *TME 10 UserLink*, which is also included in the TME 10 Framework software package. The UserLink product provides additional capabilities for software distribution options, which are discussed further in Section 4.3.4, "TME 10 UserLink" on page 100.

2.3 Resources

An important concept of the TME 10 environment is that of resources. *Resources* are the TME 10 representations of actual elements in the enterprise. These resources may correspond to physical things, like computers, or to intangible things, like a set of rules governing a computer. Resources that are subject to certain sets of rules within the TME 10 environment are called *managed resources,* and the predefined rules are called *policies*.

Managed resources are contained within *policy regions*, which are special collections of managed resources that are subject to the same set of rules. As more products are installed in the TME 10 environment, more managed resources become available for use.

This section first discusses the resources found on the TME 10 desktop and then the different types of managed resources.

2.3.1 Resources Found on the TME 10 Desktop

This section discusses the resources found in the primary or top-level window of the TME 10 desktop (the administrator GUI), along with icons that represent them.

2.3.1.1 Administrator Collection and Administrator

  The administrator collection is a container that holds the icons for all administrators defined for the TME 10 environment. It is represented by the icon shown above on the left. Within the administrator collection is an icon for each administrator, as shown on the right. The pop-up menus on the administrators' icons enable you to view and change information about the administrators, particularly their role assignments. The functions that can be performed using these resources are discussed in Section 2.6, "Administrators" on page 29.

2.3.1.2 Bulletin Board

  This resource contains notices that are sent by TME 10 applications to inform the administrators of changes in the TME 10 environment. The icon for the bulletin board can appear in two different states, one showing there are no new notices to read, shown on the left above, and one showing that there are new notices, shown on the right. The

notification facility is discussed in Section 2.7, “Notification (Bulletin Board) Facility” on page 32.

2.3.1.3 Policy Region

 The policy region resource is a collection of managed resources that share one or more common sets of rules. Policy regions also represent administrative domains that can be assigned to administrators and are discussed in Section 2.5, “Policy and Policy Regions” on page 28.

2.3.1.4 Scheduler

 The scheduler resource allows tasks performed within the TME 10 environment to be automated. This feature is discussed in Section 2.10, “Scheduler” on page 40.

2.3.1.5 Generic Collection

 The generic collection is a container on the desktop that can hold sets of resources, including other containers. Its function is to group and allow easy access to resources. The generic collection does not actually contain these resources, as policy regions do; it is only a set of pointers that link to resources located elsewhere in the TME 10 environment.

2.3.2 Managed Nodes

  TME 10 clients running operating systems able to support the TME 10 Framework are represented as *managed nodes*. Two icons are available for managed nodes, a server and a client icon. There is no difference in the way the different icons function; they differ for aesthetic purposes only and may be toggled back and forth at will. Managed nodes run the oserv daemon and maintain a local database. Managed nodes are UNIX or Windows NT systems and have the graphical TME 10 desktop capability.

The TMR server itself is configured automatically as the first managed node on the TME 10 desktop. Other managed nodes are defined and appear on the desktop when the TME 10 Framework software is installed on them. Communication is then established between the oserv daemons running on each system. Once the managed node icon appears on the desktop, the following menu options are available on a pop-up menu for that icon:

- **Open...** This menu option opens a window for the managed node and displays any relevant contents, such as local profile copies.
- **Properties...** This menu option displays physical system information such as RAM and allows changes to be made to some information, such as Internet Protocol (IP) interfaces.
- **Run xterm** This menu option opens an X-terminal session on that machine. This option is invalid for Windows NT managed nodes.
- **Toggle icon...** This option allows you to change between the server and client icon for the machine. This is for appearance only and does not change any of the functionality in the TME 10 environment.
- **Synchronize...** This option allows the synchronization of information stored in profiles with the corresponding system files. This will be discussed further in Section 2.8, "Configuration Management" on page 33.

This menu can be expanded as more TME 10 applications are installed. In particular, TME 10 User Administration adds host management options to it.

2.3.3 PC Managed Nodes

A *PC managed node* is a representation on the TME 10 desktop of a TME 10 client running PC agent software. The actual PC managed node by definition is a UNIX or Windows NT managed node that relays and keeps object information in its database about a machine running PC agent software, as shown in Figure 6.

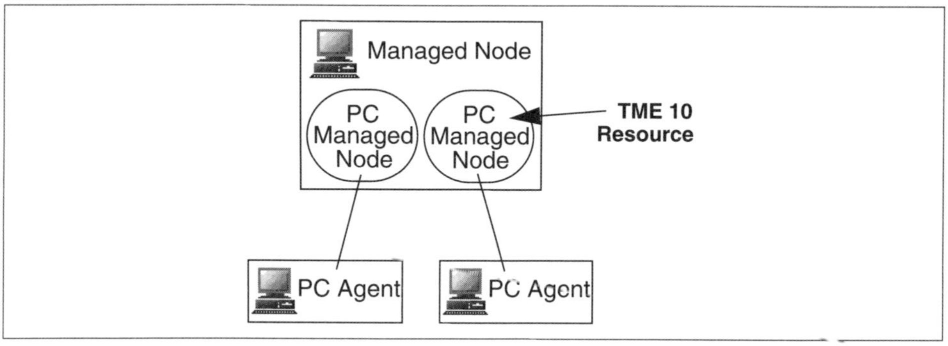

Figure 6. PC Managed Node/PC Agent Relationship

The icons for PC managed nodes are exactly the same as those of managed nodes. The label below the icon showing the machine's operating system will indicate what type of machine it is. As with managed nodes, there is no difference in functionality between the server and client icons; the icon used for a certain device is up to the user.

Icons for Windows NT

Machines running the Windows NT operating system can have different roles in the TME 10 environment. They can run the TME 10 Framework, in which case they would show up as managed nodes on the TME 10 desktop. They can also run the PC agent software and would then appear as PC managed nodes on the TME 10 desktop. Since the icons for managed nodes and PC managed nodes are the same, those Windows NT nodes running TME 10 Framework have a label reading *TMP/NT* and those running the PC agent have the label *Windows NT*.

When a PC managed node icon is added to the desktop, the following menu options appear as a pop-up menu for that icon:

- **Properties...** This displays physical system information about the PC.
- **Editable properties...** This option allows changes to be made to the icon name, operating system, and other fields.
- **Toggle icon...** This menu option allows you to change between the server and client icon for the machine. This is for appearance only and does not change any of the functionality in the TME 10 environment.

This menu can be expanded as more TME 10 applications are installed.

A Note on PC Terminology

The concept and usage of the *PC managed node* and *PC agent* terms can be confusing and often misleading. A TME 10 client running PC agent software can be called a PC agent machine. Sometimes it is also referred to as a PC managed node. In actuality, the PC managed node is a UNIX or Windows NT system that holds object information in its TME 10 database about a machine running PC agent software. Be aware that the term PC managed node is sometimes used to describe the PC client itself or the UNIX or Windows NT system sponsoring that client as a proxy.

2.3.4 NetWare Managed Sites

 The NetWare managed site (NWMS) resource icon represents a NetWare server and a group of NetWare clients. Multiple icons can be created for the same server if two different sets of clients are to be defined. The concept and terminology is the same for the PC managed node and PCs running the PC agent. The NWMS is a representation of the NetWare server and its clients. The actual object in the TME 10 database resides on a UNIX or NT managed node that acts as the liaison between the server and the

NetWare server and its clients. This relationship is shown in Figure 7 on page 24.

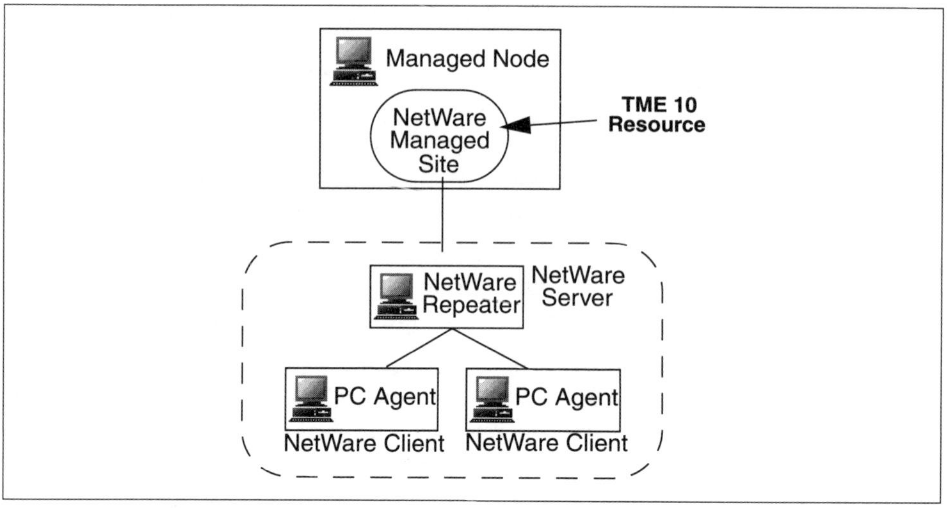

Figure 7. NetWare Managed Site

The NetWare managed site is used for software distribution and is discussed further in Section 4.5, "NetWare Configuration" on page 104.

2.3.5 Other Managed Resources

Managed resources are those resources subject to TME 10 predefined rules, called policies, and are contained within policy regions. Managed nodes, PC managed nodes, and NetWare managed sites discussed in the previous sections are the managed resources that represent computers. Other managed resources available with the TME 10 Framework are discussed below and are shown with their respective icons.

2.3.5.1 Policy Subregion

A policy subregion is a policy region located inside another policy region. A policy subregion has the same icon as a policy region. Policy subregions are discussed in Section 2.5, "Policy and Policy Regions" on page 28.

2.3.5.2 Profile Manager

A profile manager resource is a container for profiles. Managed resources, such as managed nodes, PC managed nodes, and even other

profile managers, can subscribe to a profile manager. During a profile distribution, subscribers of a profile manager receive copies of the profiles (and their contents) contained in the profile manager. Profiles and profile managers are discussed in Section 2.8, "Configuration Management" on page 33.

2.3.5.3 Task Library

A task library is a managed resource that allows an administrator to create and store tasks and jobs, which are defined below.

2.3.5.4 Task

A task is a resource that represents an action or operation that needs to be performed within the TME 10 environment. Tasks are discussed in Section 2.9, "Performing Tasks in the TME 10 Environment" on page 38.

2.3.5.5 Job

A job is a resource representing a task that is executed on specific managed resources. Jobs are discussed in Section 2.9, "Performing Tasks in the TME 10 Environment" on page 38.

2.3.5.6 Query Libraries and Queries

The query facility is represented by query libraries and queries that appear within the context of a policy region. A *query library* is a container for queries and is represented by the icon on the left. A *query* is a specific, predefined request for information from the TME 10 configuration repository, a feature of the TME 10 Inventory application. It is represented by the icon on the right. The query facility is discussed in Chapter 5, "TME 10 Inventory" on page 111.

2.4 Introduction to the Desktop

The TME 10 *graphical user interface (GUI)*, or *desktop*, is the administrator's view of the TME 10. The TME 10 desktop, or simply the desktop, allows users to graphically access resources and perform tasks. TME 10 also provides a *command line interface (CLI)* to allow many of the functions that the desktop provides to be performed from a shell. There are some functions that can be performed from the CLI only. Some functions can be performed through the desktop only.

The TME 10 desktop can be started from any machine running the TME 10 Framework software. The desktop can be configured to start from any subset of servers and clients running the TME 10 Framework. There is also a product called *TME 10 Desktop for Windows* that can be installed on machines running Windows 95, Windows NT, or Windows 3.11. The TME 10 Desktop for Windows is a graphical client/server software comparable to the X-Windows architecture. The desktop functions are performed on the TME 10 Framework (managed node), but the display window is sent across the network and displayed under Windows. To the user it appears as if the TME 10 desktop GUI is local to his/her PC. See the *TME 10 Desktop for Windows User's Guide* for more information.

The desktop has menus, icons, status lines, and other means to allow these activities. Most of the icons have been shown and defined in the previous sections on resources and managed resources. Figure 8 on page 27 shows the initial view after the desktop is started. You can see that there are pull-down menu options at the top of the window. These are accessed by clicking the left-mouse button on the option you'd like to expand. Pop-up menus can be seen by clicking the right-mouse button on any of the icons shown in the icon area. These icons represent resources in the TME 10 environment. You can also double-click on any of the icons to open a dialog window that allows more detailed options relating to that icon. A search facility is provided in the center of the window. Operational messages are shown in the message area, and other information can be shown on the status line at the bottom of the window.

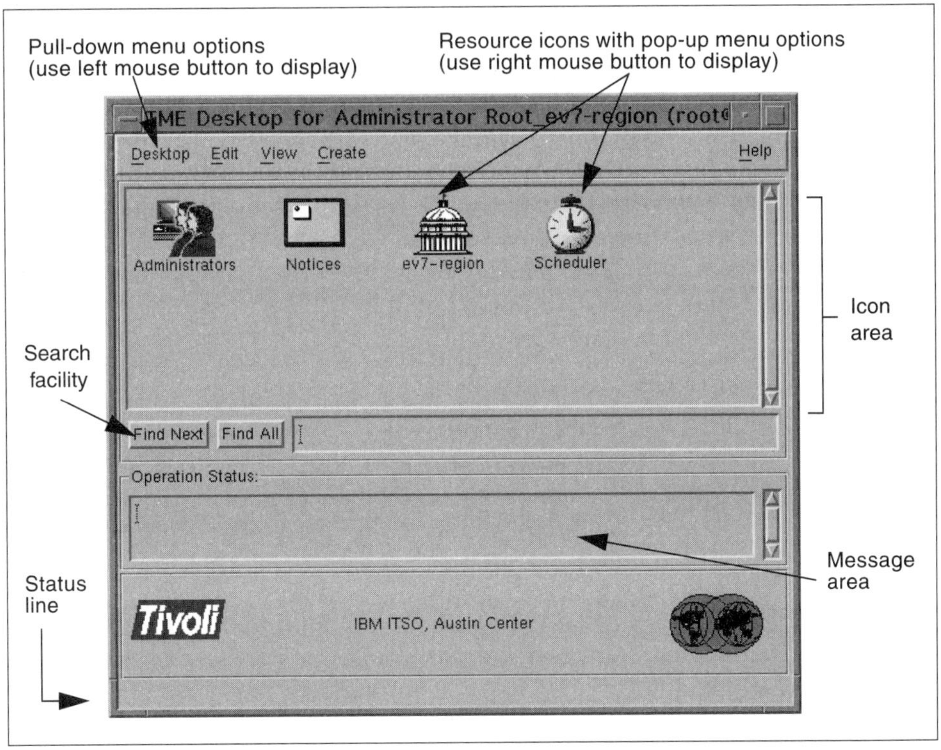

Figure 8. Initial Desktop View

There are five types of resources that can appear on the initial TME 10 desktop view: administrator collection, bulletin board, policy region, scheduler, and generic collection. The first four listed show up by default after the product's initial installation. Generic collections can be added if desired.

Many of the icons are presented in a hierarchical format, and layers of icons may be uncovered by opening new windows to reach information you may be interested in viewing. For example, policy regions can contain hierarchies of subregions within other subregions. The *desktop navigator* function of the GUI provides an alternate method of moving through the hierarchy.

The status line at the bottom of the desktop is a very helpful feature. When you place the mouse pointer over any of the icons, a brief description of that icon's function is given in the status line.

2.5 Policy and Policy Regions

In the TME 10 environment, *policy* is a set of rules that are applied to managed resources. Policy enables you to control the default values of newly-created resources (*default policy*) and to maintain the guidelines when administrators modify or operate on resources (*validation policy*). A specific rule in a policy is referred to as a policy method. A default policy method can supply a constant value or run a shell script or a program that generates a value, whereas a validation policy method usually runs a program or shell script to verify values supplied by the administrator. Administrators can define and maintain policies.

An example of TME 10 policy is a rule requiring user login names to be eight characters or less. The administrator can create a script that takes the full user name and constructs a user login name that is filled in as a default value (default policy method). He/she would also create a validation script that checks the length of a user login name before the profile is saved (validation policy method).

Policy regions, as shown in Figure 9 on page 29, are containers for managed resources that use the same set of policies. Administrator permissions or roles are assigned to administrators on the basis of policy regions. Therefore, policy regions help to organize the managed resources in the desktop and can be helpful in defining and limiting administrator access to these resources.

As shown in Figure 9 on page 29, the categories of managed resources (managed resource types) and their instances (managed resources) that belong to a certain policy region are defined by the administrator. Before a managed resource can be added to a policy region, its resource type must be added. The types available to be defined to a policy region depend on the TME 10 applications installed. The managed resource types available through the TME 10 Framework software are:

- Managed nodes
- PC managed nodes
- Task libraries
- Profile managers

Policy regions can be arranged hierarchically by creating policy subregions. Each policy subregion has its own subset of resources. When the subregion is initially defined, it has the same policies and managed resource types as its parent. After the initial definition, these things can be changed and are not at all dependent on the parent's definitions.

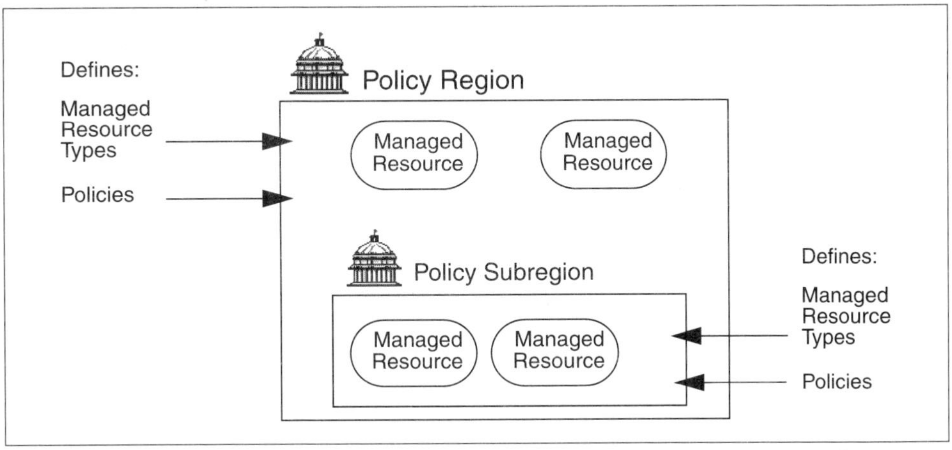

Figure 9. Policy Region with Policy Subregion

The only icons that can appear inside a policy region's window are those for the managed resource types defined for that policy region and its policy subregions. The policy region's or policy subregion's pop-up menu has the following options:

- **Open...** This option opens the policy region to show the TME 10 managed resources assigned to that policy region.
- **Region Properties...** This option displays a window that lets the administrator change the name of the policy region.
- **Managed Resources...** This option allows the administrator to view and change the types of managed resources that are defined for that policy region.
- **Managed Resource Policies...** This option allows the administrator to change the policy for the different managed resource types within that policy region.

As initially mentioned, policy regions and subregions are collections of resources for which the same set of policies apply. Different criteria can be used to build these entities, such as administrator locations, administrator permission hierarchy, geography, departments, machine types, and so on. The product is so flexible that it can be laid out to reflect each company's individual structure and policies.

2.6 Administrators

A TME 10 administrator is someone who has been given authorization to perform management tasks in the TME 10 environment. The TME 10 administrator facility provides a senior administrator the ability to create administrator accounts and assign them the authority to perform tasks. Each administrator then has his or her own TME 10 desktop that reflects the access and control he or she has been given.

2.6.1 Authorization Roles

A major concept in TME 10 security is that of *authorization roles.* Authorization roles are predefined names for sets of management task abilities. These roles are discrete, not hierarchical, meaning that each role has specific functions it can perform, and these functions cannot necessarily be performed by any of the other roles. However, some operations can be executed by more than one role.

The role or roles given to an administrator will define what that administrator can do to a particular set of resources. Following is a list of the TME 10 authorization roles and their meanings:

- ***super*** – Allows the administrator to configure the TME 10 environment. Example: Connecting and disconnecting TMRs.
- ***senior*** – Allows the administrator to create and define all of the TME 10 resources. Example: Creating a new policy region.
- ***admin*** – Allows the administrator to perform day-to-day operation, configuration, and policy tasks. Example: Distributing a set of files to TME 10 clients.
- ***user*** – Allows read-only access to the TME 10 environment. This role is required to run the graphical desktop. Example: Displaying configuration of a client machine.
- ***backup*** – Allows the administrator to back up the TME 10 databases.
- ***restore*** – Allows the administrator to restore TME 10 databases.
- ***install_product*** – Allows the administrator to install applications into the local TMR.
- ***install_client*** – Allows the administrator to install managed nodes within policy regions that support the managed node resource type.
- ***Query_edit*** – Allows the administrator to edit existing queries within a query library.
- ***Query_execute*** – Allows the administrator to perform queries using the query facility.
- ***Query_view*** – Allows the administrator to view query libraries and queries defined in the query facility.

These authorization roles can be delegated for the entire TMR and also for individual primary resources, such as policy regions or scheduler, but not for individual managed resources. Most often, roles are delegated specifically for policy regions. For example, an administrator could be given a senior authorization role in one specific policy region so that he/she could make various changes to that specific group of managed resources. The same administrator could be given user authorization for the rest of the TMR so that he/she would only be able to view TME 10 configuration, but not make any changes.

2.6.2 Creating or Modifying an Administrator

When the TME 10 Framework software is first installed on the TMR server machine, an administrator is created with the super authorization role. This administrator can create other administrators. Any administrators with the super or senior role can create new administrators and assign them authorization roles.

The *Administrators* resource icon has two options on its pop-up menu. The **Open...** option opens a window showing all of the administrators that have been created. The **Create Administrator...** option allows you to create a new TME 10 administrator. Figure 10 shows the window that appears when this option is chosen.

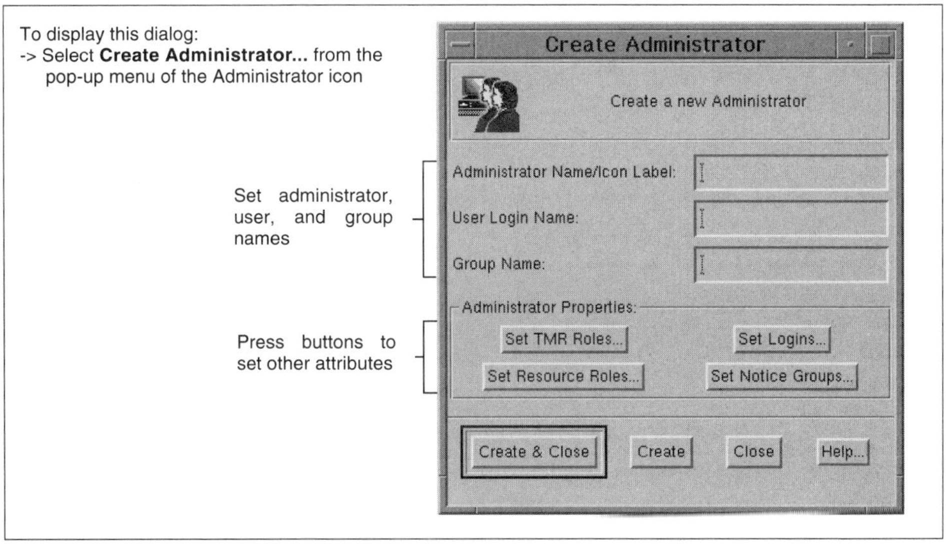

Figure 10. Create Administrator Dialog

When you create an administrator, several things must be defined:

- *Administrator Name* – Each administrator must have a unique name within the TME 10 environment. This is the name that shows up as a label for that administrator's icon in the administrator collection.
- *Login and Group Names* – Each administrator must have a valid UNIX or Windows NT user and group name on every system they are going to manage. Certain tasks run under these user and group names.
- *TMR Roles* – A TMR role provides the assigned authorization level to *all* resources in the TMR. For example, if an administrator has a senior role in the TMR, this administrator has the senior role over every resource in that TMR. TMR roles should be assigned with great care.
- *Resource Roles* – Authorization roles are given out here on a per resource basis. For example, if an administrator has been given the *admin* role for the TMR as a whole, you could give him or her the *senior* role for a specific policy region using the **Set Resource Roles...** section.
- *Logins* – You must define where the administrator will be logged in when starting the TME 10 desktop or running commands. You can define numerous logins for the same administrator.
- *Notice Groups* – You must also define which notice groups administrators will be able to access.

After a new administrator is created, it is necessary to populate the new administrator's desktop with the resources he/she should have access to. This is done by dragging and dropping resources from an existing administrator's desktop to the new administrator's desktop.

The administrator icon has its own pop-up menu that allows you to modify any of the information previously configured for that administrator.

2.7 Notification (Bulletin Board) Facility

The notification facility provides a way to keep track of what system administration activities are happening. Notices are posted to a graphical bulletin board on the TME 10 desktop.

A *notice* is a message telling the administrator that something has happened or changed in the TME 10 environment. As notices are generated, they are sent to a notice group. A *notice group* is a grouping where notices sharing common types of information are stored. For example, there is a notice group called *TME Authorization*, where notices are sent regarding additions, deletions, and changes to TME 10 system administrators.

Access to the different notices groups is given to each administrator using the administrator facility itself. Each administrator is accessing his/her own information; so an administrator performing functions on his/her notices and notice groups will not affect the other administrators. What each administrator sees, are pointers to central copies of the notices.

System administrators can read these notices and then save, delete, and forward them as desired. The notices have a time stamp, severity, administrator, identification number, and subject, and they can be filtered, combined, and sorted by many of these fields.

When the TME 10 Framework software is installed, four notice groups are set up:

- *TME Administration* – This group contains notices concerning general TME 10 functions, like creating and removing resources and installation of new applications.
- *TME Authorization* – This group contains notices related to TME 10 administrator creations, deletions, or changes and authorization errors.
- *TME Diagnostics* – This group contains notices generated by TME 10 maintenance activities.
- *TME Scheduler* – This group contains notices concerning the TME 10 scheduler.

The number of notice groups available expands as more TME 10 applications are installed.

2.8 Configuration Management

Profiles and profile managers make up the configuration management portion of the TME 10. Together, these two organize, create, and distribute information to remote systems.

Figure 11 on page 34 shows a TME 10 desktop view of a profile manager with its profiles and subscribers, all described in the sections that follow.

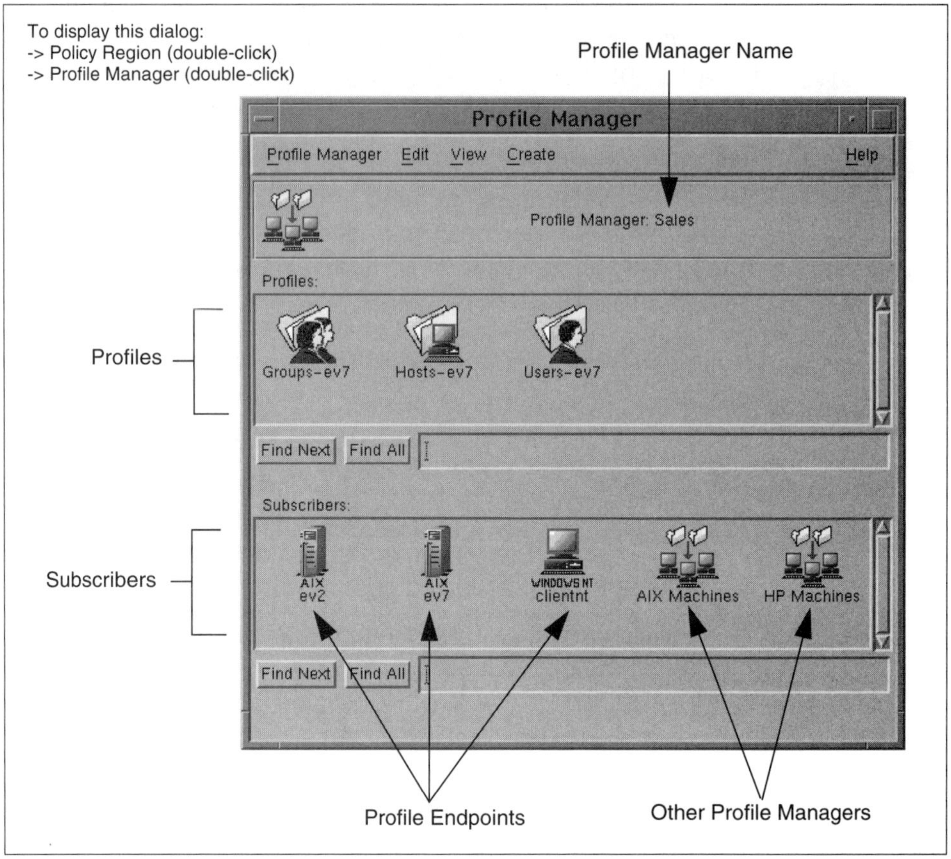

Figure 11. Profile Manager Desktop View

2.8.1 Profiles

A collection of information corresponding to a system resource is called a *profile*. It contains information that is specific to a certain application and a certain profile type. A profile is stored centrally in a profile database and can be distributed to numerous locations. An example of a profile is a *user profile* in the TME 10 User Administration application or a file package in TME 10 Software Distribution. The user profile is used with UNIX-, NT- or NetWare-based systems and contains information about users, such as the user name, user ID, and user group for each user. This profile is stored on one TME 10 machine in a platform-independent manner. The information contained in the user profile can then be distributed to NetWare, NT or UNIX machines of different types.

A Note About Profiles

The TME 10 Framework provides the profile managers and the distribution capabilities. Profile types are added as additional products are installed in the TME 10 environment. The user profile mentioned above is part of the TME 10 User Administration application and is discussed in Section 3.3, "TME 10 User Administration Profiles" on page 55.

Profiles are subject to the default and validation policies defined for them. Profiles are created and maintained in the context of profile managers. Profiles can be changed without immediately putting the changes into effect on the managed machines. The editing and distribution of the profile are two separate functions.

When creating a profile, you can enter the data by hand or populate it using existing system files or databases. To continue our example above using the user profile, you could retrieve the information for your user profile from several remote systems' /etc/passwd or NIS files. You can specify the hosts from which to obtain information and whether the information should replace or append an existing profile. The ability to do these types of operations depends on the type of profile you are creating and the information that already exists.

After profiles are created, they can then be copied or cloned. Copying a profile creates an exact copy of the profile. Cloning creates a new profile that contains the same policy definitions, but does not replicate the information contained within the profile. One profile can be used with more than one profile manager.

2.8.2 Profile Managers

A profile manager provides a place to create and organize groups of profiles and link recipients to them. A profile manager can contain multiple profiles of the same type, or it can contain profiles of more than one type. Profile managers also control the distribution of profiles and help organize resources.

Profile managers can be changed by creating new profiles, editing the profiles already contained there, and by subscribing and unsubscribing profile endpoints and other profile managers.

2.8.3 Subscribers

A *subscriber* is a profile endpoint or another profile manager that receives profile records from the profile manager. A *profile endpoint* is a system that is the final destination for a profile. Examples of profile endpoints can be managed nodes, PC managed nodes, or NIS domains. In the case of PC managed nodes, the profile would be distributed to the UNIX or Windows NT system sponsoring that PC, which would then distribute to the PC running PC agent software. The same situation would be true for NetWare Managed Sites. The profile would be distributed to the NetWare server, which would then distribute to its set of clients. Profile endpoints can subscribe to more than one profile manager. Subscribing to a profile manager is the equivalent of subscribing to all of the profiles contained within that profile manager.

Profile managers can also subscribe to other profile managers, thereby creating a subscription hierarchy. When a profile manager is a subscriber, then all of its subscribers become distribution endpoints for the top-most profile manager. This subscription hierarchy yields more flexibility options and control over definition of resources within the profile manager. An example of this hierarchy is shown in Figure 12.

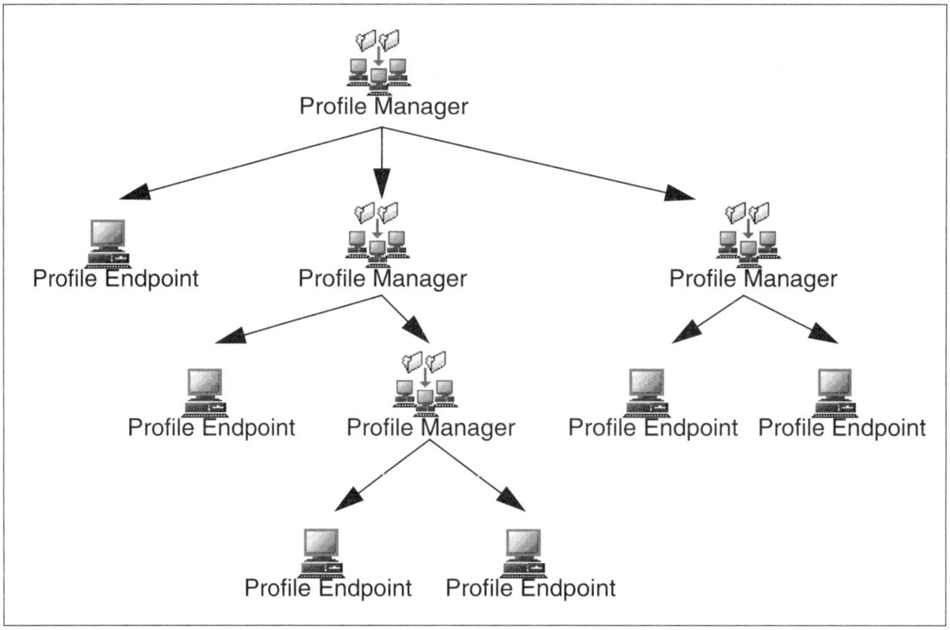

Figure 12. Profile Manager Hierarchy

Note that this subscription hierarchy is the key for simplicity in managing your environment. By creating specific profile managers containing, for example, no profiles but all machines of the same type in a department as subscribers, you build a group of machines subject to distribution of the same information. You then add this profile manager as a subscriber to another profile manager that contains profiles to be distributed. The profile manager *AIX Machines* shown as a subscriber to the profile manager in Figure 11 on page 34 is an example of this. If changes occur in the network, machines can be added to and deleted from this "grouping" profile manager easily and without affecting other TME 10 operations.

2.8.4 Distributing Profiles

System configurations on the endpoints are only changed when the profile is distributed to these machines. When profiles are distributed to other profile managers, all that is changed are the profile databases, unless you explicitly distribute to a subscriber.

When distributing the profile, you can choose whether the distribution will stop at the first level of subscribers or whether it will be distributed to all subscribers. Figure 12 on page 36 shows a hierarchy of profile managers. If the distribution is stopped at the first level, it would only be distributed to one profile endpoint and to two profile managers; both are the initial level of subscribers of the top-level profile manager. If the distribution is sent to all subscribers, each profile endpoint and profile manager would receive a copy of the profile.

The option is also given when distributing a profile of whether to keep or to overwrite local modifications. The option to preserve modification will incorporate local changes made after the last distribution into the newly distributed information. The option to overwrite will erase any previous information and replace it with the profile's information.

Another means of distribution is to have an endpoint request it to happen. The endpoint will initiate a request to get a new copy of a profile. This will cause the profile to be distributed from the profile manager located one level higher in the hierarchy.

2.8.5 Synchronizing Profiles

Sometimes system files and databases of a profile endpoint are changed without using the TME 10 functions, and it may be desired that profiles are then updated to reflect these changes. This can be done with the **Synchronize...** option of a managed node's menu. The synchronize function works by profile type. Items that exist in the profile database but do not exist in the system's files or databases are removed from the profile database. Items that exist in both places but contain different information are altered in the profile database to reflect the actual system files or databases residing on that node. For items that exist in the actual system files but not in the profile database, a prompt is given in order to choose the profile to which the items should be added.

2.9 Performing Tasks in the TME 10 Environment

A *task library* is a resource that allows an administrator to create tasks and jobs. A *task* is an operation or set of operations that needs to be done within the TME 10 environment routinely. A *job* is a task that is executed on specific managed resources.

2.9.1 Task Library

The task library allows tasks and jobs to be created and also provides a place for the storage of binaries, scripts, or programs to be run in the TME 10 environment. Task libraries are created within policy regions, and more than one may be created in any given policy region. They can be arranged arbitrarily, perhaps to accommodate different types of tasks, different types of machines, or another configuration.

2.9.2 Tasks

A task that must be performed is defined and stored within a task library, and therefore it can be used repeatedly without having to redefine it. It is also useful to define tasks that grant authority to administrators to perform certain high-level functions without giving them high-level access to the system itself. When a task is created, as shown in Figure 13 on page 39, you must define the following aspects:

- Executables to be run
- Administrator role required
- User ID and user group under which the task will be executed

To display this dialog:
-> Policy Region (double-click)
-> Select **Create Task...** from pop-up menu of task library icon

Select each platform on which the task will run, which will allow you to specify the executables to be run on each platform type

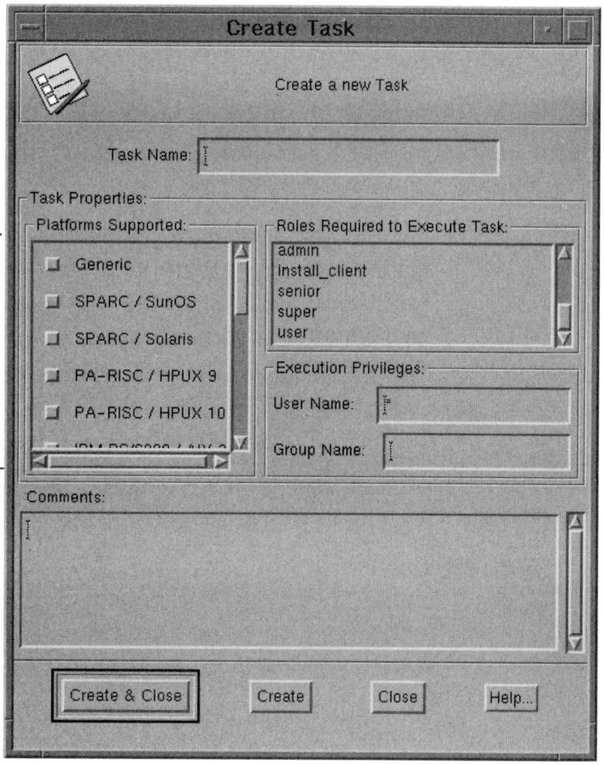

Figure 13. Create Task Dialog

Different executables may be specified for different platforms, which allows one task icon to perform work on many different operating systems. The executable files can reside on any managed node.

Changing Task Executables

An important thing to note about creating tasks is that after the task is initially created, the executable files used in the task are copied to the TME 10's binary tree. If you wish to edit the executable file after the task has been created, you should then edit the TME 10 task so that the new executable is copied again to the binary tree.

To execute the task one time without creating a job, the following must be defined:

- Task endpoints – The machines on which the task will run
- Format and destination of output

- Execution parameters – Example: time-out value
- Execution mode – Whether the job will run serial, parallel, or staged

After the task has been defined in the task library, it may then be edited or deleted.

2.9.3 Jobs

A job is simply a task that is executed on a specific set of managed resources. The task must exist before the job can be created. Several jobs can be created to run the same task, but with different sets of managed resources as task endpoints. When defining a job, the same things must be defined as when executing a task a single time: task endpoints, format and destination of output, execution parameters, and execution mode. Other than the task definitions, the job definitions contain specific target and execution parameters. Once a job is created, it may then be edited or deleted.

2.10 Scheduler

The scheduler can be thought of as a service within the TME 10 environment that will perform one-time or periodic scheduling of user-defined jobs as well as other functions, such as a profile distribution. The scheduler is helpful when you have tasks that must be performed on a regular basis or at times when administrators are not available to start the functions themselves. The window allowing the scheduling of a job is shown in Figure 14 on page 41:

To display this dialog:
-> Policy Region (double-click)
->Task Library (double-click)
-> Drag job icon and drop on
Scheduler icon in desktop

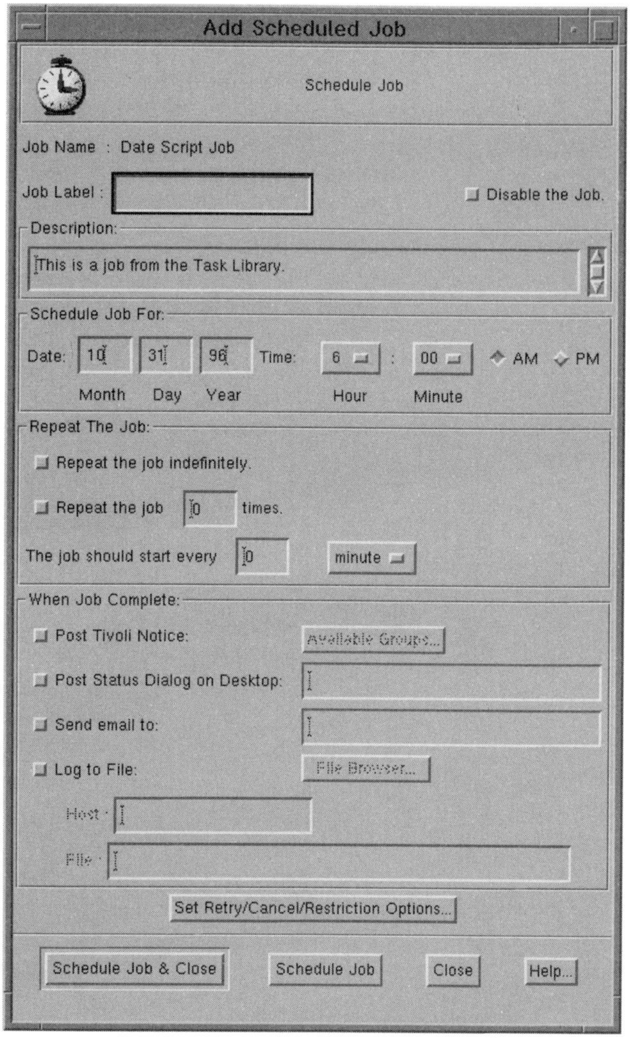

Figure 14. Add Scheduled Job Dialog

When scheduling a job to be executed, you must specify the following:

- Start date and time
- If and how the job should be repeated
- Notification that should be performed when the job is complete
- Conditions for cancelling a job
- Scheduling retries if a job fails

After the job has been scheduled, you can edit it or delete it from the scheduler.

2.11 Light Client Framework: A Glimpse Into the Future

In versions 3.1 and earlier, we have two types of TME 10 clients:

1. TME 10 client running the TME 10 Framework (managed node)
2. Limited-function TME 10 client running a PC agent

The full-function TME 10 clients possess some of the same capabilities as the TMR server, and they maintain a TME 10 database. In all, these clients have a fairly large footprint, and their maintenance and synchronization are expensive for the TMR server. A TMR server can therefore only support approximately 200 full-function clients or managed nodes.

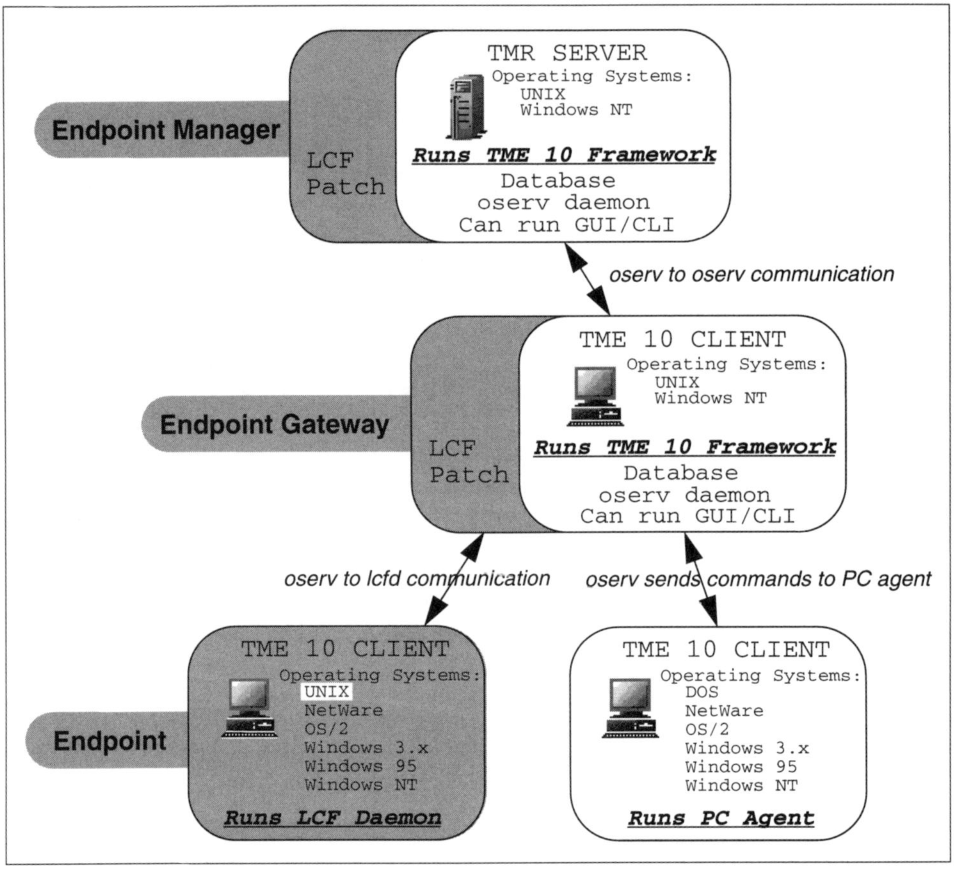

Figure 15. Light Client Framework

The current TME 10 Framework will be extended with a Light Client Framework (LCF) architecture. Figure 15 shows how the LCF elements (shaded) will be added to current TMR configurations. Compare this new environment also with the current basic configuration of a TMR as shown in Figure 5 on page 18.

The new LCF architecture elements are:

- ***Endpoint*** – A workstation running the LCF daemon, which extends TME 10 Framework functionality into PCs, thus eliminating the need for having to split the personality of a PC into a PC managed node and a 'dumb' PC agent. In addition to added CORBA intelligence, the new endpoints will receive more dynamic behavior and require less manual configuration. A machine not involved in the daily operations of managing a network computing environment is an endpoint. This includes UNIX platforms, which is new.
- ***Endpoint Gateway*** – Basically, a managed node as it exists in the current Framework with added functions to support dynamic configurations of endpoints and to take over all endpoint communications, thus relieving the TMR server from some of its control functions. An endpoint gateway is automatically configured as a repeater whose range includes all its assigned endpoints.
- ***Endpoint Manager*** – Is installed on the TMR server and assigns endpoints to endpoint gateways, either when the endpoints first log in to the TME 10 environment or when their assigned gateways become unavailable. The endpoint manager also maintains an endpoint list that contains information about each endpoint, including a unique identifier, the *odnum*, and the gateway to which it is assigned. In a small environment, the endpoint manager can also be defined as an endpoint gateway.

By extending into the endpoints, the object-oriented Framework becomes three-tiered. The LCF daemon is a small subset of the CORBA runtime that provides sufficient functionality to implement methods, such as the TME 10 Software Distribution filepack methods and the profile endpoint methods. Other parts of the LCF allow endpoint-initiated operations required for applications like TME 10 Distributed Monitoring and TME 10 Inventory.

The endpoint has no database. The information it needs is stored in its proxy managed node's database. A new endpoint logs in to the TME 10 environment with a broadcast message which is routed to the endpoint manager. The endpoint manager configures the new endpoint into the endpoint list, assigns an endpoint gateway, and informs both the endpoint gateway and the endpoint of their new relationship. From then on, all communications between the endpoint and the rest of the TME 10 environment go through that gateway.

The endpoints initially do not have any methods. When a method is called, the LCF daemon checks its cache, and if the method is not there, it is downloaded from the associated gateway.

The main benefit of the new LCF architecture extension will be:

- An huge increase in scalability. The number of managed nodes will still be limited to 200. However, the number of TME 10 clients with managed node-like functionality in a TMR can now be in the tens of thousands.
- Endpoints need not be statically configured anymore. There is strong support for DHCP-connected (dynamic host configuration protocol) clients and dynamic creation and configuration of endpoint definitions.

The new architecture will have little effect on the way TME 10 applications work. For instance, the TME 10 Software Distribution or TME 10 Inventory will work the same way with the endpoints as with PC managed nodes now. What changes is the TME 10 Framework underneath. With the introduction of endpoints, which can be considered dataless managed nodes, we will see two major differences:

- Profile distributions to subscribed endpoints will be dataless, meaning that no local profile copy is created in the endpoints as is the case with 'real' managed nodes. The actions related to the profile, however, will be performed as on managed nodes.
- More TME 10 applications will be able to run on the PC platform, such as the TME 10 Distributed Monitoring and the TME 10 Enterprise Console event adapters.

While TME 10 applications will be enhanced to support the new LCF clients, we will see a transition period in which some applications need the current PC managed node/PC agent configuration, and others, the endpoint functions. Mixed environments will be supported until PC managed nodes, and also NetWare managed sites, are not required anymore and eventually disappear.

CHAPTER 3

TME 10 User Administration

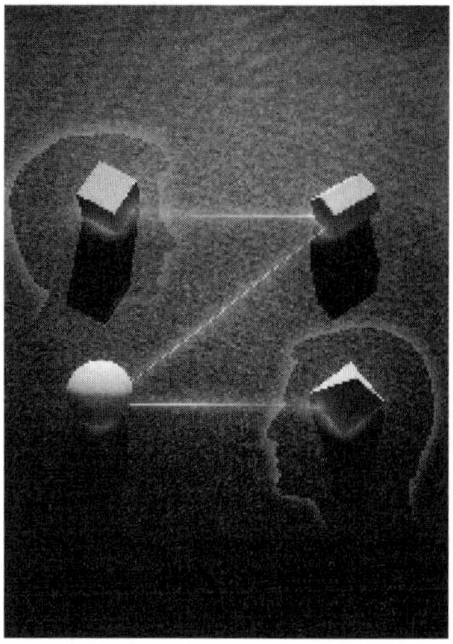

TME 10 User Administration, as shown in Figure 16, is one of the applications that can be installed on top of the TME 10 Framework. It extends the capabilities of the TME 10 environment and allows you to manage user accounts on the UNIX, Windows NT, and NetWare platforms from a single location.

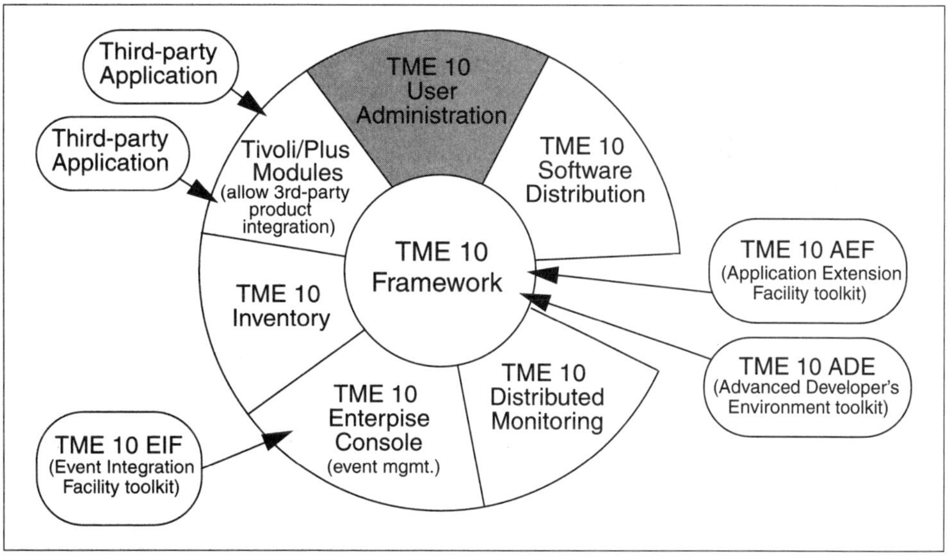

Figure 16. TME 10 Software Components

TME 10 User Administration provides your network computing environment with the following features:

- Centralized and GUI-based control of administration tasks
- Consistent administrative policy definition
- Automated repetitive administration tasks
- Parallel operations performed on many users and systems
- Delegation of administrative tasks to other administrators
- Configuration error reduction via profile-based methodology
- Single-action user management to synchronize logins and passwords

3.1 Overview and Product Information

This book covers the TME 10 User Administration at version level 3.0, or more precisely, it describes the functions and features of Tivoli/Admin Version 3.0 using the new TME 10 terminology. 3.1.2, "Features and Future" on page 49 describes what will change in TME 10 User Administration 3.1

3.1.1 Supported Platforms

The TME 10 User Administration software package consists of TME 10 User Administration for use on a UNIX managed node, as well as a separate code called PC Filepack Utilities that can be installed on a PC managed node to manage user definitions in a NetWare or Windows NT environment.

The TME 10 User Administration software has to be installed on each UNIX managed node to be able to perform the TME 10 User Administration features. The following operating systems are supported:

- AIX
- HP-UX
- SunOS
- Solaris

The TME 10 User Administration software for a PC managed node runs on the following operating systems:

- Windows NT
- NetWare

In this release, if a Windows NT server or workstation is configured as a managed node, it also has to be configured as a PC managed node to be able to perform the user administration functions.

Refer to the *TME 10 User Administration Release Notes* for disk space requirements for TME 10 User Administration.

3.1.2 Features and Future

TME 10 User Administration Version 3.0 includes user, group, and host namespace profiles. When you install TME 10 Net.Commander 3.0, aside from having the Internet Services management, it will also contain the host namespace profile capability. Obviously, there is an overlap of functions between these two products for their 3.0 versions.

Future versions of TME 10 User Administration will not contain the host namespace profile and the Message of the Day (MOTD) capabilities, which are moved to TME 10 Net.Commander. Table 1 lists where the version 3.0 functions will be available in the future.

Table 1. Current Content and Future of TME 10 User Administration

Version 3.0 Features	TME 10 User Administration 3.1	TME 10 Net.Commander 3.1
User Management	✓	
Group Management	✓	
NIS Management	✓	
Mail aliases	✓	
Process Signaler	✓	
Host Namespace Management		✓
Internet Services		✓
MOTD Services		✓
Trusted Hosts, Root, Users	✓	
Configuration File Updates	✓	

In TME 10 User Administration 3.1, Windows NT will be supported as a managed node.

3.1.3 Concepts and Architecture at a Glance

TME 10 User Administration is a profile-based application that works according to the *management by subscription* model. In this model, profiles contained in a profile manager define specific aspects of system configuration, such as user account information, group information, or host information. A profile record (or entry) represents the actual configuration information about one user, group, or host. In order to receive this configuration information, managed nodes, PC managed nodes, and NetWare managed sites subscribe to the profiles. Once data is stored in the profile or modified, you can distribute it to subscribers, thus updating their system information.

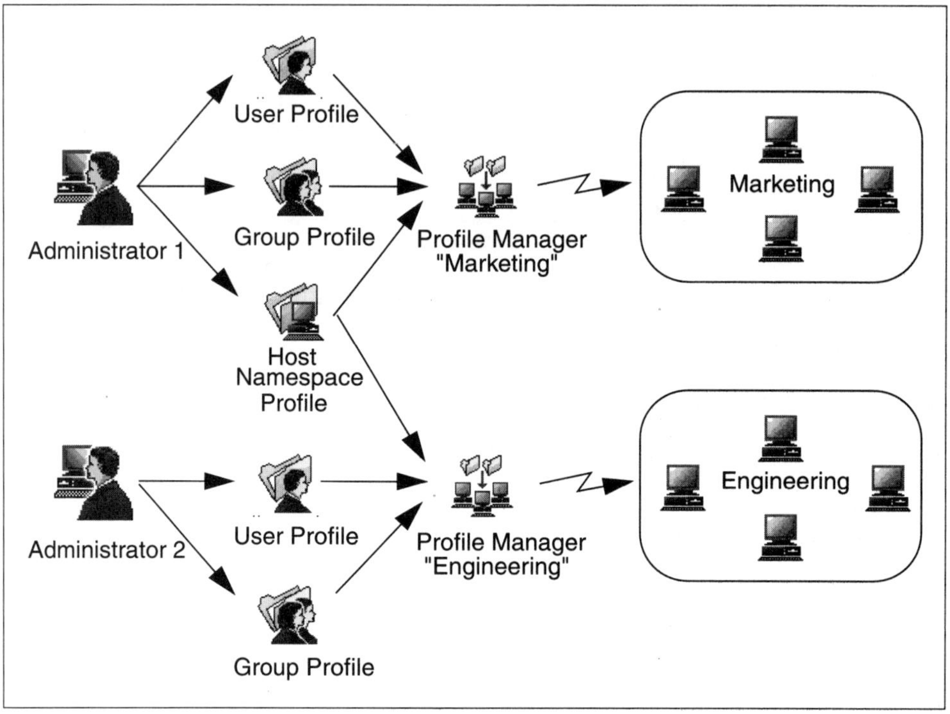

Figure 17. Relationship between Profiles, Profile Managers, and Managed Nodes

Figure 17 shows the relationship between profiles, profile managers, and managed nodes for user, group, and host namespace information as provided by TME 10 User Administration.

Profile entries can either be manually added one at a time, or they can be initially imported (*populated*) from one or more subscribed managed nodes. The profiles are stored in the TME 10 database of the TMR server. Creating profile entries will be covered in Sections 3.5.1, "Populating a Profile" on page 60, and 3.6.1, "Adding Profile Records" on page 67.

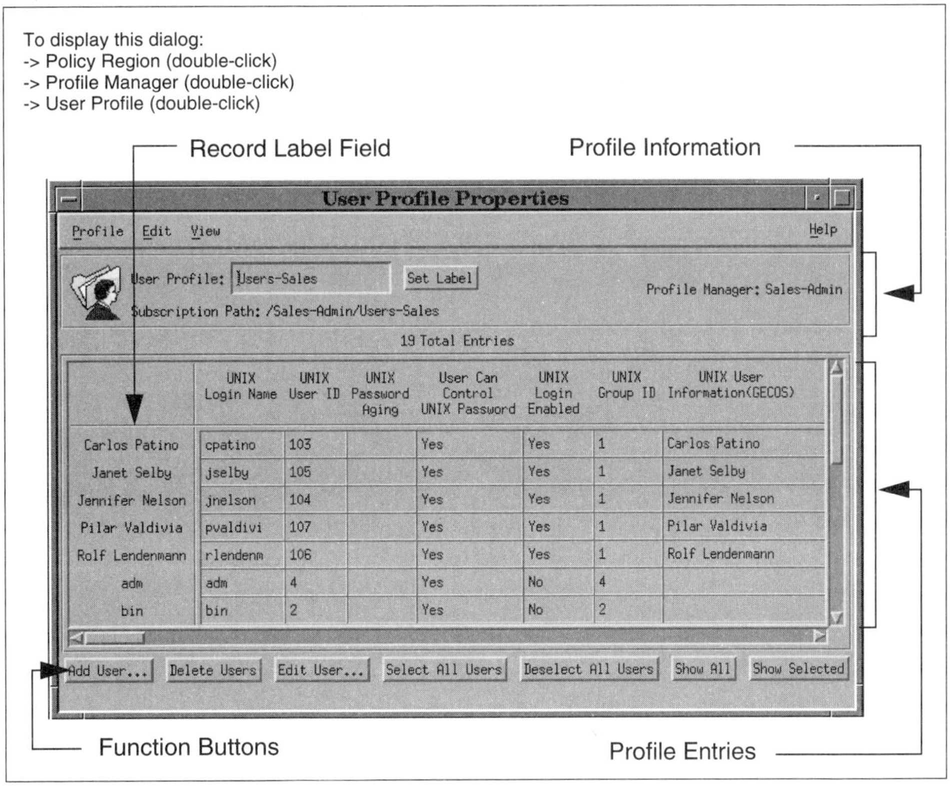

	UNIX Login Name	UNIX User ID	UNIX Password Aging	User Can Control UNIX Password	UNIX Login Enabled	UNIX Group ID	UNIX User Information(GECOS)
Carlos Patino	cpatino	103		Yes	Yes	1	Carlos Patino
Janet Selby	jselby	105		Yes	Yes	1	Janet Selby
Jennifer Nelson	jnelson	104		Yes	Yes	1	Jennifer Nelson
Pilar Valdivia	pvaldivi	107		Yes	Yes	1	Pilar Valdivia
Rolf Lendenmann	rlendenm	106		Yes	Yes	1	Rolf Lendenmann
adm	adm	4		Yes	No	4	
bin	bin	2		Yes	No	2	

Figure 18. User Profile Properties Dialog

Figure 18 shows an example of a *User Profile Properties* window that already contains several records.

The Profile Information area displays information such as the profile's name, the profile manager that contains the profile, and the profile's icon. In this example, the user profile displays all users of the Sales department. Each of the profile entries represents the information about a specific user and will create or maintain a single line in the corresponding system configuration file, the `/etc/passwd` file, of each workstation.

Any attribute contained in the profile can be designated as the record label. In this example, the *UNIX User Information (GECOS)* attribute was selected as a record label. Finally, the function buttons allow you to perform specific operations such as adding, deleting, or editing an entry as well as selecting or deselecting a set of entries.

In order to update system configuration files on the managed target machines, the profiles must be distributed to them. To be able to distribute profiles, an association has to be made between profiles and target machines (subscribers). This is done by using the profile manager's subscription list. Profile managers contain profiles and reside within a policy region. In order to get a profile manager window, you need to open the associated policy region in the TME 10 desktop.

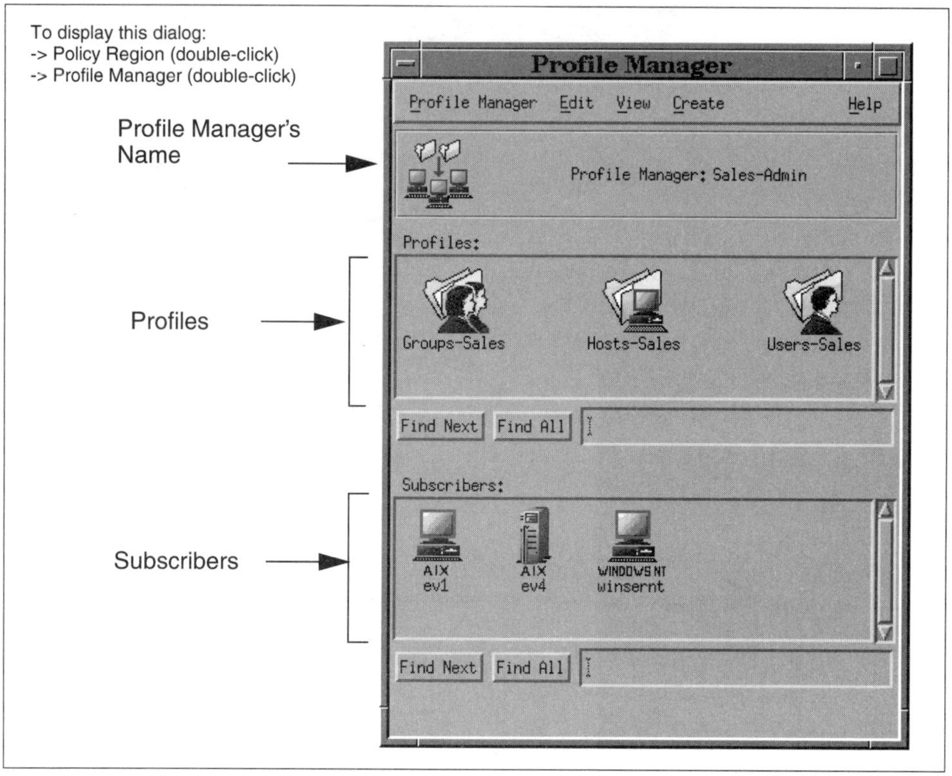

Figure 19. Profile Manager Dialog with Profiles and Subscribers

Figure 19 shows an example of a *Profile Manager* window. It is the Sales-Admin profile manager, which contains all user, group, and host namespace profiles for the sales department. The Subscribers area displays to which endpoints (managed nodes, PC managed nodes, or NIS domains) or to which other profile managers the profiles may be distributed. When a distribution is initiated, the administrator can specify whether the profile(s) go to all subscribers or to particular subscribers only. In our example the profile manager has the following subscribers:

- *ev1* and *ev4* (managed nodes)
- *winsernt* (PC managed node)

The above example shows a profile manager that deals with TME 10 User Administration profiles. Other entities, such as TME 10 Software Distribution file packages or TME 10 Distributed Monitoring profiles, could be added if the set of subscribers and policies are the same as for the TME 10 User Administration profiles.

Figure 20 summarizes the actions involved in defining and distributing system files using TME 10 User Administration. Remember that the following actions are performed within a *Profile Manager* window.

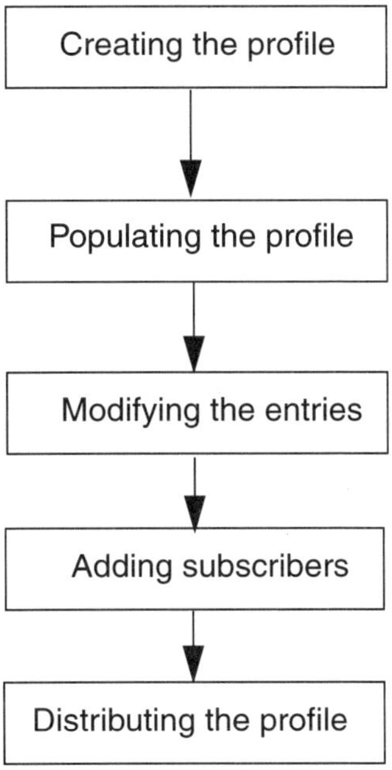

Create the TME 10 User Administration profile depending on which type of system configuration information you want to store in it. TME 10 User Administration profiles are user, group, and host namespace profiles.

The profile by itself is only a definition of the information that it will contain. Populating the profile means to get information from a system configuration file on any subscribed node in your environment.

Modify the information contained in a profile. Common operations could be adding a new entry, editing an existing entry, or deleting an entry.

Define which managed nodes, PC managed nodes, NIS domains, or profiles managers are the target of a distribution.

Send a copy of the profile to the selected subscribers in order to update the configuration files on an endpoint or make copies of the profile in a lower level of your hierarchy.

Figure 20. Tasks Involved in Customizing and Using TME 10 User Administration

3.2 Managed Resources

Like other TME 10 applications, TME 10 User Administration is based on managed resources. A managed resource in this context is a set of centrally managed definitions or parameters to be enforced in a set of target machines. The managed resources added or extended by installing TME 10 User Administration are:

 User Profile – Provides profile-based management of user account information. In a user profile each record is stored in a platform-independent format and contains information related to UNIX, Windows NT, and NetWare accounts, as well as the common login and common password. Example attributes that are stored include user name, user ID, password, home directory, and login shell. The profile resides in a profile manager and needs to be distributed to its subscribers to enforce the user account information on the managed nodes.

 Group Profile – A group profile is a collection of UNIX group-specific information such as valid groups, group IDs, and membership list. This information is typically located in the `/etc/group` file. The profile resides in a profile manager and needs to be distributed to its subscribers to enforce the group information on the managed nodes.

 Host Namespace Profile – A host namespace profile contains information related to host mapping information, typically located in the `/etc/hosts` file. It is possible to add, edit, or delete host-to-IP address entries and aliases associated with a host for any target system. The profile resides in a profile manager and needs to be distributed to its subscribers to enforce the host namespace information on the managed nodes.

 UNIX Managed Nodes – The UNIX host management facility extends the management capabilities over all UNIX managed nodes in the TMR by adding the following functions to the pop-up menus of the managed nodes' icons:

- Viewing the properties and network interface information
- Toggling the appearance of the icon that represents a managed node
- Enabling or disabling Internet services
- Viewing or signaling processes running on a managed node
- Editing local mail aliases
- Viewing or editing the remote authentication database
- Distributing or updating system configuration files
- Modifying the message of the day

The concept of host in this chapter refers to a UNIX system in a UNIX network.

NIS Domain – The NIS map management facility allows you to manage NIS domains as policy region resources. The NIS master server must be a managed node. The following operations over NIS domains are provided:

- Discovering existing NIS domains
- Adding, editing, or removing NIS maps and map data
- Checking the syntax of a map source file

TME 10 User Administration does not create NIS domains; it only creates objects that represent the domains that exist on managed hosts.

3.3 TME 10 User Administration Profiles

Since many key concepts of the TME 10 architecture are important in each of the TME 10 applications, it may be helpful to review some of them in order to understand the new concepts.

3.3.1 Key Points About Profiles

As discussed in Chapter 2, "TME 10 Framework" on page 15, a profile is an application-specific collection of information related to a specific application that lets you manage a specific type of resource. A profile also contains a list of subscribers (members of the list) to which the profile can be distributed in order to update or change system configuration information.

There is a strong relationship between profiles, profile managers, policy regions, and endpoints. Here are some key points about this relationship:

- Profile managers are created within a policy region.
- Profile managers contain profiles and subscriber lists.
- One profile can be in more than one profile manager.
- Two user profiles with the same information cannot be within the same profile manager.
- Subscriber lists may contain other profile managers, endpoints (target machines), or NIS domains.
- Profile manager hierarchies are created when profile managers have other profile managers in their subscriber lists.
- Profile manager hierarchies allow you to manage your resources from a top-down approach in your organization.

For more information about profile policy, profiles, and profile managers in general, see the *TME 10 Framework User's Guide*.

3.3.2 Profile Scope

Specifically, TME 10 User Administration profiles allow you to manage the user, group, host namespace, and NIS map configuration information.

User profiles can manage UNIX, Windows NT, and NetWare accounts, whereas group profiles and host namespace profiles can only manage UNIX group accounts and UNIX host-to-IP address mapping, respectively. When an NIS domain subscribes to profiles, its master server will get the system files on a distribution, provided that it is a managed node.

Table 2 shows the system files in a UNIX system that are modified when you use a user, group, or host namespace profile to change the configuration information:

Table 2. UNIX System Configuration Files

UNIX Information (System File)	Corresponding TME 10 Information (Profile Type)	Scope
/etc/hosts	Host Namespace Profile	Host Namespace management, such as: • Adding, editing, or deleting host-to-IP address mapping entries • Adding, editing, or removing aliases associated with a host
/etc/group	Group Profile	Group management, such as: • Defining a new group • Modifying or deleting an existing group
/etc/passwd	User Profile	User management, such as: • Creating, changing, or deleting user account information • Creating, modifying, or deleting home directories • Copying start-up files • Specifying group membership

User profiles can be populated from any managed node or PC managed node (Windows NT or NetWare) and they can be distributed to any endpoint. Possible subscribers can be:

- Other profile managers
- Managed nodes
- NIS domains
- PC managed nodes (Windows NT, NetWare NDS trees, NetWare 3.X servers)

User, group, and host namespace profiles are managed resources, and each policy region maintains a list of managed resource types that are valid for that specific policy region. In order for an administrator to create or manage a profile, the following must be true:

- The profile manager must be a managed resource of the policy region.
- The particular profile type, such as user, group, or host namespace, must be a managed resource of the policy region.
- The administrator must have the senior role to create profile managers.
- The administrator must have an administrator role to maintain the profiles in the policy region.

3.3.3 Creating a Profile

Before you can add any users, groups, or host names, you must create a profile. Initially, when you create a profile, it does not have any records. This means that you will need to manually add records one at a time, or copy records from another profile or populate your profile by getting the data from one or more endpoints. When you create a profile, you are basically creating an empty template.

Just like any other TME 10 profile, a TME 10 User Administration profile is created within a profile manager using the *Create* pull-down menu and specifying the appropriate profile type (UserProfile, GroupProfile, HostNamespace).

However, before the TME 10 User Administration profile options are presented to you in the upcoming *Create Profile* dialog, you must add the TME 10 User Administration profiles to the managed resources in your policy region. You can do this from the *Properties* pull-down menu in the policy region window when you select the **Managed Resources...** option. You can also call the *Set Managed Resources* dialog to check whether the TME 10 User Administration profiles are listed under the currently managed resource types.

3.4 Default and Validation Policies

Each profile has a set of *default policies* associated with it. The default policies determine the default values used when creating a new entry for a profile. These default values can help you minimize the amount of data that you have to enter when creating a new record. Because of the nature of the entries that a host namespace profile manages, there is no default policy values for them.

The default policy can specify a default value for one or more of the attributes associated with a profile. Therefore, any default policy values that you define will work as a template for each new record you add to the profile.

Every time you modify or create a profile entry, it is checked against a set of *validation policies* that ensure that the data you are providing complies with the current policy. Validation is performed in the same way when populating a profile. This prevents you from creating or getting an entry that does not meet your specifications. You can also request a validation for a specific profile at any time.

To display this dialog:
-> Policy Region (double-click)
-> Profile Manager (double-click)
-> User, Group or Host Namespace Profile (double-click)
-> Select the **Validation Policies** option from the *Edit* pull-down menu.

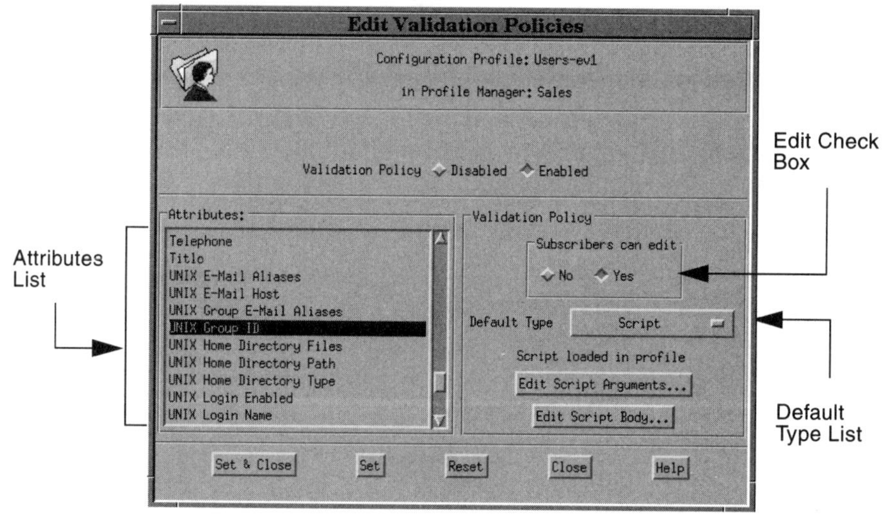

Figure 21. Edit Validation Policies Dialog

Figure 21 on page 58 shows the *Edit Validation Policies* dialog for a user profile. This dialog allows you to edit the validation policies for a user profile. The Attributes list allows you to select the attribute for which you want to define a validation policy. The *Subscribers can edit* radio button determines whether or not subscribers can change the validation policy for the selected attribute in their local copy.

The Default Type list determines the validation type used to validate the attribute. Selected is Script, which requires you to provide shell script arguments (**Edit Script Arguments...** button) and a shell script body (**Edit Script Body...** button). Other values for the default type are: *None*, *Constant*, and *Regular Expression.*

In the same way as shown in Figure 21 on page 58 for validation policies, administrators can edit default policies that implement rules for generating default values. For more information about user and group profile policies, refer to Appendix E in the *TME 10 User and Group Management Guide*.

3.5 Setting Up and Distributing TME 10 User Administration Profiles

In client/server environments, there are potentially hundreds or thousands of user accounts, hundreds of system configuration files, or hundreds of network interface configurations. To manage them with TME 10 User Administration, you need to plan your TME 10 User Administration profiles carefully.

The section covers the following operations:

- Populating a profile
- Adding subscribers
- Distributing a profile
- Other profile operations

For details on adding, manipulating, locking and unlocking profile *records*, see Section 3.6, “Managing TME 10 User Administration Profile Records” on page 67.

The operations listed above are common for every type of profile. In order not to repeat the same information for each type of profile, the following explanations will be general. From this point on to the end of the chapter, we will use the term profile to refer to any type of TME 10 User Administration profile.

Important

Remember that in order to create or maintain a profile you must have the particular profile type as a managed resource and an administrator role within your policy region.

3.5.1 Populating a Profile

Populating a profile means importing information defined in a system configuration file from one or more managed nodes. When populating a profile, you can specify which endpoints to retrieve the information from and whether this information should overwrite the original profile information or append that information to the profile. For example, you can populate a user profile with the users from one or more endpoints.

To display this dialog:
-> Policy Region (double-click)
-> Profile Manager (double-click)
-> User, Group or Host Namespace Profile (double-click)
-> Select the **Populate**... option from the *Edit* pull-down menu.

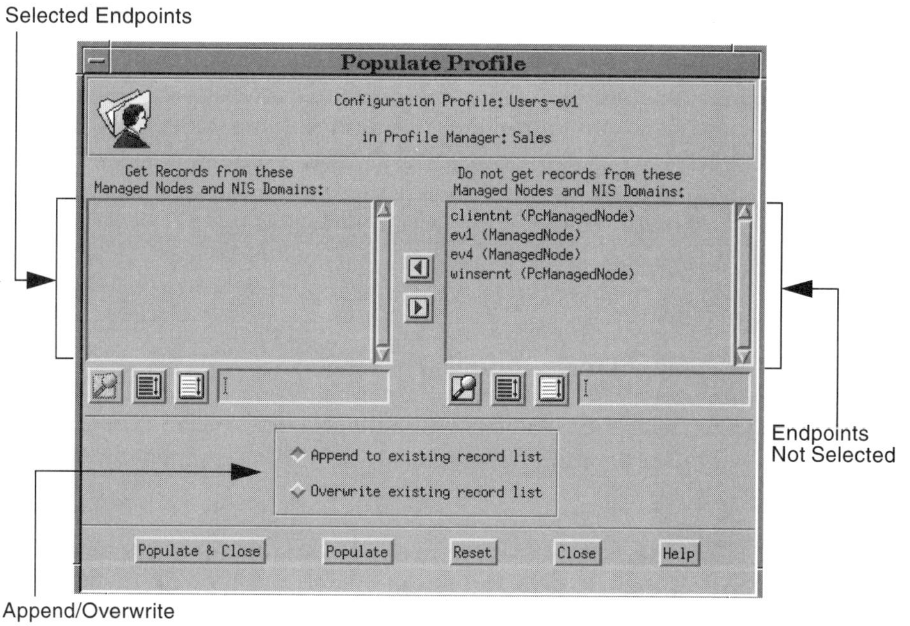

Figure 22. Populate Profile Dialog

The Selected Endpoints area in the *Populate Profile* dialog (Figure 22) lists the TME 10 resources from which to populate the profile. You can move one or more entries from the other area, Endpoints Not Selected, to the left in order to designate the source(s) for the populate operation. The **Append/Overwrite** radio buttons determine whether to add the new records to the existing records in the profile or replace the contents of the profile with the new records.

For more information about populating a profile, see the *TME 10 Framework User's Guide*.

3.5.1.1 Specialties About Populating a User Profile

When you populate a user profile, TME 10 User Administration attempts to merge duplicate user information coming from different managed nodes into the user records of the profile. The login name is used as the key to determine whether there is a match between user information. If there is a match between login names, then TME 10 User Administration verifies the operating system type. If the information comes from the same operating system type, an error is returned. Otherwise, if the operating systems are different, the new record information is merged into the existing profile record.

3.5.1.2 Specialties About Populating a Host Namespace Profile

If TME 10 User Administration finds any problems while attempting to populate a host namespace profile, it displays an error dialog. A common error is the `resource exists` error, which indicates that two or more hosts have been given the same address. To avoid this error, use one line in the /etc/hosts file to define all the host name aliases associated with a single IP address.

3.5.2 Adding Subscribers

Profiles reside in profile managers. In order to distribute the profiles to endpoints, it is necessary to subscribe endpoints to a profile manager. Possible endpoints for user and group profiles are discussed in Section 3.3.2, "Profile Scope" on page 56.

TME 10 User Administration uses the list of subscribers to determine which endpoints are the target of a distribution. Even though the subscription takes place at the profile manager level, user profiles recognize two levels of subscribers: profile manager subscribers and record level subscribers. Record level subscribers are only available for user profiles, and they are explained in Section 3.5.3.2, "Specialties About Distributing a User Profile" on page 65.

3.5.3 Distributing a Profile

After you have populated a profile or modified the records of a profile, you must distribute the profile to the subscribers to make use of the new information contained in the profile. There are two types of profile distribution:

- Next level of subscribers – When you distribute the profile, you will affect only the *TME 10 databases* of the next level of subscribers. The system files on the target machines will not be updated. To update the system files, you can then run a distribution from the individual endpoints as explained in Section 3.5.3.1, "Distributing from an Endpoint" on page 63.
- All levels of subscribers – Distribution is to all levels, and the receiving endpoint will use the information contained in the profile to modify the system configuration files or NIS maps.

To display this dialog:
-> Policy Region (double-click)
-> Profile Manager (double-click)
-> User, Group or Host Namespace Profile (double-click)
-> Select the **Distribute...** option from the *Profile* pull-down menu.

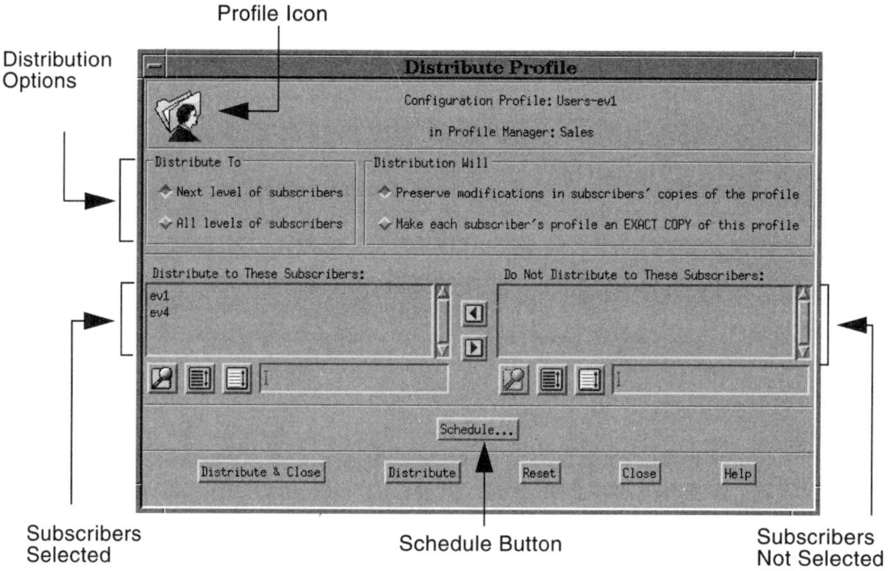

Figure 23. Distribute Profile Dialog

Figure 23 shows the *Distribute Profile* dialog that allows you to distribute the profiles. The selected subscribers will receive all records defined in the profile. The Subscribers Not Selected are subscribers to the profile manager that you want to exclude from receiving this particular profile.

If you click the **Next level of subscribers** radio button, the copy will only be sent to the next level of subscribers, and the system configuration files on the target machines are not updated. This enables you to make changes to a subscriber's copy before further distribution. On the other hand, if you click **All levels of subscribers**, all profile copies located on the subscribers will be changed, including the actual system files on the profile endpoints.

If you click the **Preserve modifications in subscriber's copy of the profile** radio button, any changes made in the local copies of the profile since the last distribution will be kept. On the other hand, if you click **Make subscriber's profile an EXACT COPY of this profile**, the distribution will overwrite the subscriber's profile with an exact copy of the profile being distributed, thereby eliminating any local changes made since the last distribution.

Caution

Requesting an exact copy literally deletes any non-matching entries.

Note that changes to local copies of profiles can be limited on a record level by locking records (see Section 3.6.2, "Locking and Unlocking the Information in Profile Records" on page 70). The distribution of the profile can be scheduled for a later time by using the *Add Scheduled Job* dialog. Pushing the **Distribute** or **Distribute & Close** buttons will execute the distribution and either leave the *Distribute Profile* window open or close it.

For more information about distributing a profile, see the *TME 10 Framework User's Guide*.

3.5.3.1 Distributing from an Endpoint

After a profile is distributed, it appears in the dialogs of its subscribers (endpoints or profile managers) as a local profile icon. You can access local profile copies by double-clicking on a managed node's icon. As shown in Figure 24 on page 64, the window presented displays the node's local profile icons.

To display this dialog:
-> Policy Region (double-click)
-> ev7 Managed Node icon (double-click)

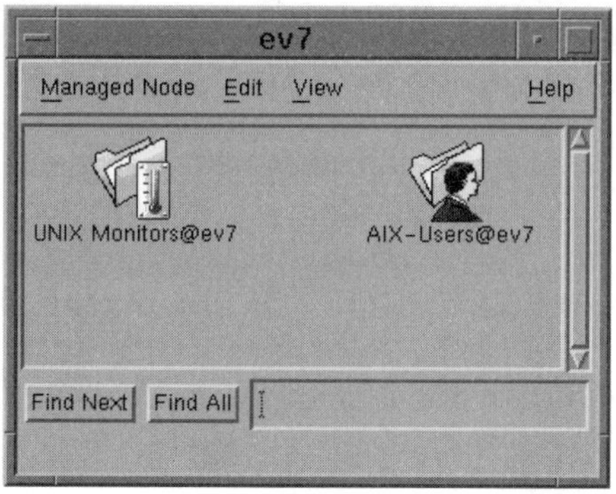

Figure 24. Local Profile Copies an on Endpoint

Distributing such a local profile updates the system files for only that node. This is also called *distributing from an endpoint* versus distributing from a profile manager.

To display this dialog:
-> Policy Region (double-click)
-> ev7 Managed Node icon (double-click)
-> User, Group or Host Namespace Profile (double-click)
-> Select the **Distribute...** option from the *Profile* pull-down menu.

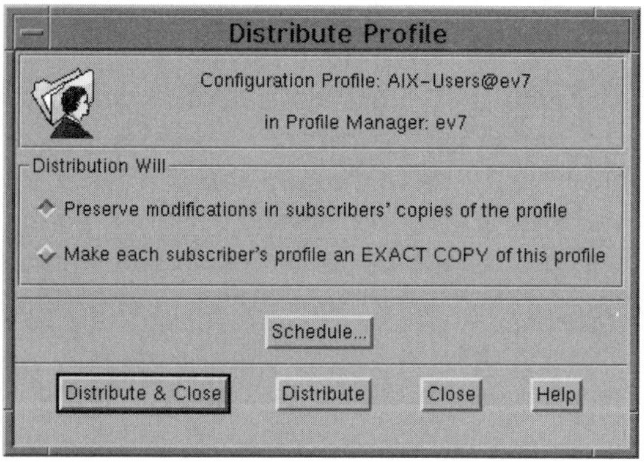

Figure 25. Distribute Profile Dialog on an Endpoint

When distributing from a local profile on an endpoint, you get the dialog shown in Figure 25. This gives you the option to replace the whole system configuration file, making it an exact copy of the profile, or you can choose to preserve the modifications made since the last distribution.

3.5.3.2 Specialties About Distributing a User Profile

User profiles offer two levels of subscribers, a feature that is only available for this type of profile:

- Profile manager subscribers
- Record level subscribers

When distributing a user profile, TME 10 User Administration first uses the profile manager level to determine to which endpoints and profile managers the profile will be distributed. Then TME 10 User Administration makes use of the record level to verify which records each particular subscriber will actually receive. For details on how to set the record level subscribers for a user profile record, see Section 3.6.1.1, "Adding User Records" on page 67.

For example, let's suppose that you have a user profile called *ITSO-Users* that has three user account records with the following record level subscribers:

- The first user record lists the managed nodes, *itso1*, *itso2,* and *itso3*.
- The second user record lists the managed nodes, *itsorus* and *itsobig.*
- The third user record lists only the managed node, *ev1.*

Also, the profile manager that contains the *ITSO-Users* profile lists the managed nodes *itso1*, *itso2*, *itso3*, *itsorus*, *itsobig*, *ev1,* and *ev4* as profile manager subscribers.

If you distribute the *ITSO-Users* profile using the **All levels of subscribers** option the following distributions occur:

- The first user record is added to the managed nodes, *itso1*, *itso2,* and *itso3.*
- The second user record is added to the managed nodes, *itsorus* and *itsobig.*
- The third user record is added to the managed node, *ev1.*
- No user records are added to the managed node, *ev4.*

3.5.4 Other Profile Operations

At this point, we have discussed the actions involved in creating and distributing information using TME 10 User Administration. In this section we will talk about additional operations that facilitate the handling of TME 10 User Administration profiles. This section covers the following operations:

- Cloning a profile

- Deleting a profile
- Navigating from one profile copy to another

The operations listed above are common for every type of profile. In order not to repeat the same information for each type of profile, the following explanations will be general.

3.5.4.1 Cloning a Profile

When you clone a profile, you create an exact copy of the profile you are cloning, including the default and validation policies associated with the original profile. However, the new profile does not have the same entries and subscribers as the original profile. The new profile has no records because it is not possible to have two profiles of the same type with the same information in the same profile manager.

3.5.4.2 Deleting a Profile

Deleting a profile deletes the original profile, the entries contained in the profile, and the copies of the profile that reside in every profile manager subscribed to the profile manager's list. Deleting a profile does not delete the information contained in the configuration files at the endpoints that were subscribed to the profile manager.

To delete the contents of the system's configuration files you must delete all the entries contained in your profile and then distribute the empty profile to the endpoints. The previous operation will delete everything, except the root entry, any NIS directives in the configuration files, and the Admin entry for Windows NT or NetWare.

3.5.4.3 Navigating from One Profile Copy to Another

From within a profile, you can display any other (distributed) copy of the profile in the subscription hierarchy. Depending on your authorization role, you can perform operations on the displayed profile copies out on the managed nodes. For more information about authorization roles, refer to Chapter 2, "TME 10 Framework" on page 15.

3.6 Managing TME 10 User Administration Profile Records

This section explains how to manage the profile records of TME 10 User Administration profiles, including:

- Adding Records
- Handling and Manipulating Records
- Locking and Unlocking the Information in Profile Records

The majority of these tasks can be performed from the corresponding Profile Properties window (*User Profile Properties* window, *Group Profile Properties* window, or *Host Namespace Profile Properties* window). Therefore, you should open the appropriate Profile Properties window (by double-clicking on a profile icon) to perform these operations.

Remember to Save Profiles

Every time you modify the contents of a group profile or a host namespace profile you must save the profile before closing the corresponding profile properties window in order to preserve the changes. If you modify the contents of a user profile, it is not necessary to save the profile.

3.6.1 Adding Profile Records

Adding records to a profile can be performed one at a time, manually, or by populating the profile, or by copying records from another profile. Populating a profile is explained in Section 3.5.1, "Populating a Profile" on page 60. Therefore, this section describes how to add records manually.

When you create a new record, TME 10 User Administration stores the information in the corresponding profile database. The new information is not applied to any system files until the profile is distributed to its ultimate destination, which is a set of subscribing systems or NIS domains.

3.6.1.1 Adding User Records

In order to add a new user, you click the **Add User...** button in the profile window. See Figure 18 on page 51 for a profile window. Figure 26 on page 68 shows the *User Properties* dialog that allows you to enter the user account information.

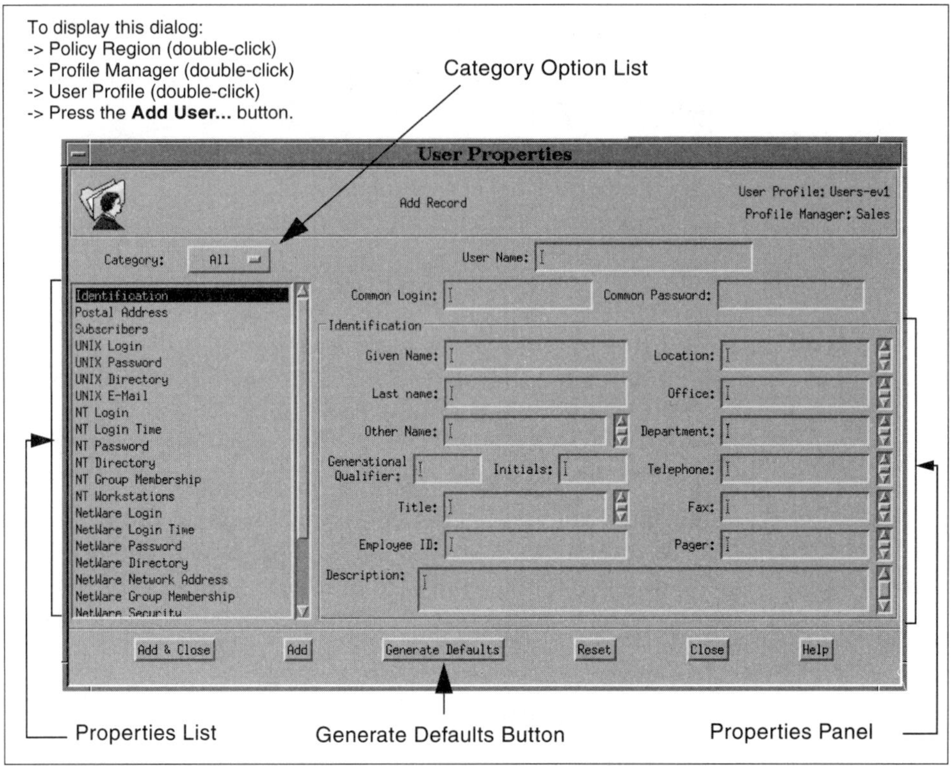

Figure 26. User Properties Dialog

The Properties Panel area is where you add the profile record information. Its content changes with what is selected in the Properties List. Figure 26 shows the panel for User Identification. With the Category Option list, you can filter what is displayed in the Properties List. The available categories are: *All*, *General*, *NT*, *NetWare,* and *UNIX*.

The **Generate Defaults** button allows you to apply (fill in) the default policy values to the fields in the properties panel. The **Add** function implicitly runs a Generate Defaults for all values left empty.

As explained in Section 3.5.3.2, “Specialties About Distributing a User Profile” on page 65, a user profile has two levels of subscribers:

- Profile manager subscribers
- Record level subscribers

If you want to specify record level subscription for the user record you are currently modifying, you must select **Subscribers** from the Properties List (third item from the top of the list in Figure 26), and then select the corresponding subscribers. Remember that the record level subscribers override the profile manager subscribers.

3.6.1.2 Adding Group Records

Figure 27 shows the *Add Record To Profile* dialog that allows you to enter the group account information.

To display this dialog:
-> Policy Region (double-click)
-> Profile Manager (double-click)
-> Group Profile (double-click)
-> Press the **Add Group...** button.

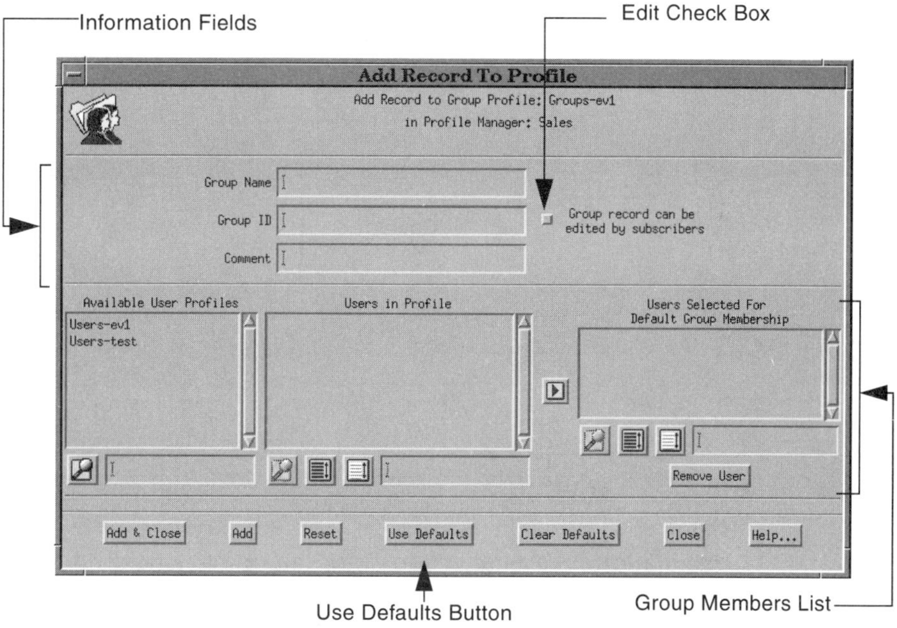

Figure 27. Add Record To Profile Dialog

The information fields allow you to enter the group name, group ID (GID), and comments about the group. The Edit Check Box specifies whether or not subscribers can change the record in their own copies of the profile.

Group members can be added by opening a profile from the Available User Profiles list and selecting users from the Users in Profile list. The **Use Defaults** button allows you to fill in the default policy values set for these fields. If you press this button after you have entered information into a field for which a default policy is defined, TME 10 User Administration replaces your information with the default information.

3.6.1.3 Adding Host Records

Figure 28 shows the *Add Host Entry to Profile* dialog that allows you to enter the host information.

To display this dialog:
-> Policy Region (double-click)
-> Profile Manager (double-click)
-> Host Namespace Profile (double-click)
-> Press the **Add Host...** button.

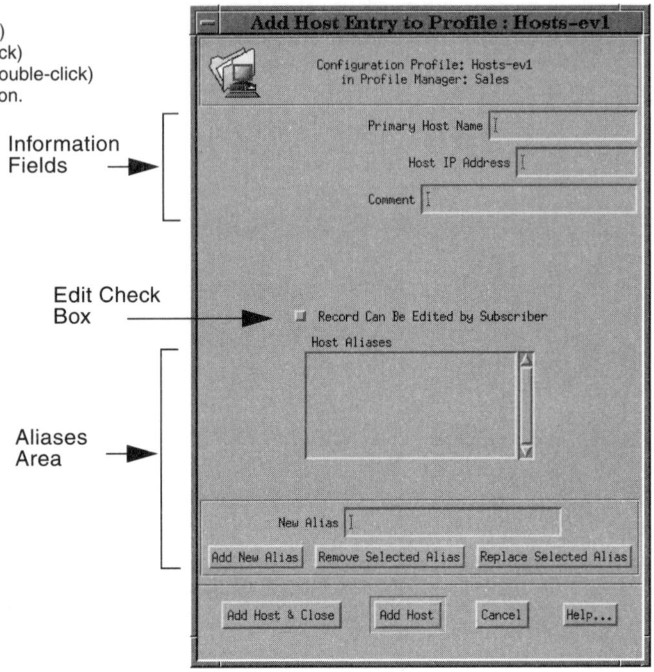

Figure 28. Add Host Entry to Profile Dialog

In the information fields you enter the primary host name, host IP address, and comments about the host you are adding. Alias names for this host entry can be added in the Aliases area. The Edit Check Box determines whether or not subscribers can change the record.

3.6.2 Locking and Unlocking the Information in Profile Records

It is possible to lock any record of the profile to prevent the local administrators of the lower levels from changing the contents of a specific record. You must distribute the profile after locking or unlocking records in order for this operation to take effect, which means you actually lock/unlock records on the target machines.

You can lock all records contained in a profile, but is not possible to lock an entire profile. In other words, administrators cannot modify the locked records, but they can add new records to a lower-level profile copy.

Unlocking the information in profile records is the opposite operation of locking the information. Unlocking records that were previously locked allows the local administrators of the lower levels to change the contents of those records.

3.6.3 Handling and Manipulating Records

This section briefly explains the available functions for manipulating profile records. It includes descriptions of the following topics:

- Viewing records
- Editing records
- Deleting records
- Copying records
- Moving records
- Validating records
- Retrieving records
- Finding records
- Sorting records
- Sorting record attributes

These tasks can be performed from the *User Profile Properties* dialog, which is shown in Figure 18 on page 51.

3.6.3.1 Viewing Records

You can view the information contained in the profile for each kind of profile in a table format. Each column contains specific information about the record. You can scroll through the window to view the records stored in the profile and the information stored in each record. The *View* pull-down menu provides you some options, such as redefining the sort order of the records and which of the many attributes are displayed for each record. See Sections 3.6.3.9, "Sorting Records" on page 76, and 3.6.3.10, "Sorting Record Attributes" on page 77, for details.

3.6.3.2 Editing Records

Double-clicking on a profile record brings back up the dialog used to add a record, such as the User Properties window shown in Figure 26 on page 68, which also allows you to modify a record. Every time a record is changed, the new information is stored in the profile database, and a notice reporting the changes is sent to the notice database. See Section 2.7, "Notification (Bulletin Board) Facility" on page 32 for more information about notification.

It's important to keep in mind that any change made in a profile record will not take effect until you distribute the profile to its ultimate destination, the endpoints subscribed to the profile.

Specialties About Editing User Records

When you edit an entry of a user profile, the entry is locked to prevent someone else from editing the same entry. Only the entry you are working on is locked, meaning that several administrators can have the same user profile open at the same time.

If you edit a user profile entry and you change the user ID (UID) of a user account, TME 10 User Administration will automatically change the user's home directory and the files owned by the user.

3.6.3.3 Deleting Records

If you no longer need the information stored in a record, you can delete the record from the profile. Remember that if you delete a specific record from a profile and if you want to update the copies on the target machines of that profile, you must distribute the profile.

Specialties About Deleting User Records

To delete a user profile record, you either click the **Delete Users** button or select the **Delete Users** option from the *Edit* pull-down menu of the profile window. TME 10 User Administration displays the following warning dialog.

Figure 29. Delete Warning Dialog

In this dialog you can click the **Delete Home Directory** button to delete the user's home directory or click the **Leave Home Directory** button to leave the user's home directory and still delete the user record from the profile.

3.6.3.4 Copying Records

It is possible to copy one or more records from one profile to another. When you copy records from one profile to another, you are creating an exact copy of the source records in the target profile. The target profile must be the same profile type as the source profile. The target profile cannot be in the same profile manager as the source profile. In other words, a single profile manager cannot have two profiles of the same type with the same information.

Figure 30 shows the *Copy Profile Records* dialog that allows you to copy records from one profile to another.

To display this dialog:
-> Policy Region (double-click)
-> Profile Manager (double-click)
-> User, Group or Host Namespace Profile (double-click)
-> Select the **Copy** option from the *Edit* pull-down menu.

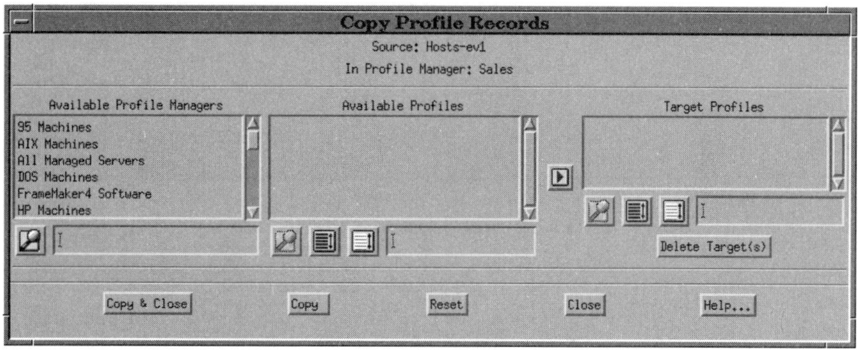

Figure 30. Copy Profile Records Dialog

In order to copy records, you highlight them in the profile window, and select the **Copy Users...** option from the *Edit* pull-down menu. In the resulting *Copy Profile Records* dialog (Figure 30), you select a target profile manager, which brings up a list of profiles. Select one or more profiles from the Available Profiles list. The selected profiles are displayed in the Target Profiles panel. Then click the **Copy** or **Copy & Close** button to perform the copy.

3.6.3.5 Moving Records

Figure 31 shows the *Move Profile Records* dialog that allows you to move records from one profile to another. To display this dialog, select the **Move Users...** option from the *Edit* pull-down menu within the corresponding profile properties window.

To display this dialog:
-> Policy Region (double-click)
-> Profile Manager (double-click)
-> User, Group or Host Namespace Profile (double-click)
-> Select the **Move** option from the *Edit* pull-down menu.

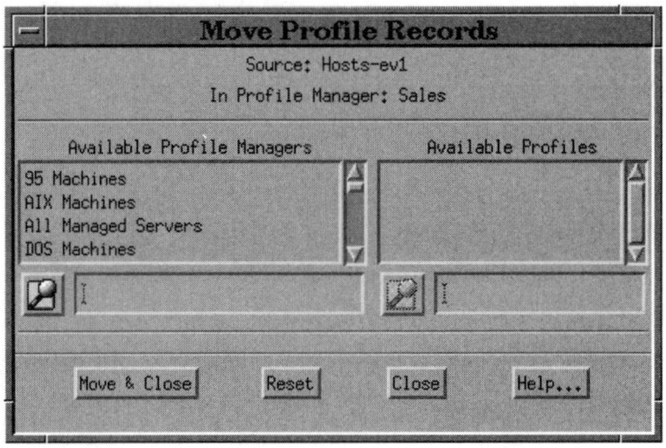

Figure 31. Moving Profile Records Dialog

When you select a profile manager, its profiles are displayed in the *Available Profiles* list. Choose one to which the selected records are moved.

3.6.3.6 Validating Records

Every time a record is changed or added, TME 10 User Administration automatically validates each attribute that has been assigned a validation policy. If you have changed the validation policy after adding or changing records, you may want to verify if the records that you had before the changes comply with the new validation policy. TME 10 User Administration provides a mechanism to validate all profile records at any time. It is important to remember that TME 10 User Administration will only validate the attributes with a validation policy assigned.

3.6.3.7 Retrieving Records

TME 10 User Administration allows you to get a copy of a profile from the profile manager one level higher in the subscription hierarchy. This operation is a request from the subscriber to its profile manager for distribution to a single subscriber.

3.6.3.8 Finding Records

Sometimes it is necessary to find a specific record that is stored in a profile. TME 10 User Administration provides a mechanism to perform this task. Figure 32 shows the *Find Records* dialog that allows you to find records stored in a profile.

To display this dialog:
-> Policy Region (double-click)
-> Profile Manager (double-click)
-> User, Group or Host Namespace Profile (double-click)
-> Select the **Find** option from the *View* pull-down menu.

Figure 32. Find Records Dialog

In order to search for records, you select an attribute from the Attribute List, enter a search string to be matched against the attribute value, and specify the search type, which can be *Contains*, *Exact match*, *Greater than,* or *Less than.* The records that match the criteria are highlighted in the *User Profile Properties* dialog shown in Figure 18 on page 51.

3.6.3.9 Sorting Records

TME 10 User Administration provides a mechanism to set the order in which the information is displayed in the table-formatted *User Profile Properties* dialog shown in Figure 18 on page 51.

To display this dialog:
-> Policy Region (double-click)
-> Profile Manager (double-click)
-> User, Group or Host Namespace Profile (double-click)
-> Select the **Users, Groups or Hosts** option from the *Sort* sub-menu which is found under the *View* pull-down menu.

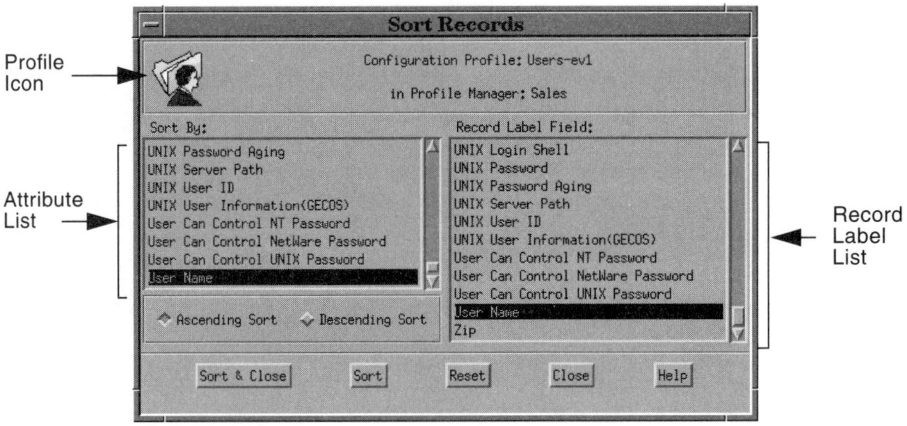

Figure 33. Sort Records Dialog

Figure 33 shows the *Sort Records* dialog that allows you to set the order in which the records are displayed (Attribute List) and to set the attribute that is used as the record label (Record Label List).

Note: When you close and then reopen a profile that has been sorted, your sort is lost.

3.6.3.10 Sorting Record Attributes

The table-formatted *Profile Properties* window provides a list of all profile records contained in the profile. However, since profiles have many attributes, only a few can be displayed. TME 10 User Administration provides a mechanism to select which attributes are displayed in the entries table of a profile and also the order in which they are displayed.

Figure 34 shows the *Display Attributes* dialog that allows you to set the attributes that are to be displayed and their display order.

To display this dialog:
-> Policy Region (double-click)
-> Profile Manager (double-click)
-> User, Group or Host Namespace Profile (double-click)
-> Select the **Attributes...** option from the *Sort* sub-menu which is found under the *View* pull-down menu.

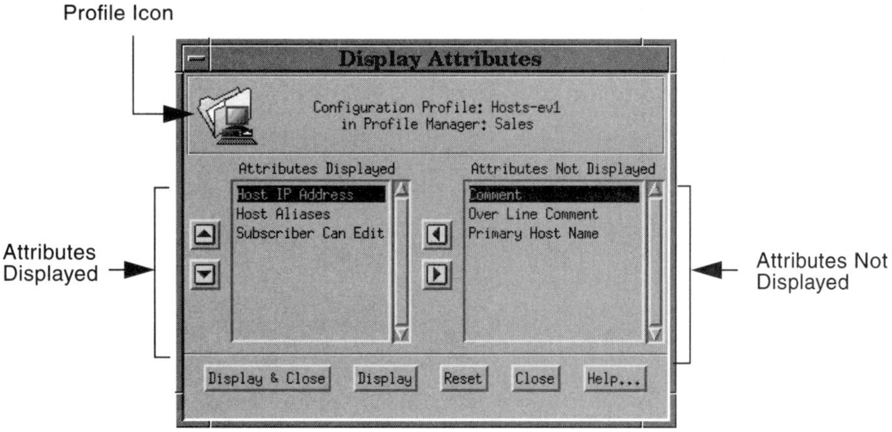

Figure 34. Display Attributes Dialog

3.7 UNIX Host Management

TME 10 User Administration extends the host management capabilities provided by the TME 10 Framework. See Chapter 2, "TME 10 Framework" on page 15 for a list of platform-provided functions. It is important to note that the host management capabilities apply only to UNIX clients and UNIX servers.

The host management section of TME 10 User Administration allows you to perform common administration tasks on TME 10 managed nodes by adding the following options to the managed node pop-up menu.

- **Internet Services and MOTD...** – Displays the status of the Internet services and allows you to change the message of the day. This function is also available in TME 10 Net.Commander and will not be available anymore in TME 10 User Administration in version 3.1.
- **Process Signaler...** – Displays the list of all processes on a managed node (host) and allows you to send a signal to one or more processes.
- **Mail Aliases...** – Displays the contents of the aliases file and allows you to modify the mail aliases database.
- **Trusted** – Displays the list of trusted hosts as well as remote root and user logins. It also allows you to control these features.
- **Configuration** – Allows you to import and export configuration files to or from the local system for emergency situations. This is not a profile operation; it directly copies files.

Since the host management capability (UNIX host and NIS domain management) is performed within the context of policy regions, it is possible to group hosts by defining them into specific policy regions. You can then establish a particular policy for that group. Then it is possible to manage the hosts according to that policy, or you can assign the responsibility to manage those hosts to another administrator.

The following subsections explain how to perform the host management operations provided by TME 10 User Administration.

3.7.1 Internet Services and MOTD

The *Internet Services and MOTD* option provides an easy way to enable or disable the major Internet services and to change the message of the day. After you modify the Internet services, TME 10 User Administration updates the /etc/inetd.conf file by commenting the disabled services or uncommenting the enabled ones. TME 10 User Administration then sends a *SIGHUP* signal to the inetd daemon to reload the configuration file so that the new changes will take effect. If you modify the message of the day, TME 10 User Administration updates the /etc/motd file.

To display this dialog:
-> Policy Region (double-click)
-> Managed Node (right-click)
-> Select the **Internet Services and MOTD...** option from the managed node's pop-up menu.

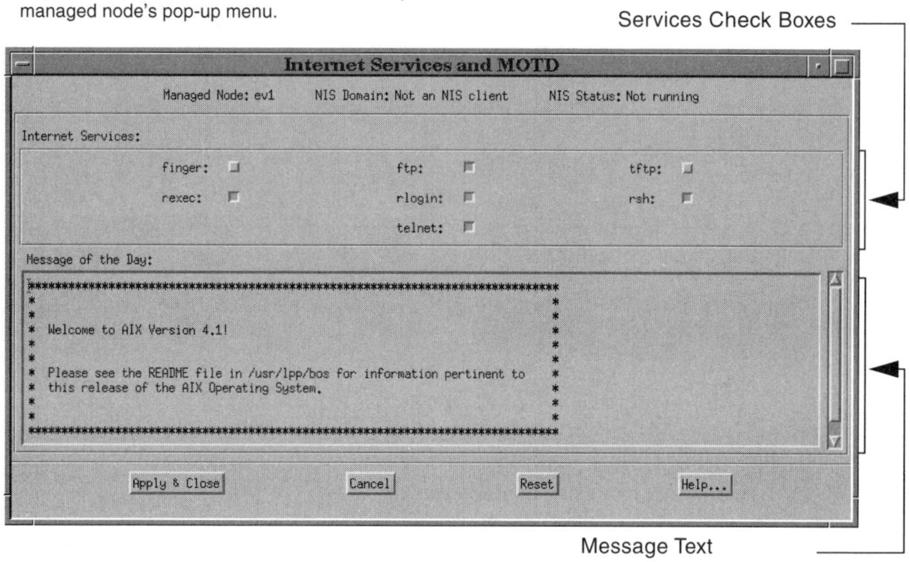

Figure 35. Internet Services and MOTD Dialog

Figure 35 shows the *Internet Services and MOTD* dialog that allows you to modify the Internet services and change the message of the day.

The Services Check Boxes specify which Internet services are enabled (if selected) or disabled (if deselected). The Message Text area allows you to edit the contents of the message of the day. The **Apply & Close** button triggers the requested configuration on that particular managed node.

3.7.2 Process Signaler

The process signaler feature of TME 10 User Administration provides a list of all processes running on a UNIX managed node. You can also send a signal to one or more selected processes.

Figure 36 on page 80 shows the *Process Signaler* dialog that allows you to view and signal processes running in a managed node.

To display this dialog:
-> Policy Region (double-click)
-> Managed Node (right-click)
-> Select the **Process Signaler...** option from the managed node's pop-up menu.

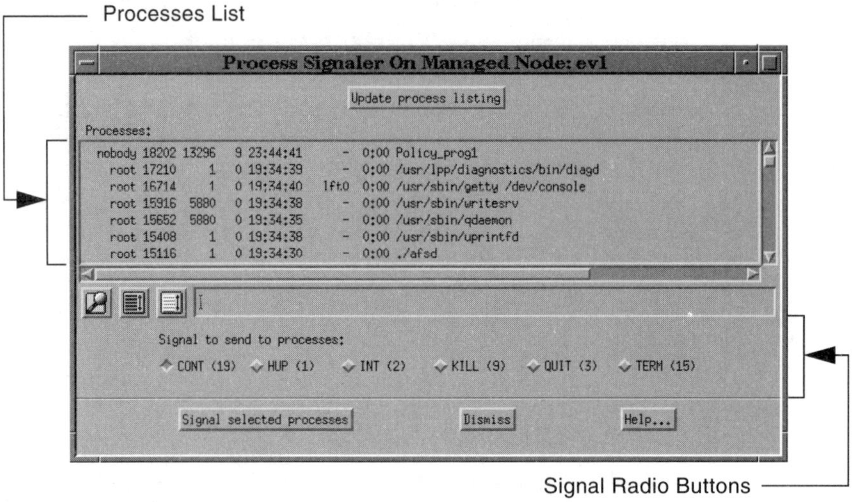

Figure 36. Process Signaler Dialog

In order to signal a process, you select the process(es) from the list, press the appropriate signal radio button, and push the **Signal selected process** button.

3.7.3 Trusted Hosts, Roots, and Users

TME 10 User Administration provides a mechanism to control remote logins from hosts, root users, and regular users by managing the host-wide remote authentication database and the root-specific database.

Table 3. UNIX System Configuration Files

UNIX Information (System file)	TME 10 Trusted Entity	Content of UNIX files and TME 10 profile
/etc/hosts.equiv	Trusted Hosts	host names (all users)
/.rhosts	Trusted Roots	host names
/etc/hosts.equiv	Trusted Users	host and user names

Table 3 shows the system files that are modified in a UNIX system when you use this feature.

Note: Comment lines starting with the # character are misinterpreted by TME 10 User Administration. Therefore, the UNIX system files (/etc/hosts.equiv and /.rhosts) should not have any comment lines.

3.7.4 Mail Aliases

This option allows you to view, create, copy, edit, and delete mail aliases and recipients through the UNIX managed node's pop-up menu.

Figure 37 shows the *View and Edit Aliases* dialog that allows you to manage the aliases file.

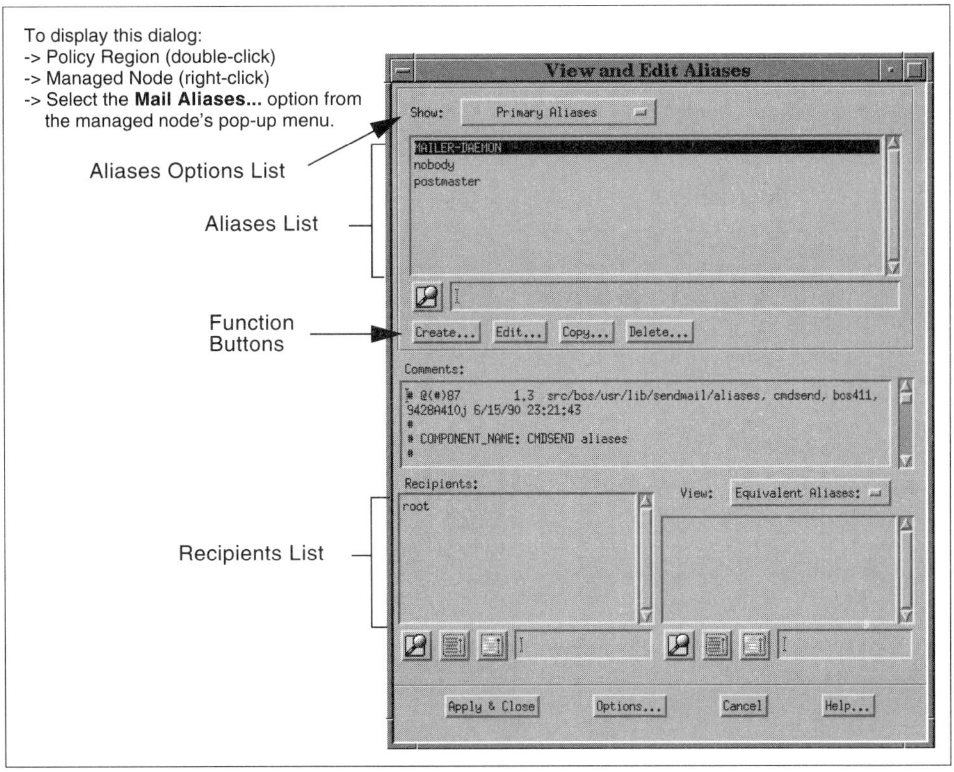

Figure 37. View and Edit Aliases Dialog

The Aliases Option List determines which aliases are displayed in the Aliases List area. The Recipients List panel shows recipients for the selected alias. In order to add new recipients to this list or modify an alias list, select the alias list, and click the appropriate button in the Function Buttons area.

3.7.5 Update/Distribute Configuration Files

This feature of TME 10 User Administration allows you to import or export system configuration files between hosts. This feature can be used in emergency situations, such as when a system configuration file has been corrupted or deleted and you need to replace it with a copy from another system.

The **Update...** option allows you to copy files from any managed node in your TMR to the managed node where you are executing this task. On the other hand, the **Distribute...** option allows you to copy files from the managed node where you are executing this task to any managed node in your TMR. These two tasks are not profile operations; do not confuse them with ordinary TME 10 profile distributions.

3.8 The User Locator

The *User Locator* is a tool that allows you to locate any user in your TME 10 environment. After you install the TME 10 User Administration product, this tool appears on the TME 10 desktop. By double-clicking on the **User Locator Icon**, you can display the *User Locator* dialog, which lists all the users in the TME 10 environment in alphabetical order (see Figure 38).

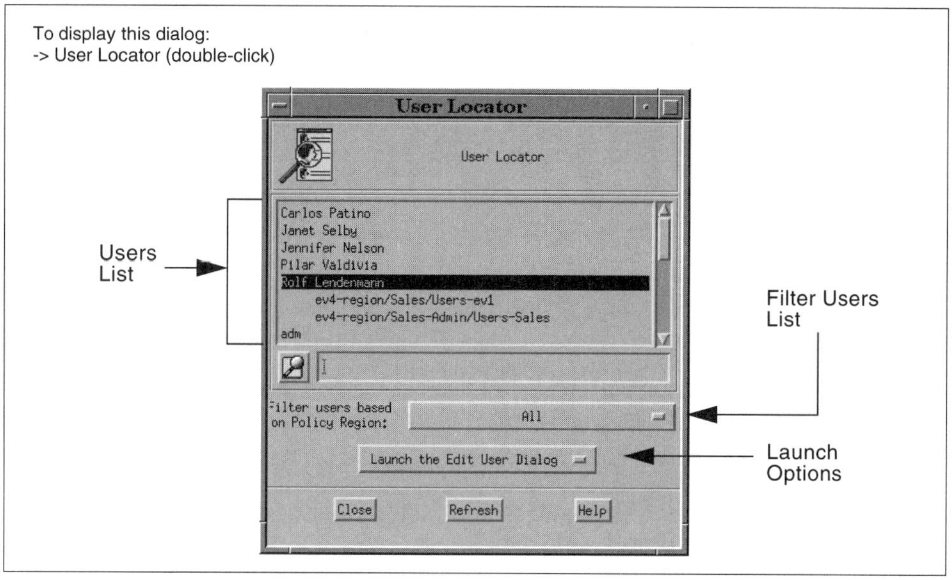

Figure 38. User Locator Dialog

The Users List panel lists all users in your TME 10 environment. Each user in the *User Locator* dialog has an expandable view that lists all the profiles to which the user belongs. The nomenclature used to display the information is the following:

```
PolicyRegion/ProfileManager/Profile
```

The search of users can be limited (filtered) to a policy region, or you can search across the TME 10 environment. Every time you change the search filter, the list of users in the Users List area is updated. The Launch Options feature allows you to determine which dialog(s) are displayed when you locate a user. Available options are:

- Display the *User Properties* dialog
- Display the U*ser Profile Properties* dialog
- Display both

After TME 10 User Administration displays the *User Properties* dialog, the user record is locked and can be edited.

CHAPTER 4

TME 10 Software Distribution

With the TME 10 Framework as the architectural framework and TME 10 Software Distribution as one of its core deployment management applications, the distribution and installation of software on machines in a heterogeneous network computing environment has never before been as efficient and as timely.

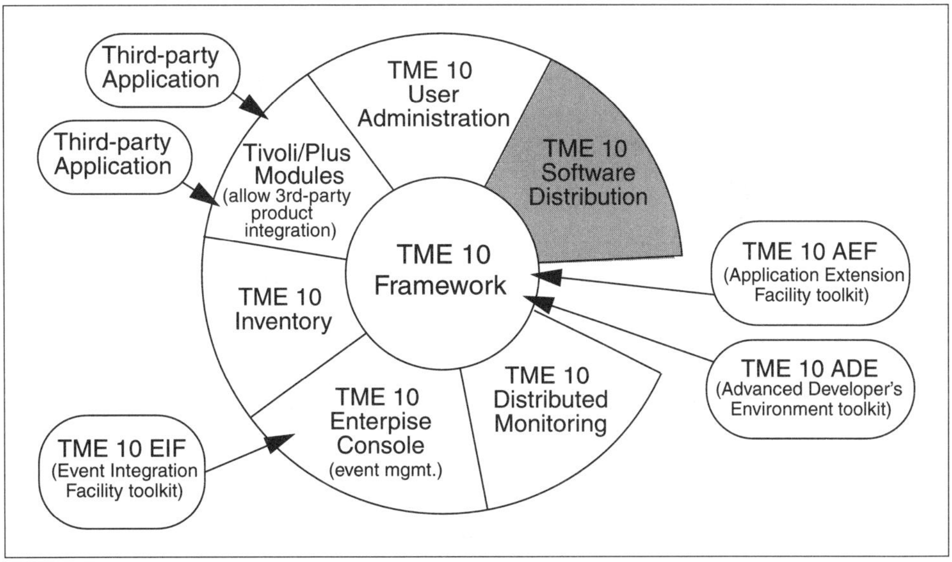

Figure 39. TME 10 Software Distribution as a TME 10 Software Component

This chapter shows how TME 10 Software Distribution lends itself to being a true enterprise solution, that it is a management system that is scalable and provides a simple, centralized point of control for automated software distribution across heterogenous network computing environments.

4.1 Overview and Product Information

This book covers the TME 10 Software Distribution at version level 3.0, or more precisely, it describes the functions and features of Tivoli/Courier Version 3.0 using the new TME 10 terminology.

The majority of the information provided in this chapter is common to the TME 10 Software Distribution 3.1 product. Section 4.6.2, "Future of TME 10 Software Distribution" on page 107 provides an insight to the new features of 3.1.

4.1.1 TME 10 Software Distribution at a Glance

This section provides a summary of the TME 10 Software Distribution distribution process and briefly reviews some of the basic TME 10 terminology in the context of the TME 10 Software Distribution product. It is assumed that the reader has reviewed Chapter 1, "TME 10 Environment" on page 3, and Chapter 2, "TME 10 Framework" on page 15, to understand the concepts surrounding the TME 10 environment and the TME 10 Framework.

4.1.1.1 TME 10 Software Distribution Machine Roles

TME 10 Software Distribution uses the generic distribution functions built into the TME 10 Framework. The TME 10 Framework's MDist (multiplexed distribution) function uses repeaters and a distribution hierarchy to optimize network resources and machines.

TME 10 Software Distribution can be installed on either UNIX or Windows NT machines configured as *TME 10 managed nodes*. In order to get the TME 10 Software Distribution functionality, TME 10 Software Distribution needs, at a minimum, to be installed on the TMR server.

Figure 40 depicts a basic TME 10 Software Distribution environment with the location of a TMR server, a TME 10 Software Distribution application, a source host, managed nodes, PC managed nodes, and an administrator defining the distribution on his TME 10 desktop. The distribution flow is marked with the dashed arrows.

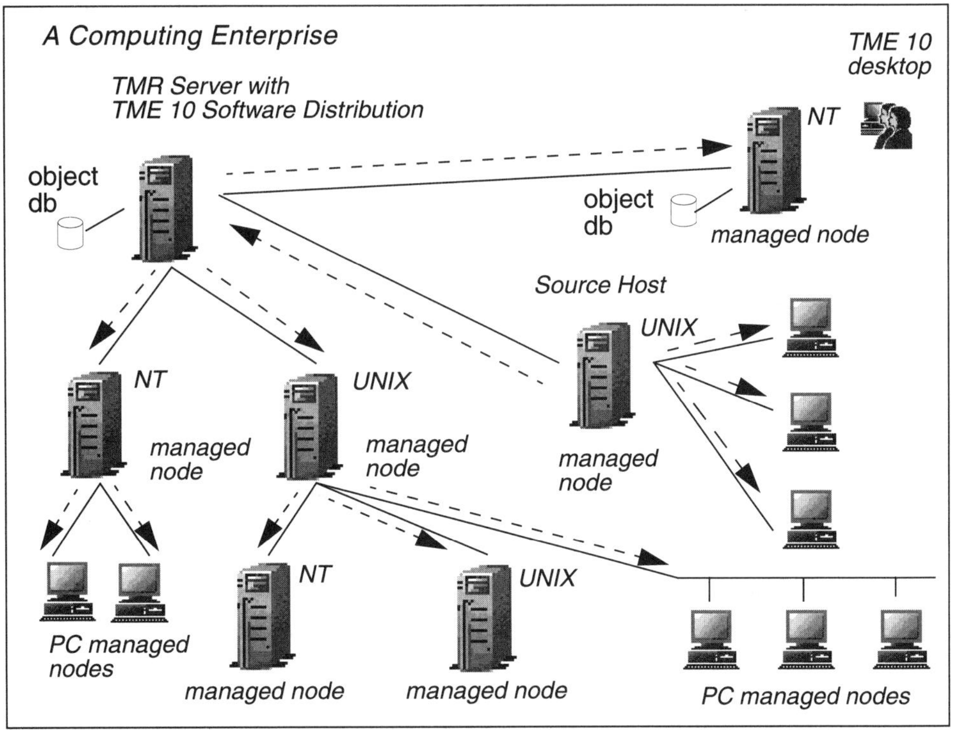

Figure 40. TME 10 Software Distribution Resources

TME 10 Software Distribution can distribute to UNIX machines, to NetWare and Windows NT servers, and to PCs running Windows, Windows 95, Windows NT, OS/2, and DOS. These *target machines are* commonly known as *endpoints* if they will receive the software and maintain it for their own use. They must be managed nodes (TME 10 client installed) or PC managed nodes (PC agent installed).

The software that will be distributed originates from a managed node. The machine that provides the software is known as the *source host.*

The managed nodes contain the TME 10 binaries, TME 10 libraries, TME 10 database, and TME 10 applications, not unlike the TMR server. They have a replicated set of services for performing management operations for the TMR server. The database on the managed node is not as comprehensive as the database on the TMR server. Managed nodes, PC managed nodes, and other resources are maintained as objects in the TMR server and/or in the managed node object database.

The location of these TME 10 clients depends on your analysis of the network and how you have optimized the performance of the network, taking into consideration bandwidth constraints along with file system space, political boundaries, and other network limitations. The personnel supporting the software distribution efforts are called *administrators*. These people would manage software distributions from their workstation or *TME 10 desktop.* TME 10 desktops may be made available on these TME 10 clients.

4.1.1.2 Introduction to the Software Distribution Process

The personnel permitted to install, tailor, and manage software distributions from TME 10 Software Distribution are known as administrators. Each administrator is assigned authorization levels, called *roles,* which are appropriate for a given management operation. For example, an administrator must have the *super* role to install TME 10 Software Distribution.

Based on the distribution requirements, the administrator defines *file packages* and associates them with a target machine or machines. The administrator can then either immediately distribute the file package or schedule the distribution for a later time. This file package does not actually contain the data to be distributed but a reference to the location where the data may be found. It also contains the characteristics of that specific distribution. All references to the data are resolved at distribution time.

As part of the definition for a specific distribution, the administrator will dictate what actions will be performed before and after the distribution, those actions performed upon committing the file package, and what actions to take when an error in the distribution process occurs. Options can be specified for notifying personnel as to the success or failure of the distribution. There is a great deal of intelligence wrapped around the distribution process. The following sections provide more details about creating file packages and the distribution process in general.

4.1.2 Supported Platforms

The TME 10 Software Distribution runs on the following operating systems:

- AIX
- HP-UX
- Solaris
- SunOS
- Windows NT

The PC agent runs on the following operating systems:

- DOS
- NetWare
- OS/2
- Windows 3.x
- Windows 95
- Windows NT

More details regarding the supported operating system versions and required patches may be found in the *TME 10 Software Distribution Release Notes.* See Section 4.6.2, "Future of TME 10 Software Distribution" on page 107, to review which other platforms will be supported in the next release of TME 10 Software Distribution, the TME 10 Software Distribution 3.1.

Several operating system platforms have prerequisite and corequisite software and TME 10 Software Distribution definition requirements that are beyond the scope of this chapter. Please refer to the *TME 10 Software Distribution Release Notes* for details.

4.2 File Packages

File packages are created by administrators from their TME 10 desktops. They designate the files, directories, configuration programs, and platform-specific options applicable for a specific distribution. TME 10 Software Distribution maintains the information regarding the file packages as objects within its object database. This section covers the following topics:

- File packages creation
- Configuration programs
- Platform-specific options
- Impact on end users
- Error handling and notification
- Nested file packages
- File package blocks
- File package customizations

4.2.1 Creating File Packages

The first step in defining a software or file distribution is to create a file package, the basic unit of a distribution. Figure 41 on page 90 shows the configuration options, also called file package properties, the administrator can specify.

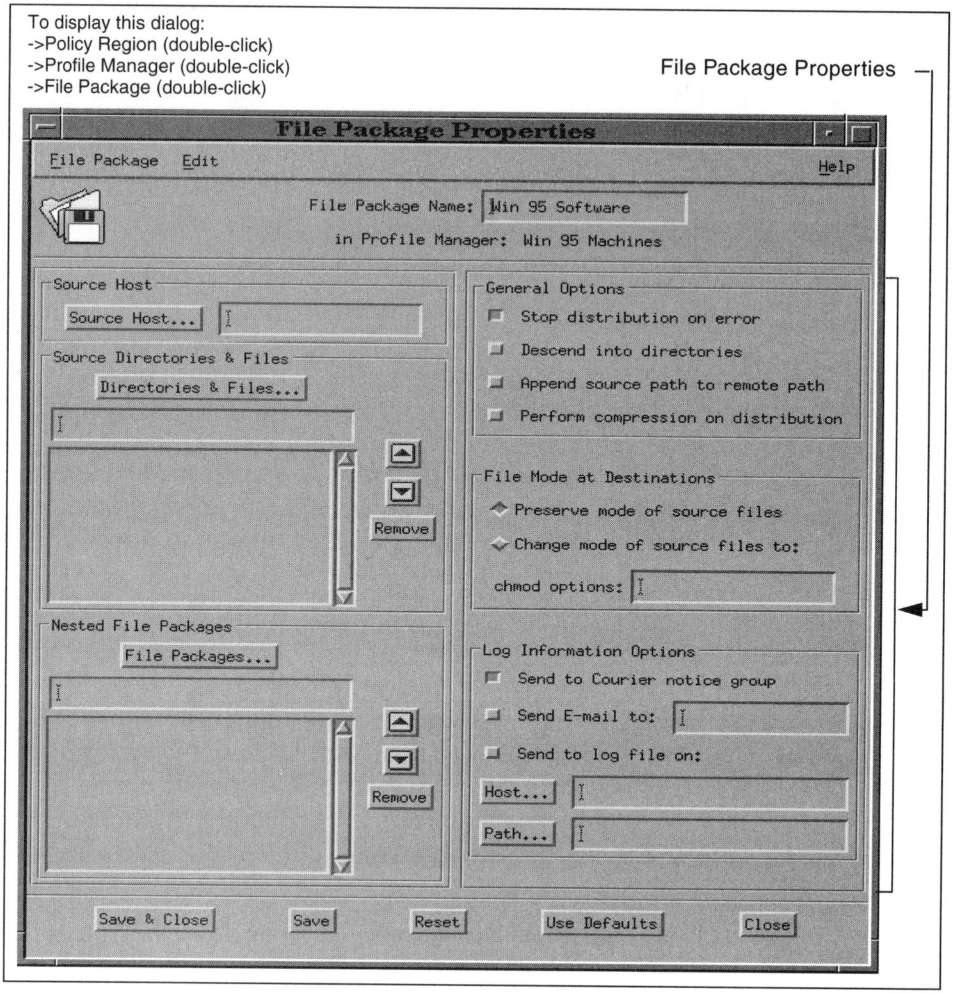

Figure 41. Distribution Options Available to All Platforms

On the left side of the window, you can define the path to the data by setting the source host as well as source directories and files. On the right side, you set more distribution properties, such as:

- **Stop distribution on error** – If selected, the distribution would stop if an error occurred on one or more target machines. This gives the administrator the opportunity to determine the cause of the problem. Error handling is discussed further in Section 4.2.5, "Error Handling and Notification" on page 94.
- **Descend into directories** – If selected, all levels of subdirectories of the designated directories will also be distributed.

- **Append source path to remote path** – If selected, the files on the target host will have the same full path names as on the source host in addition to the specified destination path.
- **Preserve mode of source files** – You can either select that the target files will have the same permission set as the source files, or you could specify the permission (chmod) values instead, using the *Change mode of source file to* option.
- **Logging options** – You can post a notice on the administrator's notice board when the file package operation is performed and request that a log entry be created or an e-mail sent.

4.2.2 Configuration Programs

Common to all platforms are the options to reference before and after programs for the distribution, as well as removal and commit programs. These *configuration programs* are identified when defining the file package. In a UNIX environment the configuration program may be a C program, shell script, Perl script, and so on. In the NetWare environment, the configuration program may be a *NetWare Loadable Module (*NLM) or an .NCF file. The available configuration programs for PCs are .BAT, .EXE, .COM or .CMD (only for OS/2) files.

The *Source Before* configuration program runs on the source host before the file package is sent to the target machine, whereas the *Target Before* configuration program runs on every target machine before any files are actually distributed. The *Target After* program runs on the target after the files are successfully placed in the target.

The *Removal* program runs on the target before the files designated in the file package are removed from the target, whereas the *After Removal* program runs on the target after the files are removed from that target.

The *Commit* configuration program runs on the target when you perform a commit operation or right after a successful distribution when you perform a *distribute and commit* operation.

The *On Error* program is run on the target machine if a fatal error occurs during a distribution or removal operation. Similarly, the *On Error* program is run if there is a non-fatal error and if the *Stop distribution on error* option is set to yes. Errors are discussed further in Section 4.2.5, "Error Handling and Notification" on page 94.

An additional feature, called AutoPack, has been added to the next release of TME 10 Software Distribution (TME 10 Software Distribution 3.1). AutoPack eliminates the need to write scripts. Section 4.6.2, "Future of TME 10 Software Distribution" on page 107, provides more detailed information.

4.2.3 Platform-Specific Options

Since every supported target platform has different characteristics, the dialogs that define what will happen on the target node are platform-specific.

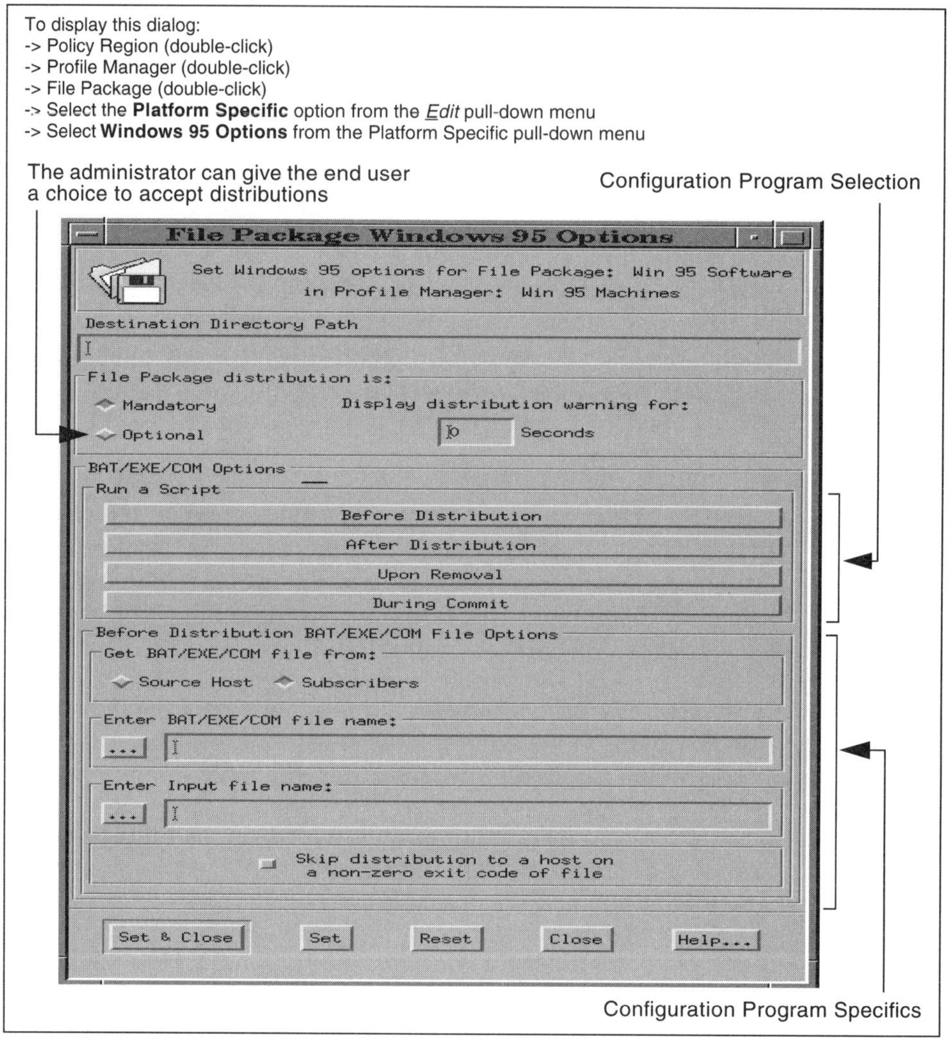

Figure 42. Options for Windows 95

As an example, Figure 42 shows what options can be defined for a Windows 95 distribution target. The lower part of the window lets the administrator enter the specifics of one configuration program, such as its file name, input file, and whether the configuration program itself is distributed from the source host or if a local copy of it will be called. What you see in the Configuration Program Specifics area depends on which pushbar is clicked in the Configuration Program Selection area.

The following list summarizes the differences between the different target platforms:

- For the UNIX environment, the administrator can specify the link resolution, the user and group ownership of the files and directories, as well as the configuration program options just discussed.
- In the DOS environment, the ability to reboot the system after distributing the file packages is offered. The PC end user has no direct control over this option. His/her work may be affected if this feature is enabled and the distributions are done during working hours.
- In the NetWare environment, the ability to set user/group rights and configure the *NLMs, NetWare Loadable Modules,* along with defining the trustee login modes, are available options.
- The Windows and OS/2 platforms simply offer the ability to define the destination directory.
- For Windows and Windows 95, the administrator may enable the reboot/restart option. The Windows 3.1 and Windows 95 operating systems provide for an end user to specify, from a pop-up window, whether or not receiving the file package is desirable. This gives these end users some degree of control over the distribution process.
- Windows NT provides the same dialog and options as Windows 3.1 and Windows 95 except for the option to make a distribution optional. A user at an NT workstation is not given a choice to accept or decline a distribution.

4.2.4 Impact on the End User

With the exception of Windows 3.1 and Windows 95 operating systems, where the end user may request that his or her PC not receive file packages, the data distribution and reception of the data is transparent to the end user. PC users, however, may experience a slight slowdown in processing at the time the file packages are received and at the time the configuration programs are run. Extensive scheduling capabilities available within TME 10 Software Distribution permit the administrator to distribute file packages at various times (days, nights, weekends, and so on) minimizing the impact on the end-user community.

Also, an administrator should schedule mass distributions at a time when there would be minimal bandwidth contention in the network. He/she can also set some tuning parameters to control the percentage of network bandwidth used during the distribution process.

4.2.5 Error Handling and Notification

Errors occur, for example, if the target machine is down or if the source files are not found at the time of distribution. The administrator has the option to define whether TME 10 Software Distribution will attempt to retry the distribution to a given target machine when an error occurs. It can retry once or any number of times over a given time period.

The distribution process may continue if the error is not a *fatal* error. A fatal error occurs if a system can no longer support the distribution process, such as when a machine is out of memory. Information regarding the errors may be written to the TME 10 log file.

There are several ways in which the administrator is notified as to the success or failure of the distribution and the success or failure of other tasks triggered as a result of the distribution process. An e-mail may be automatically created and sent to the administrator. He/she may be advised by a bulletin board entry or a pop-up window posted on the TME 10 desktop. More detailed information on the problem could be found in a log file that can be specified in the file package creation dialog. The notification options associated with the distribution ensure that personnel are well aware of the distribution activities.

4.2.6 Nesting File Packages

A file package originates from only one source host. The file package may, however, identify several files for distribution on that source host, which can be either a UNIX or Windows NT machine. To distribute files from different source hosts or to targets with different characteristics in one distribution effort, it will be necessary to *nest* file packages. Nesting file packages permits one file package (from one source host) to be imbedded or nested within a second or third file package (from another source host).

Nesting file packages is also common for situations when:

- There is only one source host, but the before and after configuration programs are different for some of the targets.
- There is only one source host, but the properties are slightly different for some targets.

There are certain behaviors that are exhibited as a result of distributing nested file packages. Properties associated with nesting file packages can be found in the *TME 10 Software Distribution User's Guide*.

4.2.7 File Package Blocks

When a file package is defined and stored in the TME 10 databases, it only *refers* to the location of the data to be distributed and does not contain the actual data. All references are resolved at distribution time. However, if it is necessary to take a snapshot of the data at, say, time A because at time B that data would be different or if the network topology dictated that it would be necessary to collect the actual data in its entirety at time A, then the administrator could create a file package block (*fpblock*).

This feature allows an administrator to *copy* the actual data from all the data and configuration files into an fpblock. The distribution of this special file package is triggered by a set of `fpblock` commands. These commands are discussed in the *TME 10 Software Distribution User's Guide* and detailed in the *TME 10 Software Distribution Reference Manual*.

4.2.8 Manually Customizing or Updating File Packages

At times, it may be necessary to include or exclude specific files and functions from the file package definition or to create another file package similar to an already existing one. For example, in a situation where there is an extensive number of files to be distributed, it may be simpler and faster to add the file list to the file package definition with a text editor rather than through the TME 10 desktop.

Once a file package is defined, it is stored in the TME 10 database. It can be *exported* into a file and manually updated to reflect the desired distribution characteristics. The changes will be saved and *imported* back into the original file package, hence preparing the file package for distribution. The changes can also be used to create a new file package.

Also, in some cases, it is not possible to set specific features through the GUI. The features may then be set using a text editor after the file package has been exported. The exported file lists keywords and their associated values. Modifying or adding to the keyword list will affect the distribution process. The *TME 10 Software Distribution Reference Manual* provides a complete list of keywords, their descriptions, their values, and the distribution operations that they are related to.

4.3 Distribution Configurations

Before a file package can be distributed, the administrator needs to associate specific target machines with the file package. Remember that defining a file package only takes care of the specifics of different target platform types, but does not determine any particular target machine. In order to make the distribution efforts simple, efficient, and secure, an administrator somehow needs to build groups of machines with the same characteristics and then distribute the file package to these groups of machines. This section discusses how a distribution is defined and executed:

- Grouping target machines
- Associating file packages with target machines (subscription)
- Distributing file packages (push operation)
- Requesting file packages (pull operation) using TME 10 UserLink

4.3.1 Grouping Together Resources

Policy regions, profile managers, and *profiles* are mechanisms provided by the TME 10 Framework to help organize resources hierarchically. An administrator will ultimately use this hierarchy to associate file packages with target machines. In the following paragraphs, we briefly repeat what this means for TME 10 Software Distribution. Details about these concepts can be found in Chapter 2, "TME 10 Framework" on page 15.

Policy regions and subregions are collections of resources for which the same set of policies apply. Different criteria can be used to build these entities, such as administrator locations, administrator permission hierarchy, geography, departments, machine types, and so on. A policy region or subregion can also be seen as a domain of an administrator within which he or she has responsibility for all machines. (Of course one administrator may be responsible for more than one such domain, or more than one administrator can be assigned responsibility for the same domain).

Profiles are the resources that are distributed. A file package is a TME 10 Software Distribution profile, and it is treated and handled as a profile. The entity that allows an administrator to group machines together within his or her domain is the profile manager. These profile managers are used as containers for machines of the same architecture. Machine containers can be created by adding the machines as subscribers to a profile manager that does not have any profiles.

Figure 43 shows an example of different platform-dependent profile managers building a subscription hierarchy.

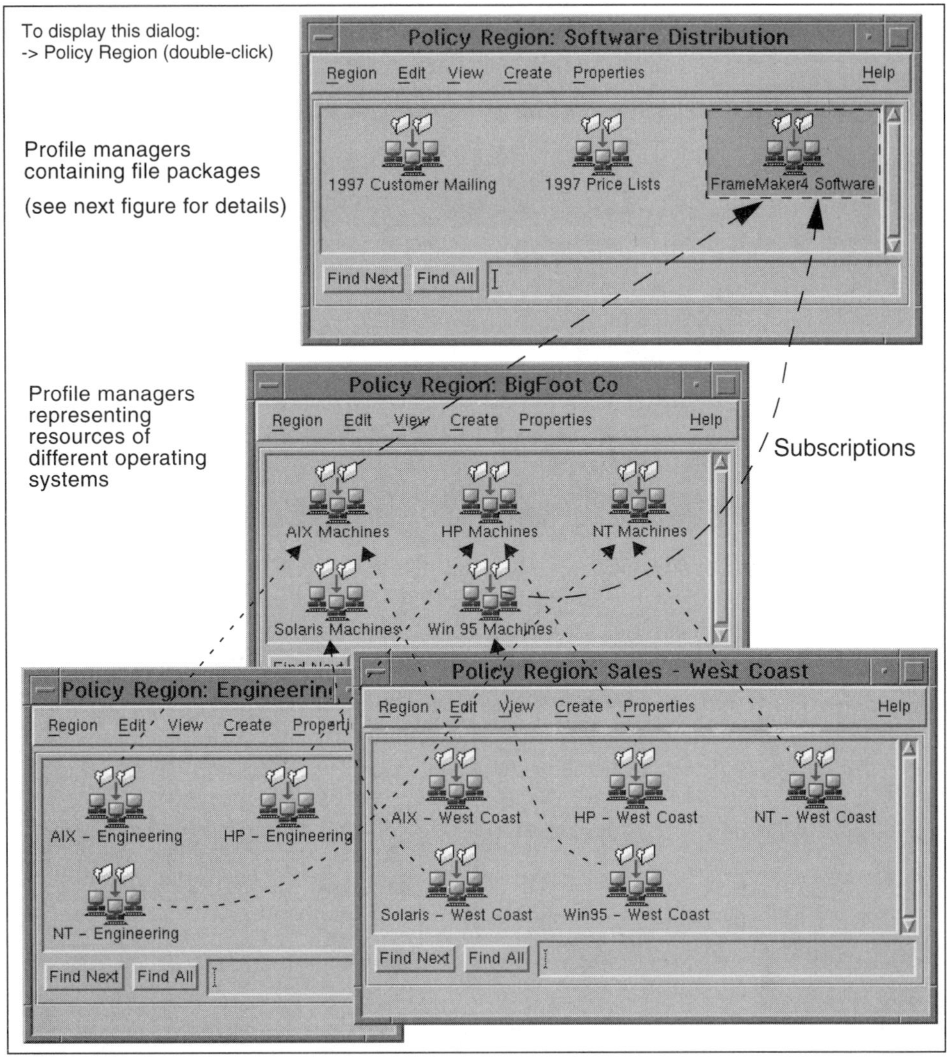

Figure 43. Profile Managers with File Packages and Computing Platforms

Given that a UNIX FrameMaker application is not identical to a Windows 95 FrameMaker application, the administrator would have created two distinct file packages or profiles that are representative of the individual operating system.

Policy regions and profile managers should be structured in such a way that it facilitates the distribution process. The division is purely arbitrary. Whatever the structure, the administrator who is responsible for that particular part of the network will associate a file package or several file packages with the appropriate target machines and initiate a distribution either automatically or manually.

4.3.2 Associating File Packages with Target Machines

From a TME 10 Software Distribution perspective, profile managers will be defined and used within a policy region to contain and associate one or more target machines with one or more profiles (file packages). The target machines *subscribe* to profiles within profile managers.

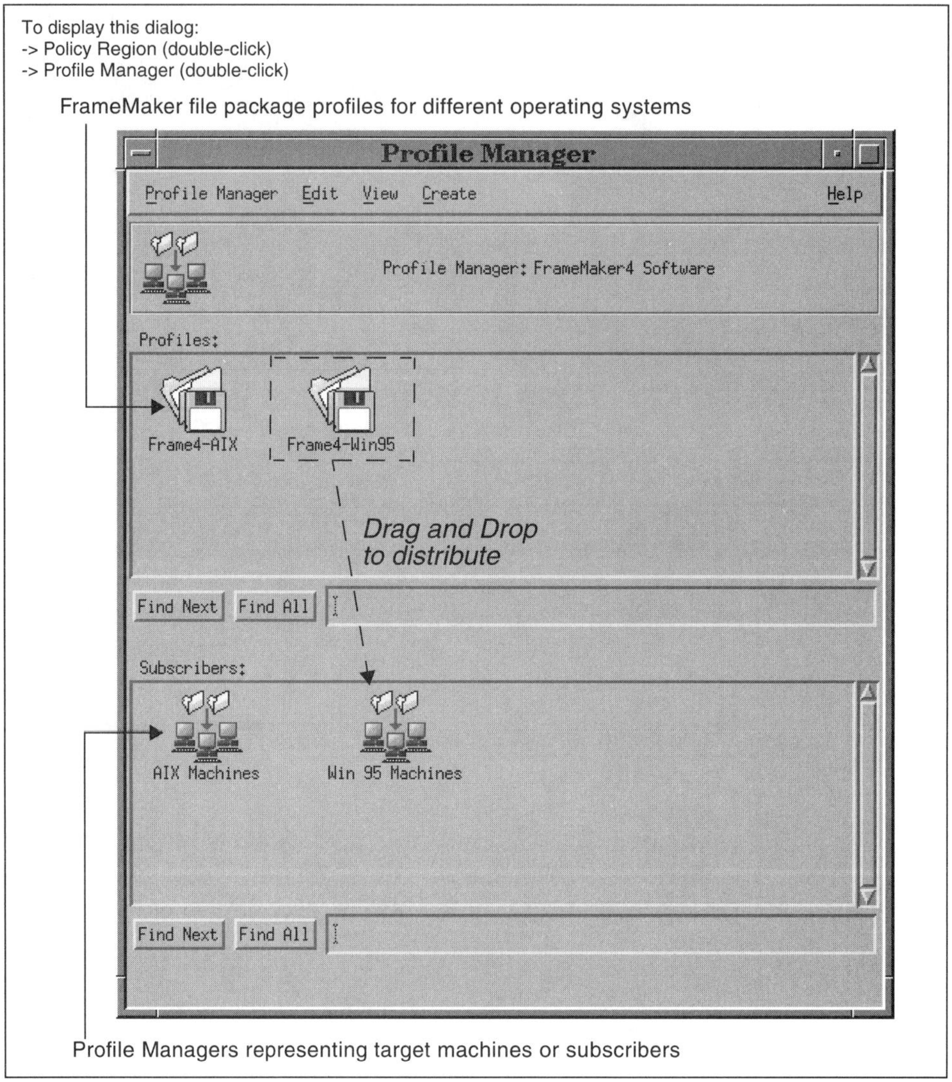

Figure 44. Associating Target Machines and File Packages

In Figure 44, each software application has been associated with an individual profile manager. This profile manager contains all the file packages for all operating systems supported by that software application. Also, each operating system platform has been associated with a profile manager that is specific for the platform that it represents.

To *associate* a set of target machines with an file package, simply drag the icon of the profile manager that represents the target machines and drop it on the profile manager icon that represents the file package. This is done on the policy region level as shown in Figure 43 on page 97. After the *AIX Machines* and the *Win 95 Machines* profile manager have been dragged and dropped on the *FrameMaker4 Software* profile manager, the *FrameMaker4 Software* profile manager presents itself as depicted in Figure 44 (double-click on a *FrameMaker4 Software* profile manager icon).

As mentioned earlier, profile managers that represent operating system platforms only contain subscribers but no profile. Such an endpoint-oriented profile manager would then subscribe to the profile manager containing file packages. This allows an administrator to reuse the profile manager for many different profiles or file packages and have a clear separation between profiles and recipients. New machines can easily be added to the appropriate profile manager and will receive all file packages to which that profile manager is subscribed.

A machine could become the target for two or more distinct distribution operations. For example, the first distribution may be directed towards all Windows 95 PCs; the second may be directed towards all Marketing personnel. A PC identified in both categories (profile managers) will receive all file packages.

4.3.3 Distributing File Packages

In order to *distribute* the software, the administrator would drag the file package icon and drop it on top of the corresponding profile manager icon that represents the subscribers (as shown in Figure 44 on page 98). This may be useful for ad hoc distribution requests.

Another approach to initiate a distribution would be to take advantage of the *Distribute File Package* dialog that comes up when you select the **Distribute...** option from the *Profile Manager* dialog's pull-down menu or from a single profile's pop-up menu. Before using the pull-down menu, you can select multiple file packages and multiple subscribers. Additional options for scheduling and distributing file packages are available from this dialog.

Temporary Problem

In the program version that we were using, the drag and drop function was not available from the TME 10 Desktop for Windows. This was a bug and should be fixed by now.

The *TME 10 Software Distribution User's Guide* provides an excellent example and a set of procedures on how to define file packages, subscribers, and profile managers. Section 2.5, "Policy and Policy Regions" on page 28, defines policy regions, profiles, profile managers, and subscribers in detail.

4.3.4 TME 10 UserLink

From an end-user perspective, the distribution process is a *push* operation. The request is made from the administration staff and not by the individual who will benefit from the data transfer. TME 10 UserLink offers the end user a *pull* operation, enabling him/her to request data distribution at his/her convenience.

TME 10 UserLink, which is another TME 10 management application, permits users on Windows, Windows 95, and Windows NT machines to download or retrieve TME 10 Software Distribution file packages from any managed node in the TME 10 environment. This pull function is performed over a TCP/IP connection.

The use of the pull operation on a PC has the following prerequisites (some of these prerequisites are not specific to TME 10 UserLink):

- TME 10 UserLink (the `usrlnkd` daemon) is installed on a TME 10 managed node in the TMR.
- The TME 10 UserLink browser and the TME 10 PC agent are installed on any PC whose end user wishes to perform this pull function.
- The name of the TME 10 UserLink managed node is configured in the TME 10 UserLink browser.
- A PC managed node is defined to the TMR server that represents the PC running TME 10 UserLink browser software.

Figure 45 on page 101 depicts a TME 10 UserLink environment.

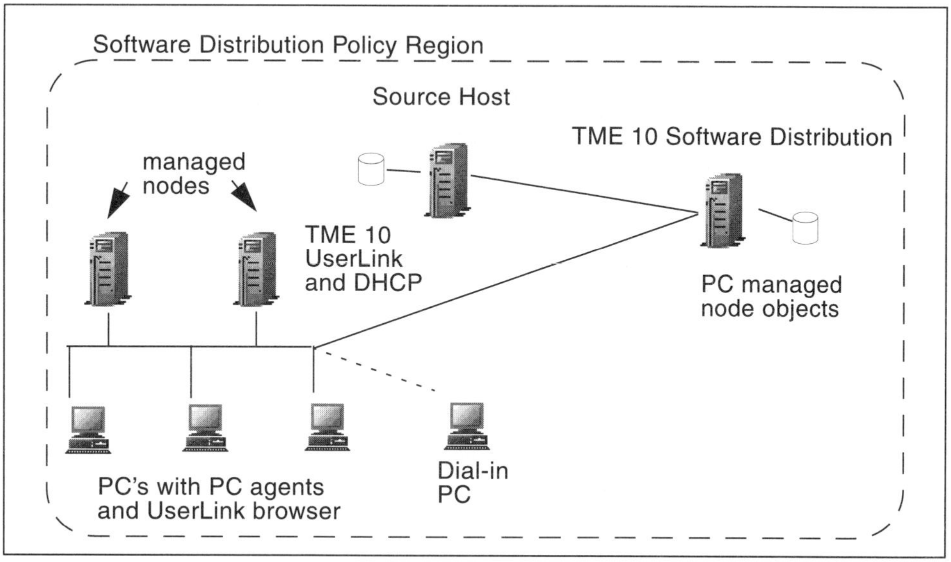

Figure 45. TME 10 UserLink Configuration

The file package must be in the same policy region to which the PC managed node is subscribed, and the PC managed node from which you are pulling the file package must be subscribed to the file package for security reasons. Therefore, you cannot pull a file package to a PC managed node that is not authorized to receive it.

The end user makes a request for a list of file packages that TME 10 Software Distribution can distribute. The list is presented to the end user via the UserLink browser, and the end user chooses the desirable file packages to download. The request is forwarded to TME 10 Software Distribution from the UserLink managed node, and the file packages are downloaded from the source host.

People who don't work at the office can also receive file packages. TME 10 Software Distribution and TME 10 UserLink work in conjunction with TME 10 UserLink/DHCP, the Dynamic Host Configuration Protocol. UserLink/DHCP provides a dynamic IP address for PCs that need to receive file packages. UserLink/DHCP services provide PC users with a list of file packages available for distribution. When the user selects the file package to retrieve, the selection is passed through the UserLink/DHCP service and then distributed to the PC managed node.

For details about installing UserLink on managed nodes, see the *TME 10 Framework Planning and Installation Guide.*

4.4 TME 10 Software Distribution Topology and Scalability

Typical distribution goals for most organizations include moving data as quickly as possible while creating as little network load as possible. The TMR server distributes the TME 10 Software Distribution file packages in parallel (simultaneously) to each local target machine. In a complex distribution chain, where there are a relatively large set of managed nodes, the organization may wish to vary the distribution topology and the flow of data.

This section discusses TME 10 Framework components, namely *TMRs* and *repeaters,* that will help optimize the distribution process. It will discuss why the arrangement of this logical structure should be mapped to a distributed network topology that incorporates varying connection and network types.

The concept of using repeaters and a repeater hierarchy is known to the TME 10 environment as MDist or Multiplexed Distribution services. These services are provided with the TME 10 Framework.

4.4.1 Subdividing Networks

It is possible to logically subdivide an enterprise network into multiple regions called TME 10 Management Regions (*TMRs*). The criteria for determining the TMR boundaries may be found in Section 1.5.3, "TMR Configuration" on page 10. TMRs may be connected to one another and may permit administrators to manage resources across several distributed networks or regions.

A TMR defines a TME 10 management server, TME 10 *management stations* (TME 10 desktops) and a set of resources it serves. The TMR server contains the TME 10 Framework software that provides a set of foundation services for many TME 10 management applications including TME 10 Software Distribution. The criteria for determining the location as well as the prerequisite hardware and software for the TMR servers and management stations may be found in the *TME 10 Framework Planning and Installation Guide.*

4.4.2 TME 10 Software Distribution Scalability

When the first TMR server is installed for a TMR, it is installed as a repeater on the TMR server. In a TMR-to-TMR connection, the repeater will send only one copy of the data to a target repeater in the remote TMR. The receiving repeater in the other TMR will distribute, in parallel, the data to all local target managed nodes or endpoints. This method of distributing the data only once between TMRs (and repeaters) versus performing the distribution multiple times between TMRs will help conserve bandwidth, minimize network delays, and improve processing times because the file package crosses the network links only once.

For performance reasons within a TMR, it may be necessary to designate some TME 10 clients as repeaters. The TME 10 client, in this case, would be a UNIX or NT machine. It has, by the virtue of the fact that it is a TME 10 client, repeater code installed. The administrator would *enable* the repeater code by setting a parameter that establishes the range of machines to which the repeater could send file packages to. This is set via the `wrpt` command. The TMR server will send *one* copy of the data to the TME 10 client acting as a *repeater site* and in turn, the repeater site will distribute, *in parallel*, the data to other managed nodes or endpoints. The software distribution will fail if either the repeater site fails or is not available. It is, therefore, very important that a repeater site be a reliable machine.

Repeaters do not have any error handling capabilities or responsibilities as far as software distribution is concerned. They just relay the files being distributed, thus taking the burden from the original TMR server. Logically, the distribution is still between the TMR server and each individual endpoint. So, when the repeater fails, the current distribution, and any further distributions, will fail.

These intermediate repeater sites may be several layers deep, as is the case in Figure 46.

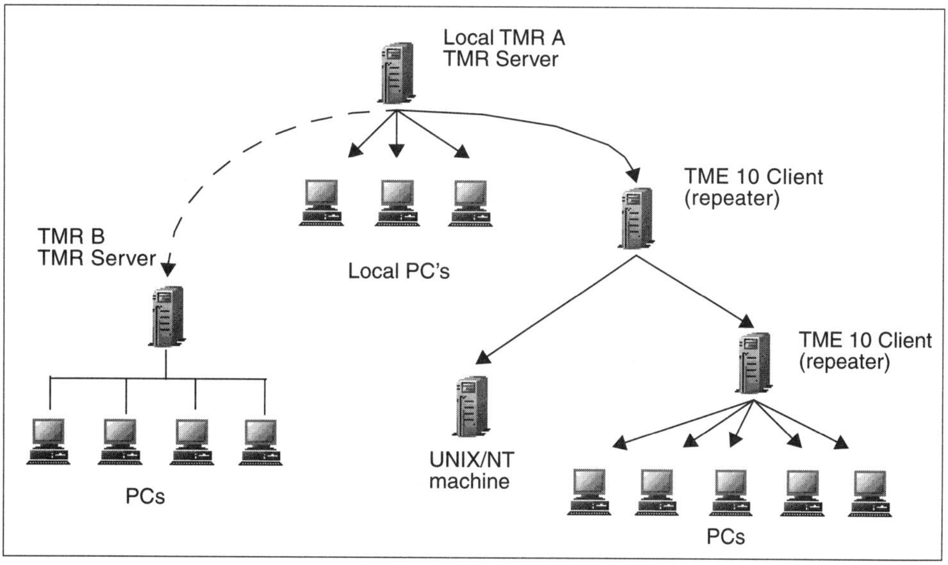

Figure 46. Distribution Configuration Between TMRs and Local Resources

Understanding an organization's distribution objectives, analyzing the system and network demands, and having an appreciation for the limitations of the network configuration should lead to a well-managed, well-tuned distribution management environment. Guidelines for positioning the repeaters and identifying the prerequisite hardware and software may be found in the *TME 10 Framework Planning and Installation Guide.*

TME 10 Software Distribution can also provide compression of data at the time of distribution. This is an option enabled by the administrator when he or she selects the distribution characteristics when creating a file package. The source of the data is left unchanged.

4.5 NetWare Configuration

TME 10 provides a way to use the powerful NetWare servers to fan out the distribution of TME 10 Software Distribution file packages.

A *NetWare managed site* (NWMS) is a TME 10 resource that *represents* a NetWare server and a set of some or all of the server's PC clients. The NetWare managed site icon appears as a managed node on the administrator's desktop and is maintained as a managed resource in the UNIX TMR server or TME 10 client object database.

The NetWare managed site performs the distribution to the NetWare environment via the TME 10 NetWare repeater (TNWR). The TME 10 NetWare repeater is a server application that is installed on a NetWare 3.12 or 4.1 server. The NetWare repeater maintains a list of available clients for this server as does the NetWare managed site. The administrator specifies which PCs the NetWare managed site will distribute the file package to. If any of the NetWare clients are unavailable, then the distribution to that PC will fail, and a message may be logged to the file package's log file as well as to the NetWare managed site's log file.

To create a NetWare managed site, you must install the TME 10 NetWare repeater on the NetWare server machine and the PC agent on the NetWare server's clients. Then you can create a NWMS to represent it and the clients.

The NetWare clients can run either the TCP/IP or IPX/SPX protocol. Each PC that will receive a file package must have either the TME 10 IPX/SPX agent or the TCP/IP agent installed. NetWare servers with NetWare repeaters installed act as repeater sites for TME 10 Software Distribution distributions for TCP/IP and IPX/SPX clients.

The NetWare server communicates to the TMR server or client over TCP/IP and therefore has an IP agent installed on the NetWare server to support TCP/IP communications. This is shown in Figure 47.

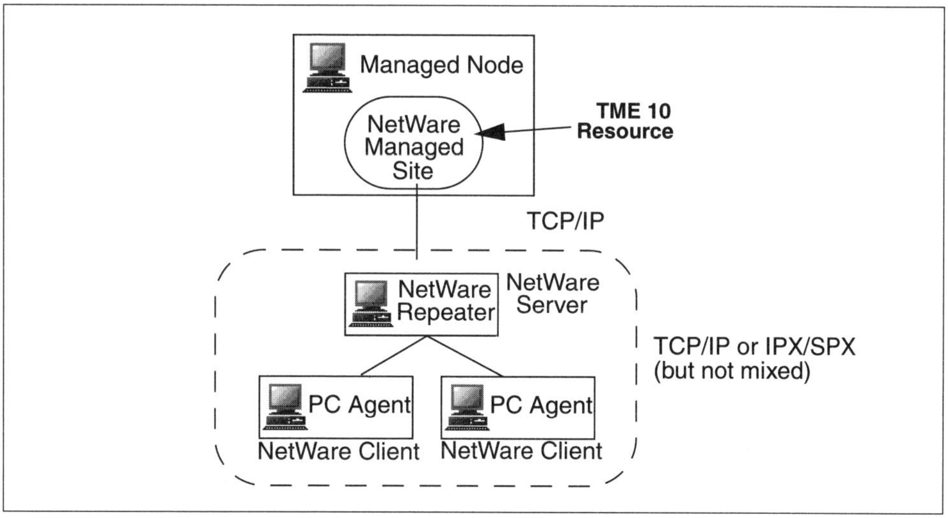

Figure 47. NetWare Managed Site

After creating the NetWare managed site on the TME 10 desktop, subscribe the NetWare managed site to a TME 10 Software Distribution file package(s). When you distribute the file package, the NetWare managed site passes the file package to the *staging area* on the NetWare server. The NetWare repeater on the NetWare server then distributes the file package from the staging area to the subscribed clients (PCs).

Although the clients of the NetWare managed site will receive the file packages distributed from the NetWare managed site, the actual NetWare server does not get to keep the file package for its own use. The file package passes from its staging area to the clients. The data in the file package is not installed on the server. In order for the NetWare server to also be a target machine or endpoint, the administrator would have to define the NetWare server as a PC managed node to the TME 10 Framework.

In order to specify configuration programs for NetWare targets (for example, before and after programs that run before or after the distribution), you must develop NetWare loadable modules (NLMs) or NetWare Command Files (NCFs) in the targeted PCs to support the programs.

See the *TME 10 Software Distribution User's Guide* for installation instructions of the NetWare managed site and the *TME 10 Framework Planning and Installation Guide* for information about the TNWR service.

4.6 Further Information

This section is a collection of some more useful information about or associated with TME 10 Software Distribution. It covers the following topics:

- Integration with other TME 10 products
- Future of TME 10 Software Distribution
- Administrative roles summary

4.6.1 Integration with Other TME 10 Products

The purpose of this section is to give a summary of a few products or features that are closely related to TME 10 Software Distribution.

4.6.1.1 TME 10 ADE

TME 10 ADE (TME 10 Advanced Developer's Environment) provides programming tools to help extend the functions of TME 10 Software Distribution. Refer to *ADE Documentations Volumes 1-4* for more information. The *TME 10 Software Distribution Reference Manual* has a section dedicated to extending TME 10 Software Distribution using ADE and AEF.

4.6.1.2 TME 10 Application Extension Facility

The TME 10 AEF product permits modifications to the GUI in terms of its presentation and functionality. Refer to the *TME 10 AEF User's Guide* for more information. The *TME 10 Software Distribution Reference Manual* has a section dedicated to extending TME 10 Software Distribution using ADE and AEF.

4.6.1.3 TME 10 Inventory

TME 10 Inventory is able to scan the machines in your TMR and manages a database with hardware and software information about the managed nodes and PC managed nodes. TME 10 Software Distribution does not automatically update the database after completing software distributions; TME 10 Inventory needs to scan the PC again to update this database. However, TME 10 Software Distribution can use the information in the database to select targets for software distribution. The TME 10 Software Distribution administrator may use queries to select machines of a certain operating system and version or to select machines with a particular application and version number installed on them. Queries can also select machines with specific hardware configurations. The names of the managed nodes and PC managed nodes that meet the established criteria are returned to the distribution dialog. The administrator can choose to designate some or all of these managed nodes as additional distribution targets.

Refer to Section 4.6.2, "Future of TME 10 Software Distribution" on page 107 to determine how TME 10 Inventory will become more tightly integrated with TME 10 Software Distribution.

4.6.1.4 TME 10 UserLink

The interface with TME 10 UserLink was described in 4.3.4, "TME 10 UserLink" on page 100.

4.6.2 Future of TME 10 Software Distribution

The following section provides specific information regarding the functions and features of the follow-on release. TME 10 Software Distribution Release 3.1 will:

- Support TME 10 Software Distribution Release 3.1 on Windows NT 4.0.
- Discontinue the support of DOS as an endpoint.
- Provide the facilities for a *scriptless install* called AutoPack. AutoPack will quickly scan a PC disk before and after the distribution of software packages. After the distribution of the software package, it will produce a list of system differences resulting from the installation of the software. It is these differences that then will be used to automatically create a file package description and a list of system files that have been modified. An AutoPack then will be created as a model for further software distributions for various target machines. A GUI component for the AutoPack facility will also provide some additional functionality.

General availability for TME 10 Software Distribution 3.1 in the United States was planned for first quarter 1997. For more information, please contact your local Tivoli or IBM office.

4.6.3 Administrative Roles

Most of the operations that an administrator can perform can be initiated from his or her TME 10 desktop, which has been assigned and customized specifically for his or her range of duties. Once the administrator has become familiar with the GUI and duties to perform via the GUI, he or she may prefer to initiate the same functions via the command line interface (CLI). Whether the function is performed from the GUI or from the CLI, the authorization roles are still in effect, and the system remains secure.

Note

When the administrator's desktop is provided by the TME 10 Desktop for Windows, the CLI commands are not available. Please refer to the *TME 10 Desktop for Windows User's Guide* for more information.

Table 4 describes the administrator roles for TME 10 Software Distribution. The roles are not cumulative; that is to say, a super role does not incorporate the authority of a senior or user role. They are distinct.

Table 4. Administrator Roles and Operations

Operation	Context	Required Role
Install TME 10 Software Distribution	Desktop view for root	super or install-product
Create a file package	Profile manager	senior or super
Clone a file package	Profile manager	senior or super
View a file package	File package	user, admin, senior, or super
Subscribe resources to a profile manager	Profile manager's policy region and subscriber's policy region	admin, senior, or super
Export a file package definition	File package	user, admin, senior, or super
Set or edit file package properties	File package	senior or super
Import a file package definition	File package	senior or super
Import a CDF	File package	senior or super
Delete a file package	File package	senior or super
Distribute a file package	Profile manager's policy region and subscriber's policy region	admin, senior, or super
Schedule a file package distribution	Profile manager's policy region and subscriber's policy region	admin, senior, or super
Calculate the size of a file package	Profile manager's policy region	admin, senior, or super
Remove a file package from a subscriber	File package	admin, senior, or super

CHAPTER 5

TME 10 Inventory

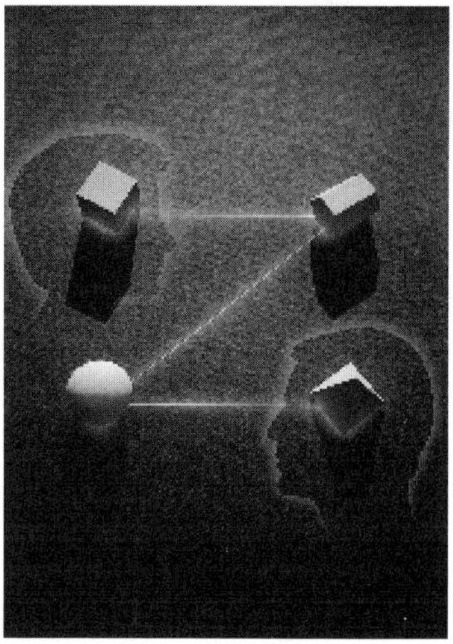

One of the difficulties in a network computing environment is keeping track of the hardware and software installed on each machine. TME 10 Inventory addresses this problem by providing the means to centrally gather the hardware and software installed on each system running a TME 10 Inventory agent and then storing that information in a relational database. From the database, queries and reports can be run to display the information.

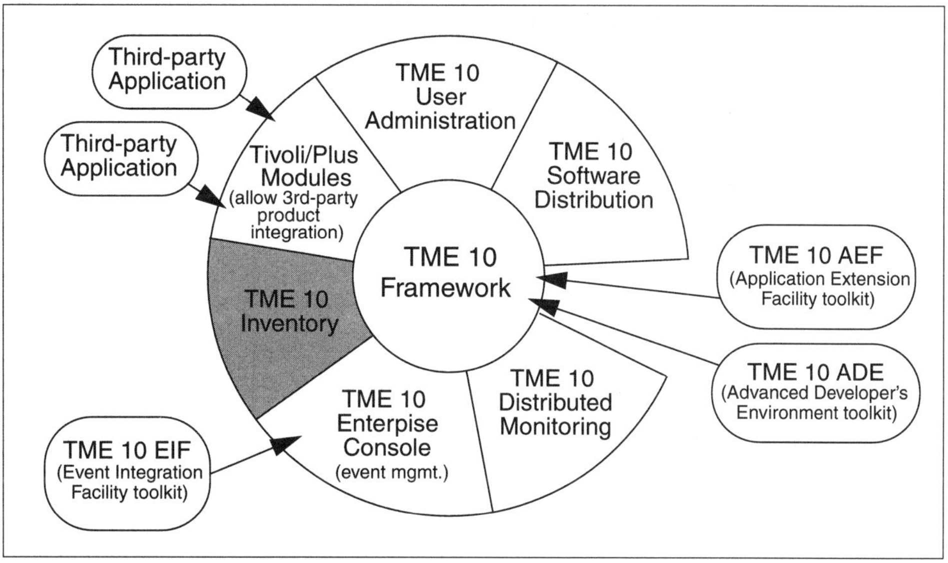

Figure 48. TME 10 Software Components

TME 10 Inventory, in conjunction with the TME 10 Framework, TME 10 Software Distribution and other tools, provides your network computing environment with the following functions:

- Selecting software distribution targets based on their installed HW/SW
- Enterprise-wide synchronization of applications and system configurations
- Detecting unauthorized installation of HW/SW on the clients
- Tracking and reporting HW/SW on clients for accounting purposes
- Monitoring and, if necessary, re-creating vital configuration files on PCs

5.1 Overview and Product Information

This book covers the TME 10 Inventory at version level 3.0, or more precisely, it describes the functions and features of Tivoli/Inventory Version 3.0 using the new TME 10 terminology.

The majority of the information provided in this chapter is common to the TME 10 Inventory 3.1 product. Future plans for TME 10 Inventory include linking it more tightly with TME 10 Software Distribution functions. TME 10 Inventory 3.1 will support Windows NT as the TME Inventory server.

5.1.1 Overview of Components

The TME 10 Inventory application can be divided into five main components:

- ***Inventory server*** – The TMR server also runs the TME 10 Inventory server piece of the TME 10 Inventory product as a whole. The server is where profiles are defined that will keep the instructions for scanning PCs. The profiles then can be distributed to remote machines on which you wish to scan for inventory information.

- ***PC scanning agent*** – The Inventory component that runs on PC platforms like Windows 95 is called the *PC scanning agent*. This agent performs the scan of the PC for information about the hardware, software, and configuration files.

- ***UNIX scanning agent*** – The Inventory piece that runs on UNIX systems to scan for hardware information is the *UNIX scanning agent*. This agent actually performs the scan of the system and generates a file with the information to be sent back to the Inventory server machine.

- ***Managed nodes*** – When a scan occurs on a PC running the PC scanning component, you can choose to store the PC's configuration files. These files are stored on the managed node that sponsors the PC and keeps its TME 10 database entry. The configuration files can be retrieved using Tivoli's RCS (Revision Control System) commands.

- ***Configuration repository*** – The configuration repository defines all of the tables and fields where the inventory information is stored and contains the stored information. This repository is a relational database, presently either Sybase or Oracle. The relational database can reside either on the same machine as the TME 10 Inventory server or on another machine. The data is stored here in standard database format and can be queried with SQL commands, with TME 10 desktop menus or with the query facility.

5.1.2 How TME 10 Inventory Works

Figure 49 shows the flow of information between the components of the TME 10 Inventory application.

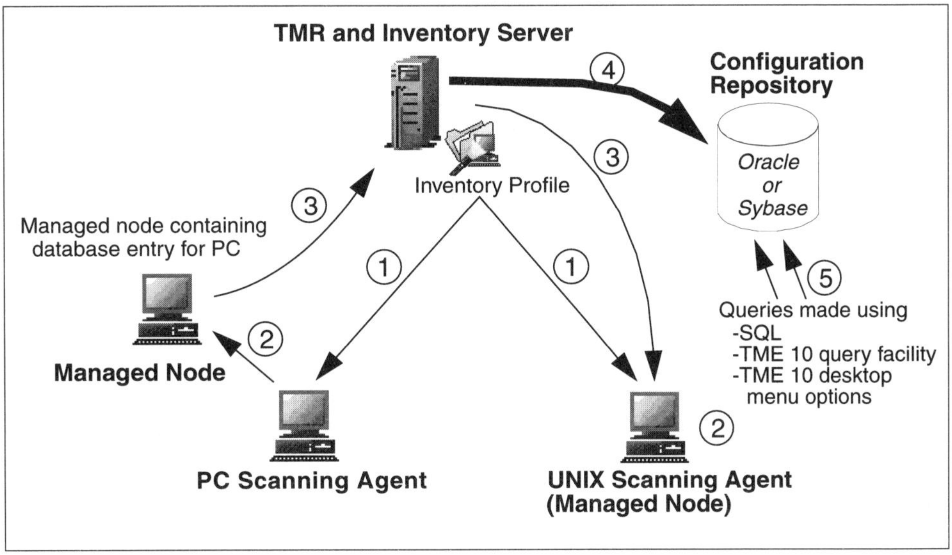

Figure 49. Flow of Information in TME 10 Inventory

The information flow consists of the following basic steps:

1. A profile is created and distributed to its subscribers. The profile contains instructions for the inventory scan.

2. The inventory data is stored in an ASCII file in industry-standard Management Information Format (MIF). PC scanning agents send their inventory information (MIF file) and their configuration files to their associated managed node.

3. The managed node parses the MIF files received from the scanning agents. If it receives PC configuration files from PC scanning agents, the managed node stores them in Revision Control System (RCS) format in its local TME 10 database directory. Eventually, the inventory information is sent to the TMR server.

4. The TME 10 Inventory server accumulates the information from all the subscribers of a single distribution action, converts it into standard database format, and stores it in the configuration repository.
5. The configuration repository can be queried in several ways for the information it now contains.

5.1.3 Information That Can Be Inventoried

The following lists show categories of information that can be scanned on PCs and UNIX systems using TME 10 Inventory. For specific details regarding each of these categories, consult the TME 10 Inventory manuals and release notes.

PCs can be inventoried for both software and hardware in the following categories:

- Component ID
- IPX LAN connections
- Processor
- Coprocessor
- System resources
- Ports
- Memory
- Mass storage
- Logical drives
- Operating system
- IPX LAN
- Environment
- Device drivers
- Configuration files
- Software

UNIX systems can be inventoried for hardware only in the following categories:

- System
- CPU
- Disk partition
- Hard disk
- Monitor

5.1.4 Supported Platforms

The platforms available to be TMR servers that also run the TME 10 Inventory server software are:

- AIX
- HP-UX
- Solaris
- SunOS

A Note About Windows NT

Please note that although Windows NT is supported as a TMR server platform, it is not yet available to run the TME 10 Inventory server or to be the access machine to the relational database. This will be possible in TME 10 Inventory 3.1.

Also, a Windows NT managed node runs the PC scanning agent.

The platforms that TME 10 Inventory can scan for information (run scanning agent software) are:

- AIX
- DOS
- HP-UX
- NetWare
- Solaris
- SunOS
- Windows NT
- Windows 3.x
- Windows 95

An OS/2 agent will be available in TME 10 Inventory 3.1.

The relational databases that can be used with TME 10 Inventory are:

- Oracle 7.x
- Sybase 10.x

For the latest and specific requirements for these operating system and database compatibilities, see the *Tivoli/Inventory User's Guide* and the *Tivoli/Inventory Release Notes*.

5.2 Managed Resources

As a TME 10 application, TME 10 Inventory is based on managed resources. A managed resource in the context of TME 10 Inventory is a set of centrally managed scanning instructions to be distributed to and run on a set of target machines. The TME 10 Inventory managed resources are described in the following definitions:

 Inventory Profile – An Inventory profile contains and controls the activities of the scanning agents on managed nodes, PC managed nodes, and NetWare managed sites. It resides in a profile manger and is distributed to the subscribed target machines that are selected for distribution.

 Managed Node, PC Manage Node, NetWare Managed Site – All machines represented by one of these resources can be scanned. These resources reside in a policy region and can be the recipients of one or more Inventory profiles if they subscribe to these profiles within a profile manager.

 Query Library – Query libraries are containers for queries; they are created in the context of policy regions.

 Query – A *query* is a specific, predefined request to the TME 10 configuration repository to find managed nodes, PC managed nodes, or NetWare managed sites that meet certain criteria. Internally, a query contains an SQL statement to be run against the RDBMS.

Note: The only resource provided by TME 10 Inventory is the Inventory profile. The other resources are part of the TME 10 Framework.

5.3 Inventory Profiles

Scanning for inventory information from remote machines is done in the context of profiles. Profiles are a main concept in the TME 10 architecture, and they are explained in Chapter 2, "TME 10 Framework" on page 15. A profile is a collection of information, and an Inventory profile contains information specific to the TME 10 Inventory application. You create Inventory profiles in the context of profile managers, which contain the profiles and also contain the subscribers, or recipients of the profiles. This is explained further in the following sections.

5.3.1 Creating an Inventory Profile

To create an Inventory profile, you must first have created a profile manager within a policy region. Once the profile manager has been created, you can set the subscribers that will belong to that profile manager, and you can also create profiles.

However, before the InventoryProfile option is presented to you in the *Create Profile* dialog, you must add the Inventory profiles to the managed resources in your policy region. You can do this from the *Properties* pull-down menu in the policy region window when you select the **Managed Resources...** option.

Subscribers can be added to the profile manager in the following ways:

- In the policy region window, drag a node icon or a profile manager icon and drop it onto the profile manager icon or into the Subscribers panel within the profile manager window.
- In the profile manager, select the **Subscribers...** option from the *Profile Manager* pull-down menu, then select the subscribers in the resulting *Subscribers* dialog.

The view of the profile manager after creation with an Inventory profile and some subscribers is shown in Figure 50.

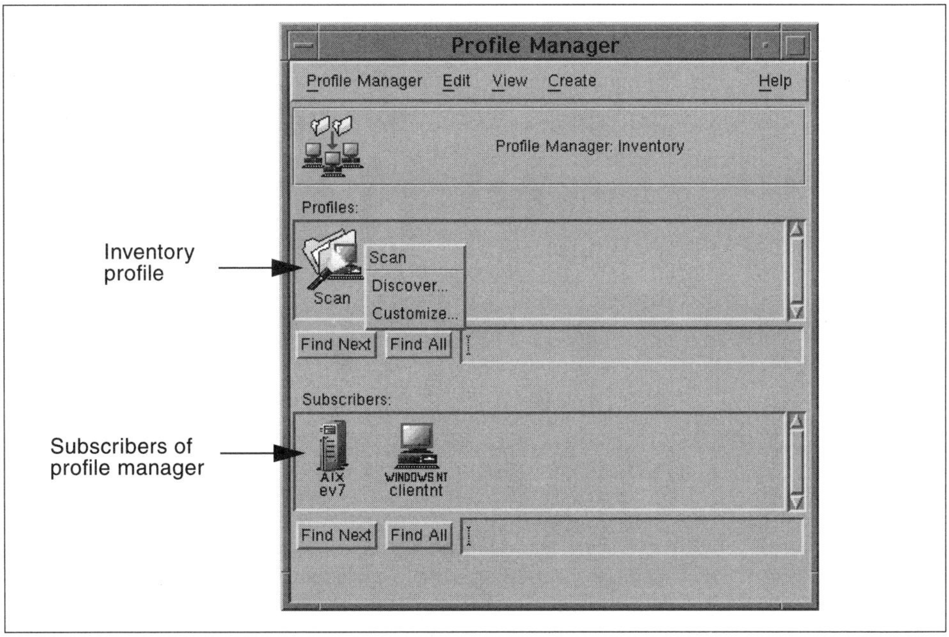

Figure 50. Profile Manager View with Inventory Profile

The types of subscribers to which an Inventory profile can be distributed are managed nodes, PC managed nodes, and NetWare managed sites as well as other profile managers containing these types of resources. In the case of NetWare sites, the TME 10 Inventory application is able to scan the clients of the site that are running the PC agent software.

5.3.2 Customizing an Inventory Profile

Once an Inventory profile has been created, you can customize some of what will be scanned. Only software scans can be customized, though. Therefore, this customization only works for PCs and not for UNIX systems. Figure 51 shows the PC software scanning options for an Inventory profile (in Figure 50 on page 117 and in Figure 52 on page 120 you can see the **Customize...** button that opens the window below).

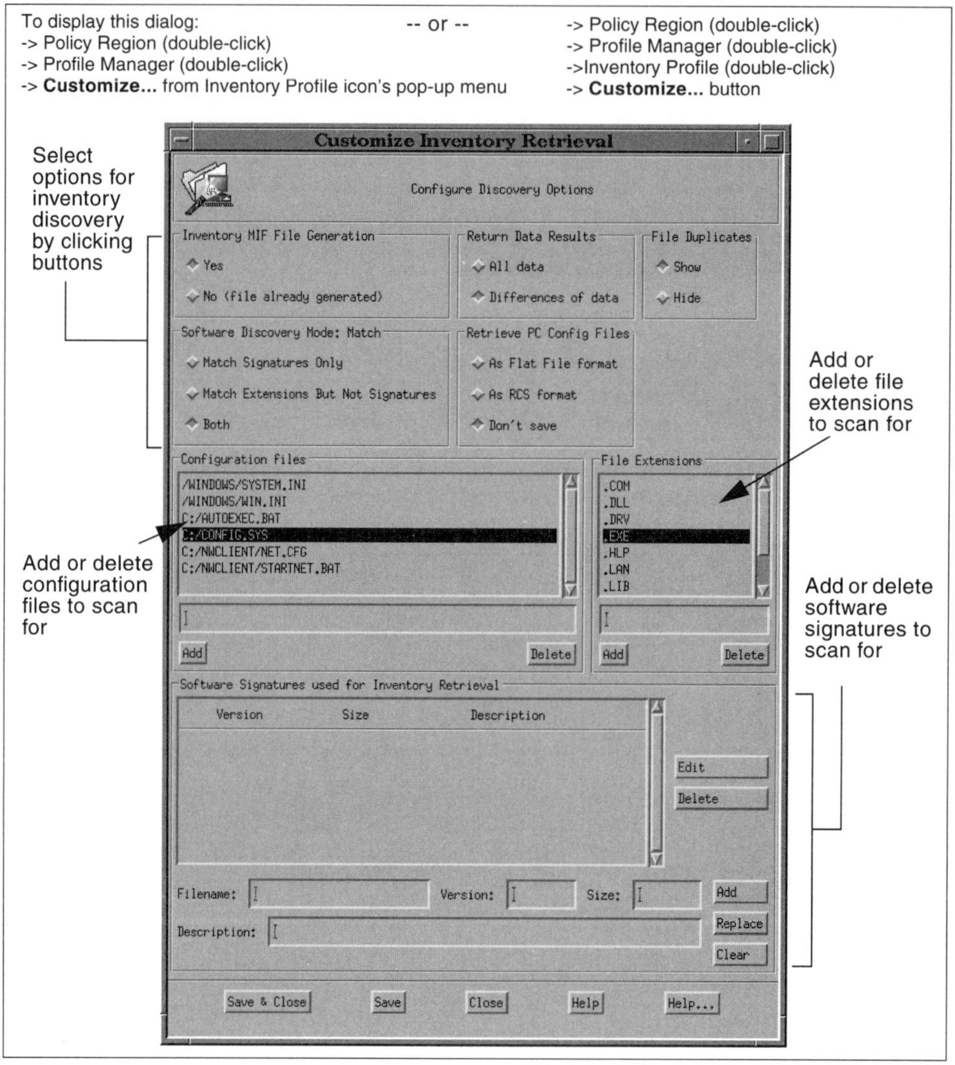

Figure 51. Window for Customizing a PC Inventory Scan

You can set the following values for customizing the TME 10 Inventory scan:

- Inventory MIF File Generation – If you select **No**, no scan is performed. An existing MIF file is retrieved from the endpoint and processed as if a scan had been performed. The information sent to the Inventory server is stored in the RDBMS.
- Return Data Results – You can decide to have only the differences between the current scan and the previous scan returned to the Inventory server. The information is then merged with the existing information in the RDBMS.
- File Duplicates – Some software packages may be installed more than once in different directories. If you select **Show**, the scan looks for all occurrences of the files or software packages that you define in the discovery options. If you select Hide, the scan ignores duplicates.
- Software Discovery Mode – A signature uniquely describes a software package. The PC scanning agent can determine what software packages, including their versions, are installed by searching for files matching the signatures. An ldappl.ini file contains predefined signatures of 16-bit and 32-bit applications and is loaded onto the PCs before scanning starts. You can also decide to look for certain file name extensions instead of or in addition to the signature matching.
- Retrieve PC Config Files – You can decide to receive the PC system configuration files as flat files or as RCS-format files, or not to receive them at all. Only when you select the RCS format can you maintain version control and history information for the configuration files stored in the database.
- Configuration files – This list contains all the file names of files you consider to be configuration files. You can edit this list by using the data entry field beneath the list and pressing the **Add** button.
- File Extensions – If you look for matching file name extensions, you need to add all relevant extensions to this list and delete unnecessary extensions. However, you should not delete extensions that are used in signature file names. For example, if you add a signature for WRITE.EXE and delete the .EXE extension, TME 10 Inventory will not detect this program.
- Software Signatures used for Inventory Retrieval – In the data entry fields at the bottom of the window, you can add signatures that are not contained in the Tivoli-provided lpappl.ini file. Fill in the file name, such as WRITE.EXE, the version number (3.1), the size of the executable (244960 bytes), and a description.

After creating or modifying the above scanning options, you need to save them. Then you can close the window. The scanning occurs when the profile is distributed to the subscribers.

5.3.3 Distributing an Inventory Profile

After the instructions for the scan are customized as desired, you can initiate the actual scan by distributing the profile to some or all of the subscribers of the profile manager. You can choose to do this immediately, or schedule it to happen later with the TME 10 scheduler facility.

Scanning machines for the first time can be very time-consuming because all information of one distribution action is collected on the Inventory server and then serially written to the RDBMS. So, for subsequent distributions, you may want to have the scan only return the differences to the previous scan. Limiting the number of subscribers for a single distribution action also helps to speed up the process.

In order to start the distribution, select the **Discover...** option of the profile icon's pop-up menu or simply double-click on it. This will bring up the window shown in Figure 52.

To display this dialog:
-> Policy Region (double-click)
-> Profile Manager (double-click)
-> Inventory Profile (double-click)

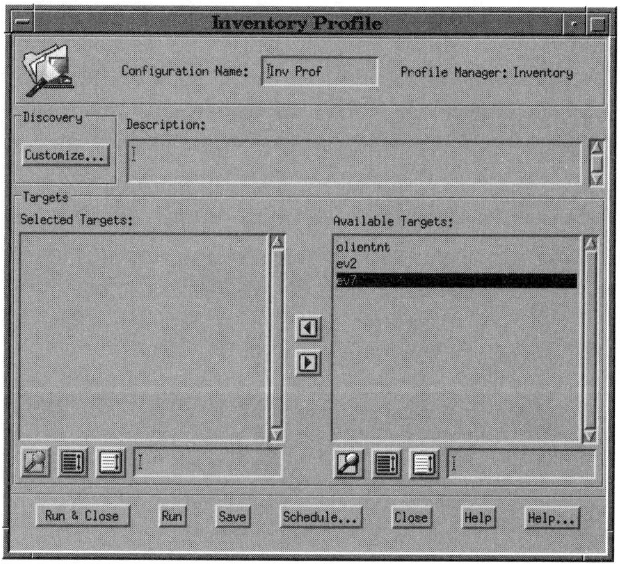

Figure 52. Inventory Profile Distribution Dialog

From this window, you select the targets for distribution. You simply move the targets from the Available Targets side of the window to the Selected Targets side of the window, and they will then be selected for distribution of the profile. You could also click the **Customize...** button to customize the scan, which would bring back up the window shown in Figure 51 on page 118. If you choose either the **Run & Close** or **Run** button, the profile will be distributed immediately. You can also click the **Schedule...** button to bring up the TME 10 scheduler facility to schedule the scan to occur at another time. For information on using the TME 10 scheduler, see Section 2.10, "Scheduler" on page 40.

5.4 The Configuration Repository

The configuration repository is a central storage for all the hardware and software inventory information in a TMR. This section discusses the following topics:

- Initial setup of the Relational Database Management System (RDBMS)
- Database tables and views
- Viewing the inventory information
- Query facility
- Selecting distribution targets using queries
- Creating and using reference models

5.4.1 Initial Setup

The configuration repository can currently be an Oracle or Sybase database. The RDBMS server does not need to be on a managed node, but one managed node in the TMR must run an SQL interface (Oracle's SQL*Plus or Sybase's isql) that provides access to the RDBMS.

The TME 10 Inventory server uses the RDMBS Interface Module (RIM) provided by the TME 10 Framework to access the database. It sends the data to the managed node that has the SQL interface installed. That managed node is called the RDBMS access host or RIM host. During the TME 10 Inventory server installation, you must specify the name of the RIM host.

The configuration repository is set up initially by running initialization scripts provided by the TME 10 software. These scripts set up the tables and fields in the relational database where the inventory information will be stored, and also a database administrator, *tivoli.*

5.4.2 Database Tables and Views

The information that builds a relational database, for instance the TME 10 Inventory database, is broken down into tables consisting of equally-structured data records with a number of data fields. Tables are put into relation with each other by means of fields that are designated to be keys. The structure of tables, fields, and keys that you design is called the data model.

The information is stored in tables that consist of an unlimited number of records. Using SQL SELECT statements, you can run database queries to retrieve and view the information. As part of the retrieval process, related data records are assembled together from multiple tables to satisfy the query. The information is presented in logical data records that consist of data fields assembled from different physical records stored in tables.

Instead of running a complex SQL SELECT statement to build these logical records every time you want to retrieve a specific piece of information, you can define a view. A view can be thought as a logical table. In fact, a view is a predefined SQL SELECT statement that presents its output in table form. Views can be treated like tables, and you can run SQL SELECT statements against views to select specific records meeting the search criteria.

The tables and views that build the TME 10 Inventory database are created by running the Tivoli-provided initialization scripts. The data model (tables, fields, keys) can be extended, and new views can be created. However, nothing should be deleted.

Additions to the data model must be performed with shell scripts or commands that interface directly with the relational database. Example scripts of adding tables to the database can be found in the $BINDIR/TAS/RIM/SQL/examples directory. Scripts for both Oracle and Sybase can be found there as examples of changing the data model.

Reference listings of the specific tables and views created as well as instructions on how to extend the data model or add views can be found in the *Tivoli/Inventory User's Guide*.

5.4.3 Viewing the Inventory Information

Once the TME 10 Inventory agents are installed, the icons for these managed nodes and PC managed nodes should now have two menu options added to each of their pop-up menus: Software Inventory and Hardware Inventory. Choosing these options will cause windows to pop up and show a predefined portion of the inventory information stored in each of these categories.

Sample windows with the results of these menu options are shown in Figure 53.

To display this dialog:
-> Policy Region (double-click)
-> **Hardware Inventory...** on pop-up menu of jnwin95 PC managed node icon

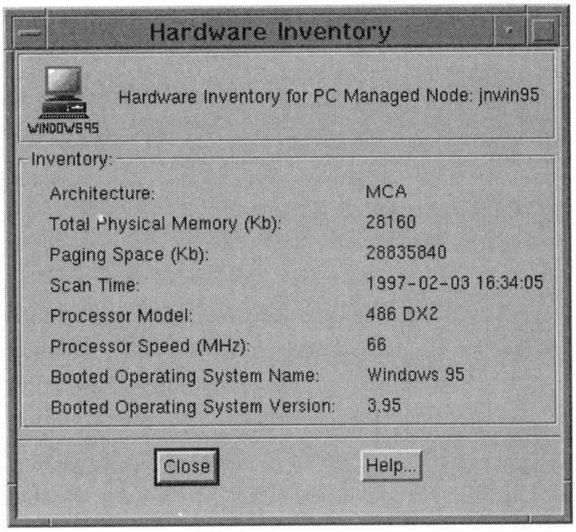

Figure 53. Software and Hardware Inventory Information Dialogs

5.4.4 Query Facility

The query facility provides a way to query the configuration repository in order to define subscribers to a profile manager. A query runs an SQL `SELECT` statement against the RDBMS and returns a list of machine resources (managed nodes, PC managed nodes, NetWare managed sites) that match the selection criteria.

This facility works by creating *query libraries* within policy regions and then creating *queries* within those query libraries. A query library is a container for queries that is created by selecting the **Query Library...** option of the policy region's *Create* pull-down menu and then specifying a name for the query library. Once the query library has been created, you can then choose the menu option to create a query, which should pop up the window shown in Figure 54 on page 124.

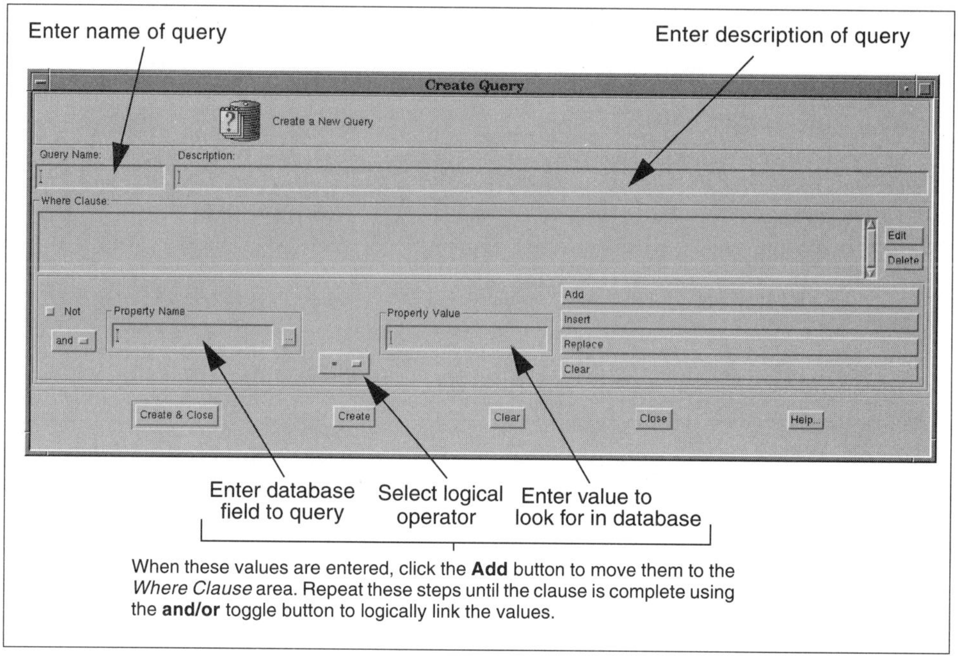

Figure 54. Creating a Query

In the top part, you enter a name and a description for the query. In the data entry fields of the lower part of the window, you can assemble selection criteria or search conditions for the query. To build the first search clause, enter a database field name in the Property Name field. You can display and choose from a pull-down list by pressing the **...** (ellipses) button. Then choose a logical operator, and enter a value to create the condition that the property needs to meet. Pressing the **Add** button adds the search clause to the Where Clause panel.

You can preface the condition with a *not* operator. When adding further search clauses, you can combine them with the logical operators *and* or *or* to build compound queries. When the clause is completed and saved, it can then be used in query operations.

5.4.4.1 View Used in Query

The Property Name list contains the field names of a database view. The default view is the INVENTORYDATA view, which is defined in the default policy method `query_def_table_name` of the QueryLibrary managed resource. You can query the currently active view and set another view, for instance YOUR_VIEW, as follows:

```
# wgetpolm -d QueryLibrary InventoryQueryLibrary query_def_table_name
```

```
INVENTORYDATA#
# wputpolm -c YOUR_VIEW -d QueryLibrary InventoryQueryLibrary \
 query_def_table_name
```

You can also change the database view of a specific query by using the `wsetquery` command. There is no GUI function to do this. Reference information about the commands and views can be found in the *Tivoli/Inventory User's Guide*.

5.4.5 Selecting Distribution Targets Using Queries

As mentioned earlier, a query returns a list of nodes, and you can use a predefined query to select subscribers that match certain hardware or software configuration criteria.

Bring up the *Subscribers* window from a profile manager with the **Subscribers...** option of either the icon's pop-up menu or from the profile manager window's *Profile Manager* menu. From there, you can click the **<<Query<<** button to start the query facility. This will pop up another window that allows you to choose the query you wish to run. These windows are shown in Figure 55.

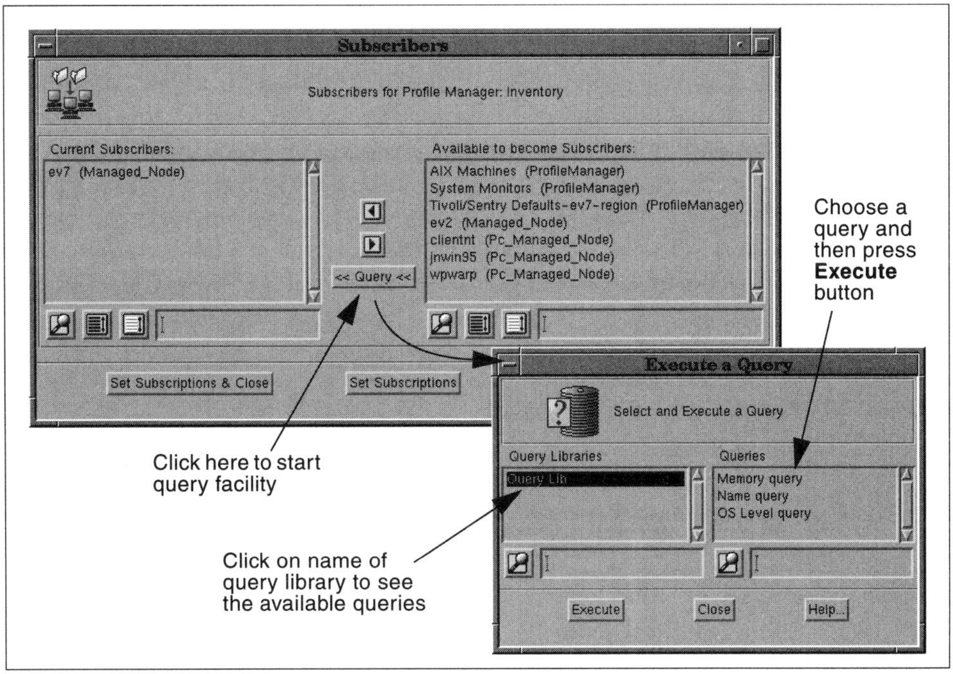

Figure 55. Starting the Query Facility

Once the query is executed, the subscribers window will now show those matching the query listed in the *Current Subscribers* section.

The query facility is also available when distributing a file package with TME 10 Software Distribution. The window for configuring the distribution also has the capability to perform a query in order to specify the subscribers that will receive the file package.

5.4.6 Data Retrieval Using SQL Commands

Because the Inventory information is stored in the relational database in standard SQL format, SQL commands can be used to run queries against the information stored, and reports can be created.

5.4.7 Creating and Using Reference Models

A reference model is a set of additional database tables representing the configuration of the ideal system against which you can compare the records of actual systems. TME 10 Inventory provides some sample SQL scripts to create a reference model for use in determining differences between the reference model and existing systems. The provided example compares the records of the reference model with the records in the repository and notifies an administrator with an e-mail message when any of the configuration records undergoes a change.

This simple example can be expanded to take almost any action you define when differences are detected, such as creating a TME 10 Enterprise Console event or a TME 10 task to create and distribute a file package that fixes the problem.

For further information about the reference model and the sample scripts, consult the *Tivoli/Inventory User's Guide*.

5.5 Authorization Roles

TME 10 Inventory provides its own set of roles for some of the Inventory-related functions but also relies on the authorization roles provided by the TME 10 Framework.

The additional authorization roles specific to TME 10 Inventory are:

- **Inventory_view** – Allows viewing an Inventory profile
- **Inventory_scan** – Allows distribution of an Inventory profile, which will cause a scan for inventory information

- **Inventory_edit** – Allows editing an Inventory profile
- **Inventory_query** – Allows querying inventory information from the configuration repository

For more information on TME 10 Framework authorization roles, see Section 2.6.1, "Authorization Roles" on page 30.

5.6 Inventory Notice Group

When the TME 10 Inventory application is installed, a new notice group becomes available in the notification facility, called *Inventory*. You can then change the administrator properties so that they can subscribe to this group and read postings concerning the TME 10 Inventory application. For more information on reading notices, see Section 2.7, "Notification (Bulletin Board) Facility" on page 32. For more information on administrators, see Section 2.6, "Administrators" on page 29.

CHAPTER 6

TME 10 Distributed Monitoring

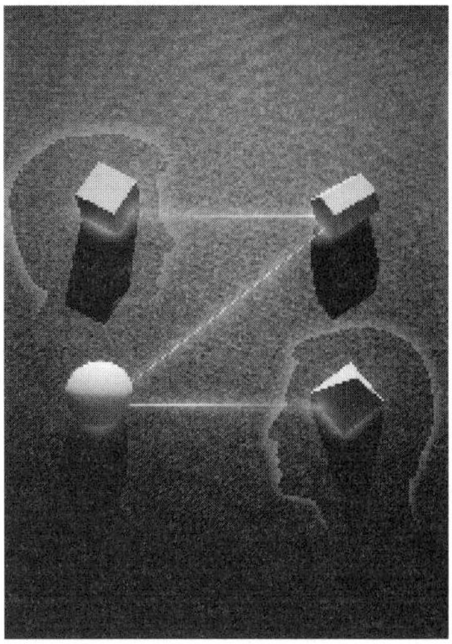

TME 10 Distributed Monitoring is an application that allows you to monitor the status of a wide range of geographically dispersed hardware from different vendors running different operating systems, including resources that are not part of your TME 10 Environment.

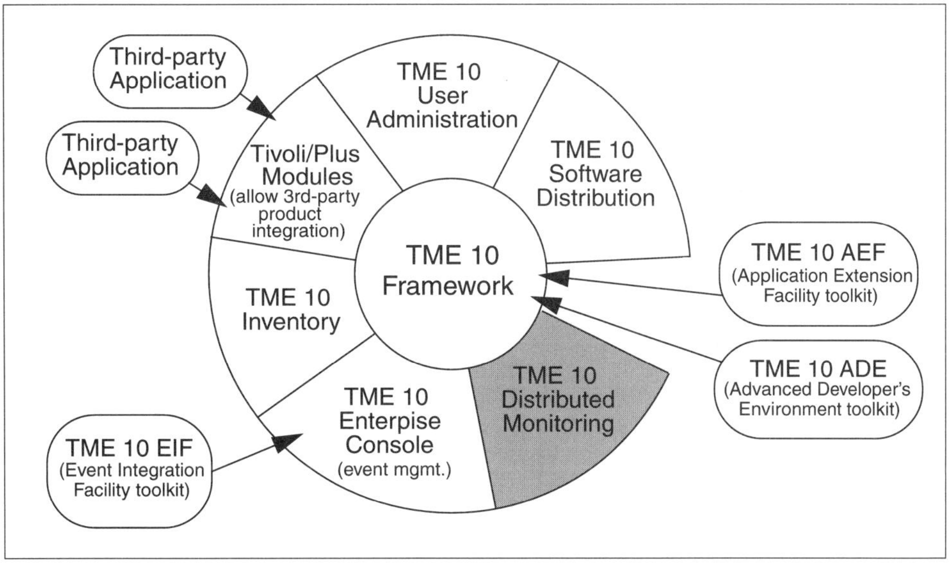

Figure 56. TME 10 Software Components

TME 10 Distributed Monitoring provides your network computing environment with the following features:

- Centralized monitoring of remote resources
- Predefined monitors for almost every resource (monitoring collections)
- Strong mechanism to generate events and alarms
- Automated decisions and actions in response to alarms or events
- Various responses (e-mail, triggering a program, sending an SNMP trap)
- Custom scripts for monitoring specific applications
- Full integration with the TME 10 Enterprise Console event server
- Data collection for statistical analysis and capacity planning

6.1 Overview and Product Information

This book discusses the TME 10 Distributed Monitoring at version level 3.0, or more precisely, it describes the functions and features of Tivoli/Sentry Version 3.0 using the new TME 10 terminology.

The former IBM product, System Monitor/6000, that performs functions similar to Tivoli/Sentry was also included in the new TME 10 Distributed Monitoring product, but is not covered in this book. System Monitor/6000 generates SNMP traps from problems it detects. This product will eventually be discontinued.

6.1.1 Supported Platforms

The TME 10 Distributed Monitoring software package consists of the TME 10 Distributed Monitoring for managed nodes as well as a separate code for each monitoring collection provided by TME 10 Distributed Monitoring.

The TME 10 Distributed Monitoring software for managed nodes (TMR server and TME 10 clients) has to be installed on each managed node that needs to perform the monitoring functions. It runs on the following operating systems:

- AIX
- HP-UX
- SunOS
- Solaris
- Windows NT

The monitoring collections are only installed on the TMR server (there is no client portion for monitoring collections). The available Monitoring Collections are shown in the following list:

- Universal Monitoring Collection
- UNIX Monitoring Collection
- Windows NT Monitoring Collection
- SNMP Monitoring Collection

- RFC 1213 Monitoring Collection
- Compaq Insight Manager Monitoring Collection

Refer to the *TME 10 Distributed Monitoring Release Notes* for disk space requirements for the TME 10 Distributed Monitoring application.

6.1.2 TME 10 Distributed Monitoring at a Glance

TME 10 Distributed Monitoring is based on the TME 10 Framework architecture. It provides fundamental tools for monitoring resources or events on an arbitrary set of managed nodes and for triggering actions based on the managed node's state. TME 10 Distributed Monitoring has two main components that enable these functions:

- The ***Distributed Monitoring engine*** – One process on each managed node that controls and oversees the resources as defined in the monitors of Distributed Monitoring profiles. It determines when to trigger a monitor and when to run the automated responses. The Distributed Monitoring engine runs autonomously on each monitored system, which makes more efficient use of network resources.
- ***Monitoring Collections*** – Monitoring sources are grouped into monitoring collections. A monitoring source represents a specific aspect of a system that can be monitored, such as percentage of disk space used. The intelligence (code and parameters) that actually enables performing these monitoring functions has to be available (installed) before a monitor can be defined. Tivoli and Tivoli partners provide predefined monitoring sources that monitor common system functions. Section 6.1.1, "Supported Platforms" on page 130, lists predefined monitoring collections that come with TME 10 Distributed Monitoring. Other collections may be installed with other applications that are TME 10 Distributed Monitoring-enabled.

A monitor is an entity that monitors a specific aspect of a resource out on a managed node, and its definitions contain threshold values and various response actions triggered upon reaching a threshold. Monitor definition is performed centrally, and the monitors are distributed to the managed nodes' Distributed Monitoring engines via Distributed Monitoring profiles. The Distributed Monitoring engine controls all the monitors on a managed node and performs the necessary checks on behalf of the monitors at the specified intervals. TME 10 Distributed Monitoring uses its own scheduler, which is different from the central TME 10 Framework scheduler.

Figure 57 on page 132 shows the interaction of the Distributed Monitoring engine with the TMR server.

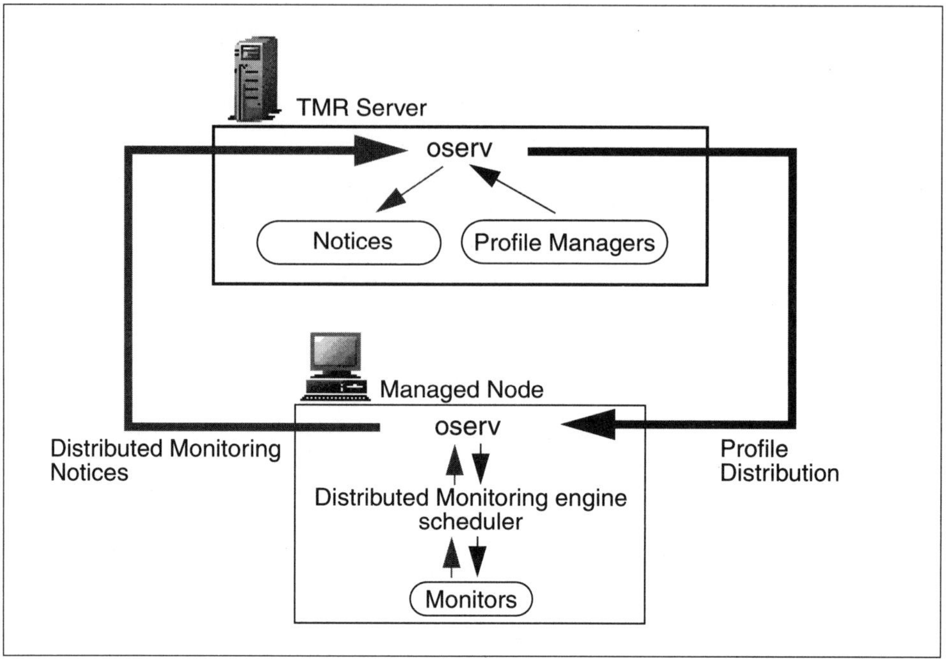

Figure 57. Interaction between Distributed Monitoring Engine and TMR Server

Like other TME 10 applications, TME 10 Distributed Monitoring works with profiles, but other than, for instance, in TME 10 Software Distribution where each file package is a profile, monitors are *records* of a Distributed Monitoring profile. Thus, multiple (usually related) monitors can be handled with one profile. Considering that Distributed Monitoring profile records are, in essence, monitors, from this point on we will use the term *monitor* to refer to a Distributed Monitoring profile record.

After a Distributed Monitoring profile has been created, monitors can be manually added one at a time or copied from another profile. Further details about adding monitors to a Distributed Monitoring profile are covered in Section 6.4.1, "Creating Monitors" on page 139. Figure 58 on page 133 shows the *Distributed Monitoring Profile Properties* dialog, illustrating the monitors as profile records.

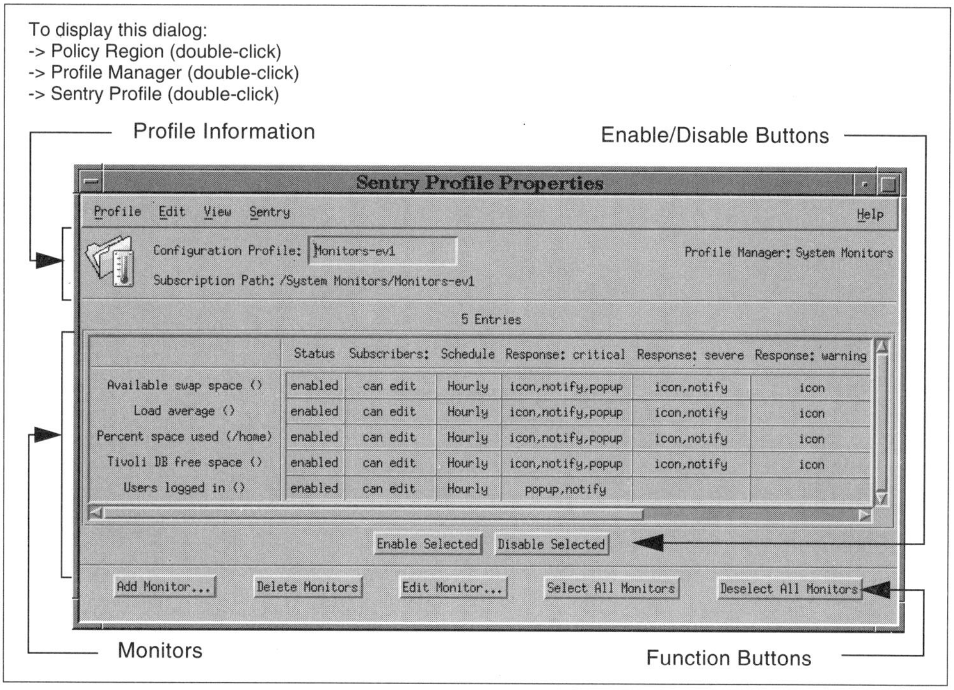

Figure 58. Distributed Monitoring Profile Properties Dialog

The Monitors area shows five monitors with some of their attributes. The *View* pull-down menu provides the option to define which attributes are displayed. The function buttons allow you to invoke operations on selected monitors. Monitors can also be disabled; by default, they are enabled.

Note

Every time you enable or disable monitors, you must distribute the profile again in order for the changes to take effect. See Section 6.6.5, "Distributing the Profile" on page 157 for more details.

To be able to distribute Distributed Monitoring profiles, an association has to be made between profiles and target machines on which the monitors need to perform their task. This is done by using the profile manager's subscription list. Profile managers contain profiles and reside within a policy region.

Figure 59 on page 134 shows an example of a *profile manager* that contains a Distributed Monitoring profile (Monitors-ev1) and two subscribers (AIX ev1 and AIX ev4). In a real environment, you would probably add operating system-specific monitors into separate Distributed Monitoring profiles and profile managers, build groups of machines that receive the same set of profiles by adding them into a profile manager without profiles, and then add these profile managers as subscribers. This concept of grouping resources together is explained in more detail for TME 10 Software Distribution in Section 4.3.1, “Grouping Together Resources” on page 96.

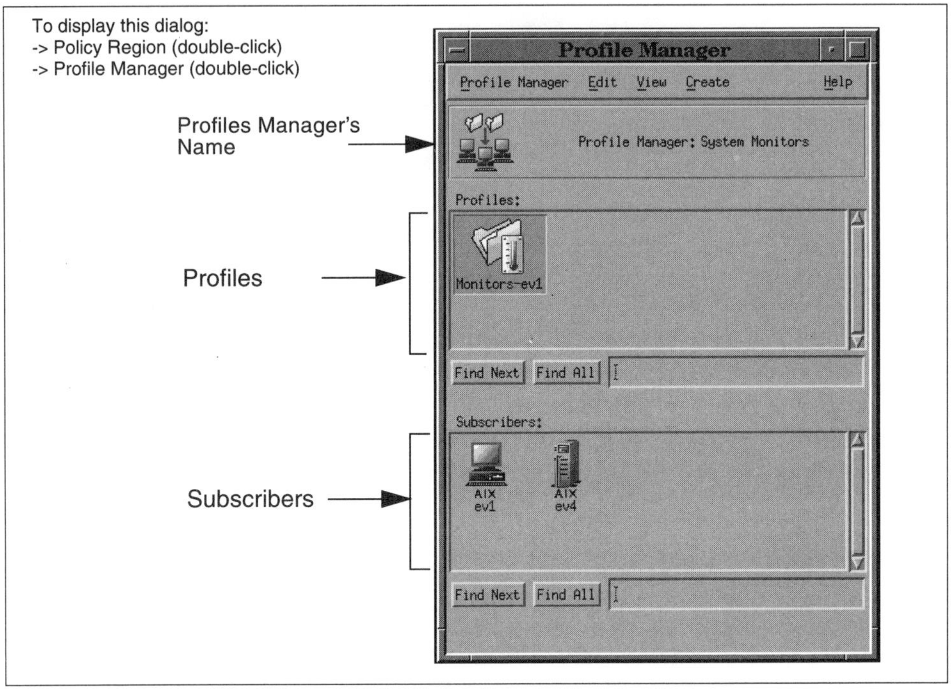

Figure 59. Profile Manager Dialog with Profiles and Subscribers

The above example shows a profile manager that deals with a Distributed Monitoring profile. Other entities, such as TME 10 Software Distribution file packages or TME 10 User Administration profiles, could be added if the set of subscribers and the policies are the same as for the Distributed Monitoring profiles.

The administrator can monitor the status of monitors using an *indicator collection*. Within an indicator collection, you can assign an indicator icon to a Distributed Monitoring profile, and when any monitor of that profile detects a problem, the gauge on the corresponding indicator icon is raised to the appropriate warning level. An indicator collection and indicators provide an easy and centralized method to check on all the Distributed Monitoring profiles in a policy region. Indicator collections are covered in Section 6.5, “Indicator Collections” on page 150.

Figure 60 provides a general outline of the tasks involved in monitoring a networked resource with TME 10 Distributed Monitoring.

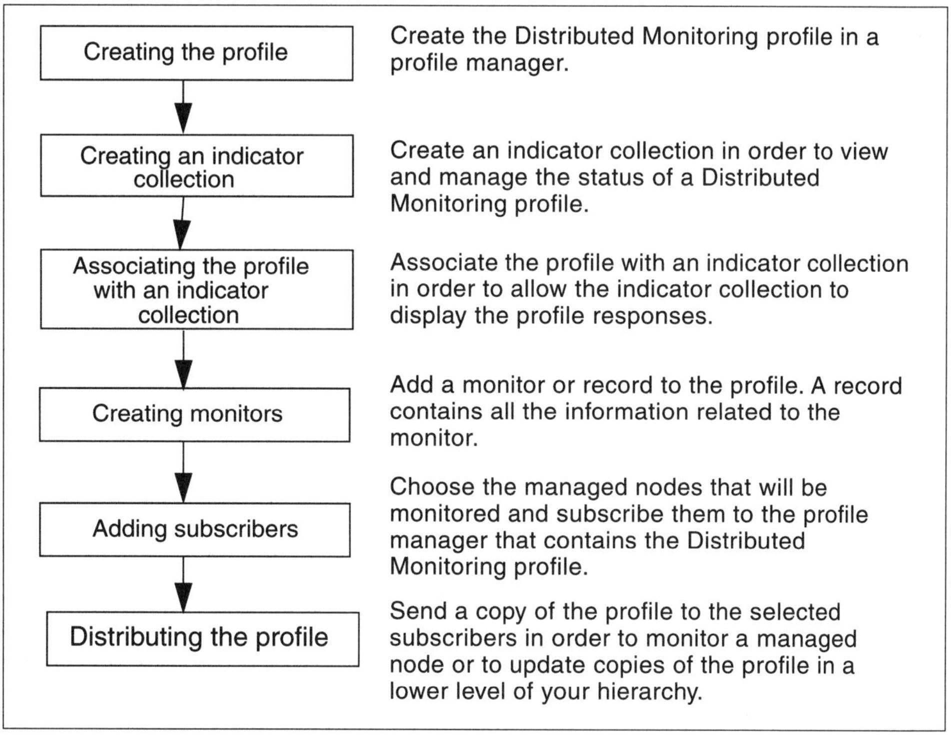

Figure 60. Tasks Involved in Customizing and Using Distributed Monitoring

6.2 Managed Resources

As a TME 10 application, TME 10 Distributed Monitoring is based on managed resources. A managed resource in the context of TME 10 Distributed Monitoring is a set of centrally managed monitors to be distributed to and run on a set of target machines. The managed resources added with this product are described in the following definitions:

 Distributed Monitoring Profile – A Distributed Monitoring profile contains and controls the activities of monitoring sources. It resides in a profile manger and is distributed to the subscribed target machines that are selected for distribution.

 Managed Node – Any host on which the TME 10 Framework has been installed. A managed node resides in a policy region and can be the recipient of one or more Distributed Monitoring profiles if it subscribes to these profiles within a profile manager.

 Distributed Monitoring Proxy – Represents a non-TME resource that functions as a subscriber for Distributed Monitoring profiles. Each Distributed Monitoring proxy endpoint is necessarily associated with an existing managed node.

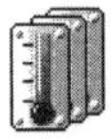 Indicator Collection – Provides a window in which you can view indicator icons and status alerts for monitors within your policy region.

 Indicator – Resides in an indicator collection and allows you to graphically display the status of the Distributed Monitoring profile that has been affiliated with it. Four different icons with different gauge levels indicate the highest severity status present in all monitors of the profile.

6.3 Distributed Monitoring Profiles

Since many key concepts of the TME 10 architecture are important in each of the TME 10 applications, it may be helpful to review some of them in order to understand the new concepts. After reviewing these general key points about profiles, this section discusses the specifics of Distributed Monitoring profiles and how to create them. Before a Distributed Monitoring profile can be distributed and perform useful monitoring, many more things have to be defined. Monitors, indicator collections and further customization of the profile are discussed in the following sections.

6.3.1 Key Points About Profiles

As discussed in Chapter 2, “TME 10 Framework” on page 15, a profile is a collection of information related to a specific application that lets you manage a specific type of resource. A profile also contains a list of subscribers (members of the list) to which the profile can be distributed in order to update or change system configuration information.

There is a strong relationship between profiles, profile managers, policy regions, and endpoints. Here are some key points about this relationship:

- Profile managers are created within a policy region.

- Profile managers contain profiles and subscriber lists.
- Subscriber lists may contain other profile managers or endpoints.
- Profile manager hierarchies are created when profile managers have other profile managers in their subscriber lists.
- Profile manager hierarchies allow you to manage your resources from a top down approach in your organization.

For more information about profile policy, profiles, and profile managers in general, see the *TME 10 Framework User's Guide*.

6.3.2 Profile Scope

Specifically, Distributed Monitoring profiles allow you to monitor resources or events on an arbitrary set of managed nodes and take preventive or corrective actions. As discussed in Section 6.1.2, "TME 10 Distributed Monitoring at a Glance" on page 131, a Distributed Monitoring profile record is a monitor definition that allows you to define the characteristics of the monitor, which are:

- Monitor name
- Resource to be monitored
- Status
- Monitoring schedule
- Automated response

Distributed Monitoring profiles also define characteristics that are valid for all records (monitors) stored in the profile, including the following:

- UID and GID required to run a script
- Default monitoring schedule
- Format of messages that are sent to notice groups
- Format of messages that are sent to the TME 10 Enterprise Console server
- Indicator collection affiliation
- Scripts to run or files to transfer when distributing a Distributed Monitoring profile

Distributed Monitoring profiles, Distributed Monitoring proxies, and indicator collections are managed resources. Each policy region maintains a list of managed resource types that are valid for that specific policy region. In order for an administrator to create or manage these resources, the following must be true:

- The profile manager must be a managed resource of the policy region.

- The particular resource type, such as Distributed Monitoring profile, Distributed Monitoring proxy, or indicator collection, must be a managed resource of the policy region.
- The administrator must have a senior role to create profile managers.
- The administrator must have an administrator role to maintain the Distributed Monitoring profiles and indicator collections in the policy region.
- The administrator must have a senior role to maintain the Distributed Monitoring proxies in the policy region.

6.3.3 Creating a Profile

Before you can create and use any monitors, you must create a Distributed Monitoring profile. Initially, when you create a Distributed Monitoring profile, it does not have any monitors. Just like any other TME 10 profile, a Distributed Monitoring profile is created within a profile manager using the *Create* pull-down menu and specifying the appropriate profile type (Distributed Monitoring Profile).

However, before the option Distributed Monitoring Profile (or SentryProfile) is presented to you in the upcoming *Create Profile* dialog, you must add the Distributed Monitoring profiles to the managed resources in your policy region. You can do this from the *Properties* pull-down menu in the policy region window when you select the **Managed Resources...** option. You can also call the *Set Managed Resources* dialog to check whether the Distributed Monitoring profiles are listed under the current resources.

6.4 Managing Profile Monitors

This section explains how to manage the monitors of Distributed Monitoring profiles and covers the following operations:

- Creating monitors
- Editing monitors
- Response levels, thresholds, and actions
- Monitoring schedule and message style
- Locking and unlocking the information in profile records
- Other operations on monitors

For more information about creating monitors, refer to Section 6.4.1, "Creating Monitors" on page 139.

Note

Every time you modify the contents of a Distributed Monitoring profile, you must save the profile before closing the *Distributed Monitoring Profile Properties* window in order to preserve the changes.

6.4.1 Creating Monitors

You must first decide which resources you want to monitor and then create the appropriate monitors to do that. Creating or adding monitors to a Distributed Monitoring profile can be performed manually, one at a time, or by copying or moving monitors from another Distributed Monitoring profile. A Distributed Monitoring profile can contain as many monitors as you want. Some monitoring sources provide predefined settings and response actions, which minimizes the amount of data you have to enter.

When you create a new monitor, Distributed Monitoring stores the information in the corresponding profile database. The new monitor will not monitor any resource until the profile is distributed to its ultimate destination.

To create a monitor, click the **Add Monitor...** button in the Distributed Monitoring profile. An example of this is shown in Figure 58 on page 133. Figure 61 on page 140 shows the *Add Monitor to Tivoli/Sentry Profile* dialog that allows you to create a monitor in a Distributed Monitoring profile.

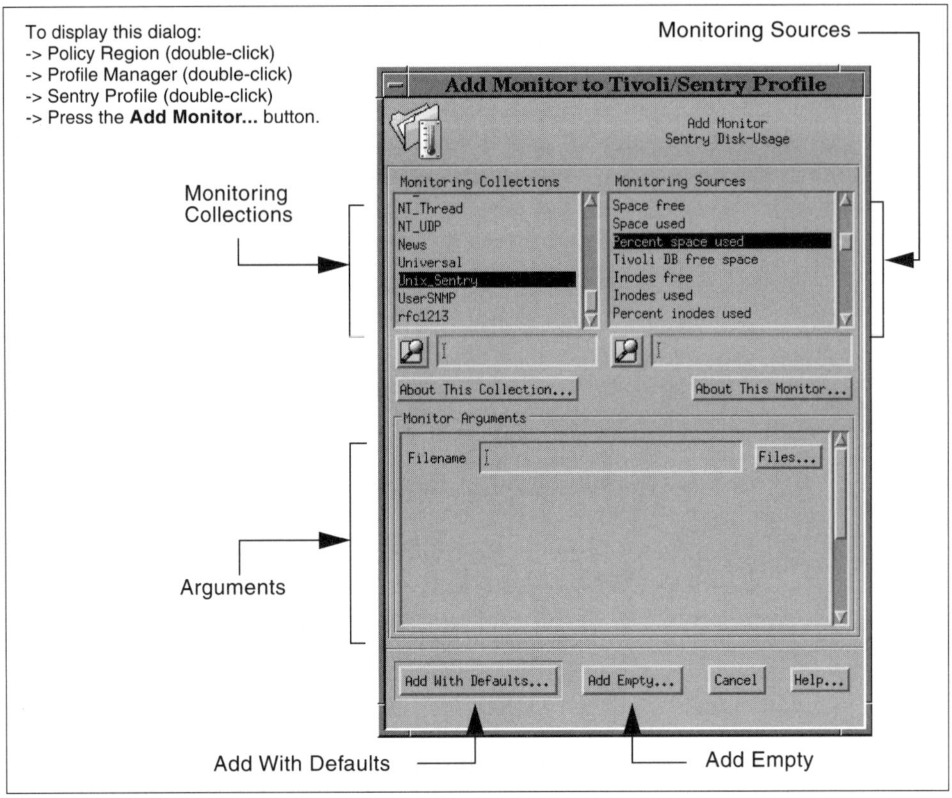

Figure 61. Add Monitor to Distributed Monitoring Profile

The Monitoring Collections area lists the installed monitoring collections. When you select a monitoring collection, the monitoring sources contained in that collection are displayed in the monitoring sources list to the right. In this example, the *Unix_Sentry* monitoring collection has been selected and, from its list of monitoring sources, the *percent space used*.

The Arguments area displays the arguments required for the selected monitoring source. Some monitoring sources may require multiple monitor arguments, and some may not require any argument. You must supply values for all arguments displayed in this area. In this example, a *Filename* argument is required for the *Percent space used* monitoring source, which determines the file or directory that will be monitored for disk space problems.

There is a *default source profile* that is used by TME 10 Distributed Monitoring as a template for getting the default values. Every time you create a new monitor by using the *Add With Defaults* button, TME 10 Distributed Monitoring tries to locate a monitor of the same type in the default source profile. If it finds a monitor of the same type, then all monitoring options are copied into the new monitor. It is possible to designate any Distributed Monitoring profile as a default source profile.

Initially, if you do not specify a default source profile, TME 10 Distributed Monitoring provides a profile called *TivoliSentryDefaults* as a default source profile for all your profiles.

Pressing the **Add With Defaults...** or the **Add Empty...** button brings up the *Edit Monitor* dialog discussed in the next section.

6.4.2 Editing Monitors

The *Edit Monitor* dialog allows you to configure or change a monitor. You can specify how often the monitor checks on a resource as well as how TME 10 Distributed Monitoring will respond when a threshold has been reached.

When you open the *Distributed Monitoring Profile Properties* window for a specific profile, that window is locked to prevent someone else from using the same properties window. This means that only one administrator can have a specific *Distributed Monitoring Profile Properties* window open at the same time.

Figure 62 on page 142 shows an example of the *Edit Monitor* dialog that allows you to configure the monitors. Display this dialog either by double-clicking on an existing monitor in the table-like *Distributed Monitoring Profile Properties* window, Figure 58 on page 133, or by adding a new monitor as explained above in Section 6.4.1, "Creating Monitors" on page 139.

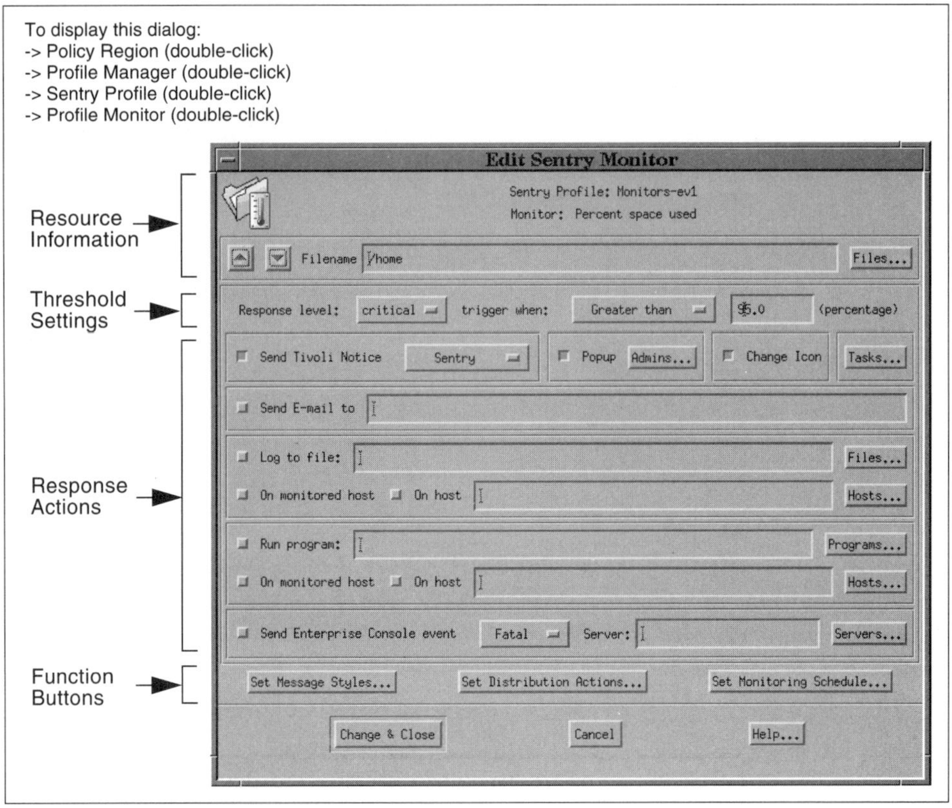

Figure 62. Edit Monitor Dialog

In the Resource Information area, you find the arguments you entered in the *Add Monitor* dialog. For the *Percent space used* monitor, it is the file name (/home). The Threshold Settings area allows you to configure the response levels as well as the circumstances in which the monitor should be triggered. In this example, the resource actions for the *critical* level are triggered when the /home file system is more than 95 percent full. For one monitor, you can set five different response levels with triggers and actions. See Section 6.4.3, “Response Levels, Thresholds, and Actions” on page 143, for a list of response levels and thresholds.

You can select one or more of the predefined actions in the Response Actions area by selecting the appropriate checkbox and providing additional information, such as the name of a program to run. For each response level, you get a separate set of actions. In this example, when the threshold is reached, a TME 10 notice is sent to the Distributed Monitoring (or Sentry) notice group, an alarm dialog is displayed on the administrator desktop, and the profile’s icon within the indicator collection is changed.

The function buttons allow you to override some profile-wide definitions for a specific monitor, such as:

- Message styles (Section 6.4.4, "Setting Message Style" on page 145)
- Distribution actions (Section 6.6.3, "Setting Distribution Actions" on page 155)
- Monitoring schedule (Section 6.6.2, "Setting the Monitoring Schedule" on page 154)

6.4.3 Response Levels, Thresholds, and Actions

For each monitor, you can define five response levels with a set of actions to be performed either unconditionally or when a threshold is reached. Response levels, thresholds, and actions are explained in the following sections.

6.4.3.1 Response Levels

TME 10 Distributed Monitoring provides five response levels. By using these response levels, you can define the automated actions that will be executed when an alarm level is reached. Table 5 shows and describes the five response levels available in TME 10 Distributed Monitoring.

Table 5. Response Levels Available in TME 10 Distributed Monitoring

Response level	Description
Critical	Indicates the highest response level. This is the first condition checked for by the *Distributed Monitoring engine* process.
Severe	Indicates the middle response level. This condition is checked for by the *Distributed Monitoring engine* process if the "Critical" level was not reached.
Warning	Indicates the low response level. This is the third condition checked for by the *Distributed Monitoring engine* process; it is only checked if the "Critical" and "Severe" levels were not reached.
Normal	Indicates the "none of the above" response level. There is no threshold checked for this level. The actions associated with this level will be executed each time the monitoring activity is performed and the "Critical," "Severe" and "Warning" levels were not reached.
Always	Indicates the "always true" response level. The actions will always be executed when the monitoring activity is performed in addition to the actions of one of the above levels.

6.4.3.2 Response Thresholds

TME 10 Distributed Monitoring provides 21 response thresholds. The thresholds available depend on the source being monitored and are defined by the monitoring collections. Table 6 shows all available response thresholds.

Table 6. Response Thresholds Available in TME 10 Distributed Monitoring

Threshold	Trigger Response When
(never)	Never.
Greater than	Current value is greater than specified value.
Less than	Current value is less than specified value.
Equal to	Current value is equal to specified value.
Not equal to	Current value is not equal to specified value.
Increases beyond	Current value increases beyond specified value.
Decreases below	Current value decreases below specified value.
Increase of	Current value has increased by specified value.
% increase	Current value has increased by specified percentage.
Changes by	Current value has increased by an absolute increment value.
Outside range	Current value falls outside specified range.
Is up/available	System resource (daemon, host, or print queue) is available.
Is down/unavailable	System resource (daemon, host, print queue) is unavailable.
Becomes available	System resource previously unavailable, becomes available.
Becomes unavailable	System resource previously available, becomes unavailable.
Same as	Returned string matched specified string.
Different from	Returned string is different from specified string.
Matches	Response from scripts matches specified value. Specified value may include wild cards.
Mismatches	Response from scripts does not match specified value. Specified value may include wild cards.
Changes to	Current value matches the specified value, but the previous value did not.
Changes from	Current value does not match the specified value, but the previous value did.

6.4.3.3 Response Actions

TME 10 Distributed Monitoring can perform preventive or corrective response actions when the threshold conditions are met at the time the Distributed Monitoring engine checks on behalf of the monitor. Table 7 shows and describes the response actions available in TME 10 Distributed Monitoring.

Table 7. Response Actions Available in TME 10 Distributed Monitoring

Response action	Description
Send TME 10 Notice	Post a notice to a specified notice group. You must subscribe to the notice group to receive the message.
Pop-up Alarm	Displays an alarm dialog on one or more administrator desktops.
Change Icon	Changes the profile's icon in the indicator collection.
Run response from Task Library	Runs a predefined task from a TME 10 task library when a threshold is reached.
Send e-mail	Sends an e-mail to a specified address. You can specify more than one address by separating them with commas. TME 10 Distributed Monitoring does not verify that the e-mail address you provide is valid.
Log to file	Adds an entry to a specified log file. If the file does not exist, TME 10 Distributed Monitoring creates the file, but you must specify an existing directory because TME 10 Distributed Monitoring does not create directories.
Run program	Runs an executable when a threshold is reached. This response is executed under the same user and group IDs as the Distributed Monitoring profile.
Send Enterprise Console event	Sends TME 10 Distributed Monitoring data to a TME 10 Enterprise Console event server.

6.4.4 Setting Message Style

TME 10 Distributed Monitoring allows you to control the format in which the notice, pop-up dialog, e-mail, log file, and Enterprise Console event responses are created. It is possible to control the response format of each monitor contained in a Distributed Monitoring profile. This feature is available by clicking the **Set Message Styles** button within the *Edit Monitor* dialog.

6.4.5 Locking and Unlocking Monitors

It is possible to lock any monitor of a Distributed Monitoring profile to prevent the local administrators of the lower levels from changing the contents of a specific monitor. You must distribute the profile after locking or unlocking monitors in order for this operation to take effect, which means you actually lock/unlock records on the target machines.

You can lock all monitors contained in a profile, but it is not possible to lock an entire Distributed Monitoring profile. In other words, administrators cannot modify the locked monitors, but they can add new monitors to a lower-level profile copy.

Unlocking the information in a monitor is the opposite operation of locking the information. Unlocking of previously locked monitors allows the local administrators of the lower levels to change the contents of those monitors.

6.4.6 Other Operations on Monitors

This section explains how to manipulate monitors in Distributed Monitoring profiles. It includes descriptions of the following topics:

- Viewing monitors
- Deleting monitors
- Copying monitors
- Moving monitors
- Finding monitors
- Sorting monitors
- Sorting monitors attributes

These tasks can be performed from the *Distributed Monitoring Profile Properties* dialog, which is shown in Figure 58 on page 133.

6.4.6.1 Viewing Monitors

You can view the monitors contained in a Distributed Monitoring profile in a table format by using the *Distributed Monitoring Profile Properties* dialog shown in Figure 58 on page 133. Each row represents a monitor, and each column contains specific information about the monitor, such as:

- Monitor status
- Response levels
- Whether or not subscribers can edit the monitor

You can scroll through the window to view the monitors stored in the profile and the configuration information stored in each monitor. The *View* pull-down menu provides you some options, such as redefining the sort order of the monitor and determining which of the many attributes are displayed for each monitor. Sections 6.4.6.6, “Sorting Monitors” on page 149, and 6.4.6.7, “Sorting Monitor Attributes” on page 149, cover the sort options in more detail.

6.4.6.2 Deleting Monitors

If you no longer need a monitor, you can delete the monitor from the profile. Remember that if you delete a specific monitor from a profile, you must save and distribute the profile in order to fully delete it.

6.4.6.3 Copying Monitors

It is possible to copy one or more monitors from one profile to another. When you copy monitors from one profile to another, you are creating an exact copy of the source monitors in an existing target profile. The target profile must be a Distributed Monitoring profile.

Figure 63 shows the *Copy Profile Records* dialog that allows you to copy monitors from one profile to another.

To display this dialog:
-> Policy Region (double-click)
-> Profile Manager (double-click)
-> Sentry Profile (double-click)
-> Select the **Copy Monitor...** option from the *Edit* pull-down menu

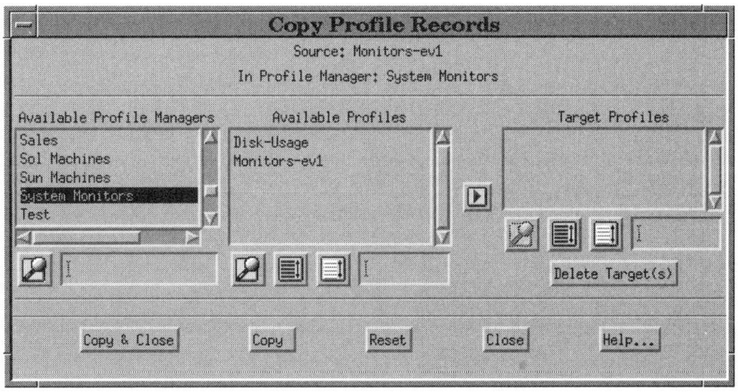

Figure 63. Copy Profile Records Dialog

The selected profile will then appear in the *Target Profiles* panel.

6.4.6.4 Moving Monitors

Moving monitors allows you to move one or more monitors from one profile to another. This operation deletes the specified monitors from the source profile and adds them to the target profile. Figure 64 shows the *Moving Profile Records* dialog that allows you to move monitors from one profile to another.

To display this dialog:
-> Policy Region (double-click)
-> Profile Manager (double-click)
-> Sentry Profile (double-click)
-> Select the **Move Monitor...** option from the *Edit* pull-down menu

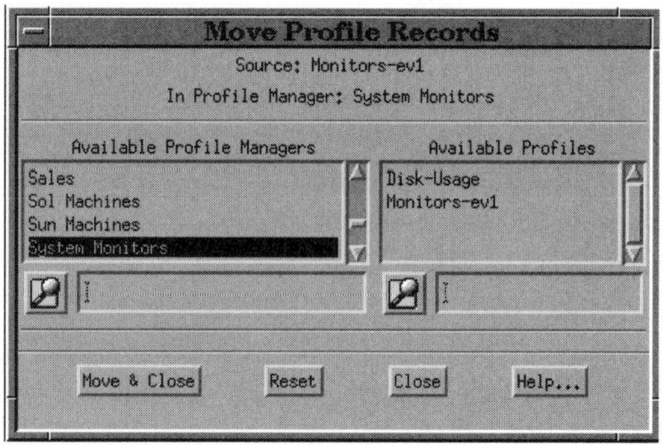

Figure 64. Moving Profile Records Dialog

When you select a profile manager, its profiles are displayed in the *Available Profiles* list. From this list, you select one to which the selected monitors are moved.

6.4.6.5 Finding Monitors

Sometimes it is necessary to find a specific monitor that is stored in a profile. This feature is very useful if your Distributed Monitoring profile stores many monitors. Distributed Monitoring provides a mechanism to perform this task. Figure 65 shows the *Find Records* dialog that allows you to find monitors stored in a Distributed Monitoring profile.

To display this dialog:
-> Policy Region (double-click)
-> Profile Manager (double-click)
-> Sentry Profile (double-click)
-> Select the **Find...** option from the *View* pull-down menu

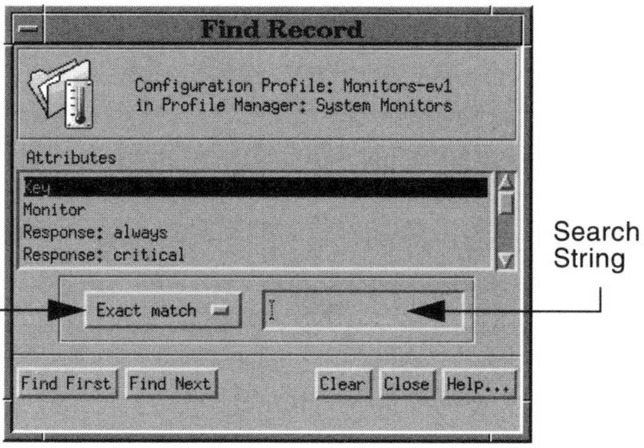

Figure 65. Find Records Dialog

In order to search for records, you select an attribute from the Attributes list, enter a search string to be matched against the attribute value, and specify the search type, which can be *Contains*, *Exact match*, *Greater than,* or *Less than.*

When the find is successful, the monitors that match the criteria are highlighted in the *Distributed Monitoring Profile Properties* dialog shown in Figure 58 on page 133.

6.4.6.6 Sorting Monitors

By default TME 10 Distributed Monitoring displays monitors alphabetically. If you want to change the order in which the monitors are displayed in the *Distributed Monitoring Profile Properties* dialog, a mechanism is provided to display the monitors in ascending or descending order.

To display this dialog:
-> Policy Region (double-click)
-> Profile Manager (double-click)
-> Sentry Profile (double-click)
-> Select the **Monitors...** option from the *Sort* submenu that is found under the *View* pull-down menu

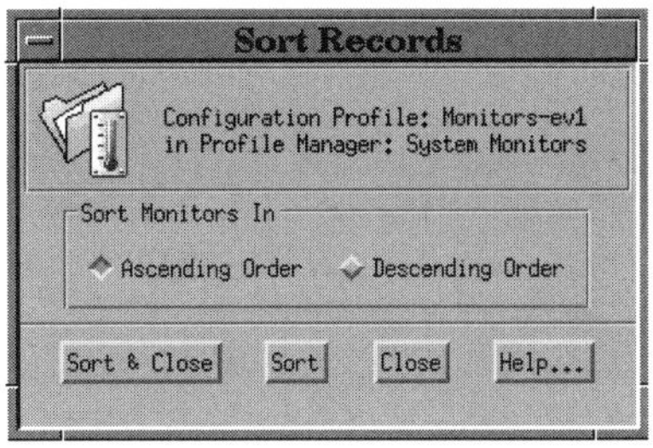

Figure 66. Sort Records Dialog

Figure 66 shows the *Sort Records* dialog that allows you to select a radio button to set the order in which the monitors are displayed in a profile.

6.4.6.7 Sorting Monitor Attributes

The table-formatted *Distributed Monitoring Profile Properties* dialog provides a list of all profile records contained in the profile. However, since profiles have many attributes, only a few can be displayed. TME 10 Distributed Monitoring provides a mechanism to select which attributes are displayed in the entries table of a profile and also the order in which they are displayed.

Figure 67 on page 150 shows the *Display Attributes* dialog that allows you to set the attributes that are displayed and their display order.

To display this dialog:
-> Policy Region (double-click)
-> Profile Manager (double-click)
-> Sentry Profile (double-click)
-> Select the **Attributes...** option from the *Sort* sub-menu which is found under the *View* pull-down menu

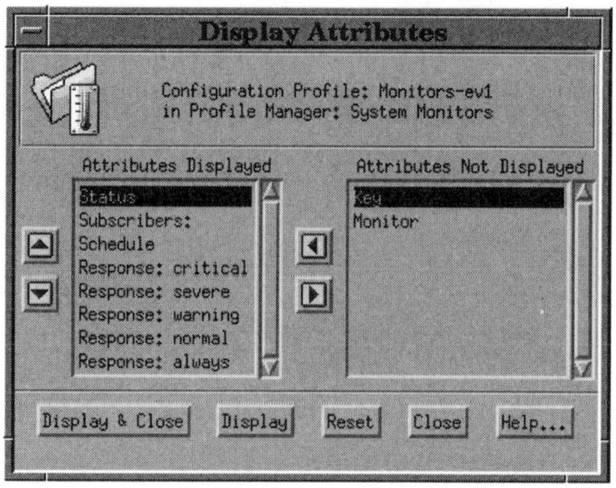

Figure 67. Display Attributes Dialog

6.5 Indicator Collections

In a large client/server environment, it is common to have numerous resources to monitor. This makes it complicated to keep control of all of them. Instead of checking every individual Distributed Monitoring profile for the state of its monitors, TME 10 Distributed Monitoring provides indicator collections.

An indicator collection is a window that has an icon for each of the profiles affiliated with it. In general, Tivoli recommends creating one indicator collection per policy region. However, you can create as many indicator collections as you want within a policy region, and a single indicator collection can be affiliated with as many profiles as desired.

The status of a monitor in an indicator collection is represented with icons. When a monitor contained in a Distributed Monitoring profile that has been associated with an indicator collection reaches one of the response levels explained in Section 6.4.3, "Response Levels, Thresholds, and Actions" on page 143, the indicator collection changes the profile icon according to the level reached. Figure 68 on page 151 shows the corresponding icons for each response level.

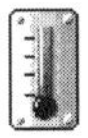	Normal
	Warning
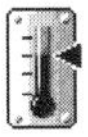	Severe
	Critical

Figure 68. Indicator Icons Within an Indicator Collection

As you can see, there is no icon for the *always* response level because this level does not indicate any abnormal state.

The following sections explain how to create and use indicator collections.

6.5.1 Creating an Indicator Collection

An indicator collection is an information resource maintained in a policy region. It is created within a *Policy Region* window by using the *Create* pull-down menu. However, before the option **IndicatorCollection...** is presented to you in this menu, you must add indicator collections to the managed resources in your policy region. You can do this from the *Properties* pull-down menu in the policy region window when you select the **Managed Resources...** option.

Configure your indicator collection such that it will deiconify or automatically come to the foreground whenever any Distributed Monitoring profile affiliated with that collection triggers.

6.5.2 Associating the Profile with an Indicator Collection

Once an indicator collection has been created, a Distributed Monitoring profile can be associated with the indicator collection. This step creates an indicator that will display the severity level of the responses coming from the monitors handled by the profile. By varying its gauge level, it displays the highest severity level found in all responses related to the corresponding profile.

Figure 69 on page 152 illustrates how an indicator collection improves an administrator's ability to monitor many resources within a policy region.

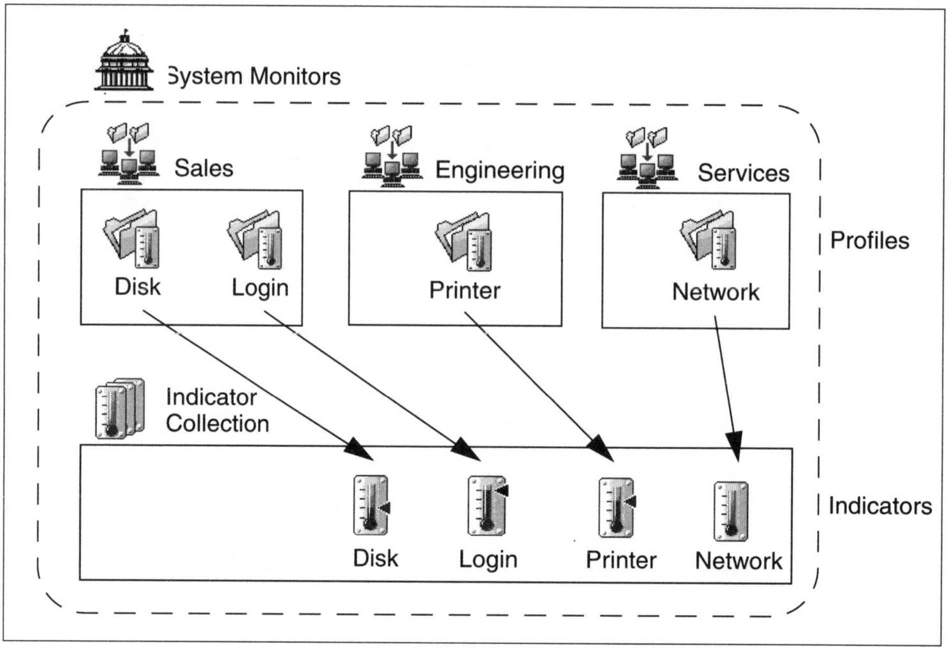

Figure 69. Using An Indicator Collection

6.5.3 Indicator Collection Functions

An indicator collection resides within a policy region and is considered an information resource. To keep control of all Distributed Monitoring profiles associated with an indicator collection, this resource allows you to perform the following tasks:

- View the status of all Distributed Monitoring profiles within a policy region from a single location by using the indicator collection icons.
- View the indicator log information of a Distributed Monitoring profile within the collection to display a history of the alarm conditions to which the profile has responded.
- Save an indicator log to a file, or mail it to any number of specified recipients.
- Reset a Distributed Monitoring profile icon to a non-alarmed state. If the condition that triggered an icon does not exist anymore, it is a good practice to reset the icon in order to easily determine when the next problem occurs.
- Clear an indicator log. This operation removes all entries from the indicator log and resets the indicator icon to its normal state.

6.6 Customizing and Distributing Distributed Monitoring Profiles

So far, we have discussed how Distributed Monitoring profiles and monitors are created, as well as how to define indicators and indicator collections that make supervising all the monitors more convenient for administrators.

This section discusses some further customization steps of Distributed Monitoring profiles that apply to all its monitors, and how to distribute the profile:

- Default policy
- Setting the monitoring schedule
- Adding subscribers
- Distributing a profile
- Other profile operations

6.6.1 Default Policy

A Distributed Monitoring profile also has a *default policy* associated with it. It consists of two attributes that determine the permissions under which a monitor executes on the remote system:

- Remote user ID
- Remote group ID

When you set the default user and group IDs, these values are automatically set for every monitor contained in the profile. These values will also be used if you add new monitors to the profile.

Figure 70 shows the *Edit Default Policies* dialog for a Distributed Monitoring profile. This dialog allows you to set the default policy values for a Distributed Monitoring profile.

To display this dialog:
-> Policy Region (double-click)
-> Profile Manager (double-click)
-> Sentry Profile (double-click)
-> Select the **Set User & Group ID...** option from the *Edit* pull-down menu

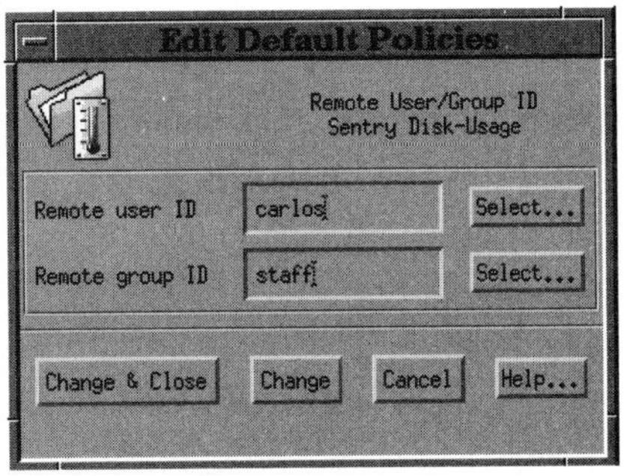

Figure 70. Edit Default Policies Dialog

6.6.2 Setting the Monitoring Schedule

Once you have created monitors in your profile and before you distribute the profile, it is important to define the monitoring schedule. This feature allows you to control how often a specific resource is monitored.

The monitor schedule option can be set at two levels:

- Profile level – To control how often all the monitors in a Distributed Monitoring profile, check the resources that are being monitored.
- Monitor level – To control how often a single monitor within a profile checks the resource that it is monitoring. The schedules set at the monitor level override those set at the profile level.

If you bring up the *Set Monitoring Schedule* dialog (Figure 71) from the *Distributed Monitoring Profile Properties* window, you will set the monitoring schedule at the profile level. Otherwise, if you bring up the *Set Monitoring Schedule* dialog from the *Edit Monitor* dialog, you will set the monitoring schedule at the monitor level.

To display this dialog:
-> Policy Region (double-click)
-> Profile Manager (double-click)
-> Sentry Profile (double-click)
To set the monitoring schedule at the profile level:
-> Select the **Set Default Schedule...** option from the *Edit* pull-down menu
To set the monitoring schedule at the monitor level:
-> Sentry Monitor (double-click)
-> Press the **Set Monitoring Schedule...** button

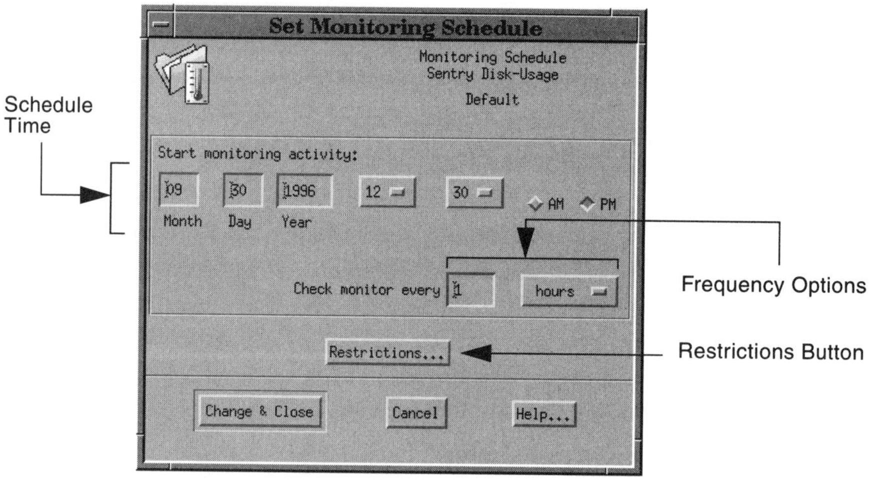

Figure 71. Set Monitoring Schedule Dialog

The schedule time determines the start date and time. If empty, the monitor starts immediately after distribution. The frequency option specifies the time interval between checks. The maximum monitoring frequency is once a minute, the default an hour. The **Restrictions...** button brings up the *Monitoring Schedule Restrictions* dialog that allows you to limit monitoring to certain periods of time (Figure 72).

To display this dialog:
-> From the *Set Monitoring Schedule* dialog, press the **Restrictions...** button

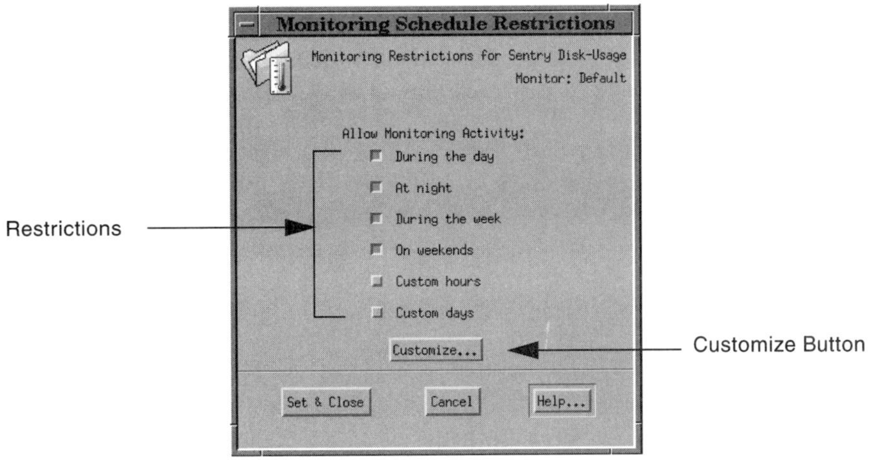

Figure 72. Monitoring Schedule Restrictions Dialog

If the default values do not satisfy your requirements, the **Customize...** button allows you to further define what is meant by *During the day*, *At night*, *During the week*, or *On weekends*.

6.6.3 Setting Distribution Actions

TME 10 Distributed Monitoring provides you with the capability to define one or more actions to be executed upon distribution of a Distributed Monitoring profile before the monitors start their operation. Figure 73 on page 156 shows the *Distribution Actions* dialog that allows you to define these actions.

To display this dialog:
-> Policy Region (double-click)
-> Profile Manager (double-click)
-> Sentry Profile (double-click)
-> Select the **Edit Distribution Actions...** option from the *Sentry* pull-down menu

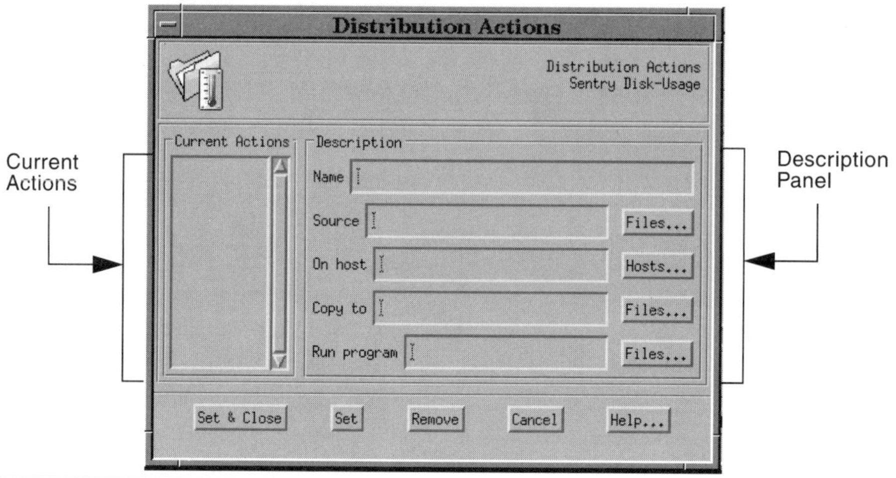

Figure 73. Distribution Actions Dialog

The *Current Actions* area lists the actions that are already defined. If you select one action, you can edit its definitions. To enter a new action, fill in its description and press the **Set** button. Its action name is added to the Current Actions area.

When running a program or script, the program or script must reside on each subscribing managed node. It is possible to copy a program/script first to a managed node and then run it. In order to do so, you specify the source host and source file path name as well as the target full path name (*Copy to* field) of the program/script.

When setting up distribution actions for a Distributed Monitoring profile, consider the following key points:

- TME 10 Distributed Monitoring uses the user ID and the group ID values as specified in the *Edit Default Policies* dialog and discussed in Section 6.6.1, "Default Policy" on page 153, to define access permissions of a file or script
- Unless system permissions prevent it, copying a file to a managed node always overwrites an existing file with the same path and name.
- A single file to be copied cannot be greater than 65536 bytes.
- If an action includes copying a file and running a script, the file is copied first.

6.6.4 Adding Subscribers

Before you can distribute the Distributed Monitoring profiles to any endpoints, subscribers must be added. Possible subscribers for a Distributed Monitoring profile can be:

- Other profile managers
- Managed nodes
- Distributed Monitoring proxies

TME 10 Distributed Monitoring uses the list of subscribers to determine which hosts will be monitored when distributing the Distributed Monitoring profiles.

6.6.5 Distributing the Profile

After you have created a profile with monitors and added subscribers, the profile must be distributed to the subscribers. This operation activates the monitors in the corresponding subscribers. It is important to bear in mind that every modification made to the characteristics of a specific profile or its monitors does not take effect until the profile is distributed again. Figure 74 shows the *Distribute Profile* dialog that allows you to distribute the profiles.

To display this dialog:
-> Policy Region (double-click)
-> Profile Manager (double-click)
-> Sentry Profile (double-click)
-> Select the **Distribute...** option from the *Profile* pull-down menu.

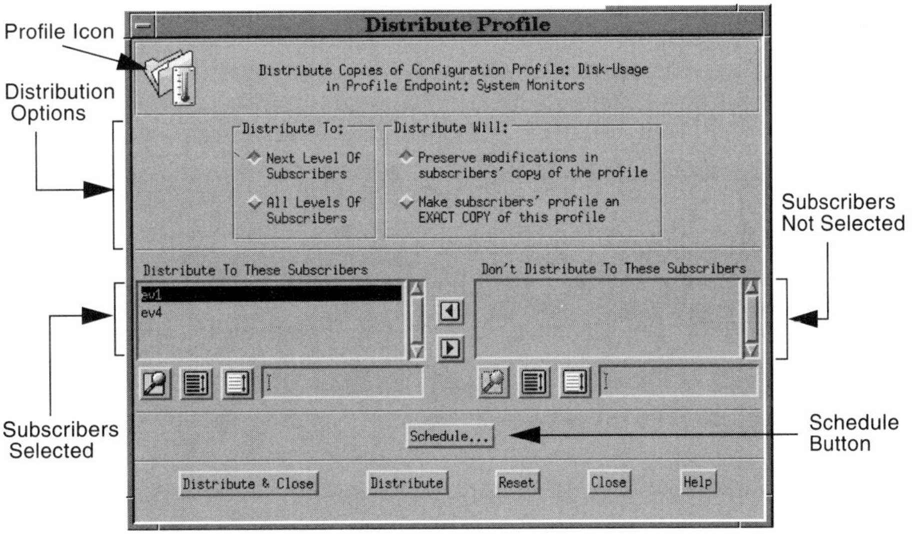

Figure 74. Distribute Profile Dialog

The Subscribers Selected will receive all the monitors defined in the profile. The Subscribers Not Selected are the ones contained in the subscription list of the profile manager, but they are excluded from receiving this particular profile.

If you select the **Next Level Of Subscribers** radio button, the copy will only be sent to the next level of subscribers, and the monitoring activity will not start. Also, it would not distribute to lower-level subscribers if there were any. Only if a profile manager were subscribed to the profile manager in Figure 74 on page 157 would you get lower-level subscribers. On the other hand, if you select **All Levels Of Subscribers**, all profile copies located on the subscribers will be changed, and the Distributed Monitoring engine at all levels of subscribed endpoints, including nested ones, will be updated with the new information.

If you select the **Preserve modifications in subscriber's copy of the profile** radio button, any changes made in the local copies of the profile since the last distribution will be kept. For example, if an administrator has changed the characteristics of a monitor, TME 10 Distributed Monitoring will not overwrite any part of the record that defines that monitor. On the other hand, if you select **Make subscriber's profile an EXACT COPY of this profile**, the distribution will overwrite the subscriber's profile with an exact copy of the profile being distributed, thereby eliminating any local changes made since the last distribution. Note that changes to local copies of profiles can be limited on a record level by locking monitors (see Section 6.4.5, "Locking and Unlocking Monitors" on page 146).

The distribution of the profile can be scheduled for a later time using the *Add Schedule Job* dialog. Clicking the **Distribute** or **Distribute & Close** buttons will execute the distribution and either leave the *Distribute Profile* window open or close it.

See also Section 3.5.3, "Distributing a Profile" on page 62, and Section 3.5.3.1, "Distributing from an Endpoint" on page 63. The profile distribution works the same way as in TME 10 User Administration.

6.6.6 Other Profile Operations

This section covers the following additional Distributed Monitoring profile operations:

- Cloning a profile
- Deleting a profile
- Navigating from one profile copy to another

6.6.6.1 Cloning a Profile

When you clone a profile, you create an exact copy of the profile you are cloning, including the default policy and the distribution actions associated with the original profile. However, the new profile does not have the same entries as the original profile; instead, it just has the definition of the profile. In other words, the new profile has no monitors.

6.6.6.2 Deleting a Profile

Deleting a profile deletes the original profile, the monitors contained in the profile, and also the copies of the profile that reside in every profile manager subscribed to the profile manager's list. It also deletes monitoring information from the Distributed Monitoring engines on the monitored hosts.

Deleting a Distributed Monitoring profile does not delete the profiles higher up in the subscription hierarchy.

6.6.6.3 Navigating From One Profile Copy to Another

TME 10 Distributed Monitoring allows you to go to and display any other copy of the profile in the subscription hierarchy from within a profile. Depending on your authorization role, you can perform operations on the displayed profile copies. For more information about authorization roles, refer to Chapter 2, "TME 10 Framework" on page 15.

6.7 Proxy Endpoints

If you want to manage resources that are not part of the TME 10 environment, you can use a Distributed Monitoring *proxy endpoint*. A Distributed Monitoring proxy endpoint represents a non-TME 10 resource entity that functions as an endpoint for Distributed Monitoring profiles. A proxy endpoint is always associated with an existing managed node. When a Distributed Monitoring profile is distributed to a proxy endpoint, the distribution is handled by the Distributed Monitoring engine on the managed node where the proxy resides.

A proxy endpoint is most useful when Distributed Monitoring profiles have been configured with monitoring scripts that make use of the different values of environment variables. A proxy endpoint contains a list of environment variables that are passed to the Distributed Monitoring engine. These variables can be pulled by the monitors established in the engine, and the variable values can be used during the data collection.

The following list gives some examples of when to use a proxy endpoint:

- To monitor a home directory which has a different physical path on each of several managed nodes. The environment variable can tell the proxy where the home path resides on each managed node.
- To define the name of a file to be used for writing debug or log messages.
- To define a host name of a non-TME 10 host to be probed.

6.8 Integration with the TME 10 Enterprise Console

TME 10 Distributed Monitoring provides a mechanism to transmit TME 10 Distributed Monitoring events of a specific severity level to the TME 10 Enterprise Console event server for handling. This feature is configured by using the *Edit Monitor* dialog as explained in Section 6.4.2, "Editing Monitors" on page 141. TME 10 Enterprise Console can then analyze the event in a systemwide context and may attempt to take corrective action to resolve the situation. No TME 10 Enterprise Console adapter application needs to be installed as TME 10 Distributed Monitoring is designed to send events in the format acceptable to TME 10 Enterprise Console. TME 10 Enterprise Console also provides the required class definition files for TME 10 Distributed Monitoring. For more information about TME 10 Enterprise Console, refer to Chapter 7, "TME 10 Enterprise Console" on page 163.

CHAPTER 7

TME 10 Enterprise Console

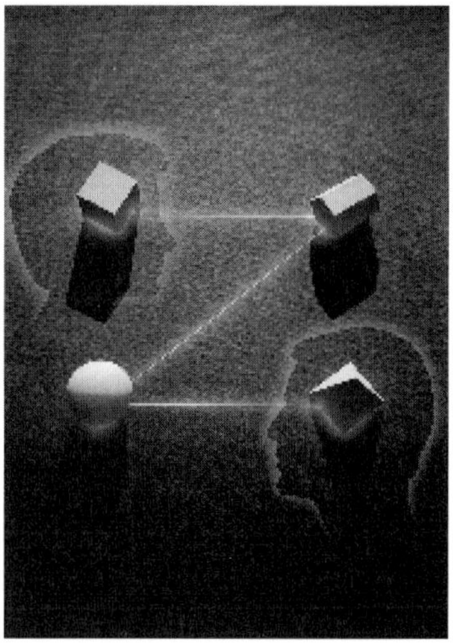

TME 10 Enterprise Console is one of Tivoli's availability-management applications. As a management tool, it assists in maintaining a high availability of the myriad of networks, systems, applications, and databases found within the realm of an enterprise and provides a centralized point of control for all major critical messages stemming from these resources.

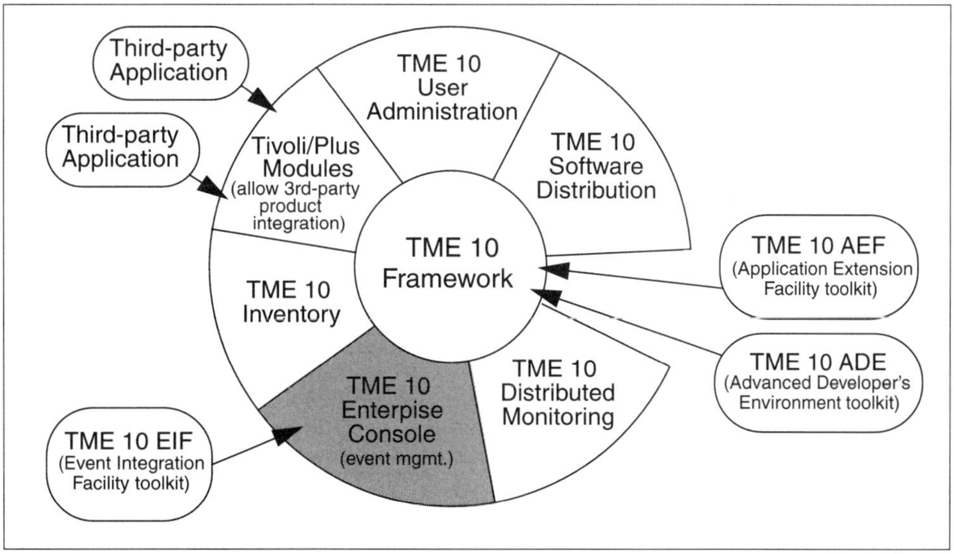

Figure 75. TME 10 Software Components

TME 10 Enterprise Console performs well in all three areas of a true Distributed Systems Management (DSM) product, which are:

- Scaling to large heterogeneous and worldwide computing environments
- Automating systems management processes and deploying applications
- Providing an integrated management view of the computing infrastructure

This chapter will show how TME 10 Enterprise Console lends itself to being a true enterprise solution that provides a simple, centralized point of control and a homogeneous approach to managing complex, heterogeneous network computing environments.

7.1 Overview and Product Information

This book covers the TME 10 Enterprise Console at version level 2.6, or more precisely, it describes the functions and features of Tivoli/Enterprise Console (T/EC) 2.6 using the new TME 10 terminology.

The majority of the information provided here will be common to the TME 10 Enterprise Console 3.1 product, which is the follow-on product to TME 10 Enterprise Console 2.6. Refer to Section 7.8.2, “Futures” on page 198, to review additional features and functions that will be available to the TME10 Enterprise Console 3.1.

7.1.1 Distributed Systems Management Requirements

For many companies, the computing enterprise is becoming more heterogeneous in nature. It is supporting a wider variety of operating system platforms and communications methods and carrying a diverse set of applications and databases. Many computing enterprises are also becoming more distributed both from a client/server and geographical perspective. It follows, therefore, that the computing enterprise is becoming increasingly more demanding to manage and control, and it is getting more difficult to attain acceptable levels of availability.

Understanding the health of our computing resources is crucial to achieving and maintaining the availability levels demanded by the end user. Availability or the lack of availability of the computing resources may be directly related to the bottom line of a company as well as to its competitiveness within the industry.

The people who created and developed the variety of resources that make up our computing environment gave the resources the ability to express the state of their well being through the creation and transmission of alarms, messages, alerts, and traps, to mention but a few. These may be created in great volumes and may flow through the network expressing both significant and truly insignificant changes in the state of the health of that resource. It has been up to the system support teams and operations staff to sort through the waves of messages in order to respond appropriately to a given situation.

Messages, alarms, traps, and the like are generated as result of a change of status in or around a computing resource. They can be purely informative in nature or denote a critical or severe situation. Unless these resources are self-correcting, some action must be initiated to restore the computing environment to an acceptable standing. This may be done via human or automated intervention.

7.1.2 Event Management Using TME 10 Enterprise Console

TME 10 Enterprise Console provides a much needed centralized point of integration and control for enterprise client/server environments. It allows administrators to monitor information about the environments for which they are responsible and provides automated responses to incidents occurring in the network and computing environment.

The amount of information contained in the enterprise varies in the way it is manifested and the forms in which it is stored. A TME 10 Enterprise Console *event adapter* located at or near to where the message originates. The adapter translates the message from its native or raw form into TME 10 Enterprise Console standard format and then ships the message to the TME 10 Enterprise Console *event server* for handling.

Once these messages are transformed into the TME 10 Enterprise Console standard format, they are known as *events.* Refer to Section 7.2, "Events and Event Adapters" on page 168, for more information regarding the event adapter and to Section 7.3, "Event Server and Event Flow" on page 175, for more information on the event server. The architecture for an event may be found in Section 7.2.1, "Event Architecture" on page 170.

The heart and soul of TME 10 Enterprise Console is the *event server,* which essentially captures, analyzes, and reacts to messages sent by the computing resources. It includes an intelligent event correlation engine for making decisions on real-time data. The decisions made and subsequent actions initiated will attempt to resolve outstanding problems. The decision could be to discard the message altogether or to trigger an automated routine or task to take corrective action. It may also require acknowledgment and intervention from an operator, and therefore the event server would permit the event to be received by the *event console* of a specified operator. See Section 7.7, "Event Console" on page 193, for complete details regarding the event console.

The operator, synonymous in this chapter with the term *administrator,* plays an important role in the management arena. The event server permits viewing of events specifically within the administrator's control range. The events may be informative, telling the administrator about the state of a resource, or they may require immediate attention and intervention. The operator can draw on a set of predefined tasks or programs to define resolutions and actions needed to restore the resource to an acceptable state.

7.1.3 Configurations and Machine Roles

Shared by all TME 10 management products is the *TME 10 Framework* which provides the framework for managing resources in a network computing environment. TME 10 Enterprise Console is tightly tied to this foundation and takes advantage of the many services that the TME 10 Framework provides. Refer to Chapter 2, "TME 10 Framework" on page 15, for more information regarding the basic framework and a review of terms like administrator and administrator roles and the concepts behind a TMR server, TME 10 clients, TME 10 desktop, CLI commands, and the notion of a TMR.

The TME 10 Enterprise Console 2.6 application, which includes the event server, is installed on either the TMR server or on a TME 10 client. It is suggested that the event server run on a machine that is dedicated to event processing and that it be a powerful machine.

Event adapters are installed on the TME 10 clients and the TMR server. It is also possible to install event adapters on non-TME 10 nodes. However, this limits the range of TME 10 commands that may be executed on this computing resource.

A Sybase relational database management system (RDBMS), which is coupled with the TME 10 Enterprise Console version 2.6 product, maintains information regarding current and historical (or already processed) events. In this release, the database should be located on the event server machine. Refer to Section 7.8.2, "Futures" on page 198, to review which relational databases will be supported in TME 10 Enterprise Console 3.1.

Operators or administrative staff may be local to the TME 10 Enterprise Console event server and Sybase database or positioned at any distributed point in the network that supports the TME 10 desktop and the TME 10 Enterprise Console event console. Note that in release 2.6 of TME 10 Enterprise Console it is necessary to install the TME 10 Enterprise Console event server on a managed node in order to run an event console from that node. However, only one event server coupled with the Sybase database is permitted in a TMR.

Recall from Section 1.5.2, "The TME 10 Management Region" on page 9 that the TME 10 environment uses TME 10 Management Regions (TMRs) to meet the needs and demands of managing resources that are geographically dispersed across networks. Each TMR has its own TMR server for managing local clients, and a set of distributed replicated services for performing distributed management operations. TMRs can be connected together across the network, enabling large-scale systems management, and remote-site management and operation. TMR connections can be either one-way or two-way.

Configurations that include TME 10 Enterprise Console may vary between enterprises. It may be sufficient to have only one copy of TME 10 Enterprise Console event server/Sybase database in a multiple TMR environment. In this case, two-way communications should be established between the TMRs to permit the flow of events to the TMR that maintains the event server database (Sybase). Operators located at various strategic points in the network may be privy to viewing and managing all or some of the events occurring in the computing environment.

In the case where each TMR supports its own TME 10 Enterprise Console application, one TME 10 Enterprise Console may act as a backup for the other in times of network communications or TMR server failures. The event adapters can automatically reroute their events to an available secondary event server as defined in the adapter configuration file.

7.1.4 Supported Platforms

TME 10 Enterprise Console currently supports the operating system release levels and event adapters listed in Table 8.

Table 8. Supported Operating Systems and Adapters

Operating System	Event Server & Event Console	HP OpenView Adapter	SunNet Manager Adapter	SNMP Adapter	Logfile Adapter	NetView 6000 Adapter
SunOS 4.12/4.13	✓	✓	✓	✓	✓	
Solaris 2.3/2.4	✓		✓	✓	✓	✓
AIX 3.2.5	✓			✓	✓	✓

Operating System	Event Server & Event Console	HP OpenView Adapter	SunNet Manager Adapter	SNMP Adapter	Logfile Adapter	NetView 6000 Adapter
AIX 4.1	✓				✓	✓
HP/UX 9.x	✓	✓		✓	✓	
HP/UX 10.0	✓				✓	
AT&T SVR4					✓	
Windows NT					✓	

Refer to Section 7.8.2, "Futures" on page 198 to review which operating systems will be supported in TME 10 Enterprise Console 3.1.

Refer to the *TME 10 Enterprise Console Release Notes* for more details regarding the operating system prerequisites and hardware requirements for TME 10 Enterprise Console and to Section 2.2, "TME 10 Machine Roles" on page 18, for more information regarding the TME 10 client.

7.2 Events and Event Adapters

Computing resources generate messages/alerts/traps and alarms in a variety of formats. Each event adapter application installed on or near the monitored computing resource is familiar with the structure of that raw data and will convert the data into the TME 10 Enterprise Console acceptable format called an *event*. Table 10 on page 172 supplies a list of supported event adapter types.

Event adapters transform the information they receive by parsing and restructuring the information before sending it on to the event server in the form of an event. The event server will discard an event if it does not arrive in an acceptable TME 10 Enterprise Console format.

The event adapter application is known as the *source* of the event. As Figure 76 shows, the adapter can be integrated with the computing resource, or it can be an add-on process.

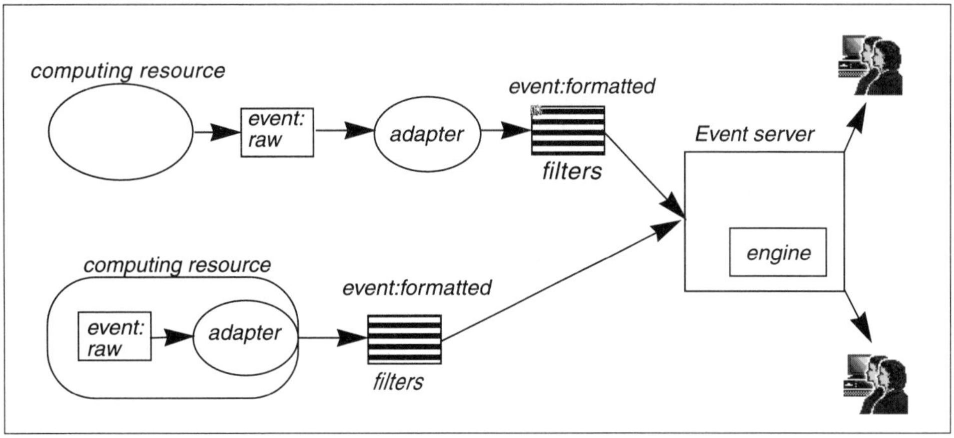

Figure 76. Formatting Messages Into Events

If a computing resource is not communicative—that is, it does not generate status messages—then in order to manage this resource, the TME 10 Enterprise Console management system will have to rely on some external processes to query and report on its health. This external process is usually a shell script or program written by the technical support group.

The event adapter application may also act proactively by interrogating the computing resource. If, for example, there was a need to check a file on the computing resource at configurable intervals, the adapter could be set up to do this. It can also run commands or applications and interpret the results prior to sending an event to the event server.

If a computing resource is overly expressive in terms of sending out copious amounts of messages, it will then be necessary to filter the extraneous information so as to forward only significant events to the event server. This will help reduce the demand on the network and the amount of processing done at the event server. *Filters* may be set at the adapter level. The filters reduce the number of messages becoming events by demanding that each message meet some predefined criteria before it is transformed into an event and sent to the event server. If the message does not pass the filter, it will be discarded.

It is invaluable for a corporation to document the situations in which the various events can be generated. Consider documenting the events that are either the cause of or effect of an original event. When events are correlated like this, that is, when the cause and effect relationships are established, it may help minimize the handling of the related (or effect) events. Establishing these relationships can be achieved by writing *rules* for the event server *rules engine*. Refer to Section 7.4, "The Rules Engine" on page 178, for more information regarding rules and the rules engine.

The event adapter also has an event buffer that will buffer the events in the case where the connection to the event server is lost. Section 7.2.4, "Communication with the Event Server" on page 173, provides details on connections between the event adapter and the event server.

7.2.1 Event Architecture

A *configuration file* is made available to the event adapter. It provides statements that will map the contents of the incoming message into the standard TME 10 Enterprise Console event format. The statements in the adapter's configuration file define all categories of problems known to that specific event adapter. The categories of known problems are called classes.

As an example, if the source of the message was NetView/6000 and it was an application type of problem, it could be categorized with a class name like `NV6K_Application_Down_Event`.

The adapter parses the incoming message and retrieves pieces of data from the original message. This data is required to build the *slot values* for the event (a slot is an attribute with a name and a value). In generic terms, an event may look somewhat like this:

```
Class=ClassName;slotname=slotvalue;slotname=slotvalue;slotname=... etc.
```

The only information that is absolutely necessary prior to sending an event is `Class=ClassName`. In general, an event is not longer than 512 bytes. Table 9 on page 171 lists several valid slot names along with a brief description of what the slot represents. In order to handle the events, the event server must also know the class names as well as slots and slot values for each event. For this purpose, the event server uses class definition files, also called BAROC files. BAROC is a language, Basic Recorder of Objects in C, that is used for event classes and instance descriptions. See Section 7.5, "Class Definitions" on page 183, for more details on BAROC files.

Once the event is sent to the event server, it is validated by the *reception engine* component and given a unique ID, time stamp, and server_handle slot value equal to 1. The ID, time stamp, and server_handle are used in conjunction to uniquely identify the event. The event server processes the event by interrogating the class name and slot names and by making decisions based on their assigned values. The event server may add additional information as it processes the event. Other event server components may also update slot values.

Table 9. Slot Names and Their Descriptions

Slot Name	Description
class	Event class is checked against event server's list of valid classes
server_handle	A number used to internally by the event server
date_reception	Date and time the event was *received* by the event server
event_handle	A number used to reference the event (assigned by event server)
source	Source of the event as defined by the adapter type (for example, NV6K, HPOV, and so on)
sub_source	Further categorization of the source
origin	IP address of the resource that generated the event; the event adapter assigns this value
sub_origin	Further categorization of the origin
hostname	Name of the system on which event occurred
adapter_host	Host on which the adapter is running
date	Date and time the event was *generated*
status	Status of the event (OPEN, ACK, or CLOSED)
administrator	Administrator who acknowledged event and assumed responsibility
acl	List of authorization roles that enables an administrator to modify an event
credibility	'Believability' of the source of the event (assigned by event server)
severity	Severity of the event (FATAL, CRITICAL, MINOR, WARNING, HARMLESS, UNKNOWN)
duration	To be used in version 3.1 of TME 10 Enterprise Console as the time the event is left open
msg	Default message displayed on event consoles
msg_handle	Message ID used to obtain the internationalized message
msg_catalog	Message catalog used for internationalization

Slot Name	Description
msg_index	Offset within the event message catalog
duration	A number used internally by the event server
num_actions	Number of actions currently being tracked by response engine
repeat_count	Counter for keeping track of the number of times a duplicate type of event has been received
cause_date_reception	date_reception slot value as identified in the cause event
cause_event_handle	Unique identifier for the new event

7.2.2 Sample Event Adapters

Table 10 lists the sample event adapters provided by TME 10 Enterprise Console along with the designated source names. The source names will be used by the event server as criteria to filter the events that will be forwarded to specific operators.

Table 10. Sample Event Adapters with Source Names and Reference Manuals

Sample Event Adapters	Source Names	Reference Manuals
SunNet Manager	SNM	TME 10 Enterprise Console Event Adapter Guide - SunNet Manager
SNMP traps	SNMP	TME 10 Enterprise Console Event Adapter Guide - SNMP
IBM NetView/6000	NV6K	TME 10 Enterprise Console Event Adapter Guide - NetView
HP OpenView	HPOV	TME 10 Enterprise Console Event Adapter Guide - HP OpenView
Microsoft NT	NT	TME 10 Enterprise Console Event Adapter Guide - Windows NT
Logfile	LOGFILE	TME 10 Enterprise Console Event Adapter Guide - Logfile
TME 10 Distributed Monitoring*	SENTRY	Information found within the TME 10 Enterprise Console application
* TME 10 Distributed Monitoring automatically creates the event in the desired TME 10 Enterprise Console format. No event adapter is required.		

7.2.3 Tools and Utilities

The TME 10 EIF (Event Integration Facility) toolkit provides the necessary tools to create a new and customized adapter application.

There are also two utilities available for configuring and modifying existing adapters. The Adapter Configuration Utility provides a graphical user interface (GUI) that allows for customizing and configuring event adapters more easily. Rather than editing the actual adapter configuration file on each computing resource that maintains an adapter, it becomes possible to create an adapter configuration file at the TME 10 Enterprise Console event server location which can then be distributed to a designated destination.

A utility also exists for the Logfile adapter called the TME 10 Enterprise Console Logfile Configuration Facility (LCF), or Logfile Format Editor (LFE) in future versions. This facility provides a GUI to facilitate adding new definitions of event messages that will then will be mapped to TME 10 Enterprise Console events.

7.2.4 Communication with the Event Server

There are four different ways in which the event adapter can connect to the event server. Choosing a connection mode will depend upon the quantity of events that will be sent and whether or not the connections will be made between two TME 10 managed nodes.

Table 11. Connection Modes Between Event Adapter and Event Server

Many events?	Is adapter on a managed node?	Connection type required
YES	YES	Secure connection based
YES	NO	Unsecure connection based - TCP/IP IPC
NO	YES	Secure connectionless
NO	NO	Unsecure connectionless - TCP/IP IPC

The following list explains the four different connection types and how they are used by TME 10 Enterprise Console:

- A *secure connection-based* type of connection uses the services provided by the TME 10 management framework to establish a connection between the event adapter and the event server. This is possible because the event adapter runs on a managed node and therefore has the TME 10 client code installed. Once the communication between the event adapter and the event server is established, the connection remains available indefinitely for further event forwarding.

- A *secure connectionless* type of connection also uses the services provided by the TME 10 management framework to establish a connection between the event adapter and the event server. Once the event is forwarded to the event server, communication between the event adapter and event server is disconnected. Communications are reestablished the next time the event adapter wishes to forward another event to the event server.
- An *unsecure connection-based* type of connection uses standard interprocess communications mechanisms to establish a connection between the event adapter and the event server. As the event adapter is not running on a managed node, the TME 10 management framework cannot be the one to establish communications. Once the communication between the event adapter and the event server is established using the standard interprocess communication mechanisms, the connection remains available indefinitely for further event forwarding.
- In an *unsecure connectionless* type of connection, the standard interprocess communication mechanisms are used to establish a connection between the event adapter and the event server. However, once the event is forwarded to the event server, communication between the event adapter and event server is disconnected. Communications are reestablished the next time the event adapter wishes to forward another event to the event server.

The event adapters maintain a specific file, called the *tecad_xxxx.conf* file (for Windows NT it is the *tecad_nt.con* file), that defines the behavior of the event adapter as it relates to default values, defining primary and secondary event servers and connection types. The *xxxx* represents the source name of the adapter.

In the case where the event adapter is unable to connect to the event server, or in the case where the connection has been unexpectedly severed, the events are buffered by the event adapter. The adapter's *tecad_*xxxx*.conf* file (for Windows NT it is the *tecad_nt.con* file) can be configured to discard specific events rather than buffering them. For this purpose, the administrator can define event buffer filter entries (*FilterCache* entries) in the configuration file. Events meeting the filter criteria are discarded. The *xxxx* represents the source name of the adapter. Once the connection is reestablished, any buffered events are sent to the event server for handling.

The time stamp given to the buffered event is the time it was sent to the event server and not the actual time the event first occurred. Personnel responsible for writing the logic to handle the events in the event server should provide for these discrepancies.

If the connection between event adapter and event server (called the *primary server*) is severed, the adapter will wait some 120 seconds (this is the default value) before it attempts to reestablish communications. It will try only once to connect to the primary event server. If that attempt fails, the adapter will try to connect with another or a *secondary* server. If necessary, it will run through a predefined list of secondary servers attempting a connection with each server until a connection is successfully established.

Once the connection is established with a secondary event server, the event adapter will wait until it has collected some 64 events (this is the default value) before it once again attempts a connection with the primary server.

7.3 Event Server and Event Flow

The event server is comprised of several components, each having its own set of functions to perform. For example, when an event arrives, it is validated by the *reception engine* and given a unique identifier. If the *reception engine* is busy, the *reception buffer* maintains the event until the reception engine is once again available. The *reception log* will record the event so that in case of a system or event server crash, no events will be lost. (The reception log is a Sybase relational database.)

The event, now to be called the *event under analysis*, is then passed to the *rules engine* for processing. The event is processed according to the logic defined in the *rule base.* The rules engine may, as a result of its analysis of the event, request the *dispatch* component to assist in triggering several *tasks* or actions. These are handled by the *task* component. In addition, the rules engine may solicit, via the dispatch component, some reaction by the operators. As the event server continues processing the event, it may create additional slots (attributes) and slot values and may also update previously defined slot values. The event is ultimately recorded in the *event repository,* which is a Sybase database. Details on how a set of rules are applied to the event under analysis is discussed in Section 7.4.4, "Rule Processing Flow" on page 180.

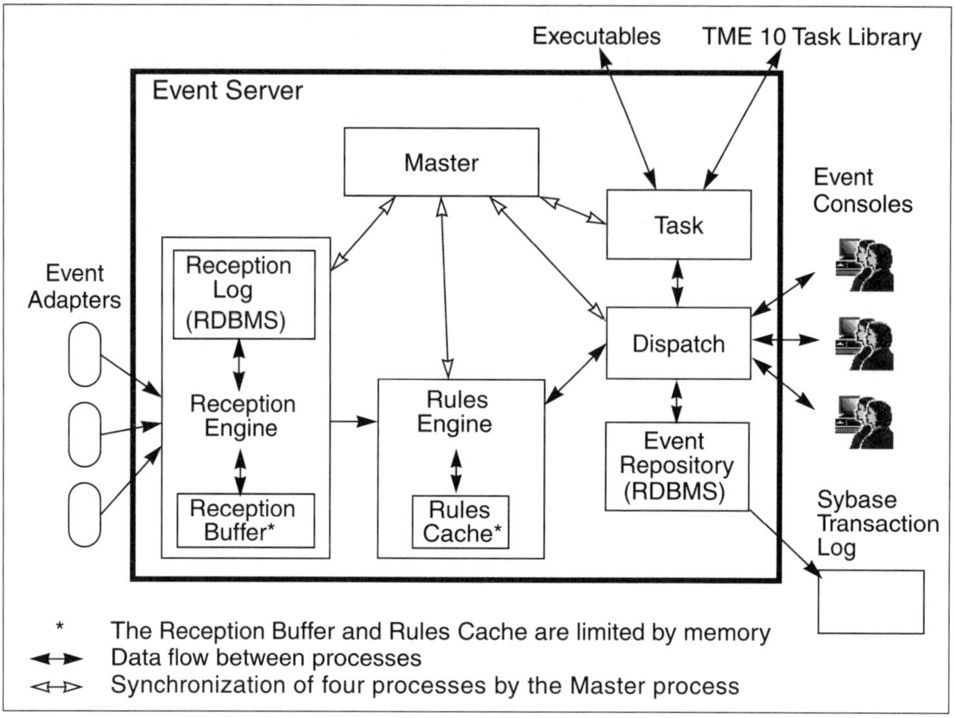

Figure 77. Components of the Event Server

The rules engine may need access to some events that have been already processed by the rules engine. The *rules cache* holds some previously processed events that are easily accessible by the rules engine. The rules cache is useful if it becomes necessary to:

- Correlate the event under analysis with some event(s) in the rules cache
- Update some slot value(s) of an event in the rules cache
- Reanalyze an event in the rules cache by reapplying all the rules

Parameters are set to define how many events will be maintained in the event cache as well as how old the events may be before they are overwritten with newly arrived events. The event may be discarded based on its age, status, or arrival date. The size of the rules cache (that is, the number of events it may maintain) is determined at installation time. Table 12 briefly describes the role of each event server component.

Table 12. Components and Functions of the Event Server

Component	Function	Process name
Master	Synchronizes the four event server processes	tec_server
Reception Engine	Receives and stores events until they can be processed by the rules engine	tec_reception
Reception Buffer	Stores events if the reception engine is busy	
Reception Log (RDBMS)	Stores all events in the reception log	
Rules Engine	Analyzes and processes events	tec_rule
Rules Cache	Stores current events in memory-resident cache	
Task Engine	Performs tasks as requested by the dispatch engine	tec_task
Dispatch Engine	Updates event consoles and receives event status changes from event consoles, rules engine, and task engine; also requests tasks be executed by task engine	tec_dispatch
Event Repository (RDBMS)	Stores all processed events	

The Sybase transaction log is configured when the RDBMS is installed and records all Sybase transactions. It may expand up to the defined maximum size, at which point writing the events to the Sybase database is prohibited. It is therefore recommended that the customer either disable the Sybase transaction log or perform regular maintenance on it so as to avoid potential problems when the log is full. Refer to Section 7.8.2, "Futures" on page 198, to see the changes to the database support for TME 10 Enterprise Console 3.1.

A TME 10 Enterprise Console task library is made available to the task component. It maintains a collection of predefined tasks that may be invoked by the operator from the operator's event console, manually or automatically.

7.4 The Rules Engine

The TME 10 Enterprise Console rules engine is a rules-based event processor. It is driven by the arrival of a new event, by an historical or already processed event held within the rules cache, or by the expiration of a timer associated with an event. The events are evaluated against a set of *rules*. Rules are used to assess the received event and determine the appropriate actions to perform. The rules engine and other components of the event server control the execution of any applicable rules. Rules are grouped together in *rule sets*.

7.4.1 Rules

Rules are executed one at a time, based on their order of definition. A rule consists of:

- The name of the rule, unique per rule set
- A description of the rule
- A set of expressions used to determine if the event meets the rule conditions (The rule can examine any slot name and slot value pair to determine if the event meets the rule conditions)
- A set of actions to take when the event meets the rule conditions

The event will be recorded in the Sybase database once all applicable rules have been executed. If the event is purposely discarded, then there will be no recording of it in the database.

Rules are sometimes referred to as business rules because they may implement the policies and procedures that are decided upon by the management organization in order to meet business goals. For example, if an event that represents an outstanding problem has not been acted upon by any operator within a specific time limit, then it is possible that established response time or service time agreements may not be met by the support team. A rule may be implemented to invoke escalation procedures to ensure a timely response.

Rules can recognize various combinations of events in a preset time window. In the situation where one event causes another event to be generated, a rule may be written to correlate these events by searching for these events in the event cache.

Rules are written in an external syntax (Prolog programming language), and when compiled, they are translated into internal syntax to be used by the rules engine. The *TME 10 Enterprise Console Rule Builder* provides a number of features and capabilities to make the process of writing rules in external syntax easier. Refer to Section 7.6, "Creating Rules" on page 187, for details of the Rule Builder.

7.4.2 Rule Sets

The following list provides some key points about a rule set. It is:

- Made up of one or more rules
- Independent of all other rule sets
- Found as a single file in the TEC_RULES directory
- Active or inactive; if designated as being active, it will be processed by the event server when its associated rule base is loaded into the event server

An individual rule set may be dedicated to taking charge of a particular type of problem, therefore allowing for multiple rule sets to be created. This division into multiple rule sets helps to organize the *rule base* and also allows for the assignment of writing rule sets to different support people.

7.4.3 Rule Base

The following list provides some key points about a rule base. It is:

- Made up of one or more rule sets. The file *rule_sets*, located in the TEC_RULES directory, defines the order in which the rule sets will be evaluated by the rules engine.
- Made up of one or more *class definitions*. The order of the class definitions is maintained in the *.load_classes* file and is located in the TEC_CLASSES directory.

  The files with the extension .baroc represent class definitions for the individual event adapters that have been installed. Class definitions are further explained in Section 7.5, "Class Definitions" on page 183.
- Loaded when the event server is started or loaded immediately after a specific TME 10 Enterprise Console command is issued.

Several rule bases may be maintained; however, only one rule base is loaded and active on an event server. One rule base can be valid for normal business hours, another for evenings, weekends, and holidays. The administrator can switch between them using the `wloadrb` TME 10 Enterprise Console command. The event server should be stopped gracefully prior to issuing the command to load the new rule base, and then restarted. Stopping the event server in this manner ensures that processing of the event under analysis and any other outstanding tasks complete properly. The commands for stopping and starting the event server are `wstopesvr` and `wstartesvr`.

Figure 78 shows the directory structure of a single rule base. When you build and load a rule base, you specify its directory name.

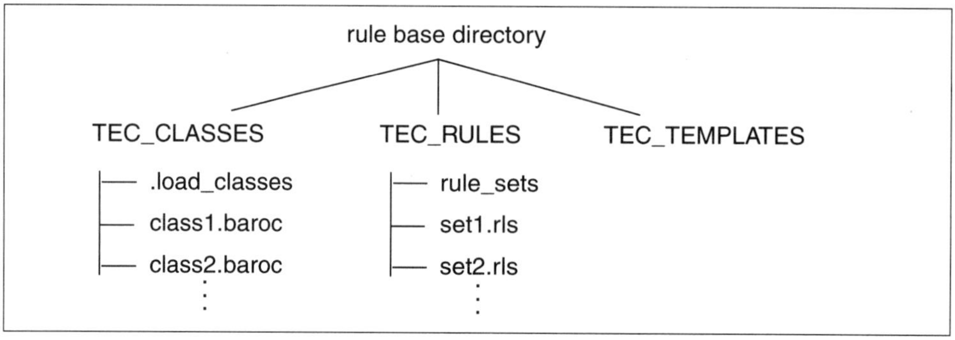

Figure 78. Locating Rule Classes and Rule Sets

TME 10 Enterprise Console provides default rule bases that are installed at the same location as the event server during the installation of the event adapters.

It will be necessary to recompile and load a rule base if rules have been created or modified. In most cases, adding a new adapter type implies adding new rules. In the case where class definitions have been modified, it will be necessary to import the new class definitions using the `wimprclass` CLI command followed by a stop and a restart of the event server.

The TEC_TEMPLATES directory may maintain Tivoli-supplied templates that are predefined operations or actions that are performed on a regular basis. It is suggested that customers explore the existing templates before considering writing home-grown routines.

7.4.4 Rule Processing Flow

Figure 79 represents a simple processing flow in the rules engine for the event under analysis.

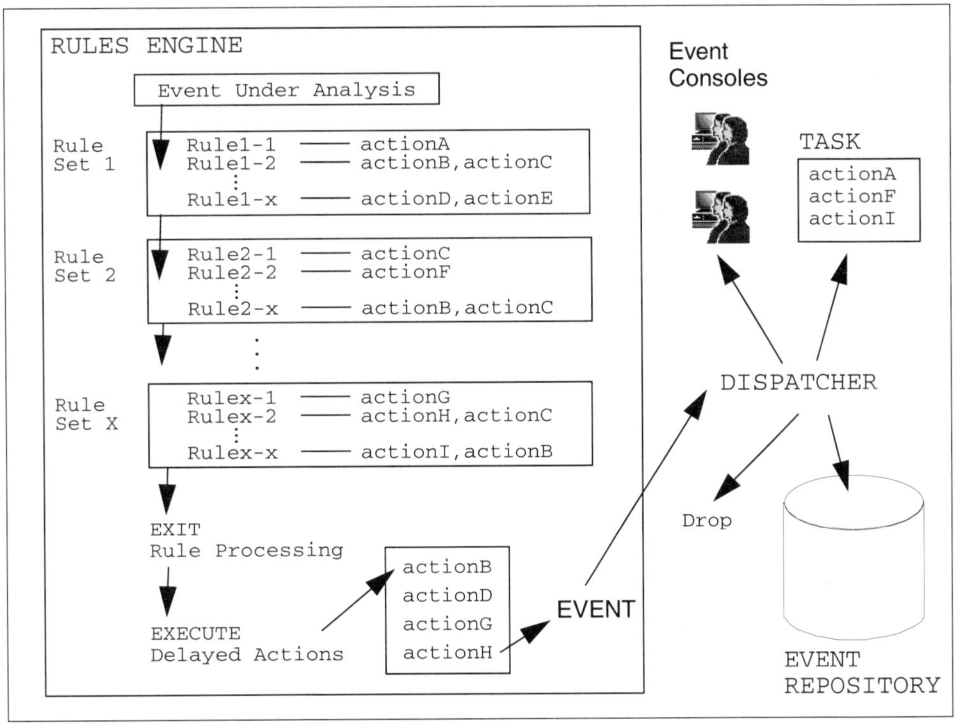

Figure 79. Event Processing and Assembling Actions

The event under analysis is evaluated sequentially by *each* rule in *every* rule set in the active rule base. The evaluation is performed sequentially starting with the first rule in the first rule set followed by the second rule in the first rule set and so on progressing from one rule set to another until the last rule in the last rule set is evaluated. Should the event under analysis meet the criteria specified in a rule, an action or a set of actions is triggered. In some cases, the actions are performed immediately. However, in most cases the execution is delayed so that the event is processed by all rules while still having its original attributes.

Once an event has completed rule processing, the rules engine performs the delayed actions (B, D, G, H in Figure 79), which may be for example:

- Setting a new severity level or status for the event
- Generating another event
- Changing already received events that are related to this event
- Forwarding the event to another event server

Control is then passed to the dispatcher who stores the event in the repository (or drops it if requested) and sends it to the event consoles. The dispatcher also calls the task engine of TME 10 Enterprise Console to asynchronously execute the *external* actions (A, F, I in Figure 79) specified in the rules, which are TME 10 tasks or any program that is executable in the operating system. The task engine tracks the outcome of these actions and feeds it back into the event that is now in the event cache and in the event repository.

If the current event generates other events or creates *change* or *redo* requests, then all these are processed as subtransactions within the same transaction. Only after the encompassing transaction is executed does the rules engine take on the next event from the reception engine.

Once an action or set of actions have been assigned or executed for the event, it may be pointless to continue evaluating other rules. Actions (such as C and E in Figure 79) can be defined to skip processing further actions, rules, or rule sets and continue with executing the delayed actions and forwarding the event to the dispatcher.

It is worthwhile to note that related events (cause and effect relationship) can be found and processed when more complex event analysis techniques and rules definitions are implemented. For instance, when a *Host_Up* event is received, you could identify all *NFS_No_Reponse* events caused by that host and discard them using more complex rules.

7.4.5 Rule Base Commands

The following table presents some TME 10 Enterprise Console CLI (Command Line Interface) commands that can be executed against rule sets, class definition files, and rule bases. Complete details may be found in the *TME 10 Enterprise Console User's Guide, Volume II* for Release 2.6. Several of these commands may be executed at the operator's event console.

Table 13. CLI Commands for Rule Bases

CLI commands	Activity
wlsrb	Lists the known rule bases configured at the TME 10 Enterprise Console server
wlscurrb	Lists the currently loaded rule base name
wlsrbrules	Lists the rule sets in a specified rule base
wlsrbclass	Lists the rule base classes
wcrtrb	Creates a rule base at the event server
wcprb	Copies a rule base
wimprbclass	Imports a file of event class specifications into a rule base
wimprbrules	Imports a rule set into the rule base
wcomprules	Compiles the rules in a rule base
wloadrb	Loads a rule base into the event server
wdelrbrules	Deletes a rule set from a rule base
wdelrbclass	Deletes a class file from the rule base
wdelrb	Deletes a rule base from the event server
wsetrb	Changes the properties of the rule base (name and directory path)
wchkclass	Checks an event class definition file for validity
chkclass	Checks an event class definition file for validity in a non-TME 10 environment

7.5 Class Definitions

A class definition file is a file that is maintained on the event server. There is one class definition file for each adapter type known to TME 10 Enterprise Console. The class definition file is written in the BAROC format. BAROC stands for BAsic Repository of Objects in C. This language implements the classical concepts of data structuring from the object-oriented paradigm, such as objects, data members (called slots), inheritance, instantiation, and specialization. The class definition file is subdivided into class definitions. A class definition presents the architectural layout of an event. It identifies the class name and slot name/slot value pairs.

The class name identifies a specific problem that the adapter may recognize. Each adapter reference manual supplies a complete listing of the supported class names.

When an event arrives at the event server, it must arrive with a class name as part of its definition. The class name given to the event at the adapter level will be matched with the same class name as defined in a class definition found within the class definition file. The event will be discarded if there is no match for the class name anywhere in the event classification file.

Upon its arrival, caused by definitions made in the class definition files, the event may be given new slot names and slot values. The addition of slot names and slot values extends the contents of the event. Similarly, existing slot values may be given a new value. Recall that the rules in the rules engine assess the slot names and their slot values in order to decide if the event matches the given criteria. Extending the contents of an event permits more explicit rules to be written.

The following describes a class definition in the class definition file with a class name of TEC_CLASS. This specific class definition represents the base event from which all other events are derived:

```
TEC_CLASS :
        EVENT
        DEFINES {
                server_handle:  INTEGER,
                                        parse = no;
                date_reception: INT32,
                                        parse = no;
                event_handle:   INTEGER,
                                        parse = no;
                source:         STRING;
                sub_source:     STRING;
                origin:         STRING;
                sub_origin:     STRING;
                hostname:       STRING;
                adapter_host:   STRING;
                date:           STRING;
                status:         STATUS,
                                        default=OPEN;
                administrator:  STRING,
                                        parse = no;
                acl:            LIST_OF STRING,
                                        default = [admin],
                                        parse = no;
                credibility:    INTEGER,
                                        default = 1 ,
                                        parse = no;
                severity:       SEVERITY,
                                        default = WARNING;
                msg:            STRING;
                msg_catalog:    STRING;
                msg_index:      INTEGER;
                duration        INTEGER,
                                        parse = no;
```

```
            num_actions:     INTEGER,
                                    parse = no;
            repeat_count:    INTEGER;
            cause_date_reception: INT32,
                                    parse = no;
            cause_event_handle: INTEGER,
                                    parse = no;
            };
END
```

Some slot names were given absolute values in the class definition file that would override the slot values of the incoming event given by the event adapter. For example, the following excerpt from the event class definition sets the default status to OPEN:

```
.
     status:  STATUS;
                 default=OPEN;
.
```

New slot values may be assigned when the event enters the event server (by specifying an absolute value in the class definition file), when the rule actions are processed against a particular event, and/or when the operator takes some action against the event.

Figure 80 on page 186 shows an event that has already been written to the event repository. It is comprised of slot names and slot values supplied by the event adapter as well as new slot names and slot values provided by the class definition file. The event represents a failed login attempt, and it appears on the administrator's event console after more details about the event have been requested.

To display this dialog:
-> Event Console (double-click)
-> Event Group icon (click)
-> Select an event and push **View Message...** button

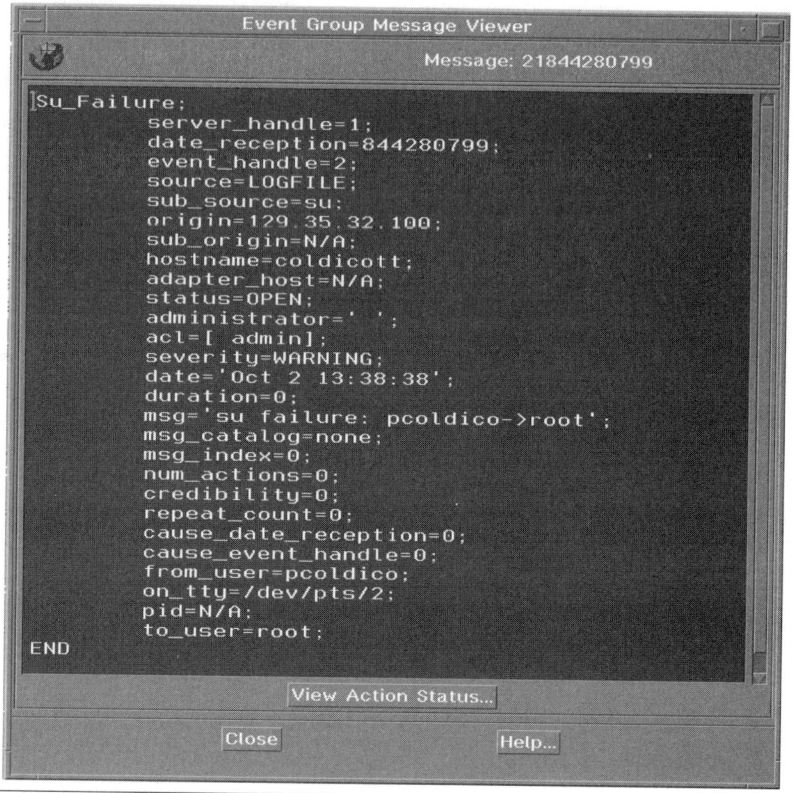

Figure 80. An Su_Failure Event

7.6 Creating Rules

TME 10 Enterprise Console includes a very powerful and comprehensive rules definition language that is based on Prolog. However, because of its power, this language can be overwhelming. The *TME 10 Enterprise Console Rule Builder* can generate rules to cover a large number of situations without any need to understand the syntax of the language or the internals of the rules engine.

7.6.1 The TME 10 Enterprise Console Rule Builder

The Rule Builder helps the user build macro-level rules from a point-and-click interface. This Rule Builder tool is accessible from the *event server* icon on the TME 10 desktop. Refer to Section 7.7, "Event Console" on page 193, for details on the event console.

Recall that rules are created in a rule set. Rule sets are associated with a rule base. Once a new rule set is created and updated with rules, it is written to the TEC_RULES subdirectory. In order to take advantage of this new or updated rule set, the rule base needs to be recompiled and then loaded. Figure 81 shows the defined rule bases.

To display this dialog:
-> Select **Rule Bases...** from pop-up menu of Event Server icon on Desktop

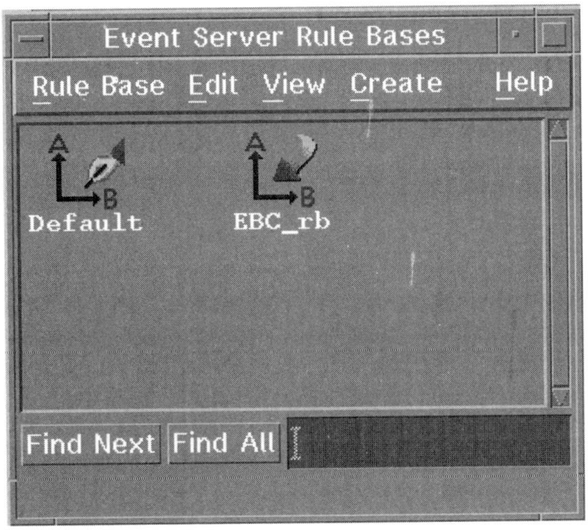

Figure 81. Accessing the Event Server Rule Base

The Rule Builder permits the user to create new rule sets as well as list and modify existing rule sets for a given rule base, as shown in Figure 82. Should a rule set be edited with a text editor, it will no longer be possible to use the Rule Builder to make further modifications to that rule set. Novice rule writers will benefit from using the Rule Builder. It is a good way to become familiar with the underlying concepts surrounding rule writing.

To display this dialog:
-> Select **Rule Bases...** from pop-up menu of Event Server icon on Desktop
-> Rule Base (double-click)

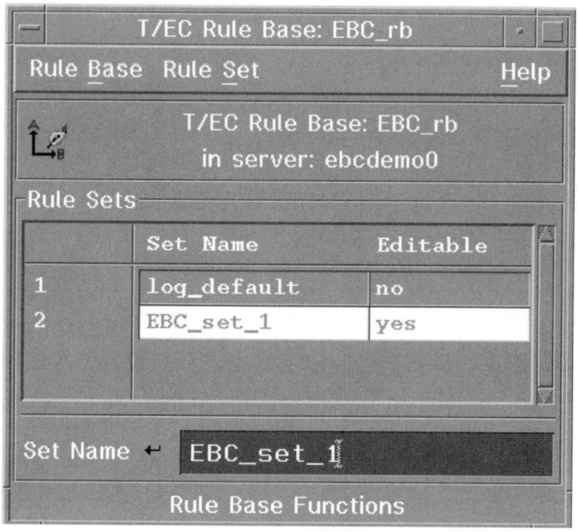

Figure 82. Listing Rule Sets within the Rule Base

7.6.1.1 Rule Types

There are two types of rules that may be created via the TME 10 Enterprise Console Rule Builder: *simple* rules and *compound* rules.

A simple rule specifies conditions that an incoming event must meet before a designated action or set of actions are applied for that event. The very first condition or *filter* that must be met is the event class name.

It may be desirable to logically associate events when one event causes another or is caused by the occurrence of another event. A compound rule is written in order to establish a relationship or a *correlation* between events that fall into one of two specified event classes. No actions can be defined for this rule type. Compound rules are used solely for correlating events.

7.6.1.2 Defining a Rule

For both simple and compound rule types, the user will specify the class name (for a simple rule) or two class names (for a compound rule), a description of the rule, and the conditions which will restrict events for which this rule is applicable. Actions are defined only for simple rules.

For each type of rule, you select the class name from a scrolling list that the Rule Builder tool provides.

Then you may build the conditions or filters from a list of available attributes and provide the attribute (slot) values that will help satisfy the condition. The attributes are based on the slot names of the incoming event. The scrolling lists made available when selecting class names and attributes come from the BAROC class definition files in the TEC_CLASSES subdirectory of the specified rule base. Figure 83 represents the *Simple Rule* dialog.

To display this dialog:
-> Select **Rule Bases...** from pop-up menu of Event Server icon on Desktop
-> Rule Base (double-click)
-> Select **Edit RuleSet...** from *Rule Set* pull-down menu
-> Select **New Rule > Simple...** from *Rule* pull-down menu

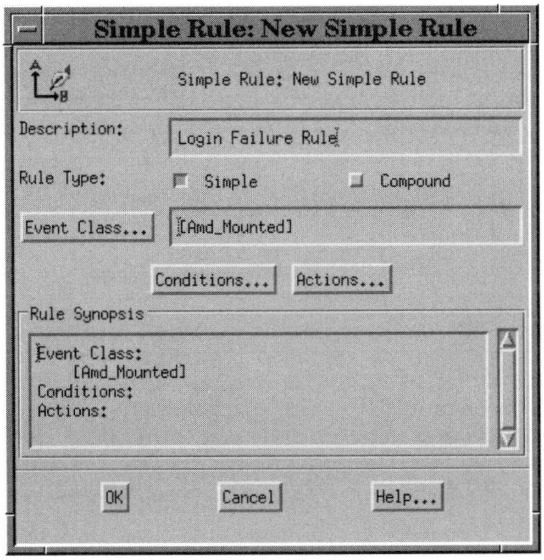

Figure 83. Creating a Simple Rule

The **Actions...** button allows you to specify the actions and when they should be executed. An *action* specifies what to do when all the rule conditions are met. For simple rules, the actions may be set as shown in Table 14 on page 190:

Table 14. Actions to be Fired

Action
Set severity
Set status
Set the message attribute
Forward the event to another event server
Drop the duplicate event
Launch a task
Launch a system command or shell script

Tasks and commands that are launched are, by default, run on the node where the event server is running. Arguments may be passed to the tasks and commands at execution time.

For simple rules, it is necessary to indicate at what point in the life cycle of the event an action or set of actions will be triggered. Table 15 presents the options:

Table 15. The Life Cycle of an Event

When to Run the Action
When event is received (into event cache of rules engine)
X minutes after event is received
When the severity of the event is upgraded
When the severity of the event is downgraded
When the event is acknowledged
When the event is closed
When the number of duplicate events received is greater than the specified limit

The Rule Builder presents the GUI dialog shown in Figure 84 on page 191 to allow the administrator to specify the actions to be triggered and when to run the actions.

To display this dialog:
-> Select **Rule Bases...** from pop-up menu of Event Server icon on Desktop
-> Rule Base (double-click)
-> Select **Edit RuleSet...** from *Rule Set* pull-down menu
-> Select **New Rule > Simple...** from *Rule* pull-down menu
-> Push **Actions...** button

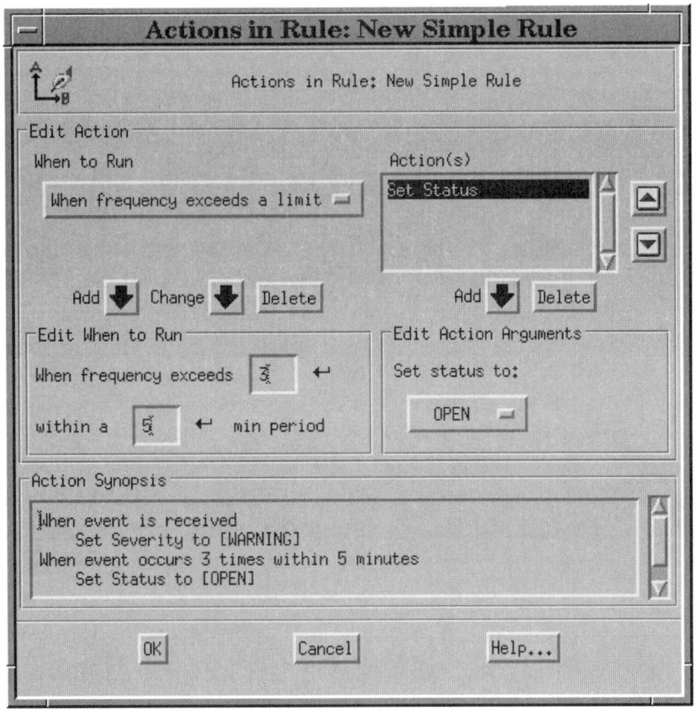

Figure 84. Specifying Actions to be Fired

When the rule definition is completed, it is incorporated into the designated rule set. The Rule Builder provides the GUI dialogs to compile and load the rule base containing the modified rule set.

7.6.2 Rule Programming

Situations may arise which the Rule Builder cannot adequately handle. Rule programming outside the Rule Builder can prove to be a challenging proposition, but it offers greater flexibility. Competency with the Prolog programming language and an understanding of BAROC definitions is required.

Some of the concepts that were applicable to the Rule Builder also apply to writing rules by hand. Before they write rules, programmers must:

- Identify the problem and the event classes
- Understand the definition of the event, including class names and the slot names and slot values that are relevant to the problem
- Identify which events are related or correlated and in which context they are related
- Identify the actions required to resolve the problem
- Identify when the actions will be triggered

In order to create or add customized rules, the rules programmer can export an existing rule base into a set of files, edit these files, and re-create the rule base. Recreating the rule base involves compiling and testing it and finally loading it in order to make it the active rule base. Instead of modifying an existing rule base, the modified files can be compiled into a new rule base, thus leaving the original base unchanged.

The advantage of writing your own rules becomes apparent with the discovery of the extensive capability of manipulating and processing events in the event cache.

Rule programming is beyond the scope of this chapter. Refer to the *Tivoli/Enterprise Console Rule Builder's Guide Version 2.6* for more details.

7.7 Event Console

The *event console* is the interface that an administrator uses to present notifications of events and to respond to events. Access to the event console is provided by yet another icon on the administrator's TME 10 desktop.

The event console can be installed on TME 10 managed nodes on UNIX or Windows NT. A Windows or Windows NT PC that has the TME 10 Desktop for Windows installed can also provide access to an event console. Refer to Chapter 2, "TME 10 Framework" on page 15, for discussions on the TMR server, TME 10 client, and TME 10 desktop.

The event console or consoles may be installed in a remote TMR (remote to where the TME 10 Enterprise Console event server/Sybase database is installed) provided that two-way communications between TMRs have been established. This configuration permits the management staff at the remote location to manage resources in the other TMR.

The Graphical User interface (GUI) of the event console is configurable and permits administrators with the *super* authorization role to customize the event console interface of other staff members according to their job function. Different staff members may have different views of the events. It is suggested that this event console be supported by a color monitor because color provides an important visual cue for indicating the severity level of events.

7.7.1 Setting Up the Event Console for Administrators

Once the event console is customized, it initially provides a high-level view of the events generated in the computing environment. The event console is divided into two windows, namely the *Enterprise Console for Source Groups* window and the *Enterprise Console for Event Groups* window.

7.7.1.1 Source Groups

The Enterprise Console for source groups has icons and supporting information (date stamp, severity level, and severity indicator) that represent the events that have arrived from computing resources.

Each icon depicts a specific event adapter. For example, if the Logfile adapter is known to the event server, then an icon representing the Logfile would be defined and therefore displayed on the administrator's event console. See also Table 10 on page 172 for a list of available source names and event adapters. In Figure 85 on page 194, there is a source group for HP OpenView, TME 10 Distributed Monitoring, NetView 6000, and Logfile events.

To display this window:
-> Event Console (double_click)

Figure 85. Source Groups on the Administrator's Event Console

When an event is displayed on an administrator's event console, the information surrounding the specific event icon gets updated. This information tells the administrator when the last event arrived, its severity level, and what is the highest severity of any event reported from that adapter. At a glance, the operator can quickly size up the health of the computing environment for each source type. Double-clicking on an icon provides a list of events for that adapter type. Selecting one of the events in the list will present the event details.

7.7.1.2 Event Groups

The Enterprise Console for event groups window also has icons and supporting information (date stamp, severity level, and severity indicator) that represent the events that have arrived from computing resources. Other than with the event sources, the events in this window are logically grouped for the administrator's convenience and assigned event group icons. For example, it may be more convenient for an administrator if the icon represented all network problems, security problems, or problems coming from a particular department.

A GUI dialog permits the administrator with the super authorization role to assign events to event groups. Event filters are used to categorize events. These filters are completely independent of the filters used by the event adapter applications we discussed earlier in this chapter. The event group filters demand that events match specific criteria (such as a specific event class, source name, origin, suborigin, and/or subsource values) before it can be associated with the event group. Events not matching any filter criteria are not made available in a particular event group.

Once the assignments are complete, and all known events have been associated with an event group, the administrator with the super role will assign individual event groups to the administrator staff. Administrators may have some event groups in common if responsibilities are shared among operators.

To display this window:
-> Event Console (double_click)

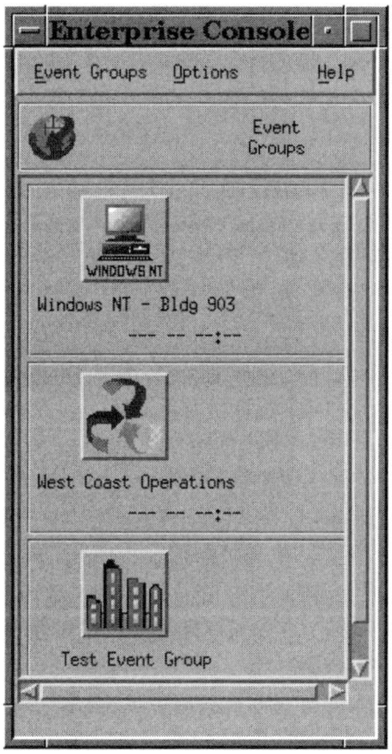

Figure 86. Event Groups on the Administrator's Event Console

Figure 86 represents three categories of problems that an administrator may encounter. The first collects events for all Windows NT problems in a given building. The second is concerned about any type of event reported from the West Coast Operations Center, and the third icon represents an icon used by the technical support team to test newly written rules.

7.7.1.3 Events and Administrative Roles

Each event group is assigned one or more *administrative roles,* just as roles are assigned to administrators. In addition, each incoming event identifies what level of administrative role the administrator must have in order to acknowledge receipt of the particular event and to take responsibility for the event. The administrator is only permitted to view the events and may not acknowledge or close the event if none of the roles assigned to the administrator's event group match the administration role assigned to the event.

After double-clicking on an icon, the administrator quickly drills down to a list of events specific to the chosen category. In the following example, the Su_Failure events that report to the event group called EBC_903_group are shown. The administrator selects an event from the event list and is provided with details concerning the chosen event.

To display this dialog:
-> Event Console (double-click)
-> Event Group icon (click)

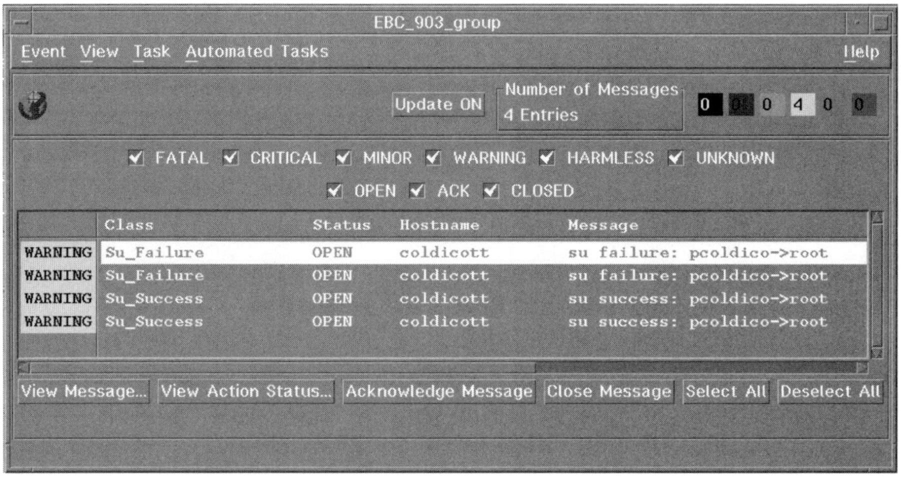

Figure 87. Event List for EBC_903 Event Group

7.7.2 Customizing the Event Console

Each operator has the option to change the types of events that will be displayed on the event console and the contents of the display by:

- Selecting the events by severity and status.
- Setting which fields should be displayed in the event message list. By default, the event message displays the Status, Class, Severity, Hostname, Message and Date fields. The operator can pick and choose the information to view.
- Sorting event messages by status, class, severity, hostname, message, date, and so on. By default, messages are sorted by status and then by severity with highest or most severe cases appearing first.

7.7.3 Commands and Tasks

While monitoring the health of the enterprise from the event console, the operator may find it necessary to execute a command or a series of commands in response to a newly arrived event. The GUI provides pull-down menus and options to control many operations. Similarly, CLI commands may be executed from the command line.

Neither the TMR server or the event console provides an audit trail of operator commands. The 'Log Requests From Event Console' setting, which the installer may have seen when TME 10 Enterprise Console was installed, is not operative in TME 10 Enterprise Console 2.6.

The range of commands that an operator can initiate against a network or system resource depends upon whether the resource has been defined as a TME 10 managed node. Refer to Chapter 2, "TME 10 Framework" on page 15, for more discussions on TME 10 managed nodes.

For repetitive administrative procedures, it is possible to package the sequence of commands and store them as Enterprise Console tasks in the Enterprise Console task library, a TME 10 task library found in the TEC25Region policy region. The tasks may be triggered manually or automatically. There are a number of existing administrative tasks available in the Enterprise Console task library. For example, the administrator who wishes to change the severity of an event, close an event, or page another administrator, may do so simply by invoking a predefined task.

Note: If the administrator chooses to automatically trigger a task or a program when a specific event is received on the event console, the administrator who wrote this task must be logged on or the task will fail. To avoid this failure, have the administrator who wishes to trigger this task create a copy of the task and have it appear as if it were created by that administrator.

One important CLI command is the `wpostemsg` command. This command sends an event to the event server. Rule programmers can test newly created or modified rules as well as the processing flow through the rules engine with this 'dummy' event. Similarly, administrators who are customizing event groups can test their event group definitions.

7.8 Further Information

This section is a collection of useful information about and associated with TME 10 Enterprise Console. It covers the following topics:

- Integration with other TME 10 products
- Future releases

7.8.1 Integration with Other TME 10 Products

The purpose of this section is to give a summary of a few products or features that are closely related to TME 10 Enterprise Console.

7.8.1.1 TME 10 Distributed Monitoring

TME 10 Distributed Monitoring can transmit Distributed Monitoring events of a specific severity level to the event server for handling. The option is set in a monitor within a Distributed Monitoring profile. The TME 10 Enterprise Console can then analyze the event in a system-wide context and may attempt to take corrective action to resolve the situation. No event adapter application needs to be installed for TME 10 Distributed Monitoring, as this product is designed to send events in the format acceptable to the TME 10 Enterprise Console. The TME 10 Enterprise Console also provides the required class definition files for TME 10 Distributed Monitoring. For more information on TME 10 Distributed Monitoring, please review Chapter 6, "TME 10 Distributed Monitoring" on page 129.

7.8.1.2 TME 10 EIF

The TME 10 EIF (Event Integration Facility) toolkit provides the necessary tools to create a new and customized adapter application.

7.8.1.3 Remedy/ARS

TME 10 Enterprise Console may be tightly integrated with Remedy/ARS (Remedy/Action Request System). Remedy/ARS is a trouble-ticketing software application that will permit operators to efficiently track and manage problems.

Trouble tickets may be automatically issued as a result of a TME 10 Enterprise Console rule being triggered or manually created by an operator at a TME 10 Enterprise Console event console. It is also possible to update the trouble ticket in Remedy/ARS and to automatically have an update performed to the corresponding TME 10 Enterprise Console events. TME 10 Enterprise Console operators are notified of newly created trouble tickets by a variety of notification mechanisms.

7.8.2 Futures

The following highlights reflect changes to the next release of TME 10 Enterprise Console, namely the TME 10 Enterprise Console 3.1. It is planned to be available in May 1997 and will have, at minimum, the new features and functions described in the following sections.

7.8.2.1 Database Support

TME 10 Enterprise Console Version 3.1 will support both Sybase 10/11 and Oracle 7 relational databases. It will be up to the customer to provide the desired RDBMS. As Sybase will be decoupled from TME 10 Enterprise Console and not provided on the installation media, the option to include Sybase at installation time will be removed, as will its installation instructions. TME 10 Enterprise Console 3.1 will access the RDBMS through the RIM (RDBMS Interface Module). Other TME 10 management applications will share the RDBMS with TME 10 Enterprise Console. The database access routines will be modified to use RIM to access the RDBMS. A set of standard queries for running reports against the data base will be made available. Please consult the TME 10 Framework release notes for current information on RIM when it becomes available.

7.8.2.2 Supported Platforms

Table 16 provides the complete list of supported platforms. Note that TME 10 Enterprise Console will now be ported to Windows NT 3.51 and 4.0.

Table 16. Supported Platforms for TME 10 Enterprise Console 3.1

Product	SunOS	Solaris	HP-UX	AIX	NT
RDBMS support	Sybase Oracle	Sybase Oracle	Sybase Oracle	Sybase Oracle	Sybase Oracle
Event Server	✓	✓	✓	✓	✓
Event Console	✓	✓	✓	✓	✓
Adapter Configuration Facility	✓	✓	✓	✓	✓
Logfile Format Editor	✓	✓	✓	✓	✓
Rule Builder	✓	✓	✓	✓	✓
Event Integration Facility	✓	✓	✓	✓	✓
SNMP Adapter	✓	✓	✓	✓	✓
Logfile Adapter	✓	✓	✓	✓	✓
SunNet Manager Adapter	✓	✓			
HP OpenView Adapter		✓	✓		
NetView 6000 Adapter				✓	
Windows NT Adapter					✓

7.8.2.3 TME 10 Enterprise Console Event Consoles

In Release 3.1 of the TME 10 Enterprise Console, it will no longer be necessary to install the complete TME 10 Enterprise Console event server code on the managed node in order to support the event console.

7.8.2.4 Support for AIX 4.2

In Release 3.1 of the TME 10 Enterprise Console, AIX 4.2 will be an officially supported platform.

7.8.2.5 New Adapters

New adapters are being developed:

- Performance Manager
- AS/400®
- TME 10 NetView for OS/390 V1R1 Alert Adapter
- TME 10 NetView for OS/390 V1R1 Message Adapter

The existing TME 10 NetView/6000 Adapter will be called the TME 10 NetView Adapter.

Part 2

Hands-on Examples

CHAPTER 8

Installing and Using the TME 10 Framework

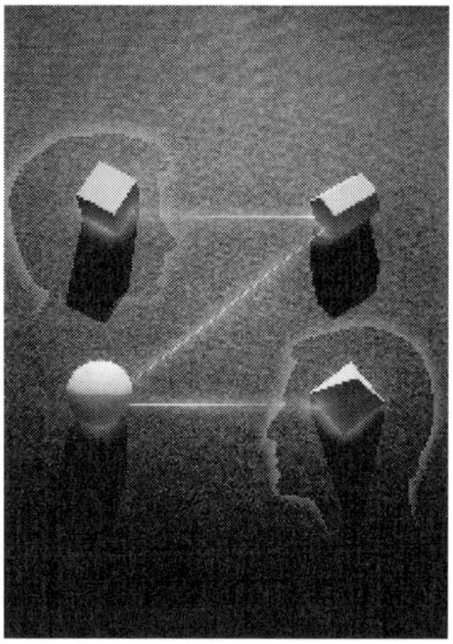

This chapter provides you with step-by-step installation instructions for the TME 10 Framework. The first section discusses the installation of a TMR server as well as managed nodes and PC agents. Once the initial TME 10 environment is set up, the following sections permit you to exercise the basic functions provided by the TME 10 Framework.

The purpose of this chapter is to familiarize you with the way these functions work, and to deepen your understanding of the concepts explained in Chapter 2, "TME 10 Framework" on page 15. It does not cover every facet and option of this product. In the last section, 8.3, "Helpful Hints" on page 242, you can find more useful information, such as how to start and stop the oserv daemon or how to back up your TME 10 environment.

TME 10 Terminology

Please note that the former name of this product was Tivoli Management Platform 3.0. When you follow these steps using the TME 10 Framework 3.1 or later, some dialogs might show slightly different titles and/or content, particularly in the installation sections. Most dialogs, however, are common to both versions of software.

8.1 TME 10 Framework Installation

When installing the TME 10 Framework in your environment, the binaries, libraries, and TME 10 database or PC agent software are installed on the machines you choose. These files take up disk space and system resources, so the initial planning is an important step in performing the TME 10 installation. After the installation plan is set, the machines can be installed using the steps in this section.

8.1.1 Installation Considerations

Before installing the TME 10 Framework software, be sure to check the TME 10 documentation for current disk space and memory requirements for your types of systems. The TME 10 Framework installs many binary and library files that require disk space and system resources, along with the TME 10 database. Please consult the latest manuals and release notes for the TME 10 Framework to determine hardware, disk space, and memory requirements for the TME 10 Framework as well as for other TME 10 applications to be installed.

On UNIX machines, the main portion of software is installed into two directories: /usr/local/Tivoli for the binaries and libraries, and /var/spool/Tivoli for the database. You may want to consider making separate filesystems for these files. You may also choose to conserve space by using the Network File System (NFS) to mount some of the directories before installing the TME 10 Framework on client machines. The libraries, binaries, manual pages, X11 resource files, and message catalogs can all be safely shared within the boundaries of a TME 10 Management Region, with the following exceptions:

- The libraries should be local to a UNIX TMR server because the server's root user must have write access to that directory.
- The subdirectory with the task libraries and oserv.exe should always be local on NT managed nodes.

The database (the files in /var on UNIX, the oserv directory on Windows NT) cannot be shared. This is true for the TMR server as well as for all other managed nodes. If using NFS for sharing, simply mount the directories before the installation process begins.

Also on UNIX machines, two setup files are created after installation that establish the correct paths and environment variables for the TME 10 Framework. You may want to add these files to your administrative users' login processes. The files are:

- /etc/Tivoli/setup_env.sh for Korn shell or Bourne shell
- /etc/Tivoli/setup_env.csh for C shell

Another consideration is that of host name to IP address conversion. Name lookups must be able to be performed from the server both ways (name to address, address to name) for all hosts that will be defined as clients in the TMR.

A license key is needed to install each TMR server. This license key is obtained directly from Tivoli.

8.1.2 Installing the TMR Server

The TMR server may either be a UNIX or Windows NT system. There are two separate CD-ROMs, one for each type of platform. Instructions for installing the TME 10 Framework on your TMR server follow.

8.1.2.1 UNIX Systems

To install the TME 10 Framework on UNIX systems, use the following steps:

1. Make sure you are a root user in a windowed environment and that your `$DISPLAY` variable is properly set.
2. Mount the CD-ROM containing the TME 10 Framework software for UNIX.
3. Create an installation directory called /usr/local/Tivoli/install_dir and then change to that directory. It may be necessary to create lower-level directories first.

   ```
   # mkdir /usr/local/Tivoli/install_dir
   # cd /usr/local/Tivoli/install_dir
   ```

4. The following command will copy some installation software onto your disk:

   ```
   # /<cdrom_path>/<mgmtplatform_path>/WPREINST.SH
   ```

   <cdrom_path> is the mount point for the CD-ROM, and <mgmtplatform_path> is the path to the TME 10 Framework software on the CD-ROM. We mounted the CD-ROM on the /cdrom directory, and the wpreinst.sh is found on the top-level directory there. So we need to run the following command:

   ```
   # /cdrom/WPREINST.SH
   to install, type ./wserver -c /cdrom
   ```

5. Begin the installation with the following command:

   ```
   # ./wserver -c /cdrom
   ```

6. This will bring up a window to start the installation (shown in Figure 88 on page 206). The top portion of the window allows you to change the directories in which the TME 10 software will be installed, if desired. There are also three options at the bottom of the window that allow you to decide whether or not the directories you have chosen will be created automatically, and to set the start-up characteristics of the oserv daemon.

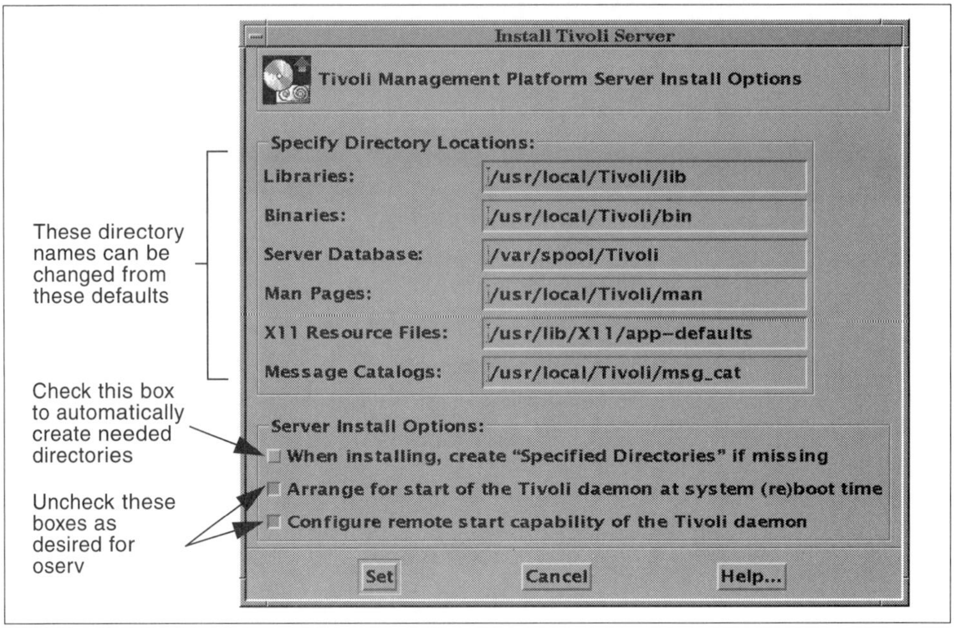

Figure 88. Setting TMR Server Installation Options

Click the **Set** button to continue.

7. In the next window that appears, shown in Figure 89, you will be asked to enter the TME 10 license key for your software. This is the only mandatory step for this window.

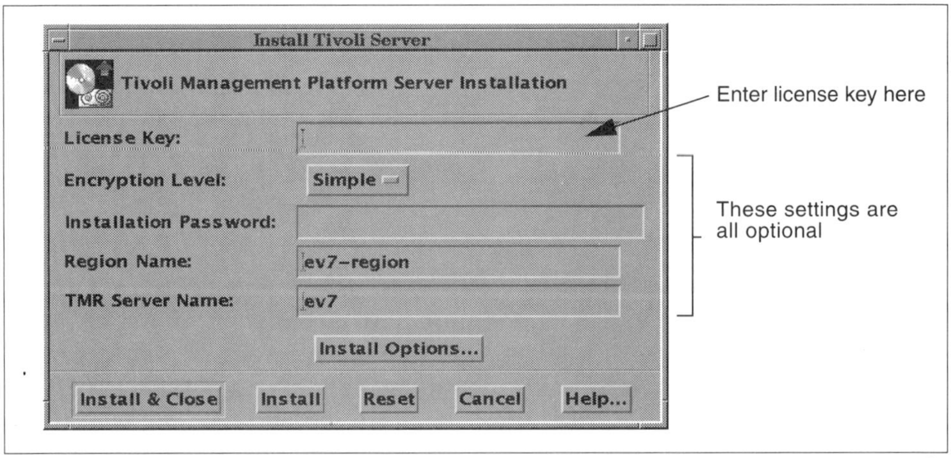

Figure 89. More Server Installation Options

You can set the encryption level for the TMR as well as an optional installation password at this point. The initial policy region's name can be changed as well as the TMR server's name to be shown on the desktop. You can also click the **Install Options...** button to bring up the window shown in Figure 88 again. Click the **Install & Close** button to continue.

A window will then show the procedures that will be performed on your system (shown in Figure 90). This window provides the last chance to cancel the operation. Click the **Continue Install** button to continue.

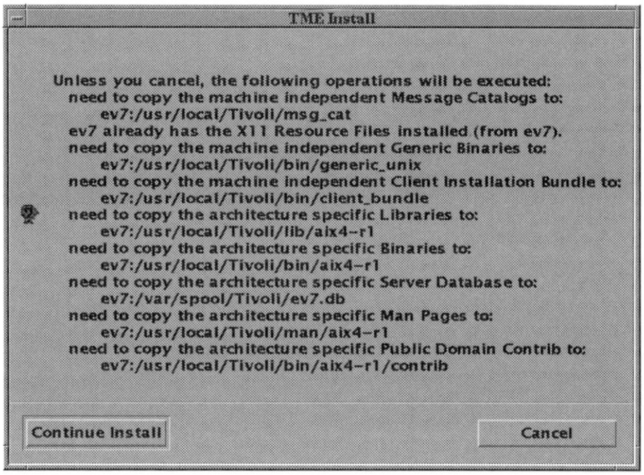

Figure 90. Server Installation Verification Dialog

8. The installation begins and a window will show the status of the installation. Wait for the "`Completed`" message to appear at the bottom of this window and for the **OK** button to appear. Click the **OK** button to make the window disappear. The TME 10 Framework has been installed on the server. The TME 10 desktop will also appear and will be ready to use (see Figure 104 on page 223).

8.1.2.2 Windows NT Systems

To install a Windows NT system as a TMR server, you must install the Desktop for Windows product as well as the TME 10 Framework software.

Installing Desktop for Windows

To install a Windows NT system with the Desktop for Windows software, use the following steps. This may be done before or after the installation of the TME 10 Framework software on this server.

1. Make sure you are logged in as Administrator.

2. Make sure the CD-ROM containing the TME 10 Framework software for Windows NT is accessible.
3. Install the Desktop for Windows product using the following command from the window generated by using the **Run...** option of the Program Manager's *File* menu (if `f:` is your CD-ROM drive):

   ```
   F:\PC\DESKTOP\DISK1\SETUP
   ```

   This will bring up a window in which you are to select your destination path for the software, and then a second window where you select the folder where the icons for this product will be stored. Then the installation will proceed. A status bar will be shown, and a message will display when the installation is complete.

Installing TME 10 Framework on Windows NT

To install the TME 10 Framework software on a Windows NT system, use the following steps:

1. Log in as Administrator.
2. Make sure the CD-ROM containing the TME 10 Framework software for Windows NT is accessible.
3. Install the TMR server using the following command from the window generated by using the **Run...** option of the Program Manager's *File* menu (if `f:` is your CD-ROM drive):

   ```
   F:\SETUP
   ```

   This brings up the first installation window shown in Figure 91.

Figure 91. Welcome Dialog for Windows NT Installation

Click the **Next** > button to continue.

If you are installing TME 10 for the first time, you are asked whether you want an account called tmersrvd and a local group Tivoli_Admin_Privileges to be created. Answer with yes.

4. You should now see the User Information dialog, which asks you to supply a user name and company name for the license agreement. This dialog is shown in Figure 92. Click the **Next** > button to continue.

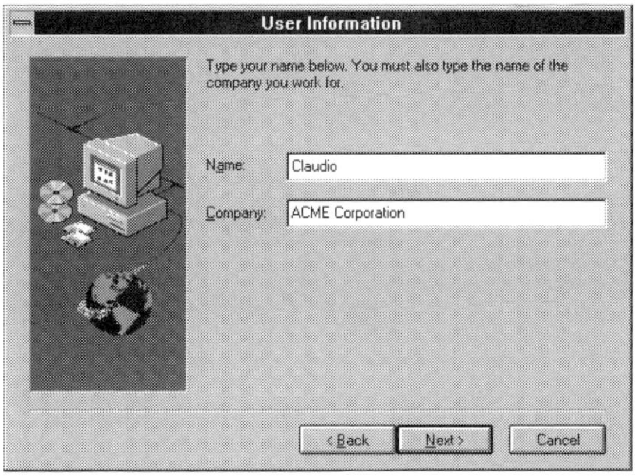

Figure 92. User Information Dialog

5. The next dialog to appear will allow you to set an installation password, if desired. This password is optional. This dialog is shown in Figure 93.

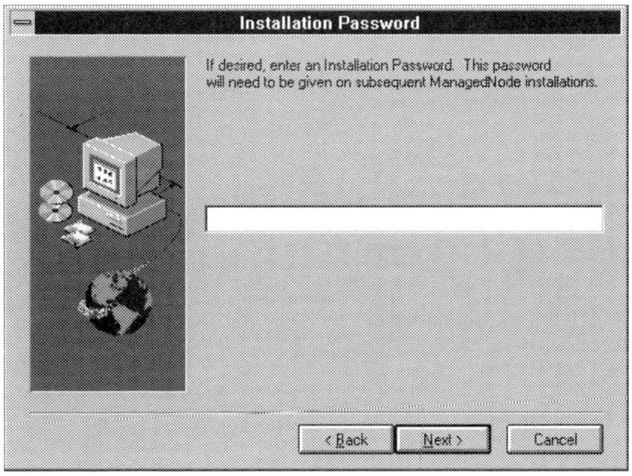

Figure 93. Installation Password Dialog

Once the information has been entered, or if you decide not to enter a password, click the **Next** > button to continue.

6. The next window to appear will allow you to configure remote user file access. You can either enter the name and password of the account through which the TME 10 functions will access remote file systems, or enter nothing if the TME 10 functions will not have access to remote file systems. This dialog is shown in Figure 94.

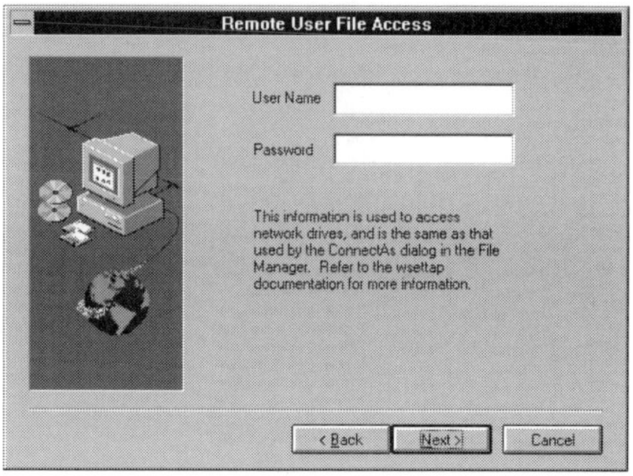

Figure 94. Remote User File Access Dialog

When the information in this window is complete, click the **Next >** button to continue.

7. The next window allows you to choose the type of installation that will be performed. You can select **Typical** for the most common options, **Compact** for the minimum required options, or **Custom** to choose your own options. This dialog is shown in Figure 95.

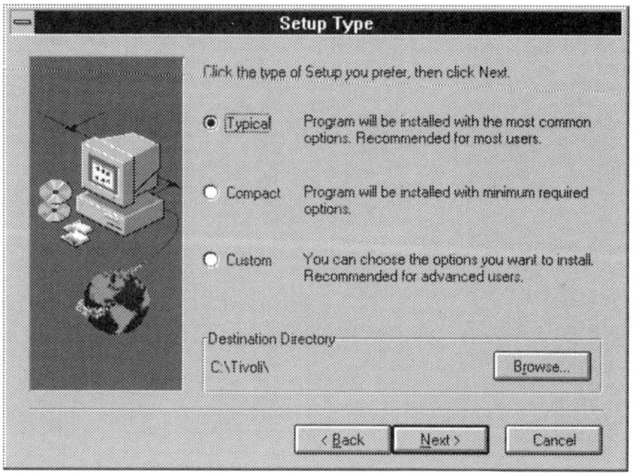

Figure 95. Setup Type Dialog

When the choice has been selected, click the **Next** > button to continue.

8. On the next window, you must enter your TME 10 license key. This is a unique character string supplied by Tivoli to allow the software to be installed. This dialog is shown in Figure 96.

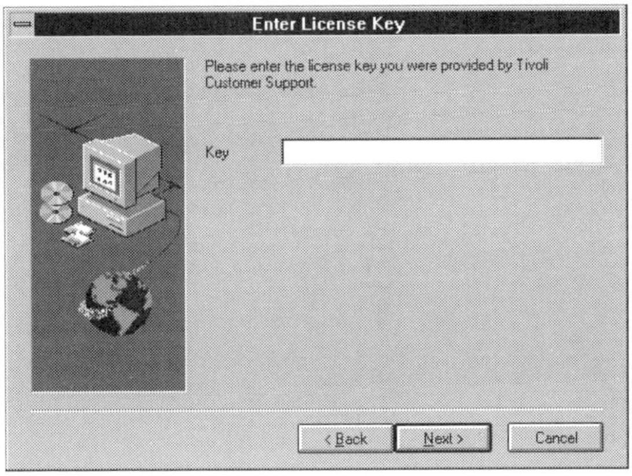

Figure 96. License Key Dialog

After the license key has been entered, click the **Next** > button to continue.

9. The next window to appear allows you to choose the directory in which the TME 10 database will be stored. You can choose to leave the default, or click the **Browse...** button to select another. This window is shown in Figure 97.

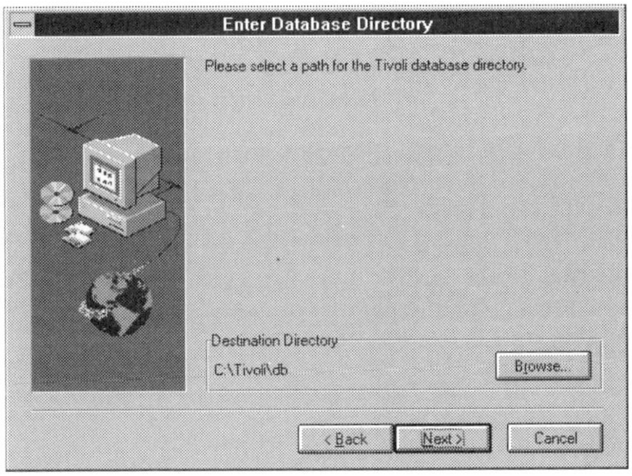

Figure 97. Database Directory Dialog

10.Now the actual installation begins, and status bars are shown on screen to show you how far the installation has gone. When close to completion, a DOS window will appear that says the server installation has completed and that you should press any key to continue. Press a key, and you will see a window telling you that the TME 10 installation is complete. You can choose to restart the computer at this point or to wait (See Figure 98).

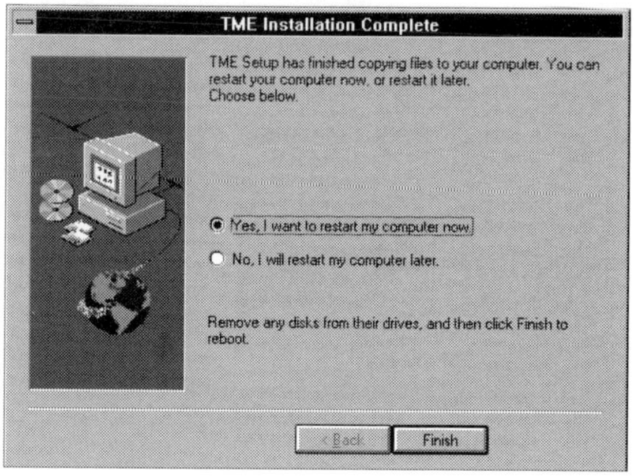

Figure 98. Installation Complete Dialog

Click the **Finish** button after the choice has been selected.

8.1.3 Installing and Configuring Clients Running the Framework

UNIX and Windows NT machines can be configured as managed nodes in the TME 10 environment, in which case they would run the TME 10 Framework software. Instructions for installing the software on these types of machines follow.

8.1.3.1 Installing UNIX Systems as TME 10 Clients

Installing the client version of the TME 10 Framework on UNIX systems is done by creating a managed node icon within the TME 10 desktop. Assume that the TMR server is on a system named ev7, and you are going to install the UNIX client on ev2. The steps for doing this follow:

1. Start the TME 10 desktop using the `tivoli` command.
2. Open the policy region on the TME 10 desktop where you would like to add the managed node icon. This is done by double-clicking on the policy region icon.

3. From the policy region window's *Create* pull-down menu, select the **ManagedNode...** option. The window shown in Figure 99 on page 213 will appear.

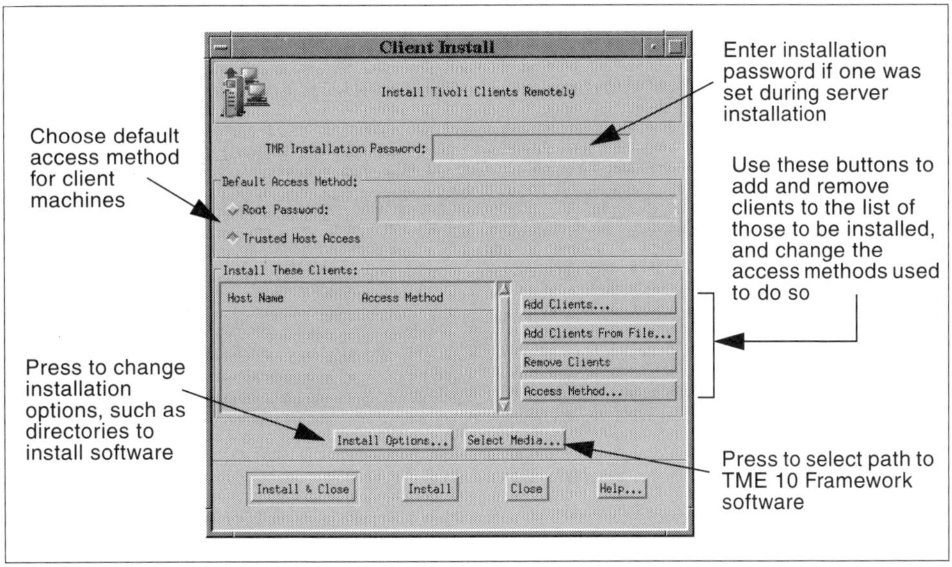

Figure 99. Client Installation Dialog

You must set the following:

- TMR Installation Password – Can be left blank if a password was not set during the TMR server installation process.
- Default Access Method – This can either be the remote machine's root password, or you can have defined previously a trusted relationship between the server and the clients using the .rhosts file, for example. If not already done, define a .rhosts file in the root user's home directory on ev2, and add root on ev7 in it. Test the trusted host access by issuing the following command on ev7:

  ```
  # rsh ev2 ls
  ```

  If you get a listing of the home directory of root on ev2, you can check the Trusted Host Access radio button.
- Clients – You must define one or more clients on which to install the TME 10 Framework, and whether they will use the default access method or something different. Click the **Add Clients...** button and enter ev2.
- Installation Options – Sets the remote directories in which to install the software, whether or not these directories will be created automatically,

and characteristics of the oserv daemon's behavior. You get the same window as shown in Figure 88 on page 206 for the TMR server.

- Select Media – Lets you define where the TME 10 Framework software can be found to use for installation. If the CD-ROM is still mounted on the TMR server, you don't have to set anything here.

When information in this window is properly entered, click the **Install** or **Install & Close** option.

4. The client install window appears, letting you know the actions that will be performed if you continue with the installation. Click the **Continue Install** button to continue.

5. The same window will remain on the screen, showing you the status of the installation. Wait for the "`Finished client install`" message to ensure completion of the client installation. You should then click the **Close** button to close the status window. The managed node icon for this machine should now appear in your policy region.

8.1.3.2 Installing Windows NT Systems as TME 10 Clients

Because the scripts used in creating managed nodes rely on the `rsh` and `rexec` commands, it is not possible to perform installations on Windows NT systems without doing some initial preparation. Windows NT systems do not allow these commands to be run on them. So, the TME 10 Remote Execution Service must be installed on the Windows NT system first, then the system can be installed from the TMR server as a managed node. The TME 10 Remote Execution Service is referred to as TRIP, and instructions for installing it follow:

1. Make sure you are logged in as Administrator and you have the CD-ROM containing the TME 10 Framework software for Windows NT is accessible.

2. From the Program Manager's *File* menu, select the **Run...** option, and enter the following command if `f:` is your CD-ROM drive:

   ```
   F:\TRIP\SETUP
   ```

3. This will bring up an installation *Welcome* window, as shown in Figure 100 on page 215.

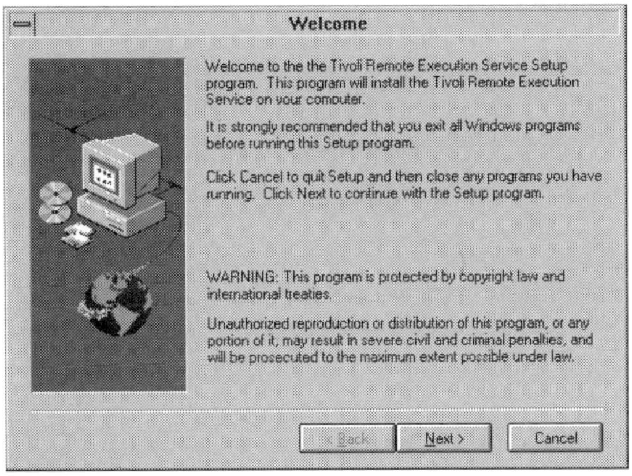

Figure 100. TRIP Welcome Dialog

Click the **Next** > button to continue the installation.

4. Another window, shown in Figure 101, will appear that allows you to choose the destination directory for the TRIP installation. You can choose the default, or click the **Browse...** button to enter your own directory.

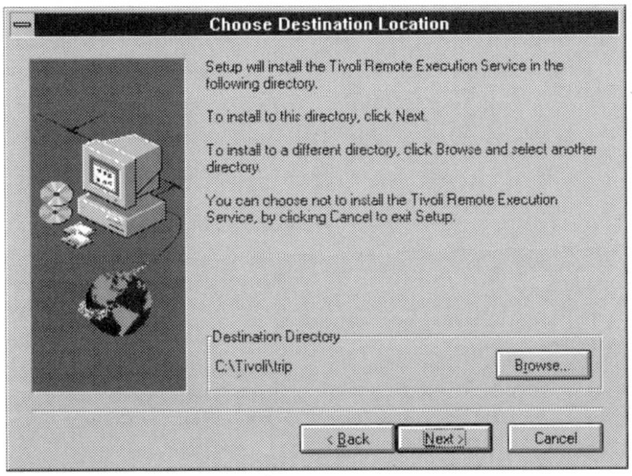

Figure 101. Destination Location Dialog

After the directory has been chosen, click the **Next** > button to continue.

5. A status window will then appear, showing the status of the TRIP installation. Near the end of the installation, a DOS window will appear instructing you to press any key to continue the installation. It will ask if you'd like to view the `README` file, and eventually you will see a window saying the installation of TRIP is complete.

6. Now that TRIP has been installed, you can go to the TMR server and create a managed node using this NT device as your target, just as you would for a UNIX system. For details on how to do this, see the previous section.

Note about TRIP Installation

An important thing to note about the installation of the TME 10 Remote Execution Service is that it needs to be installed once per TMR only. After the initial installation, as new NT managed nodes are created, the TRIP software will be installed from this initial NT node.

8.1.4 Installing the PC Agent and Creating PC Managed Nodes

To install PC agent software, you must either do this directly on the PC using the TME 10 CD-ROM, or you must create installation diskettes from the TME 10 CD-ROM to be used on the PC. There are two types of PC agents, one for running with the TCP/IP protocol and one for running IPX/SPX. The latter is used only with clients of a NetWare server running the NetWare repeater software. Be sure that the time zone variables are set properly for all PCs before installing any PC agent software.

In general, Tivoli recommends that you install the PC agent software before you create the PC managed node for it. However, PC agents that are clients of a NetWare managed site need to be installed after you install the TME 10 NetWare repeater on the NetWare server.

8.1.4.1 Installing PC Agent from CD-ROM

To install from CD, mount the CD on the PC's local CD-ROM drive and run the `setup.exe` program from either the \PC\SPXAGENT\CD directory for the IPX/SPX agent or from the \PC\TCPAGENT\CD directory for the TCP/IP agent.

8.1.4.2 Making and Installing from Diskettes for TCP/IP PC Agent

To make diskettes to be used for installation of the TCP/IP agent, copy the contents of the following directories to four diskettes:

```
PC\TCPAGENT\DISK1
PC\TCPAGENT\DISK2
PC\TCPAGENT\DISK3
PC\TCPAGENT\DISK4
```

In order to do this, place the CD-ROM into a PC's CD-ROM drive and run an `xcopy` command. For example, to create diskette 2, use a formatted diskette and run the following command if `d:` is your CD-ROM drive:

```
c:> xcopy d:\PC\TCPAGENT\DISK2 a: /s /e
```

Run the `setup.exe` program from the first disk to start the installation. The installation process allows you to choose what type of operating system you have and will adjust itself accordingly.

On OS/2, you must start an OS/2 command shell window and run the `setup` command in that window. Also on OS/2, you must then start the agent with the following command:

```
c:> \tivoli\tmeagent\os2\tivos2.exe -n c:\tivoli\tmeagent\os2\msgcat
```

In order to start the agent automatically on reboot, enter the above command in a START statement into your TCP/IP start-up file, which is usually the \tcpip\bin\tcpstart.cmd file.

8.1.4.3 Making and Installing from Diskettes for IPX/SPX PC Agent

To make diskettes to be used for installation, copy the contents of the following directories to two diskettes for the IPX/SPX agent code:

```
PC\SPXAGENT\DISK1
PC\SPXAGENT\DISK2
```

Run the `setup.exe` program from the first disk to start the installation.

Just as for the TCP/IP agent code, the installation process allows you to choose what type of operating system you have and will adjust itself accordingly.

8.1.4.4 Configuring the PC Agent

The PC agent machine may be configured for different things, such as:

- Client name and operating mode changes
- Dynamic Host Configuration Protocol setup
- NetWare agent security setup

The configuration changes for the PC agent software are all made in the C:\ETC\TMEAGENT.CFG file for all operating systems except NetWare. NetWare's PC agent configuration is held in the ETC directory of the SYS volume, also with the name TMEAGENT.CFG. See the TME 10 Framework manuals for details on setting values to the entries in this file.

8.1.4.5 Creating a PC Managed Node

The PC managed node resource can be created on the TME 10 desktop either before or after the PC agent code is installed on the PC. It is a good idea to perform this function after the agent code is installed because the software will check connectivity to this node as it creates the PC managed node.

To create the PC managed node icon on the TME 10 desktop, open the window of the policy region where you want to create the PC managed node and follow the steps shown in Figure 102.

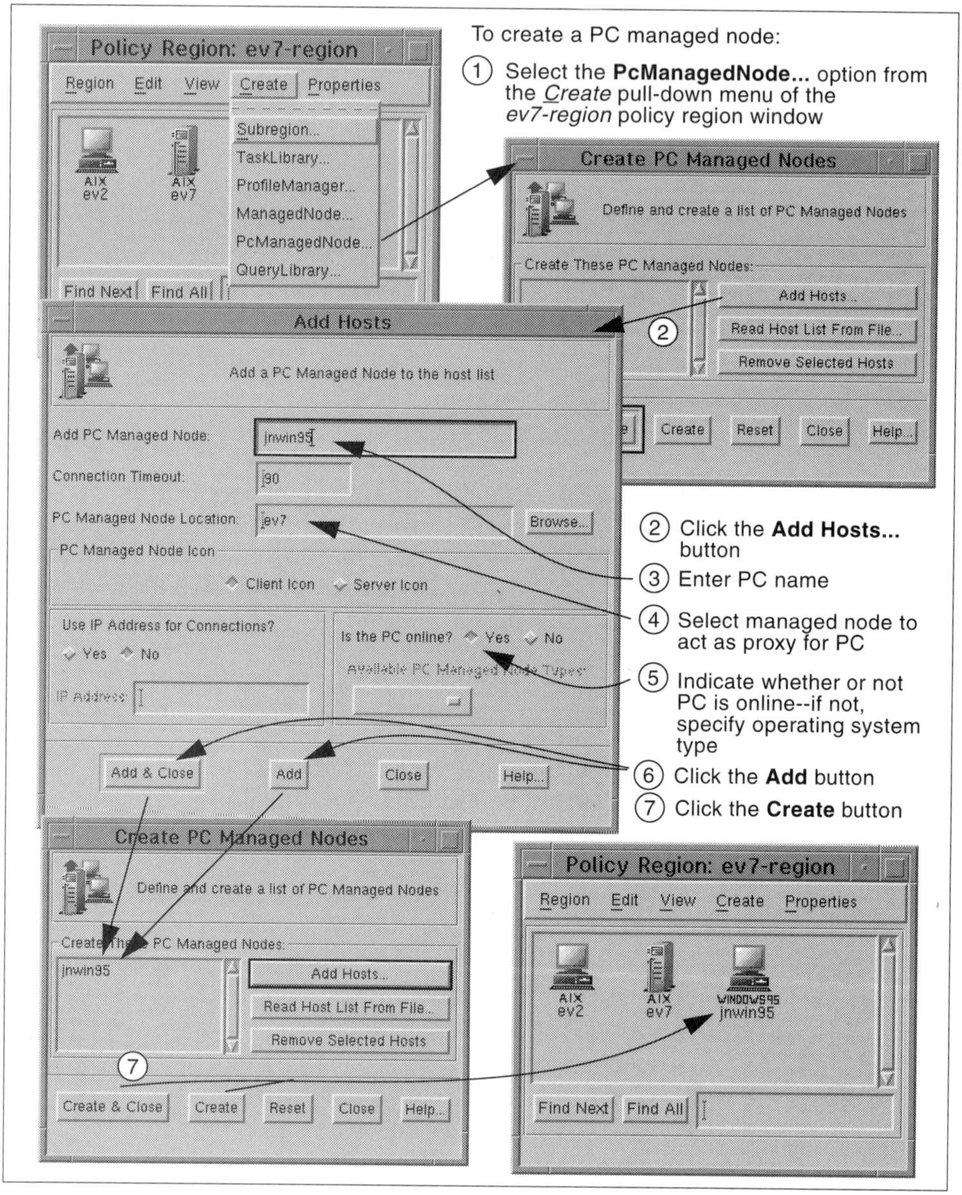

Figure 102. Create PC Managed Nodes Dialog

In the *Add Hosts* dialog in Figure 102 on page 218, you can define the following:

- Add PC Managed Node – Name for the PC managed node, usually the host name of that PC.
- Connection Timeout – Time-out value for the server trying to connect with the PC.
- PC Managed Node Location – Name of the server or client running the TME 10 Framework that you wish to have sponsor the PC and store information about the PC in its database.
- PC Managed Node Icon – Lets you choose whether you would like the client or server icon to appear on the desktop when created (this can be changed after creating the icon).
- Use IP Address for Connections? – Choose whether or not you would like to use the IP address for communicating with this system. If you choose Yes, you must supply the IP address of the PC; otherwise the connection is made to the IP host name specified in the top-most field using regular IP address resolution.
- Is the PC Online? – Indicate whether or not the PC is currently reachable by the server. If it is, the server will query the PC to find out its operating system type. If it is not, you must supply the operating type.

8.1.5 Installing Patches

Tivoli releases groups of fixes, or patches, to solve problems with the TME 10 software. These are known as Service Packs. To install TME 10 Service Packs, use the following instructions.

1. From the TME 10 desktop's *Desktop* menu, select **Install**, then **Install Patch...**
2. You may see an error about the media not being properly set. This is normal and will start the *File Browser* window that allows you to select the proper media. Search the available directories for a *patches.lst* file. When you find one, you have found the installation media, and you can click the **Set Media & Close** button.
3. The patch installation window should then appear as shown in Figure 103 on page 220. Select the patch and the clients on which you wish to install the patch. You can click the **Select Install Options...** button or the **Select Media...** button on this screen for more options.

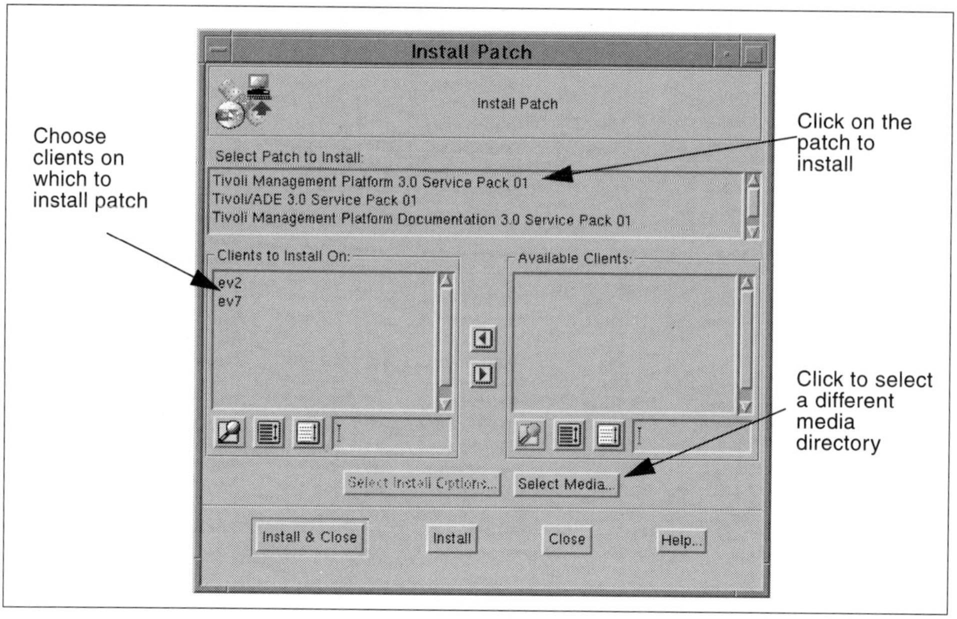

Figure 103. Patch Installation Dialog

Choose the **Install & Close** button to install the close the installation window or the **Install** button to install and keep the installation window open after completion.

4. Another window should then appear that will list all of the software that will be installed. Click the **Continue Install** button to continue or the **Cancel** button to cancel. This is your last chance to cancel the installation of the patch.

5. The window will then display the status of the patch installation. Wait for the "`Finished patch installation`" message to appear. It is then safe to click the **Close** button; the installation is complete.

8.1.6 Deinstallation of TME 10 Framework

To remove the TME 10 Framework from a machine, perform the following steps.

A Word of Caution about Removal

These steps will remove ALL TME 10 software installed on the system, not just the TME 10 Framework software. For example, if you have the TME 10 Framework and also TME 10 User Administration installed on a client, and you perform the steps listed above, TME 10 Framework and TME 10 User Administration will both be removed.

8.1.6.1 Removal from a UNIX System

Use the following steps to remove the TME 10 Framework from a UNIX system:

1. If the machine is a TME 10 client, or managed node, first remove the managed node from the TME 10 database by removing it from the desktop.
2. Kill the oserv process running on the machine from which you wish to remove the software.
3. Clean out and remove several directories with the following commands:

```
# rm -rf /var/spool/Tivoli
# rm -rf /usr/local/Tivoli
# rm -rf /usr/lib/X11/app-defaults/Tivoli
# rm -rf /etc/Tivoli
```

4. Clean up the initialization files that were modified to automatically start the oserv daemon. For example, on AIX systems you must remove some lines from the /etc/inittab, /etc/inetd.conf, /etc/rc.nfs, and /etc/services files. For lists of files modified on specific operating systems, consult the TME 10 Framework documentation and release notes.

8.1.6.2 Removal from a Windows NT System

To remove the TME 10 Framework from a Windows NT system, simply click the **Uninstall** icon located in the Tivoli folder and follow the steps given.

8.2 Practical Examples of Using the TME 10 Framework

In this section, we look at some practical uses of the TME 10 Framework to get a better idea of how it can be used in a real user environment.

8.2.1 Our Lab Environment

The lab environment to be used throughout the tutorials in this book is as follows:

TMR Server

- ***ev7*** – RS/6000® running AIX 4.1.4 (TME 10 Framework installed)

TME 10 Clients

- ***ev2*** – RS/6000 running AIX 4.1.4 (TME 10 Framework installed)
- ***clientnt*** – PC running Windows NT 3.51 (PC agent installed)
- ***cpwarp*** – PC running OS/2 Warp (PC agent installed)
- ***jnwin95*** – PC running Windows 95 (PC agent installed)

All of these machines communicate with each other via the TCP/IP protocol over a token-ring network.

For this tutorial, we show examples from an environment that contains only the TME 10 Framework software; no additional applications are installed. As we go through the chapters in Part 2 of this book, the applications discussed in this book will be added.

8.2.2 Starting the Desktop

As the root user on our server machine (*ev7*), we start up the TME 10 desktop using the `tivoli` command. Make sure you have run the */etc/Tivoli/setup_env.sh* to set the correct environment for using TME 10. Figure 104 on page 223 shows this initial view. Please note that you would normally see two Tivoli logos and that we have changed one of them by using tools that come with the AEF.

Figure 104. Initial Desktop Dialog

The appearance of the notices icon tells us that there are no new notices to read.

One policy region is defined, *ev7-region*. If we double-click on this icon, we will see the window containing the contents of that policy region, shown in Figure 105.

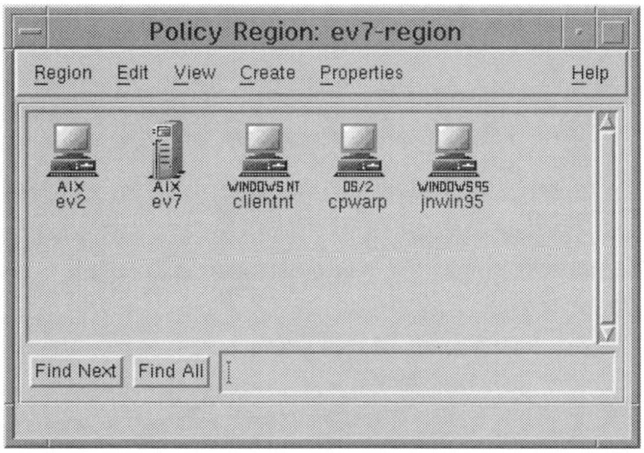

Figure 105. Policy Region Contents for ev7-region

We can see in the policy region view that five machines are defined in our policy region. Four appear with the client icon, one with the server icon. These icons can be changed and differ only in appearance. The labels below the icons show the operating system of the machine and the host name for managed nodes or the name given by the operator for PC managed nodes.

8.2.3 Managed Node and PC Managed Node Functions

Let's say we would like to change the icon of *ev2* to be a server, so that both of our AIX machines have server icons, and the PCs have client icons. Follow the instructions in Figure 106 to make this change.

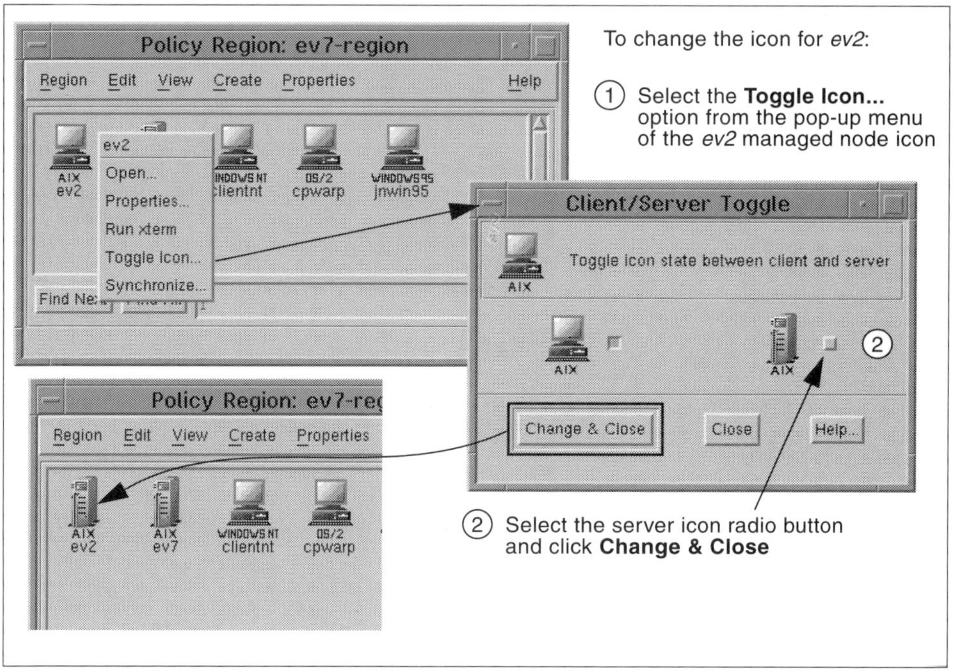

Figure 106. Client/Server Toggle Dialog

Now suppose we would like to see what version of OS/2 our system, *cpwarp*, has installed. We would place the mouse over this icon, click the right mouse button to see the pop-up menu, then choose the **Properties...** option. This is shown in Figure 107 on page 225.

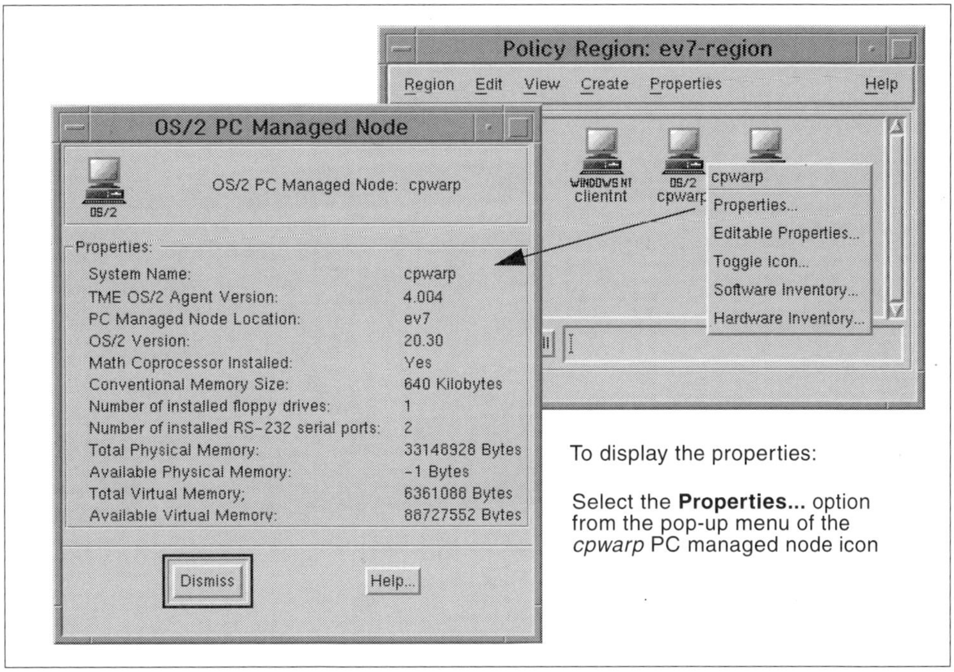

Figure 107. Properties Dialog of an OS/2 Workstation

8.2.4 Creating and Populating a Policy Region

Now let's create a new policy region to help us organize our TME 10 environment. This will be necessary to do with larger networks than our test situation. Let's say we would like our Windows 95 machine, *jnwin95*, to stay in the ev7-region policy region, but we want to move all of the other machines to a new policy region, called *ACME PR*.

To create the new policy region, we need to go to our initial desktop window and follow the steps shown in Figure 108 on page 226.

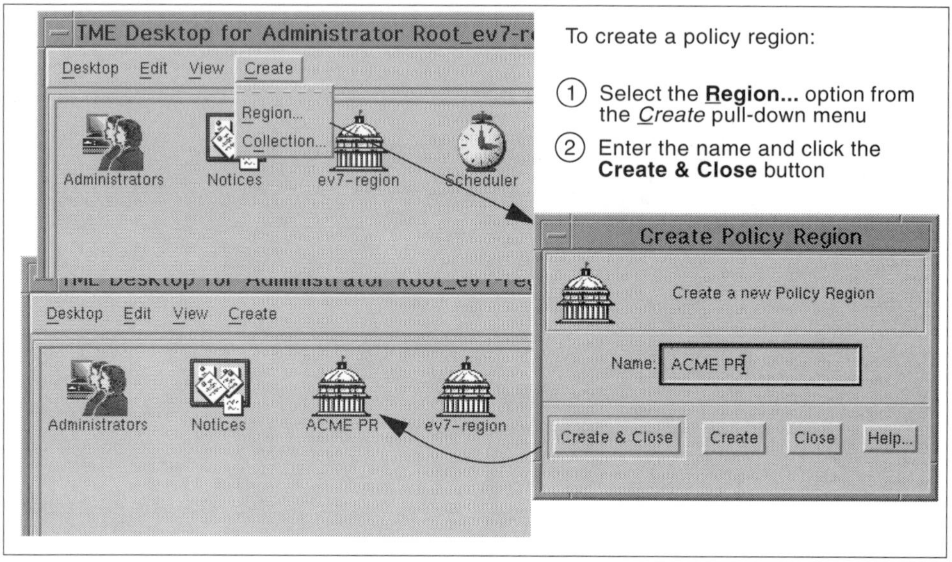

Figure 108. Creating a New Policy Region

At its initial creation, the policy region contains no resources, and there have not yet been any resource types assigned to it. So, our next step will be to set the types of resources that can be in this policy region (Figure 109).

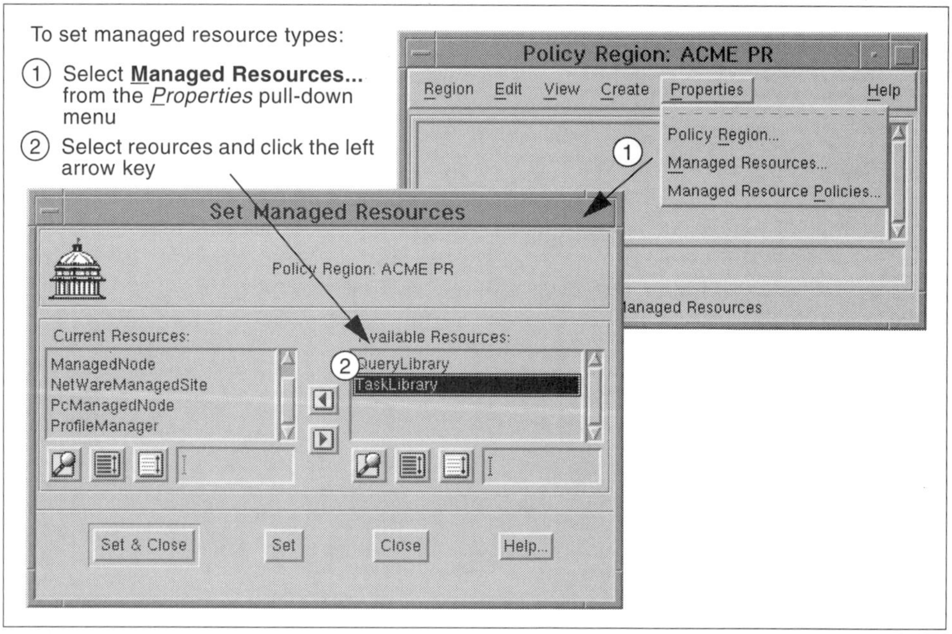

Figure 109. Setting Managed Resources for a Policy Region

As you can see in Figure 109, we have set our policy region to allow the following resource types: Managed Nodes, PC Managed Nodes, NetWare Managed Sites, Profile Managers, and Task Libraries. With this set, we should now be able to move resources into this policy region.

Moving resources from one policy region to another is done by dragging the resources from the first policy region and dropping them into the destination policy region. For our example, we are moving all of our managed nodes and PC managed nodes to the new policy region, except for one machine, *jnwin95* (see Figure 110).

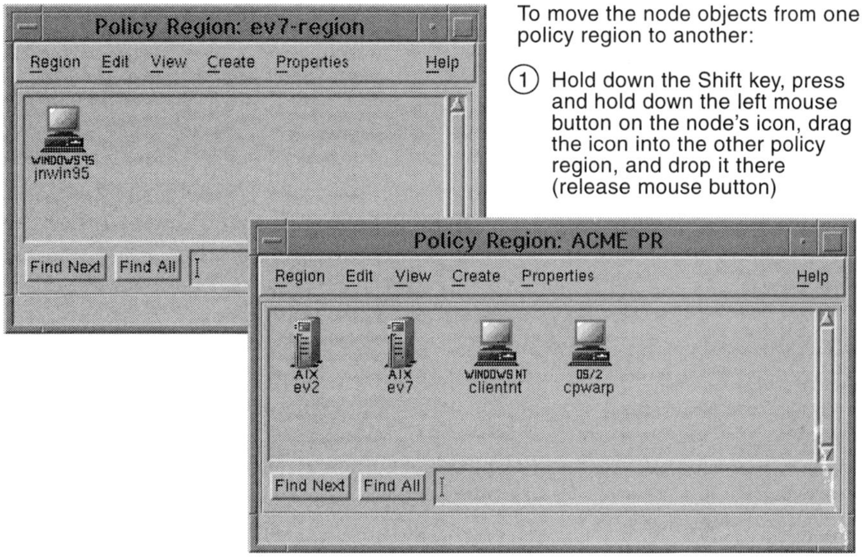

To move the node objects from one policy region to another:

(1) Hold down the Shift key, press and hold down the left mouse button on the node's icon, drag the icon into the other policy region, and drop it there (release mouse button)

Figure 110. Views of New and Old Policy Regions

8.2.5 Creating and Populating a Generic Collection

After resources are divided between different policy regions for purposes of administering them, it may become necessary to logically group resources of a certain type for easier access by the administrator. Suppose we want to create a grouping of all machines running Microsoft Windows products of any kind. This can be done by using a generic collection. Remember that the generic collection does not really contain resources; it only contains icons pointing to resources.

From the main desktop we create a collection called *MS Windows* (see Figure 111 on page 228).

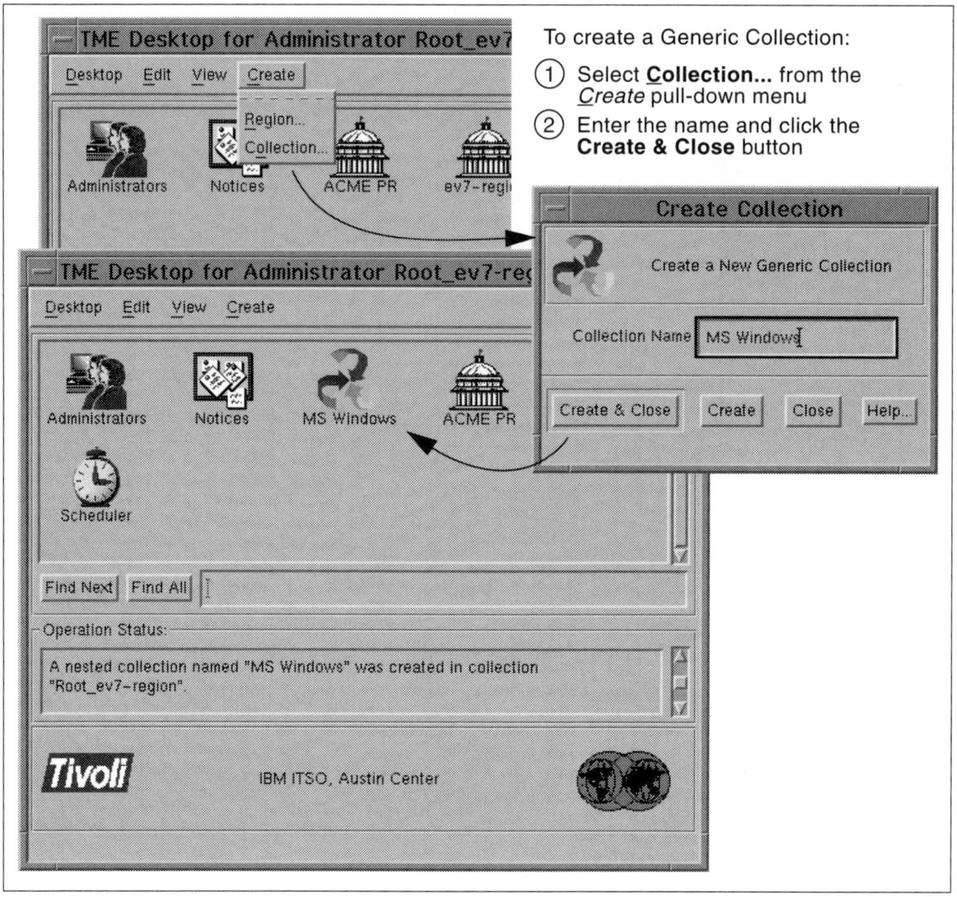

Figure 111. Creating a Generic Collection

We can then open the individual policy regions and place resources into the collection using the left mouse button to drag and drop them. We drag the *jnwin95* machine from the *ev7-region* policy region and the *clientnt* machine from the *ACME PR* policy region onto the collection icon. This is done in Figure 112 on page 229.

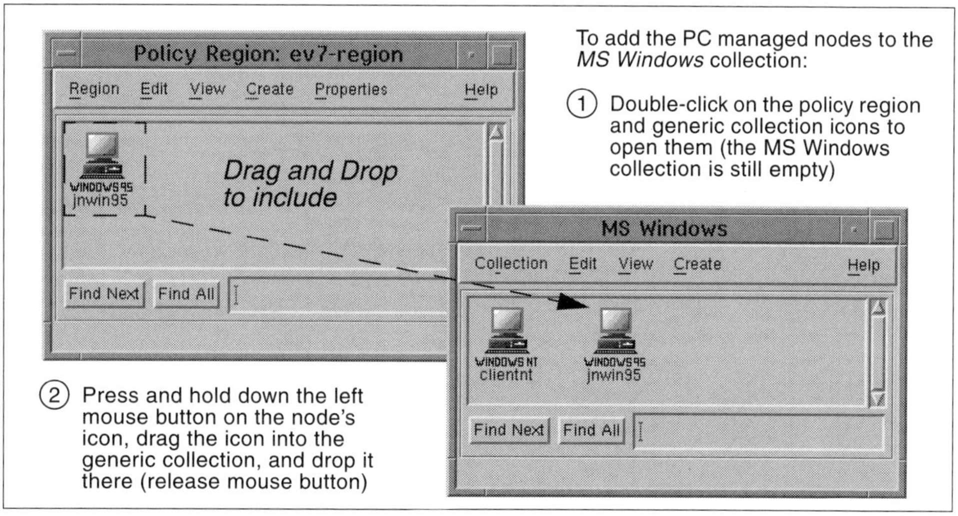

Figure 112. Populating the Generic Collection "MS Windows"

8.2.6 Creating a New Administrator

Currently, there is only one administrator defined in our TME 10 environment. This is the administrator that was defined for the root user ID when the TME 10 Framework was installed on our server.

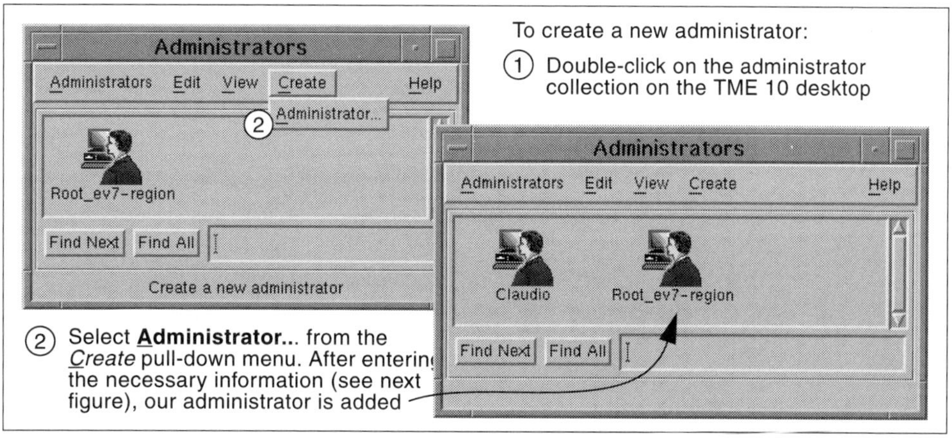

Figure 113. View of Defined Administrators

Selecting **Create->Administrator** brings up a window where you supply the administrator's name login name, and group name. Also on this screen are four buttons that allow you to set TMR roles, resource-specific roles, login names, and notice groups for that administrator. All of these windows and their settings are shown in Figure 114 on page 230.

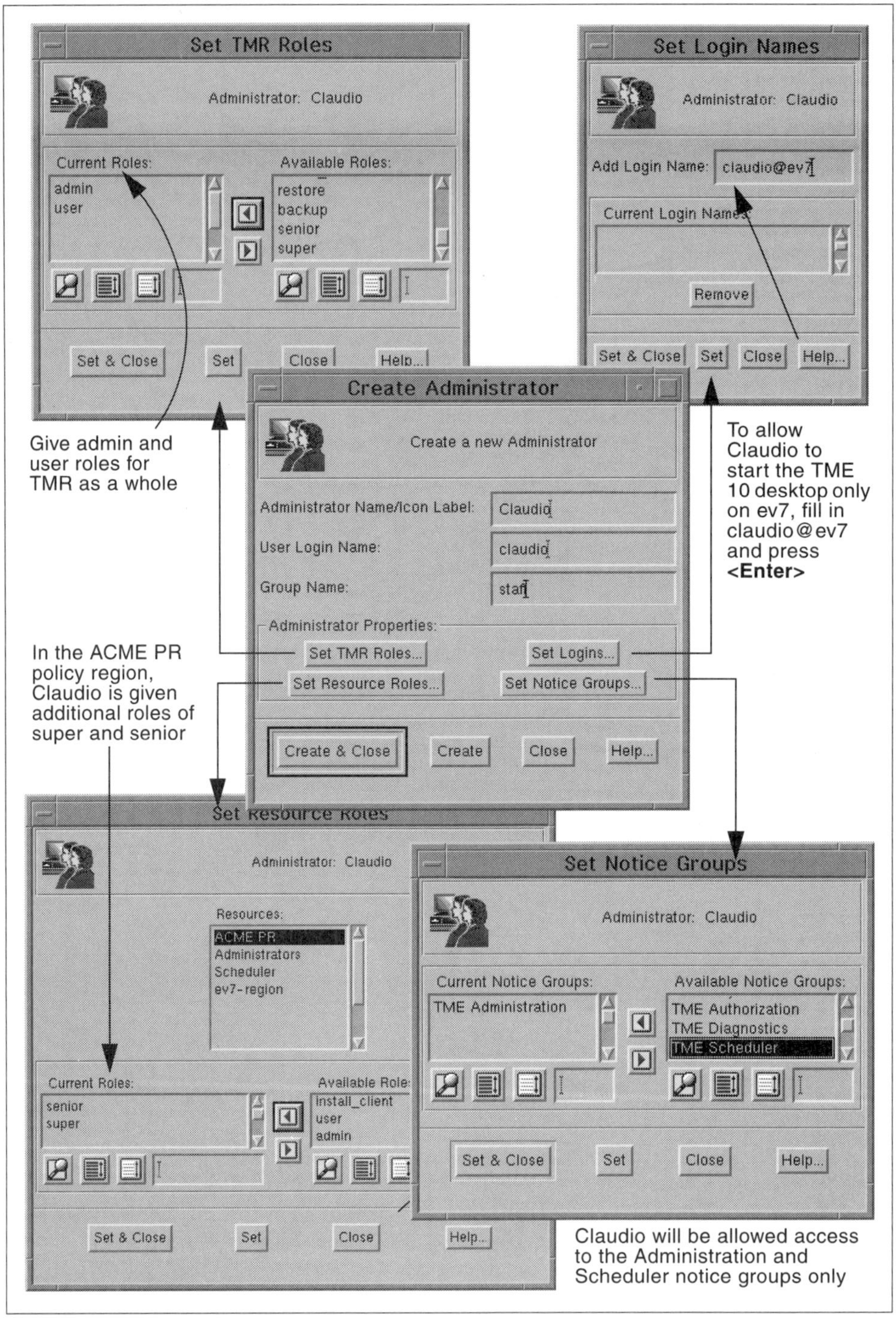

Figure 114. Multiple Windows for Creating a New Administrator

8.2.7 Reading Notices

While we have been performing functions within the TME 10 desktop, some notices have been sent to our notification facility. The bulletin board icon now appears with many notes attached to it. You can double-click on this icon to bring up the notification facility's window shown in Figure 115. This window tells us that there are unread messages in two of our notification groups, the Administration group and the Authorization group.

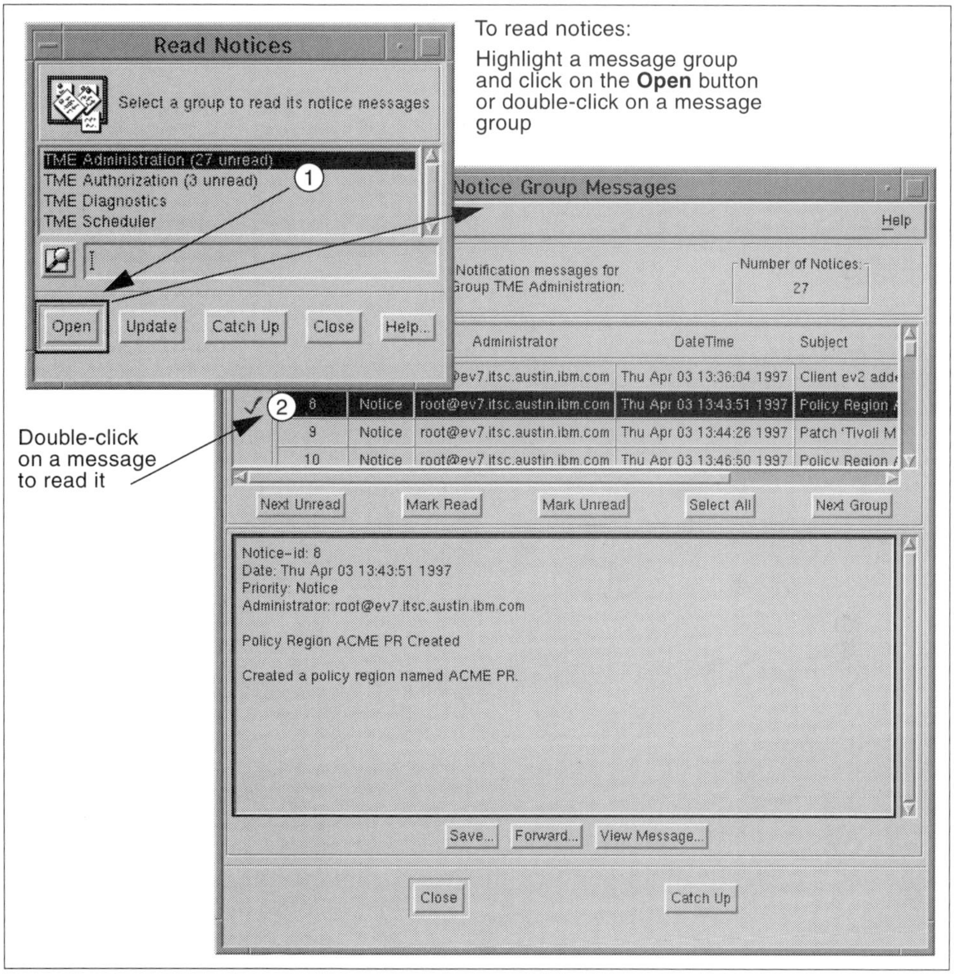

Figure 115. Reading Notices

The note we are reading, id number 8, is informing us that the *ACME PR* policy region was created. From this window, you can continue through the rest of the notes in this group and move on to the next group. While reading, you can decide to forward or save any of the notices. After all notices have been read and this window is closed, the bulletin board icon will change back to its original state.

8.2.8 Creating a New Profile Manager

Now let's suppose we would like to create a new profile manager containing all of the AIX machines in our TMR. We would do this from a policy region's window (double-click on the policy region to get this window). The policy region must be set for having profile managers as a valid managed resource type, which we have done earlier in this tutorial. We are creating a profile manager in the context of our *ACME PR* policy region, using *AIX Machines* as the name (Figure 116).

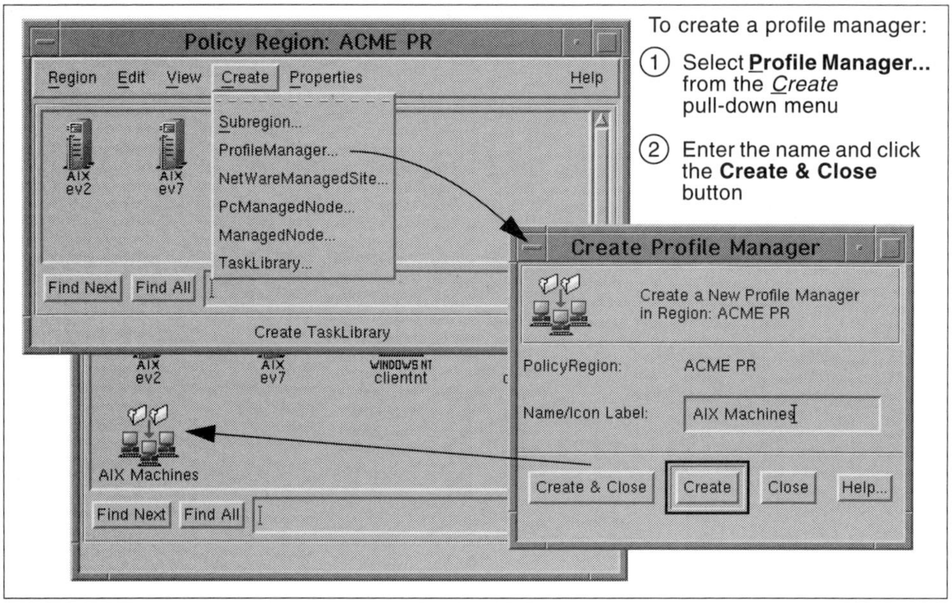

Figure 116. Creating a Profile Manager

8.2.9 Adding Subscribers

Next we want to add the two AIX machines, *ev2* and *ev7*, as subscribers. There are several ways to add subscribers to a profile manager:

- You can double-click on the new profile manager icon to bring up its window, and from its *Profile Manager* pull-down menu you can choose the **Subscribers...** option to start the *Subscribers* dialog shown in Figure 117.
- From the profile manager icon's pop-up menu you can choose **Subscribers...** and follow the steps shown in Figure 117.
- Drag a node icon and drop it onto the profile manager icon.

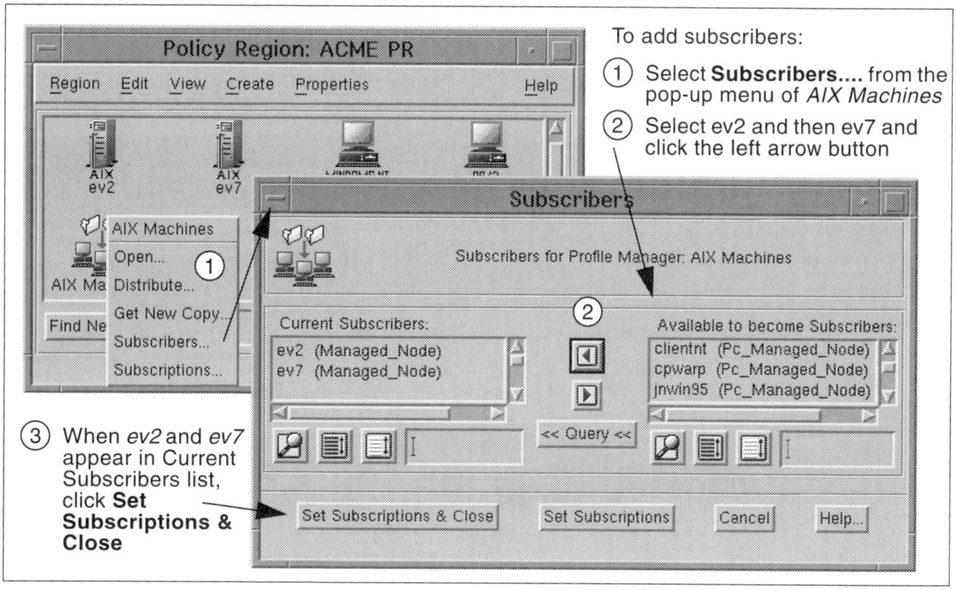

Figure 117. Adding Subscribers to a Profile Manager

Now our view of this profile manager, *AIX machines*, appears with two subscribers in the subscribers section of the window.

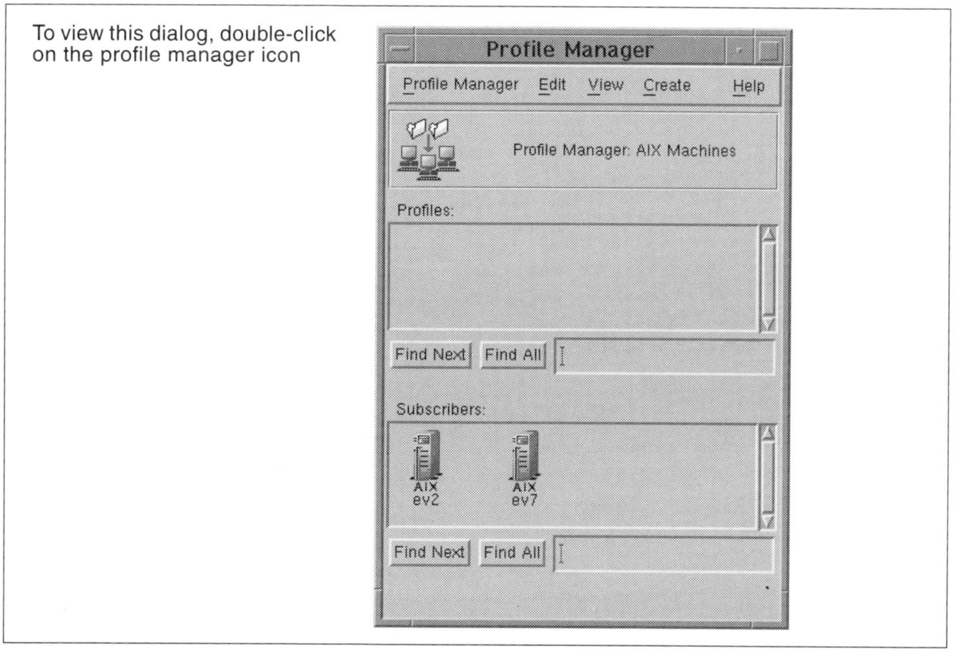

Figure 118. View of Profile Manager after Subscribers Have Been Added

We cannot yet create profiles for our profile manager because the TME 10 Framework software does not have any profiles of its own. This will be shown in the next chapter on the TME 10 User Administration application and in other chapters as well.

8.2.10 Creating Tasks and Jobs and Scheduling a Job

Before creating tasks and jobs, a task library must be created to contain these items. This is done within the context of a policy region, so you must be sure that the policy region allows task libraries as a valid managed resource type. Follow the steps shown in Figure 119 to create a task library called *Some Tasks* in the ACME PR policy region.

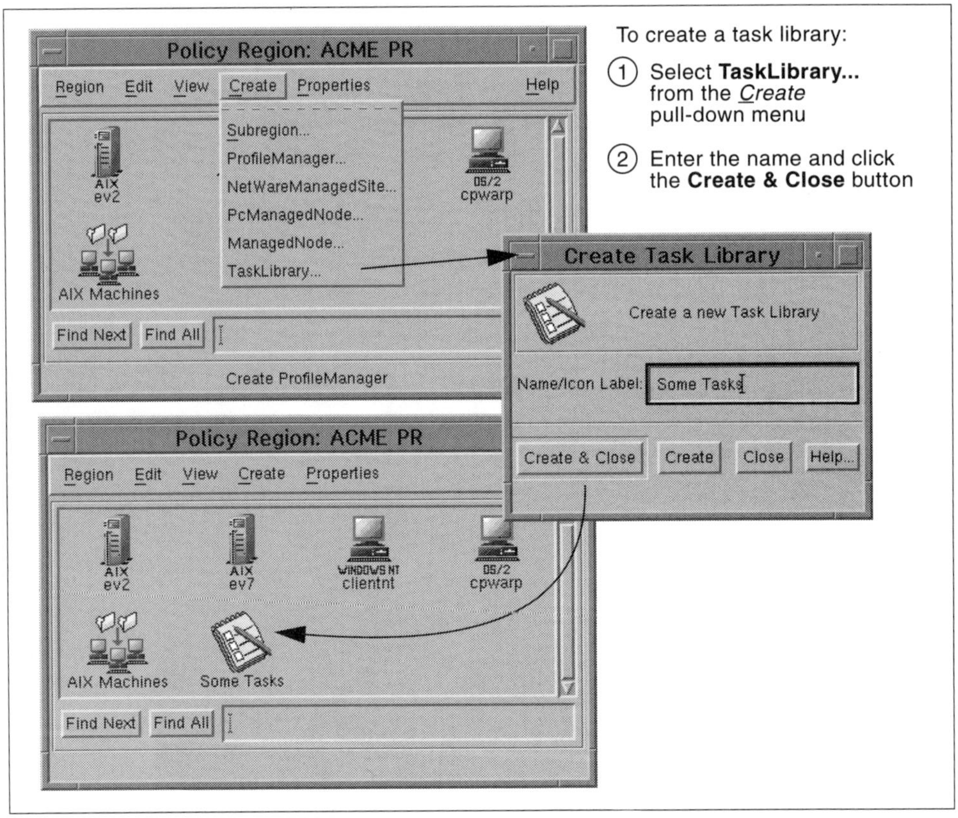

Figure 119. Creating a Task Library

Before we can create a task that executes a shell script on a UNIX node, we must create the shell script. For our testing purposes, we create a shell script `/tmp/test.script` that writes the output of the date command to a file:

```
# cat <<EOF >/tmp/test.script
> #! /bin/ksh
> echo "Task date: \c" >>/tmp/task.out
> date >>/tmp/task.out
> EOF
# chmod +x /tmp/test.script
```

Note: The `#!/bin/ksh` line is important. Although a shell script will run without it when invoked from the command line, it would not work within a TME 10 task. Whenever you edit the shell script, you also need to rebuild the task because the script is incorporated into the task for distribution when the task is created or updated.

Figure 120 sets out the steps necessary to create the task *Date Script*.

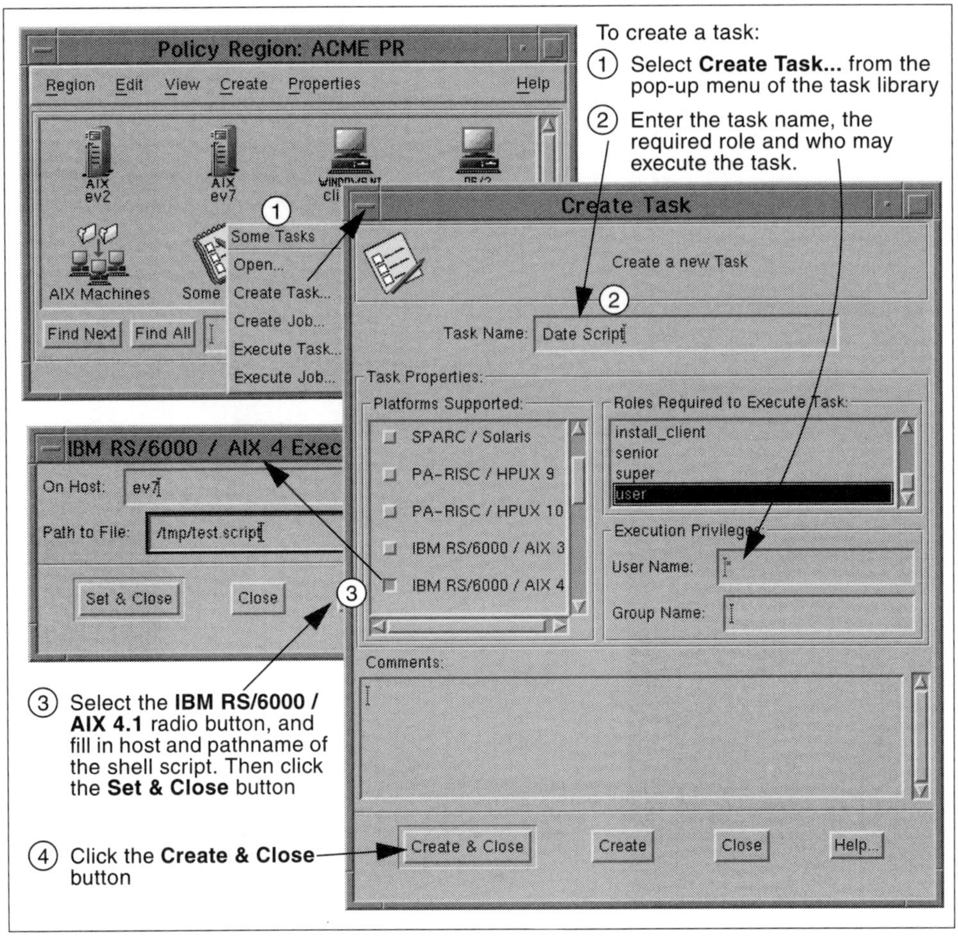

Figure 120. Creating a Task

The job will run under the user ID and group of the administrator running it if we leave those fields blank. The task is now created under the task library icon's hierarchy.

If we would like to take this task and run it on both of our AIX machines, *ev2* and *ev7*, we should create a job. This is shown in Figure 121.

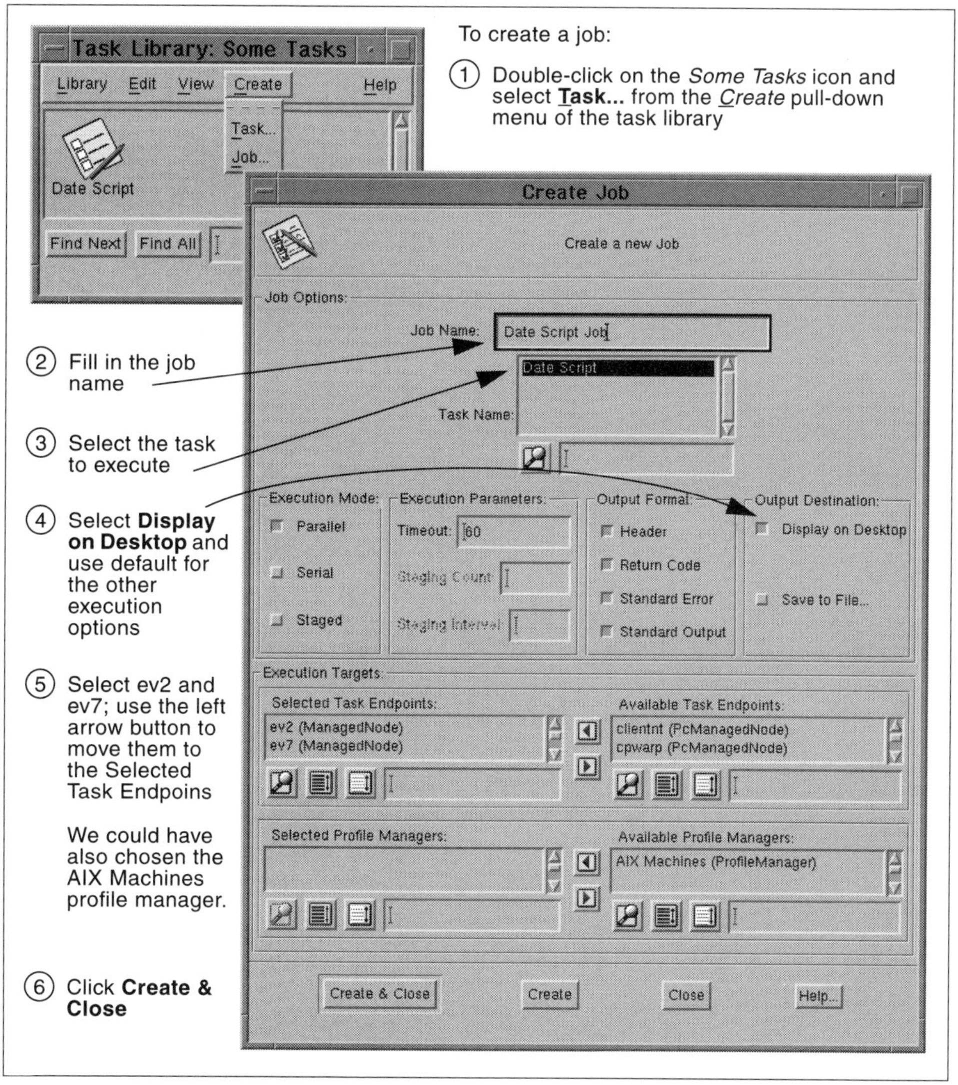

Figure 121. Creating a Job

The job will then appear in the task library window, as shown in Figure 122 on page 238. This figure also shows the task that was created earlier.

Figure 122. View of Task Library Contents

We can then double-click on the job icon to actually execute the job. Because we chose to have the output display on-screen, we see the window shown in Figure 123 appear.

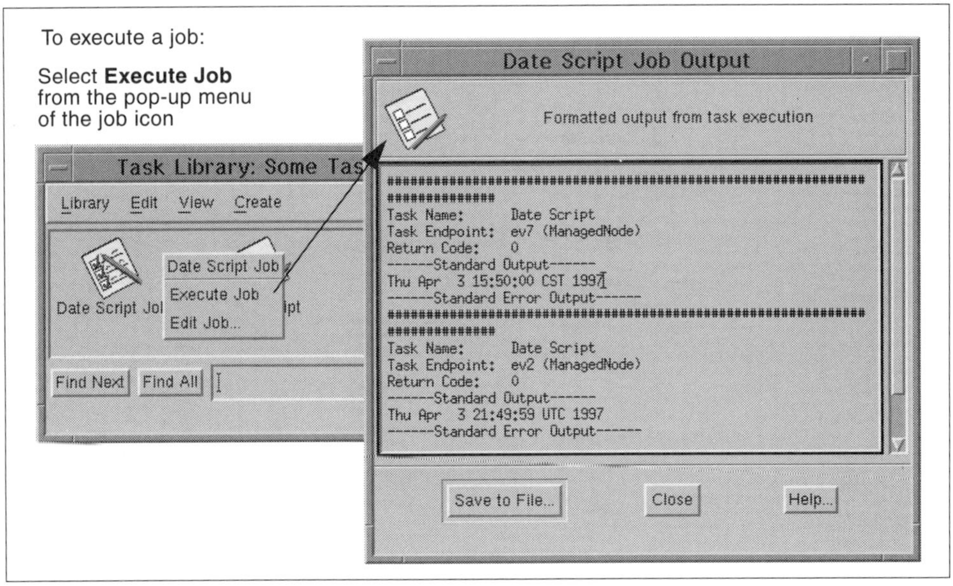

Figure 123. Window to Display Output from Job

From here, you can choose to save the output to a file or close the window. Now let's say that instead of running the job immediately as we just did, we want to schedule it to run several times. We would drag the icon for the job and drop it on top of the scheduler icon that appears on the main desktop window. When doing this, the window shown in Figure 124 on page 239 appears on the screen. You can set specifics on when the job will run and if it will be repeated. We choose to have the job run for 7 consecutive days, once per day, at 11:00 p.m. When the job runs, it will send an e-mail to our administrator, Claudio.

To schedule a job:

(1) Drag and drop the job icon onto the scheduler icon, which opens up this dialog

(2) Fill in a description

(3) Fill in day and time the job is to run for the first

(4) Enter that the job should be repeated 7 times, once a day

(5) Click **Schedule Job & Close**

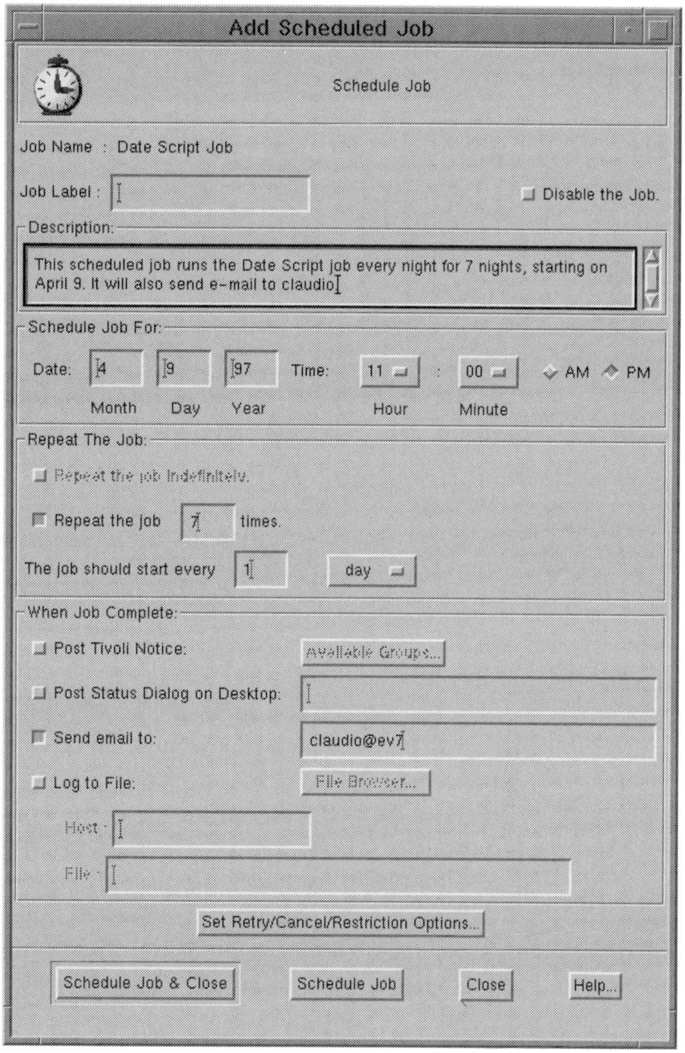

Figure 124. Scheduling a Job for Execution

When all of the information is entered, this job is entered into the TME 10 scheduler for execution at a later time. Now suppose we scheduled the job, but cannot remember exactly when it was scheduled to run. If you double-click the scheduler icon, it will bring up a window that allows you to browse all of the jobs currently scheduled. This window is shown in Figure

125. We see our job there, and can double-click on it to get more information, if necessary.

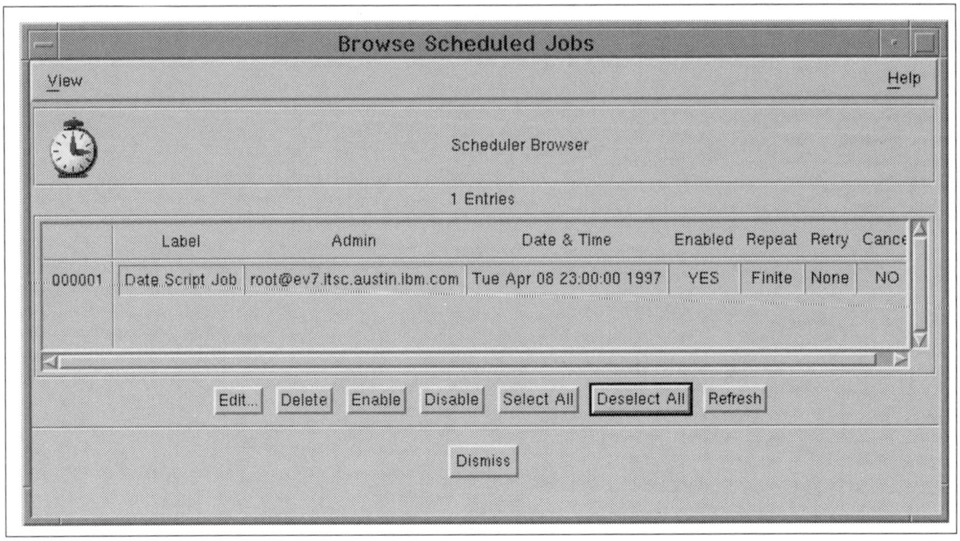

Figure 125. Browsing a Scheduled Job's Information

You can press the **Dismiss** button when you are finished browsing the jobs.

8.2.11 Using the Desktop Navigator

You can use the desktop navigator to maneuver throughout the TME 10 environment without going through layers of windows. Let's say we wanted to again find out the version of the operating system running on our OS/2 machine, but we could not remember the policy region in which it was contained. The **Navigator...** option is available from several pull-down menus, for example from the *Region* menu in any of the *Policy Region* dialogs. This will bring up the *Desktop Navigator* dialog shown in Figure 126 on page 241. From there, we can click on the radio button for **PCManagedNode(os2_client)**. This will list all of the OS/2 machines in our TME 10 environment on the right. We can click once on **cpwarp**, the machine we are interested in, and then click the **Go To** button. This will cause the window showing machine information about that machine to appear. The desktop navigator is very useful in quickly getting to resources.

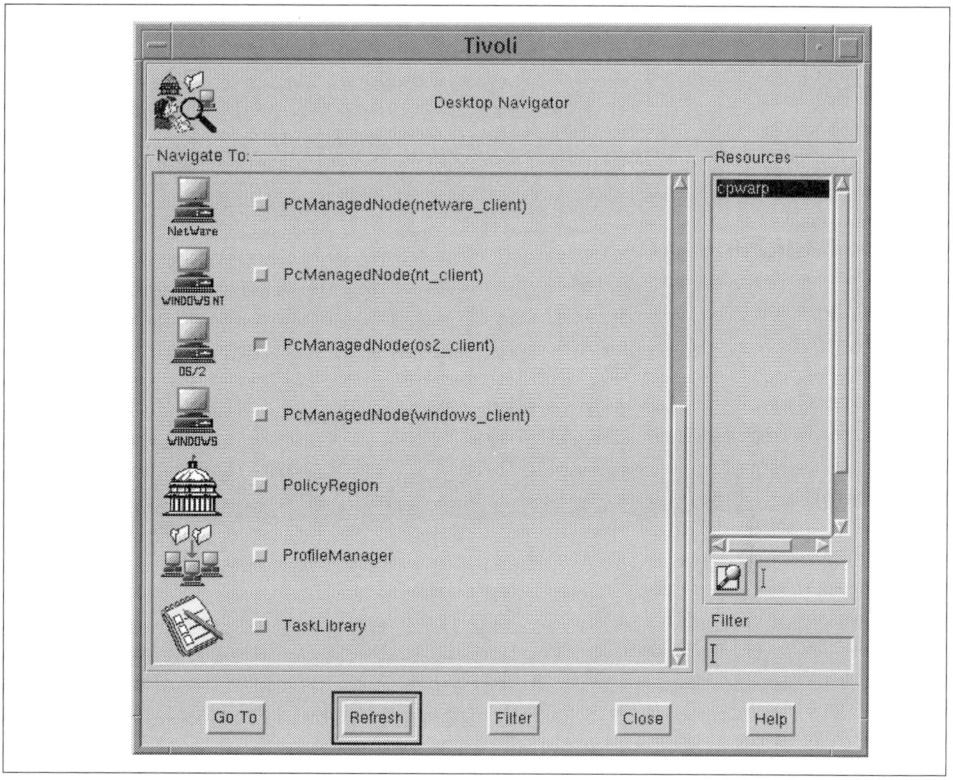

Figure 126. Using the Desktop Navigator

You can press the **Close** button when you are finished using the desktop navigator.

8.2.12 Exiting the TME 10 Desktop

When you are finished using the TME 10 desktop, choose the **Quit** option of the *Desktop* pull-down menu on the main desktop window. It will ask you to confirm that you want to close the session, and if so, it will exit the program and remove all TME 10 windows from the screen.

8.3 Helpful Hints

The following sections provide some more useful information, such as how to start and stop the oserv daemon and how to backup the TME 10 environment.

8.3.1 Getting Help from Tivoli

To contact Tivoli support, you can telephone them at (800)TIVOLI8. This number is for callers with valid support contracts only.

You may also wish to consult the Tivoli web site for marketing information, at `www.tivoli.com`.

8.3.2 Showing Installed Products

An easy way to show the products installed in your TME 10 environment is to use the *Desktop* pull-down menu of the main TME 10 desktop window; then choose the **About...** option. This will bring up a window that shows some license information, but this window also contains an **Installed Products...** button. If you click on this button, another window will come up that lists the products installed in your TME 10 environment.

8.3.3 Software Logging

There are logs kept by the TME 10 software that may contain helpful information when having problems. The oservlog is a logging file kept in the database directory and that contains information pertaining to the oserv daemon and its ability to communicate.

When TME 10 products are installed, they keep track of their installations in the /tmp directory (UNIX only). For example, when installing the TMR server with the TME 10 Framework software, you could check the /tmp/tivoli.sinstall file for information about this installation. So, you may wish to check the files in the /tmp directory for installation information.

8.3.4 Stopping and Starting the TME 10 oserv Daemon

To stop, start, or restart the oserv daemon locally or on specific machines in a TMR, you can use the `odadmin` command. This is a powerful command that has many options and uses. Basically, you want to use the `odadmin` command with either the `shutdown`, `start`, or `reexec` option to stop, start, or restart the daemon, respectively. This option is followed by either no argument, the ID number of a specific client, the word `clients`, or the word `all`. This specifies either the local machine only, the ID number of a specific client, all clients in the TMR, or all machines in the TMR including the server, respectively. Some examples follow:

- `odadmin shutdown` – Shuts down the local machine's oserv only.
- `odadmin start clients` – Starts the oserv daemon on all clients in the TMR.
- `odadmin reexec all` – Restarts the oserv daemon on all clients and the server in the TMR.

Please refer to the TME 10 documentation and man page on the `odadmin` command for more information on this and other functions of `odadmin`.

8.3.5 Repairing and Backing Up the TME 10 Database

System problems can sometimes cause inconsistencies in the TME 10 database. These types of problems can be resolved using the `wchkdb` command. For more information, see the TME 10 documentation or the man page.

It is a good idea to periodically back up the TME 10 databases, especially before performing major functions like installing new products or patches. If problems arise, you can restore the information on your system and not have to install everything again.

To back up the database, choose the **Backup...** option of the *Desktop* menu in the main window. This will allow you to perform the backup graphically and includes a function to estimate the size of the backup files. You can also use the `wbkupdb` command to perform the backup. This is the command you would use to restore backed up data on your system. See the man page for this command for more information on how to use it.

To back up the database, choose the **Backup...** option of the *Desktop* menu in the main window. This will allow you to perform the backup graphically and includes a function to estimate the size of the backup files. You can also use the `wbkupdb` command to perform the backup. This is the command you would use to restore backed up data on your system. See the man page for this command for more information on how to use it.

CHAPTER 9

Installing and Using TME 10 User Administration

This chapter provides you with step-by-step installation instructions for the TME 10 User Administration. The first section discusses the TME 10 User Administration installation on the TMR server and on managed nodes. Once the installation is complete, the following sections permit you to exercise the basic functions provided by TME 10 User Administration.

The purpose of this chapter is to familiarize you with the way these functions work and to deepen your understanding of the concepts explained in Chapter 3, "TME 10 User Administration" on page 47. It does not cover every facet and option of this product.

TME 10 Terminology

Please note that the former name of this product was Tivoli/Admin 3.0. When you follow these steps using the TME 10 User Administration 3.1 or later, some dialogs might show slightly different titles and/or content, particularly in the installation sections. Most dialogs, however, are common to both versions of software.

9.1 TME 10 User Administration Installation

You must have TME 10 Framework installed and running on the TMR server and on any UNIX systems that are to be TME 10 clients before trying to install the TME 10 User Administration application. See the *TME 10 User Administration Release Notes* for disk space requirements to install the TME 10 User Administration application.

9.1.1 Installation on UNIX Managed Nodes

TME 10 User Administration has to be installed on each managed node to be able to perform the TME 10 User Administration features. Therefore, you must repeat these installation instructions for each managed node, including the TMR server, that you plan to manage with TME 10 User Administration. Remember that in this release NT is not directly supported if it is a managed node. An NT managed node needs to be also defined as a PC managed node in order to get the user and group administration functionality.

Use the following steps to install the TME 10 User Administration application from the TME 10 desktop:

1. From the *Desktop* pull-down menu, select **Install->Install Product...**
2. You may see an error about the media not being properly set; this is normal and will start the window that allows you to select the correct path to the TME 10 User Administration application.
3. The *Install Product* dialog should then appear as shown in Figure 127. Select the **TME 10 User Administration** and the clients on which you wish to install the product. You can click the **Install Options...** button or the **Select Media...** button on this screen for more options.

.

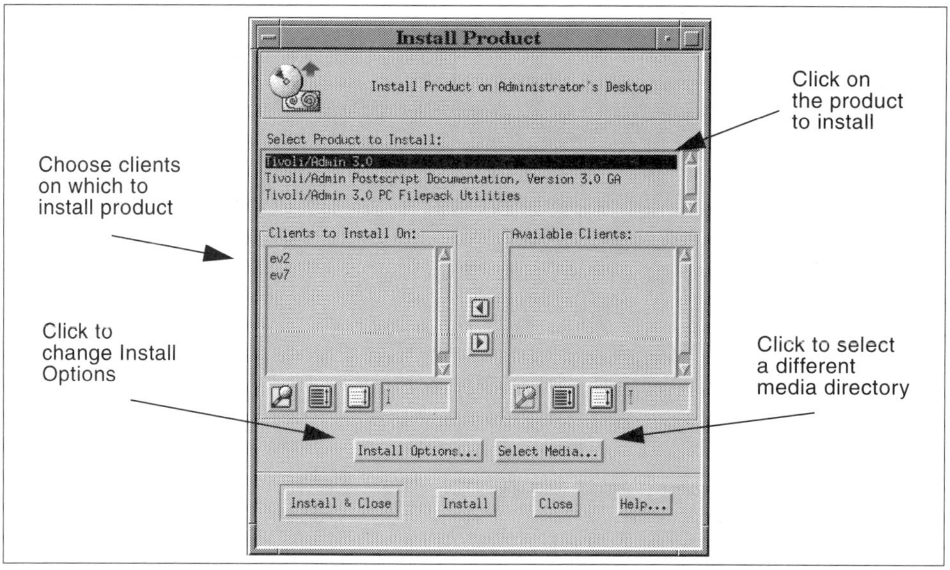

Figure 127. Install Product Dialog

Click the **Install & Close** button to install and close the installation window or the **Install** button to install and keep the installation window open after completion.

4. The *Product Install* dialog should then appear as shown in Figure 128 on page 249. This window lists all of the software that will be installed. Click the **Continue Install** button to continue or the **Cancel** button to cancel. This is your last chance to cancel the installation of the product.

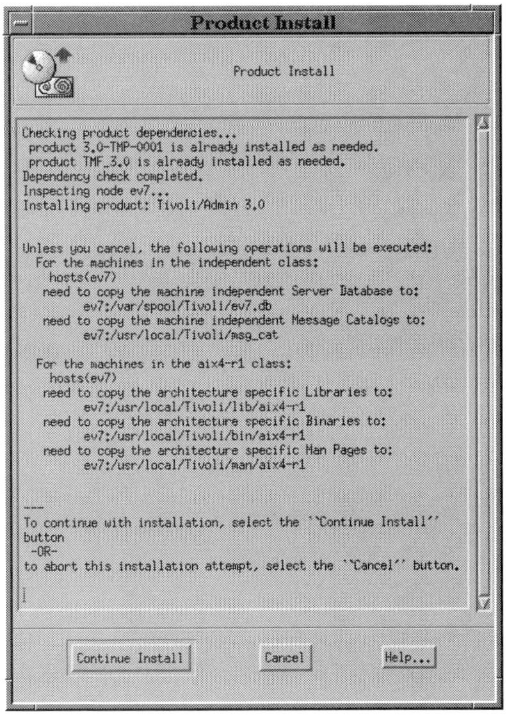

Figure 128. Product Install Dialog

5. The window will then display the status of the product installation. Wait for the `Finished product installation` message to appear. It is then safe to click the **Close** button; the installation is complete.

9.1.2 Installation on PC Managed Nodes

Remember that TME 10 User Administration can be installed for PC managed nodes that are either NT servers or NetWare servers. Installation is not needed for regular PC managed nodes if users are administered on the NT or NetWare server.

You can install the TME 10 User Administration application from the TME 10 desktop using TME 10 Software Distribution and TME 10 Software Distribution file packages, or you can install on a server-by-server basis using the installation diskette. Consider the following key points when installing TME 10 User Administration on a PC managed node.

- When installing TME 10 User Administration on a Windows NT server from the installation diskette, you can run the installation directly on the server.
- When installing TME 10 User Administration on a NetWare server from the installation diskette, you must run the installation on a Windows workstation that is connected to the server.

9.1.3 Using TME 10 Software Distribution File Packages

To install TME 10 User Administration on a PC managed node by using TME 10 Software Distribution file packages, you need to first install PC Filepack Utilities onto a UNIX managed node. You can then create the file packages by using the CLI (command line interface) scripts provided by TME 10 User Administration PC Filepack Utilities after the installation, and you can distribute them to the PC managed nodes from the UNIX managed node by using the TME 10 Software Distribution application.

Use the following steps to install the PC Filepack Utilities: from the TME 10 desktop:

1. From the *Desktop* menu, select **Install ->Install Product...** and set the media properly to be the location of the TME 10 User Administration application.
2. The *Install Product* dialog should then appear as shown in Figure 127 on page 248. Select the **TME 10 Admin 3.0 PC Filepack Utilities** from the *Select Product to Install* scrolling list. The *Install Options* dialog should then appear as shown in Figure 129.

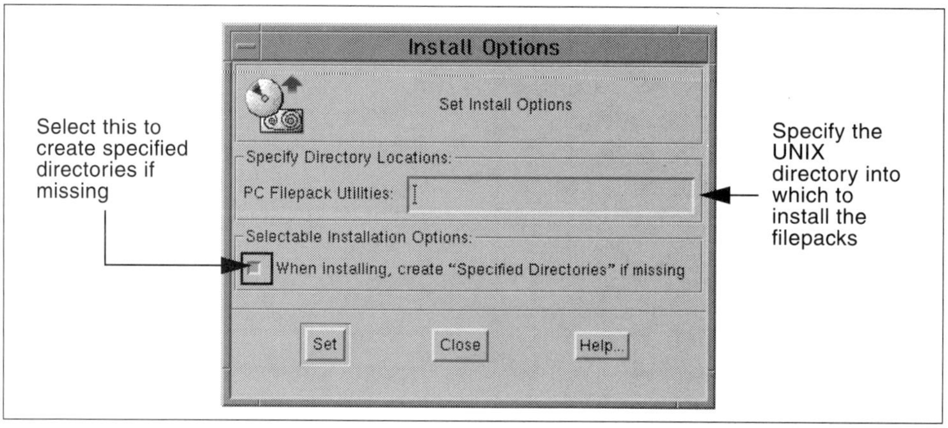

Figure 129. Install Options Dialog

Click the **Set** button to set the installation options and return to the *Install Product* dialog.

3. Select the clients onto which you want to install the file packages.

   Click the **Install & Close** button to install and close the installation window, or click the **Install** button to install and keep the installation window open after completion.

4. The *Product Install* dialog should then appear like the one shown in Figure 128 on page 249. This window will list all of the software that will be installed. Click the **Continue Install** button to continue or the **Cancel** button to cancel. This is your last chance to cancel the installation of the product.

5. When the installation is complete, use the `cd` command on the command line to go to the directory you specified in Figure 129 on page 250. This directory contains the subdirectories for the Windows NT and NetWare binaries as well as the CLI scripts to create the filepacks.

6. Create the filepacks that you want to distribute. The following CLI scripts are available to make the appropriate filepacks:

   `make_umbo_nt_fp` – Makes the Windows NT Filepack

   `make_umbo_nw4x_fp` – Makes the NetWare 4.X Filepack

   `make_umbo_nw3X_fp` – Makes the NetWare 3.X Filepack

   These commands all require three arguments: the policy region, the profile manager the TME 10 Software Distribution file package will be created in, and the managed node name that will be the source host for the distribution. The following is an example of the usage of the file package creation scripts:

   ```
   # make_umbo_nt_fp "ACME PR" distribution ev7
   ```

   The previous command line creates the Windows NT Filepack in the *distribution* profile manager of the *ACME PR* policy region using the binaries on the *ev7* UNIX managed node.

7. Use the TME 10 Software Distribution application to distribute the appropriate file packages to the appropriate PC managed node. For more information about the TME 10 Software Distribution application, refer to the Chapter 4, "TME 10 Software Distribution" on page 85.

9.1.4 Connecting to NetWare 4.X Endpoints

TME 10 User Administration requires that you run the `wsetnds` command in order to communicate with a NetWare 4.X endpoint. This command allows the application to log in to the NetWare Directory Services (NDS) tree. You need to run this command for each NDS tree that you want to manage. Once you run this command, you do not need to run it again unless you change the login name or password of the specified account. The wsetnds command is not applicable to NetWare 3.X, since NetWare 3.X does not support NDS trees.

When you populate from a NetWare PC managed node, you can only populate the user information that has an account type less than or equal to the account type associated with the wsetnds command.

Use the following syntax to use the wsetnds command:

```
# wsetnds [-l <login>] [-p <password>] -c <NDS_context> \
<@PcManagedNode:netware_endpoint>
```

where:

-l <login>	Specifies the login name of the account to use to log in to the NDS. The default is the Admin account.
-p <password>	Specifies the password for the account.
-c <NDS_context>	Specifies the NDS context for the account.
<@PcManagedNode:netware_enpoint>	Specifies the name of the NetWare PC managed node.

9.2 Practical Examples of Using the TME 10 User Administration

In this section, we look at some practical uses of the TME 10 User Administration application to get a better idea of how it can be used in a real user environment.

9.2.1 Our Lab Environment

The lab environment to be used throughout the tutorials in this book is as follows:

TMR Server

- ***ev7*** – RS/6000 running AIX 4.1.4 (TME 10 Framework and TME 10 User Administration installed)

TME 10 Clients

- ***ev2*** – RS/6000 running AIX 4.1.4 (TME 10 Framework and TME 10 User Administration installed)

- ***clientnt*** – PC running Windows NT 3.51 (PC agent installed)
- ***cpwarp*** – PC running OS/2 Warp (PC agent installed)
- ***jnwin95*** – PC running Windows 95 (PC agent installed)

All of these machines communicate with each other via the TCP/IP protocol over a token-ring network.

For this tutorial, we show examples from an environment that contains the TME 10 Framework and the TME 10 User Administration software installed. Figure 130 shows the desktop after these two applications are installed.

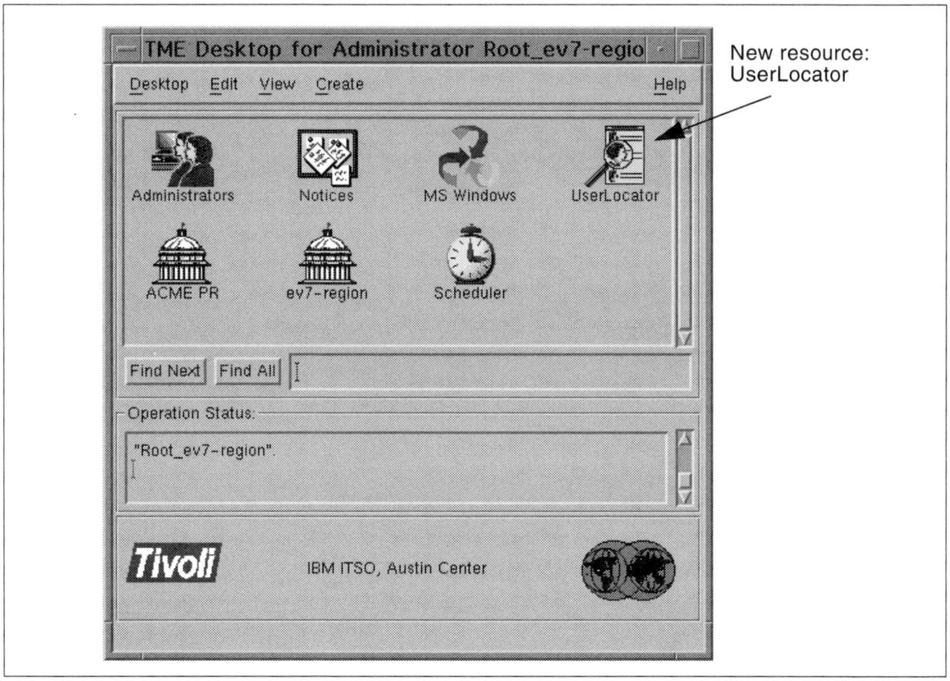

Figure 130. TME 10 Desktop after TME 10 User Administration Installation

9.2.2 Creating Profiles

In order to create TME 10 User Administration profiles, you must have at least one profile manager that can be the container for the profiles. In Chapter 8, “Installing and Using the TME 10 Framework” on page 203, we created a profile manager called *AIX Machines,* and we also subscribed the *ev1* and *ev4* managed nodes to this profile manager. Therefore let’s use the *AIX Machines* profile manager as a container of our TME 10 User Administration profiles.

Before we can create profiles, we must add their managed resource type to the list of resources that the *ACME PR* policy region can manage. Figure 131 illustrates how you add the UserProfile, GroupProfile, and HostNamespace resources to the policy region.

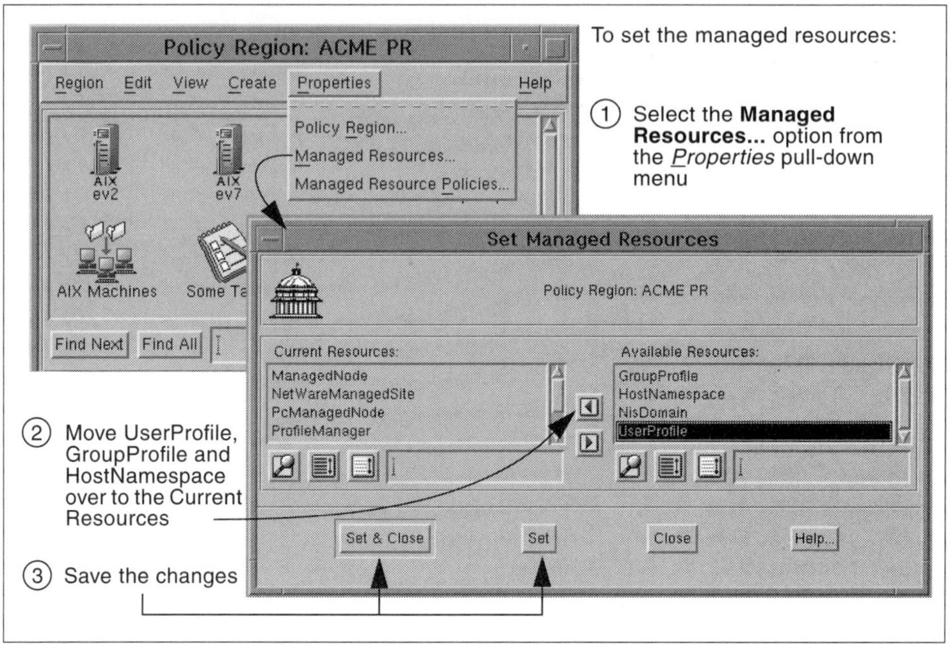

Figure 131. Set Managed Resource Dialog

Let's create a user profile called *AIX-Users* in the *AIX Machine*s profile manager of the *ACME PR* policy region. Figure 132 on page 255 shows you how to do that. Remember that the profile name must be unique in that policy region. You cannot have two profiles with the same name within a specific policy region even if both profiles are of different types.

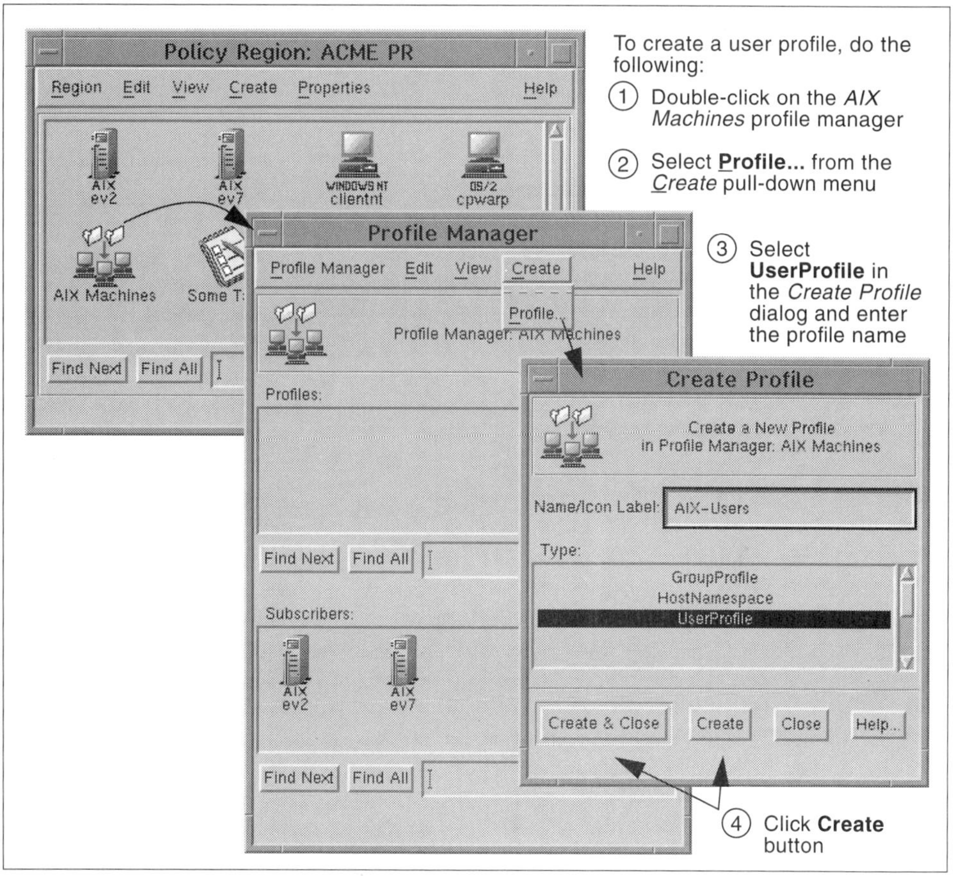

Figure 132. Creating a User Profile

Now, let's create a group profile called *AIX-Groups* and a host namespace profile called *AIX-Hosts* from the TME 10 desktop. We can follow the steps listed in Figure 132, but we need to select the appropriate profile type in the *Create Profile* dialog.

After creating the three profiles, the *AIX Machines* profile manager looks like the window in the upper-left corner of Figure 133 on page 256.

9.2.3 Populating Profiles

To get the entries of our new user profile, let's populate the *AIX-Users* profile from the *ev7* and *ev2* UNIX systems. To populate the user profile from the TME 10 desktop, follow the steps shown in Figure 133 on page 256.

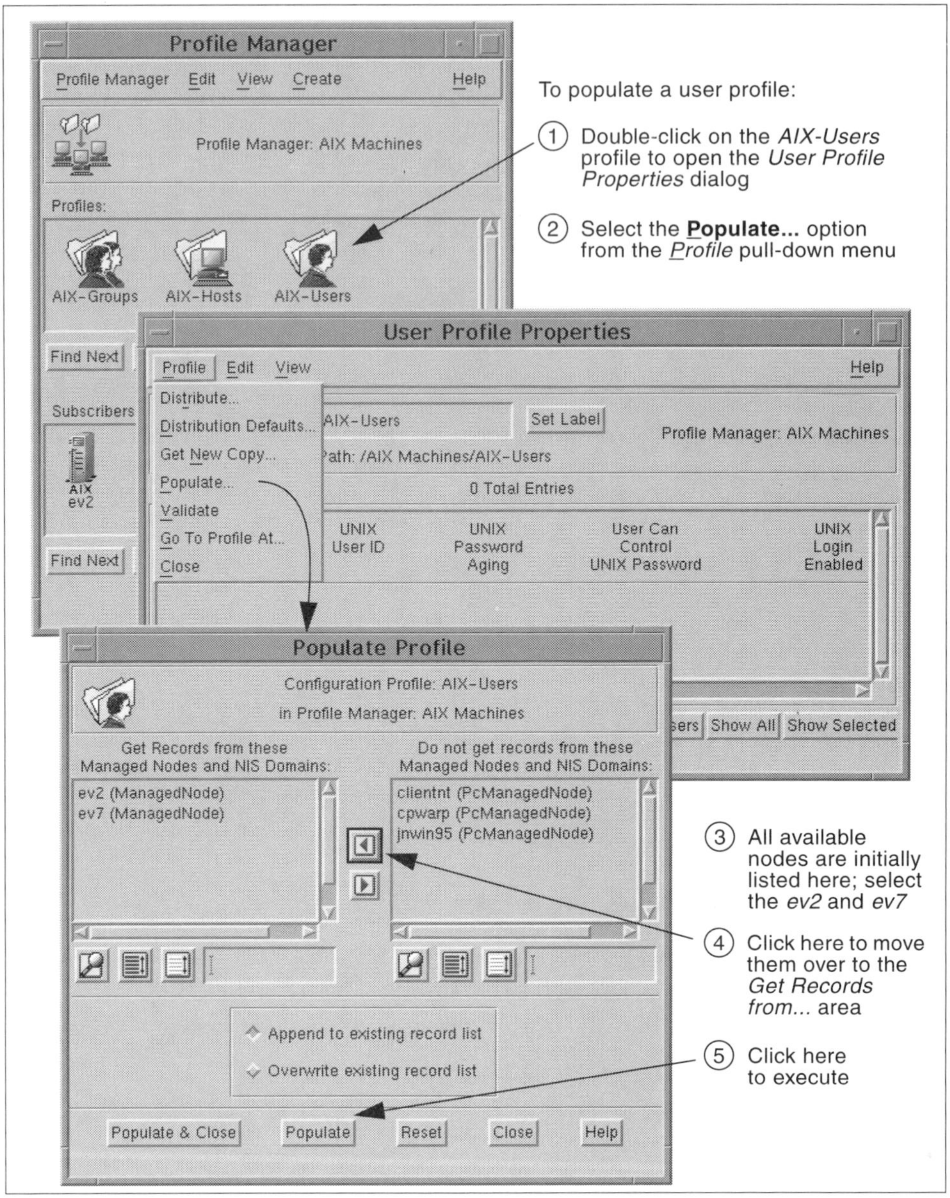

Figure 133. Populating a User Profile

Now, let's populate the *AIX-Groups* group profile and the *AIX-Hosts* host namespace profile from the TME 10 desktop. Follow the same steps as listed above for the user profile. After populating the *AIX-Users* profile, the *AIX-Groups* profile and the *AIX-Hosts* profile, the *Profile Properties* window for each profile should look like those shown in Figure 134 on page 257.

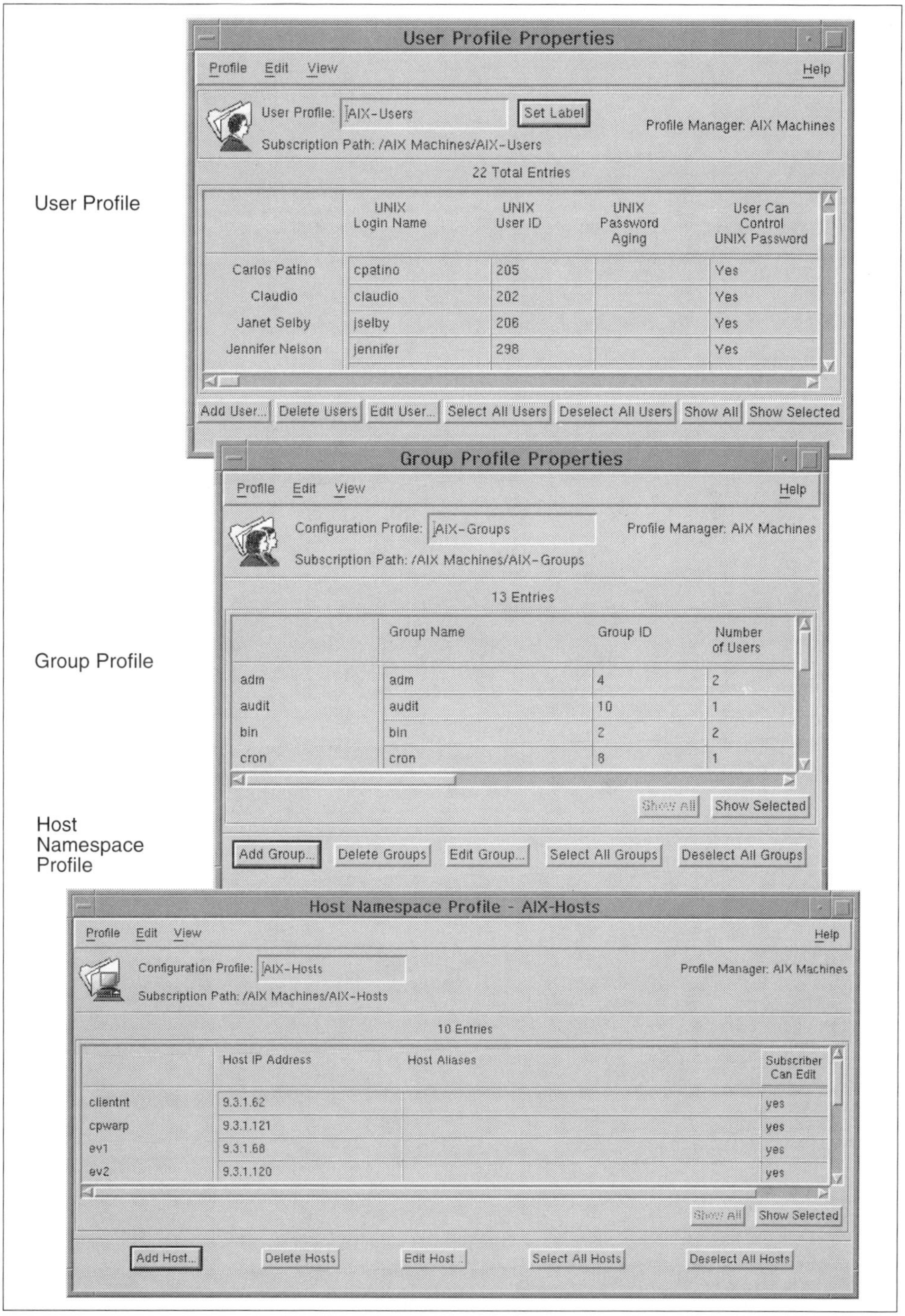

Figure 134. Profile Properties Dialogs

9.2.4 Adding Profile Records

In this section, we explain how to add single records to each type of TME 10 User Administration profiles. First, we add a new user account for Jack Martineau. As you can see in the *User Properties* dialog in Figure 135, you could add many different attribute categories. We decide to only add his UNIX Login name and have the entry generated with default attributes.

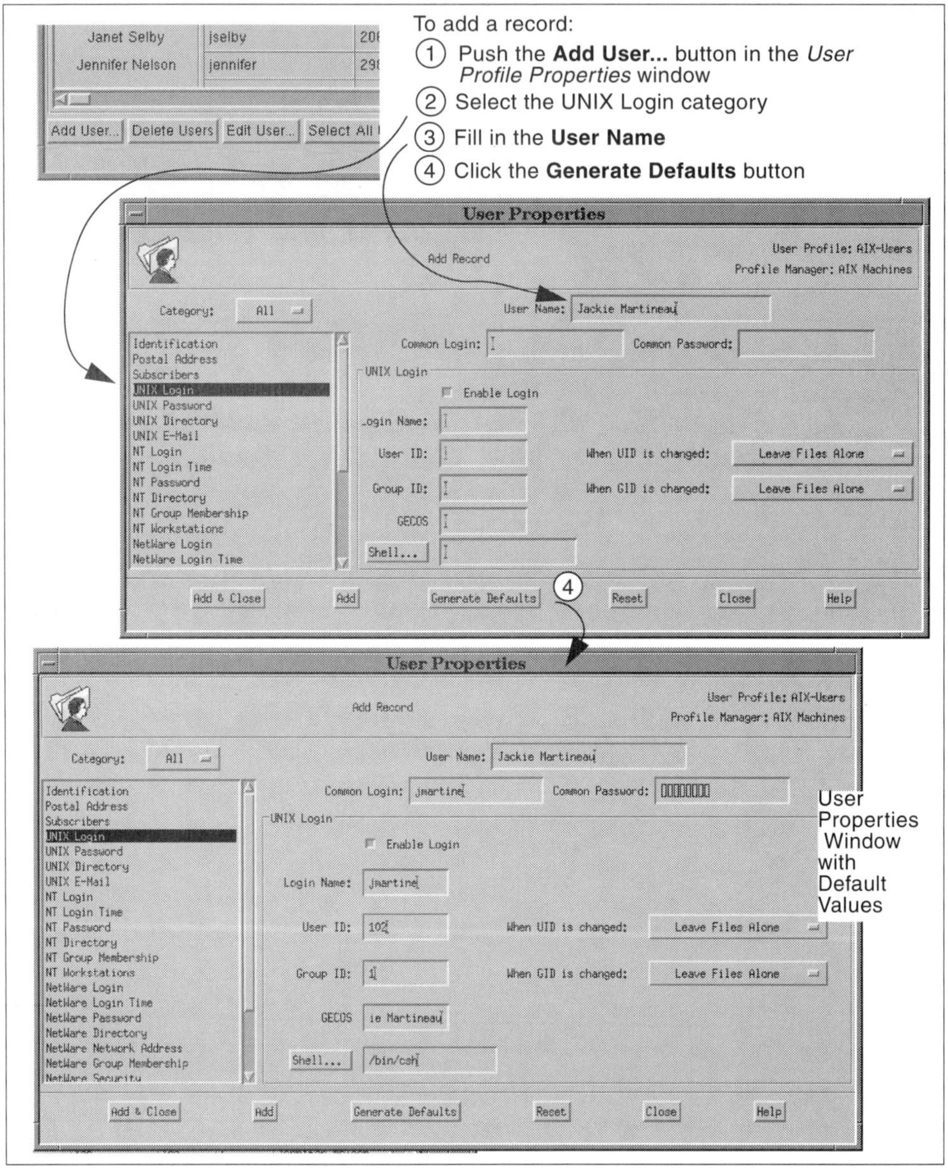

Figure 135. Adding a User Record

Secondly, we create a group record named *Tivoli* that is to contain all administrators (claudio, jennifer, pvaldivi, rlendenm) on our AIX machines. Figure 136 shows how to do this.

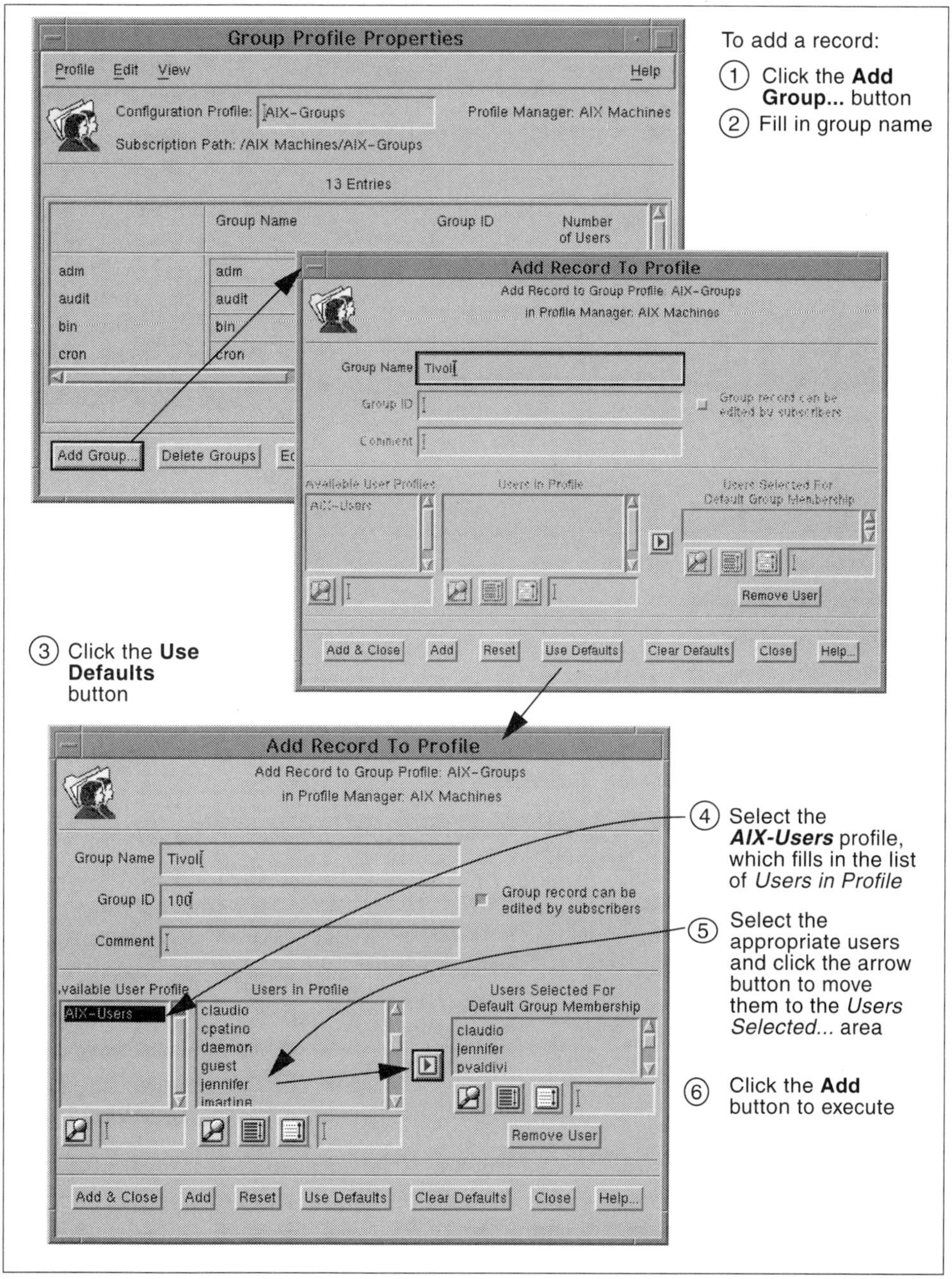

Figure 136. Adding a Group Record

Now let's suppose we want to create a new host entry in our *AIX-Hosts* profile. The new host entry's name should be `itsobig.austin.ibm.com`, and its IP address should be `129.35.224.165`. Also, this host should receive an alias of *itsobig*. See how this is done in Figure 137.

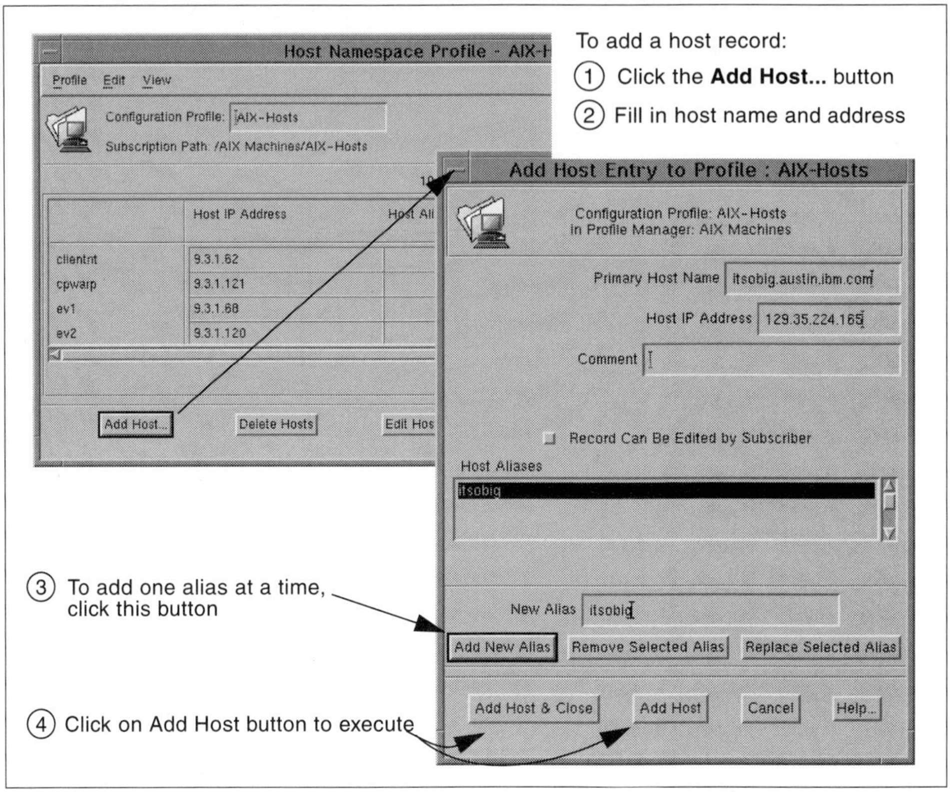

Figure 137. Adding a Host Record

9.2.5 Distributing Profiles

After we have created and populated the profiles, we must distribute them to the subscribers in order to update the configuration files on the managed nodes.

First, we distribute the *AIX-Users* user profile to the subscribers, but the distribution must comply with the following conditions:

- The *AIX-Users* profile should be distributed to the managed nodes *ev7* and *ev2*.
- User *cpatino* should not be distributed to the managed node *ev2* since this user should not get access to that machine.

Figure 138 shows how to set the record-level subscribers for the user *cpatino* in order to prevent this user from being distributed to the managed node *ev2*.

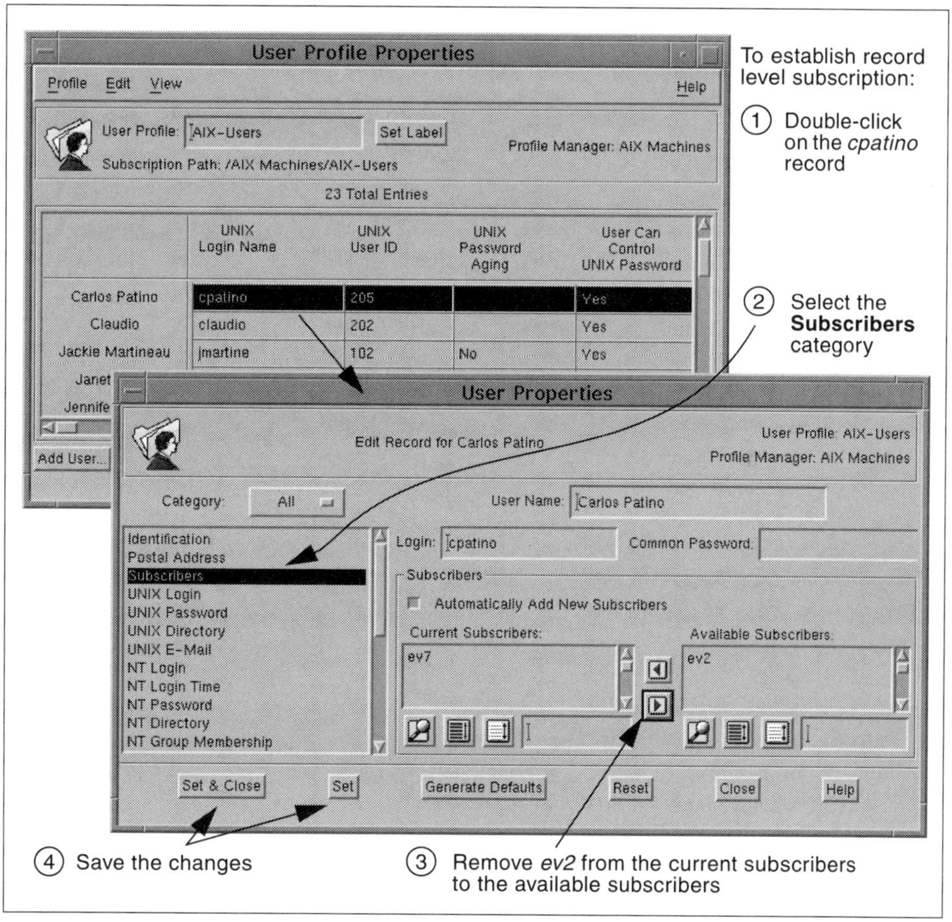

Figure 138. Setting the User Record-Level Subscribers

Now you can distribute the profile to the managed nodes. Figure 139 on page 262 illustrates how to distribute to all levels of subscribers, thereby also updating the corresponding system configuration files.

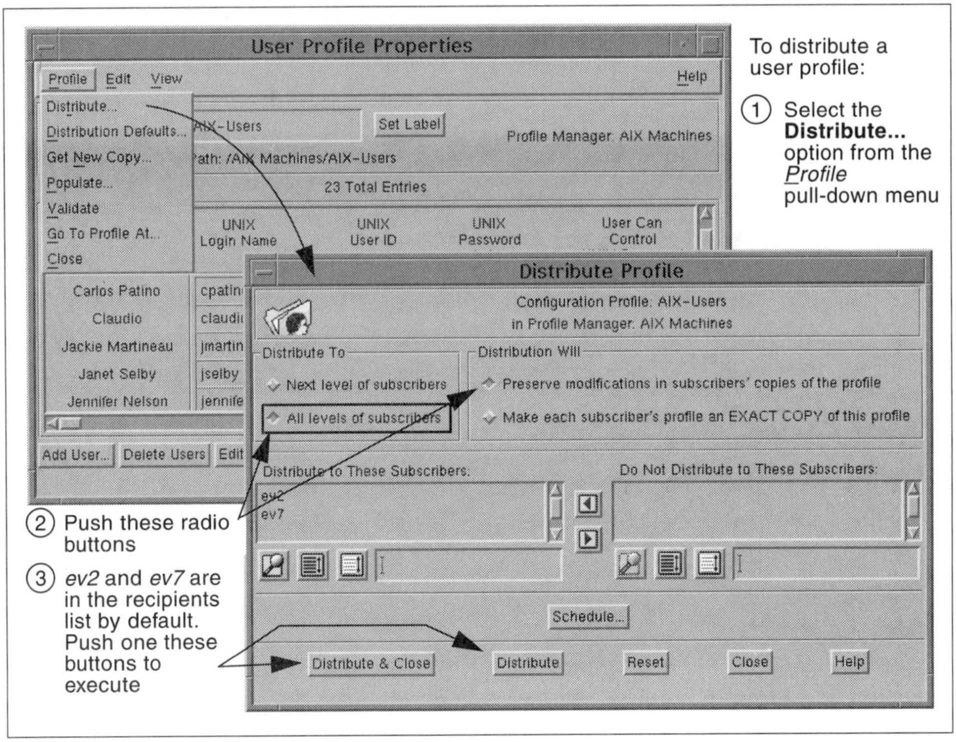

Figure 139. Distributing a User Profile

Distributing a group or host namespace profile works exactly the same as shown in Figure 139 for the user profile. There are no record-level subscribers for these types of profiles.

9.2.6 UNIX Host Management

In this section, we will look at some of the functions that the TME 10 User Administration application provides to manage UNIX hosts. The following list shows the actions that we will perform in order to explain some of the features of the host management capability of TME 10 User Administration. These following actions will be applied to the *ev2* managed node:

- Disabling the *rexec* and the *ftp* services
- Changing the message of the day (MOTD) to *Welcome to the ev2 AIX system*
- Listing all processes running and killing the process *script.sh* owned by user *rlendenm*
- Creating a mail alias called *rlen* for the user *rlendenm*

- Adding the *root* user from *itsobig.austin.ibm.com* as a trusted root on *ev2*

To disable the *rexec* and the *ftp service,* and to change the MOTD on *ev2* from the TME 10 desktop, perform the steps outlined in Figure 140.

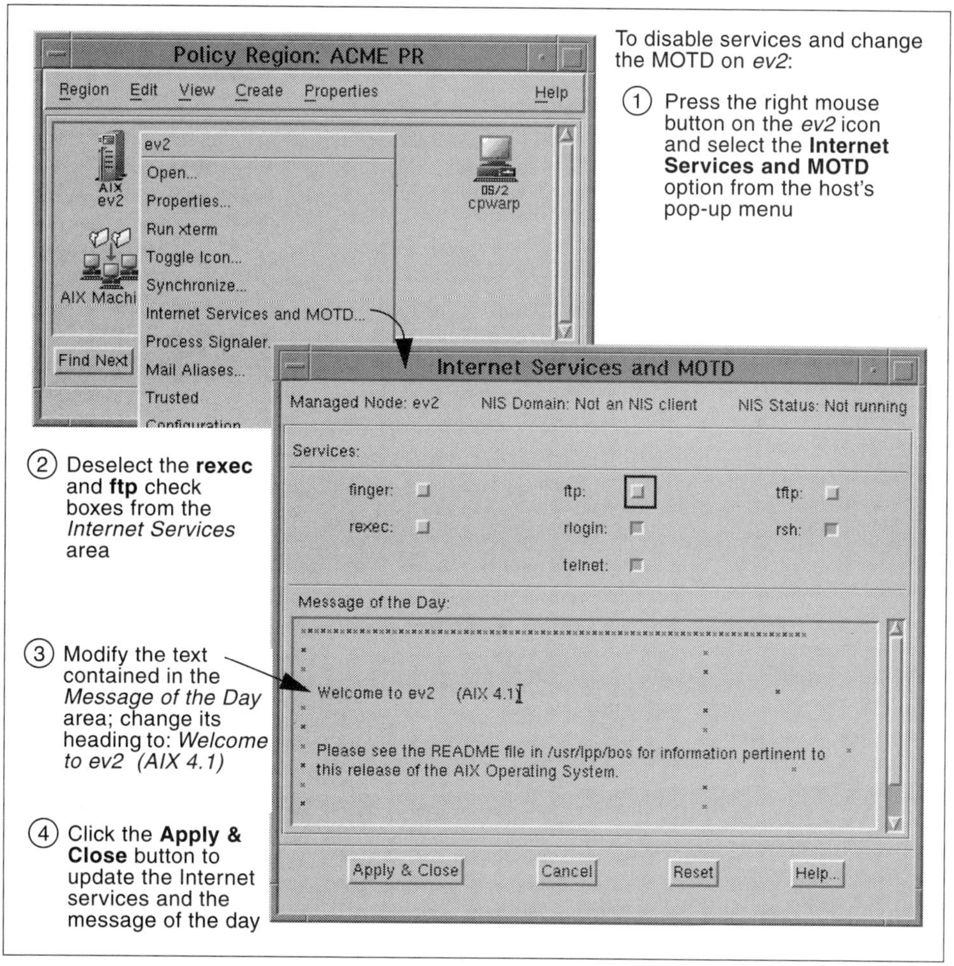

Figure 140. Modifying Internet Services and the Message of the Day

To list all processes running on *ev2* and kill user *rlendenm*'s process *script.sh,* see Figure 141 on page 264.

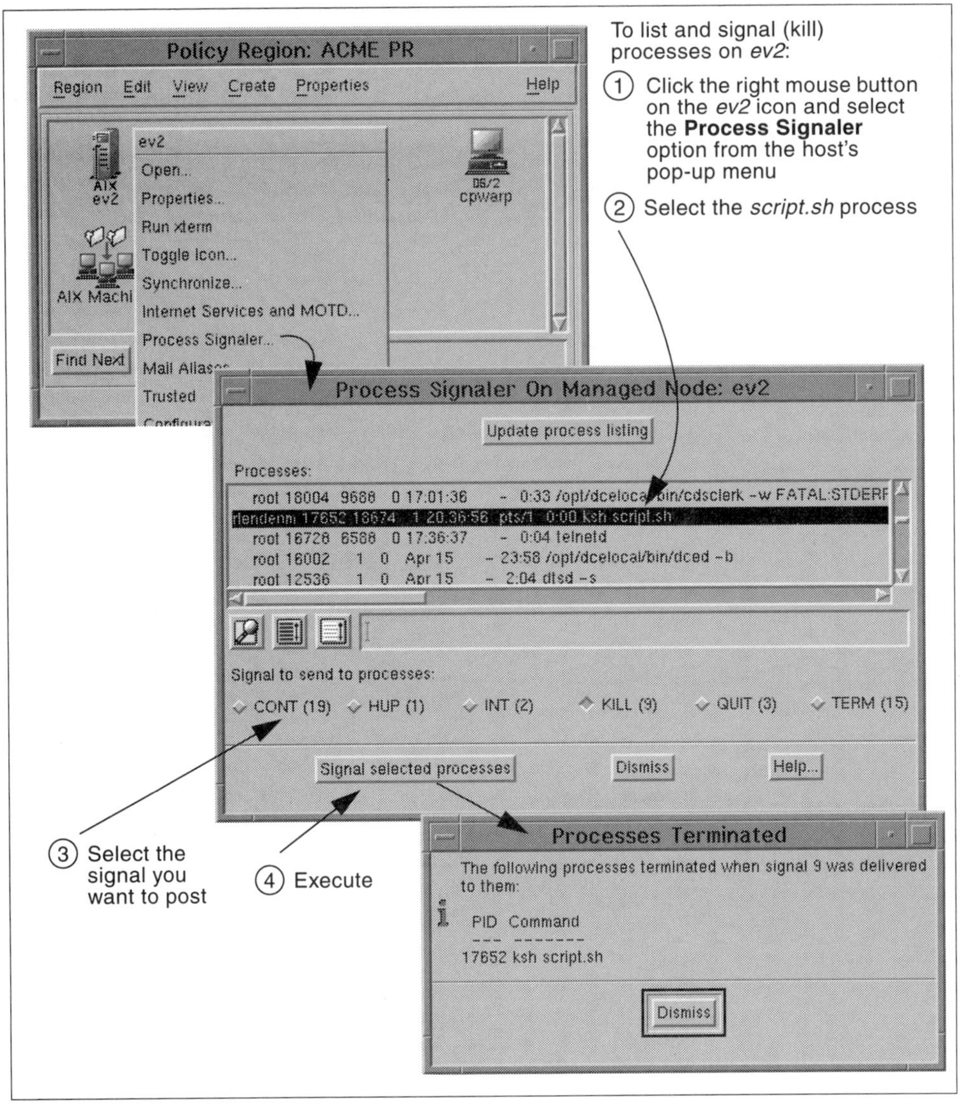

Figure 141. Using the Process Signaler

To create the mail alias called *rlen* for the user *rlendenm* from the TME 10 desktop, see Figure 142 on page 265.

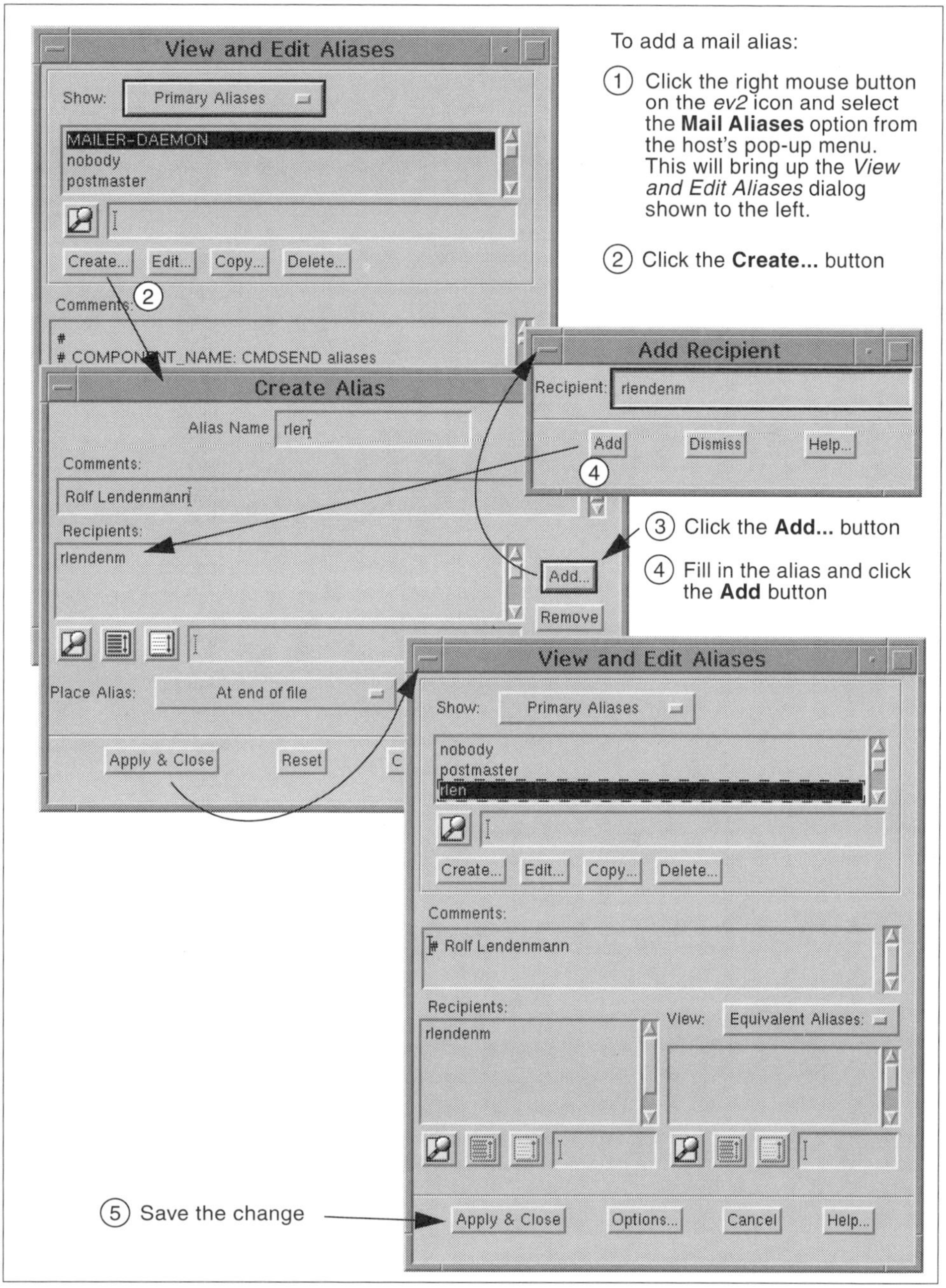

Figure 142. Creating a Mail Alias

To add the *root* user from *itsobig.austin.ibm.com* as a trusted *root* user on *ev2,* see Figure 143 on page 266.

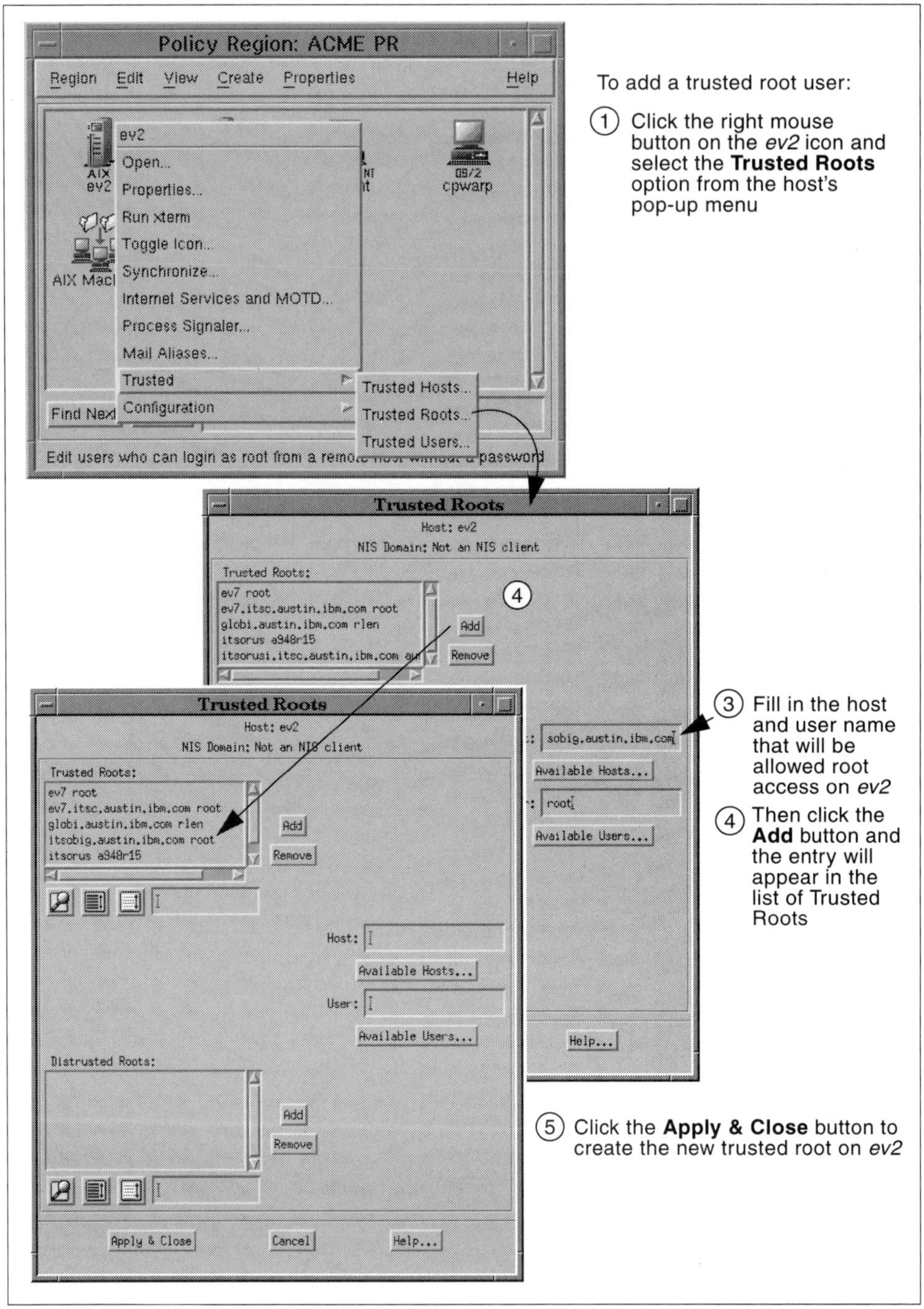

Figure 143. Creating a Trusted Root

CHAPTER 10

Installing and Using TME 10 Software Distribution

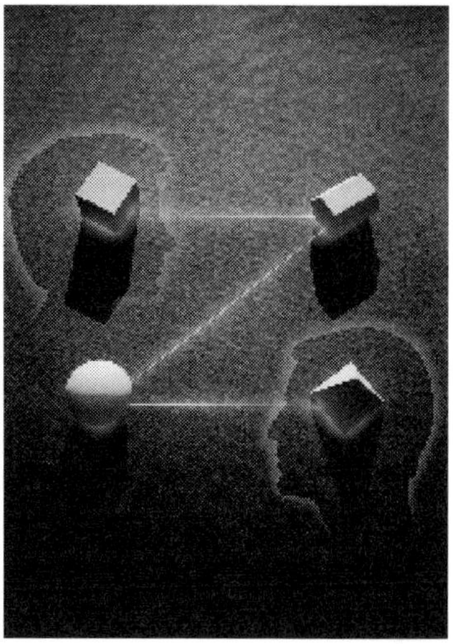

This chapter provides step-by-step installation instructions for the TME 10 Software Distribution product. The first section discusses its installation on the TMR server. Once the installation is complete, the following sections permit you to exercise the basic functions provided by TME 10 Software Distribution.

The purpose of this chapter is to familiarize you with the way these functions work and to deepen your understanding of the concepts explained in Chapter 4, "TME 10 Software Distribution" on page 85. It does not cover every facet and option of this product. In particular, the configuration programs and MDist are not discussed here. For more information on the practical use of these features and other planning issues, refer to the TME 10 Software Distribution User's Guide.

TME 10 Terminology

Please note that the former name of this product was Tivoli/Courier 3.0. When you follow these steps using the TME 10 Software Distribution 3.1 or later, some dialogs might show slightly different titles and/or content, particularly in the installation sections. Most dialogs, however, are common to both versions of software.

10.1 TME 10 Software Distribution Installation

Before installing TME 10 Software Distribution in the TME 10 environment, you must first have the TME 10 Framework and PC agent code installed on the machines you wish to use with TME 10 Software Distribution. There are instructions for doing this in Chapter 8, "Installing and Using the TME 10 Framework" on page 203.

10.1.1 Installing TME 10 Software Distribution on the TMR Server

To install TME 10 Software Distribution on your TMR server, use the following steps:

1. Make sure you have brought up the TME 10 desktop as an administrator with the *install_product* authorization role capability. Make sure you have the TME 10 Software Distribution CD-ROM mounted.

2. From the TME 10 desktop's *Desktop* pull-down menu, choose **Install**, then **Install Product...** This will pop up the window used to install new products in the TME 10 environment. Click the **Select Media...** button if the media is not set correctly for the location of your TME 10 Software Distribution software. Once the media has been set correctly, you should see the window shown in Figure 144.

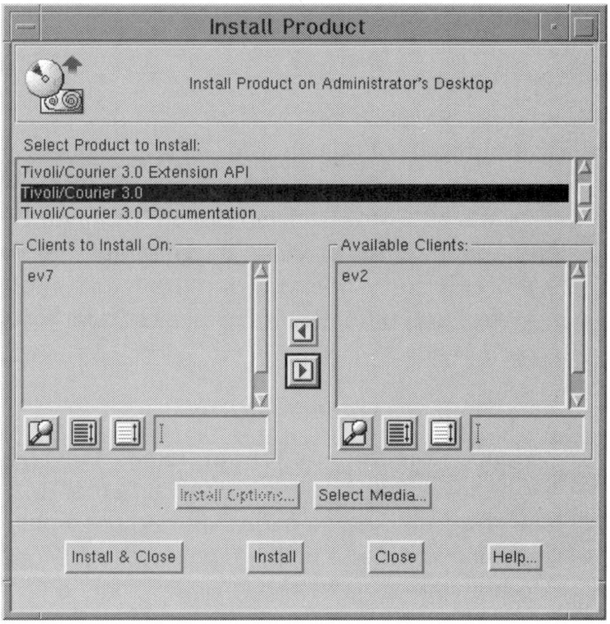

Figure 144. Install Product Dialog for TME 10 Software Distribution

As you can see, there are three choices for the software to choose. You want to install the TME 10 Software Distribution application (or Tivoli/Courier). Move *ev2* to the *Available Clients* section of the window, then click the **Install** or **Install & Close** button to install the software.

3. A status window will appear showing what is going to be installed. You will be asked to press the **Continue Install** button to continue the installation or the **Cancel** button to cancel. Continue the installation and wait for the `Finished product installation` message to appear indicating that the installation is complete. The status window is shown in Figure 145.

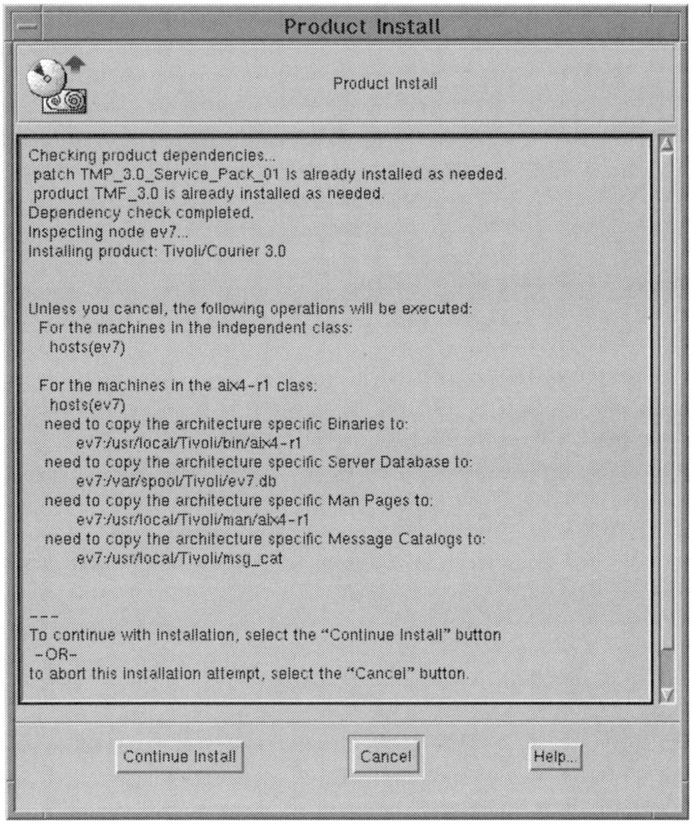

Figure 145. TME 10 Software Distribution Installation Status Dialog

Click the **Close** button on the status window. The installation of TME 10 Software Distribution is now complete on your server and UNIX machines.

AIX 4.1 on POWER2

On POWER2 architecture-based RS/6000 machines that run AIX 4.1, you need to install patch cou30001 found on the Tivoli/Courier 3.0 CD-ROM.

10.2 Practical Examples of Using TME 10 Software Distribution

We now go through some practical examples of using the TME 10 Software Distribution product. These examples assume that one is familiar with setting up the TMR, creating a policy region, setting managed resource types for a policy region, and creating a profile manager. These steps were explained in:

- Section 8.2.4, "Creating and Populating a Policy Region" on page 225
- Section 8.2.8, "Creating a New Profile Manager" on page 232

For our example, we have created a policy region called *Software Distribution* on TME 10 desktop level and assigned *ProfileManager* and *FilePackage* to be a valid managed resource type for this policy region. We have also created a profile manager called *FrameMaker* in the new policy region.

10.2.1 Our Lab Environment

The lab environment to be used for this tutorial is as follows:

TMR Server

- ***ev7*** – RS/6000 running AIX 4.1.4 (TME 10 Framework, TME 10 Software Distribution with patch cou30001 installed)

TME 10 Clients

- ***clientnt*** – PC running Windows NT (PC agent installed)
- ***jnwin95*** – PC running Windows 95 (PC agent installed)
- ***cpwarp*** – PC running OS/2 (PC agent installed)
- ***ev2*** – RS/6000 running AIX 4.1.4 (TME 10 Framework installed)

10.2.2 Creating a TME 10 Software Distribution File Package

Two of the three client workstations used to write this book run FrameMaker locally, whereas the OS/2 platform is not directly supported by FrameMaker. So, Carlos runs FrameMaker off an AIX server, *ev2*, using the X Windows emulation under OS/2. The book is written in a new 7" x 9" FrameMaker template. The files comprising these templates are in the /fp/RB_small directory on *ev7*. The templates need to be distributed to all AIX machines as well as *jnwin95* and *clientnt*.

We create a TME 10 Software Distribution file package called *RB Small* in the profile manager *FrameMaker*. This step is shown in Figure 146 on page 273.

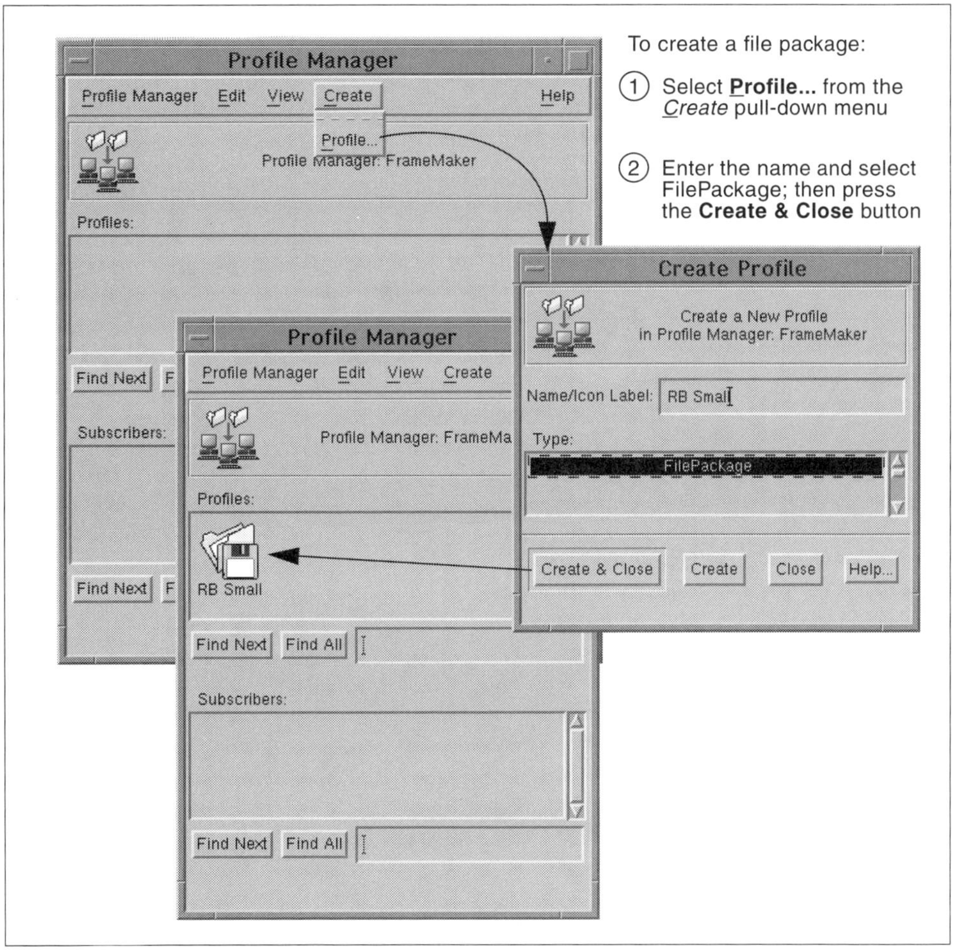

Figure 146. Creating a TME 10 Software Distribution File Package

10.2.3 Customizing the File Package

Once the file package is created, we can customize it. The /fp/RB_small directory on *ev7* holds the FrameMaker templates that we want to make available on *ev7* and *ev2* (AIX) as well as on *jnwin95* (Windows 95) and *clientnt* (Windows NT). On the target systems we need to specify the parent directory into which the RB_small directory will be copied with its subdirectories.

The /fp/RB_small directory must exist on the source host *ev7*, whereas the target directories are created if necessary. Figure 147 on page 274 shows how a file package is created.

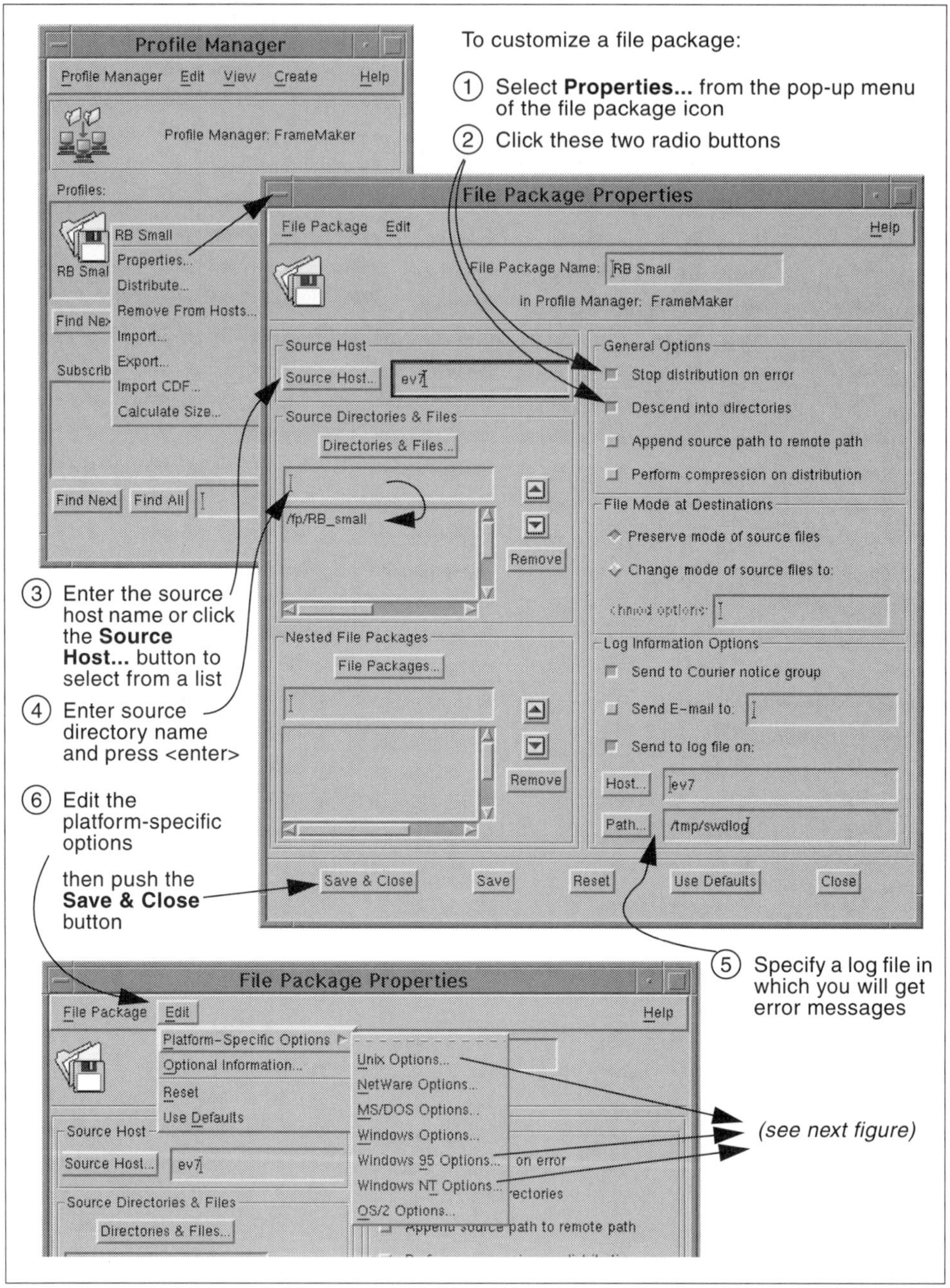

Figure 147. Customizing the TME 10 Software Distribution File Package

Figure 148 on page 275 shows the different platform-specific file package option dialogs in which we need to specify the target directory path.

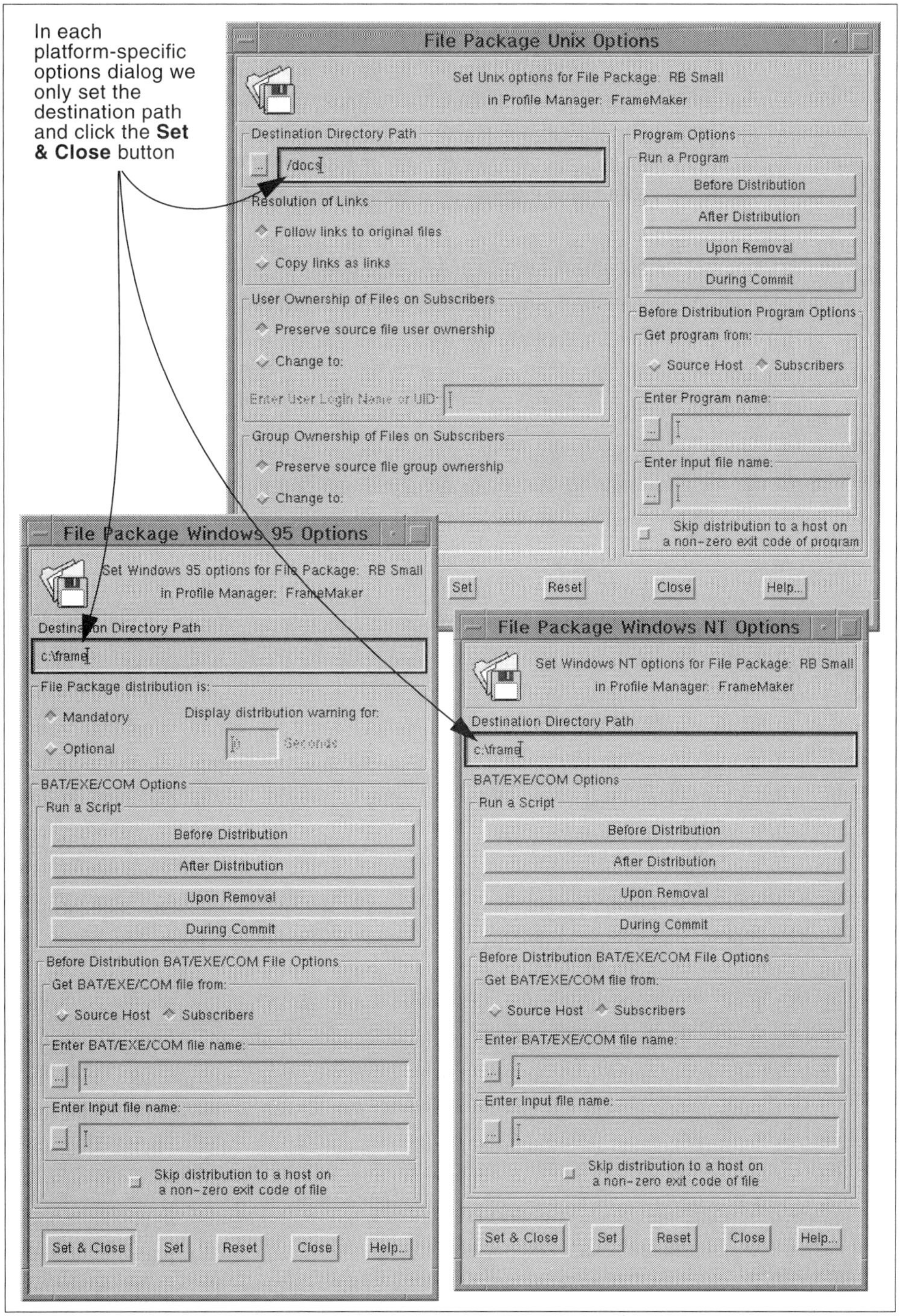

Figure 148. Customizing Platform-Specific Options

Note: All files are copied in binary. If ASCII text files are to be transmitted, we have to have separate source directories for distributions to, for instance, UNIX and Windows 95 systems, due to the different handling of line ends. Since one file package cannot distinguish between different sources, we would have to have different file packages and possibly nest them into one higher-level file package. Our example only contains files in FrameMaker's binary document format, and we get away with just one file package.

10.2.4 Distributing the File Package

Before we can distribute the file package, we need to add subscribers to the FrameMaker profile manager. In Section 8.2.9, "Adding Subscribers" on page 232, we explained the different methods for adding subscribers. In Figure 149 we drag and drop subscribers into the FrameMaker profile manager.

In order to simplify the distribution configuration, we use the AIX Machines profile manager created in Section 8.2.8, "Creating a New Profile Manager" on page 232, as a subscriber. It contains the *ev2* and *ev7* UNIX nodes and no profiles.

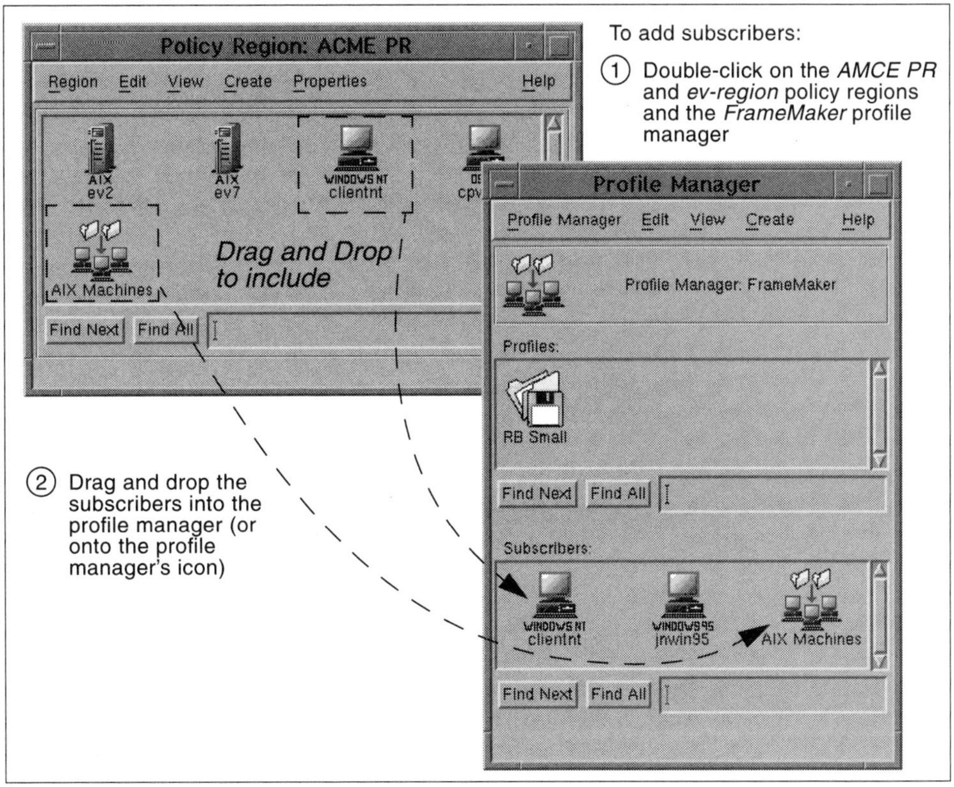

Figure 149. Adding Subscribers to a Profile Manager

Now our view of this profile manager, *FrameMaker*, appears with three (partially nested) subscribers. Next, we distribute the file package to all subscribers. Figure 150 explains how this can be done.

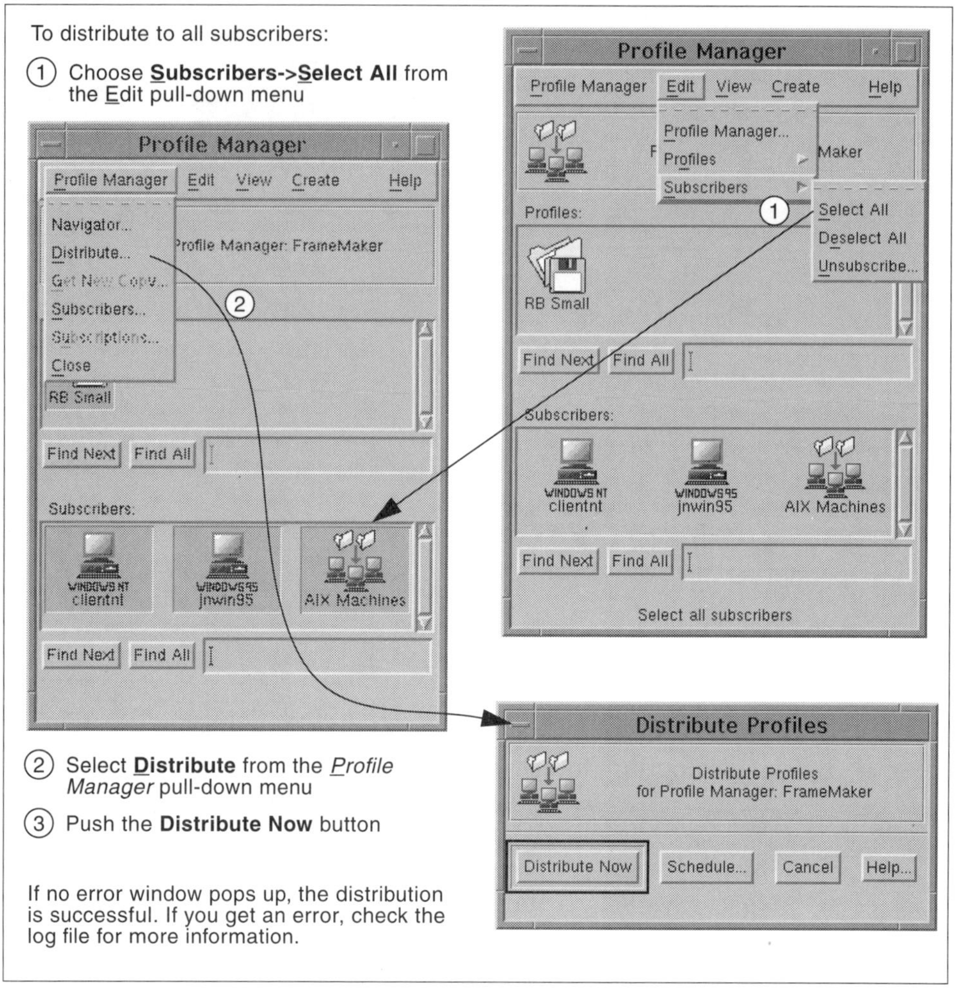

Figure 150. Distributing a File Package to All Subscribers

Instead of distributing to all subscribers, you could just drag a file package and drop it onto a specific subscriber.

10.2.5 Subscribing to the Software Distribution Notice Group

An administrator that deals with software distribution must subscribe to the appropriate notice group. Notice groups are one way to check success or failure of a software distribution. Figure 151 shows how to assign notice groups to an administrator.

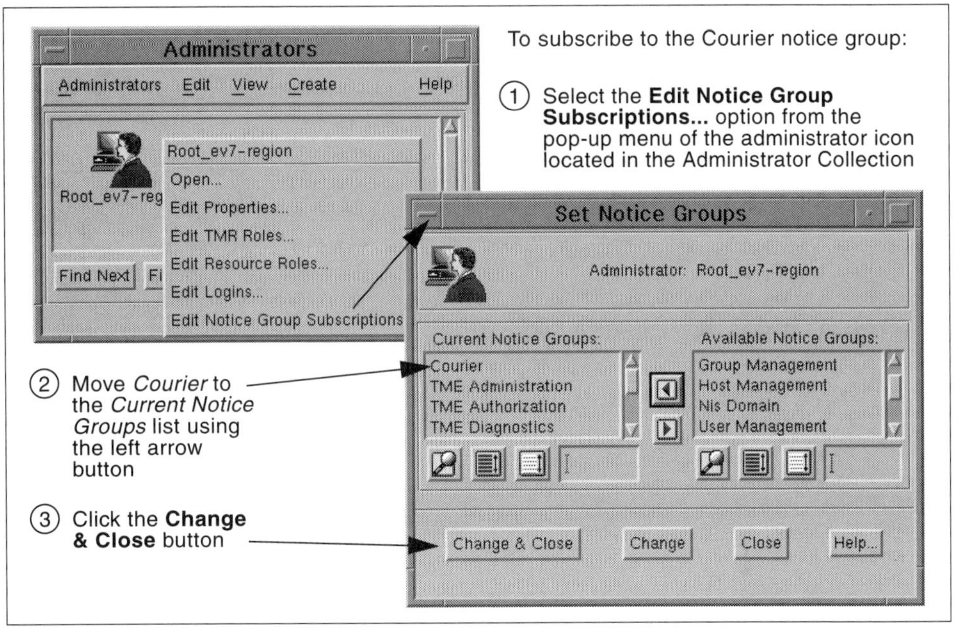

Figure 151. Selling Notice Groups for Software Distribution

10.2.6 Checking the Log File and the Notice Group

It is important to activate the logfile option in the file package because it contains more detailed information in case an error occurs. The pop-up window that the administrator gets only says that something went wrong but not exactly what. Let's look at the logfile first:

```
# cat /tmp/swdlog
File Package:   "RB Small"
Operation:      install  (m=5)
Finished:       Tue Apr  8 09:42:02 1997
--------
Source messages:
<none>
--------
ev2:SUCCESS
--------
ev7:SUCCESS
--------
clientnt:SUCCESS
c:\frame: creating path
--------
jnwin95:SUCCESS
c:\frame: creating path
================
```

The log file proves that the distribution was successful. On the Windows 95 and the Window NT system, the directory had to be created. The templates are now under c:\frame\RB_small.

Now let's check what we received in the notice group. See the example in Figure 152.

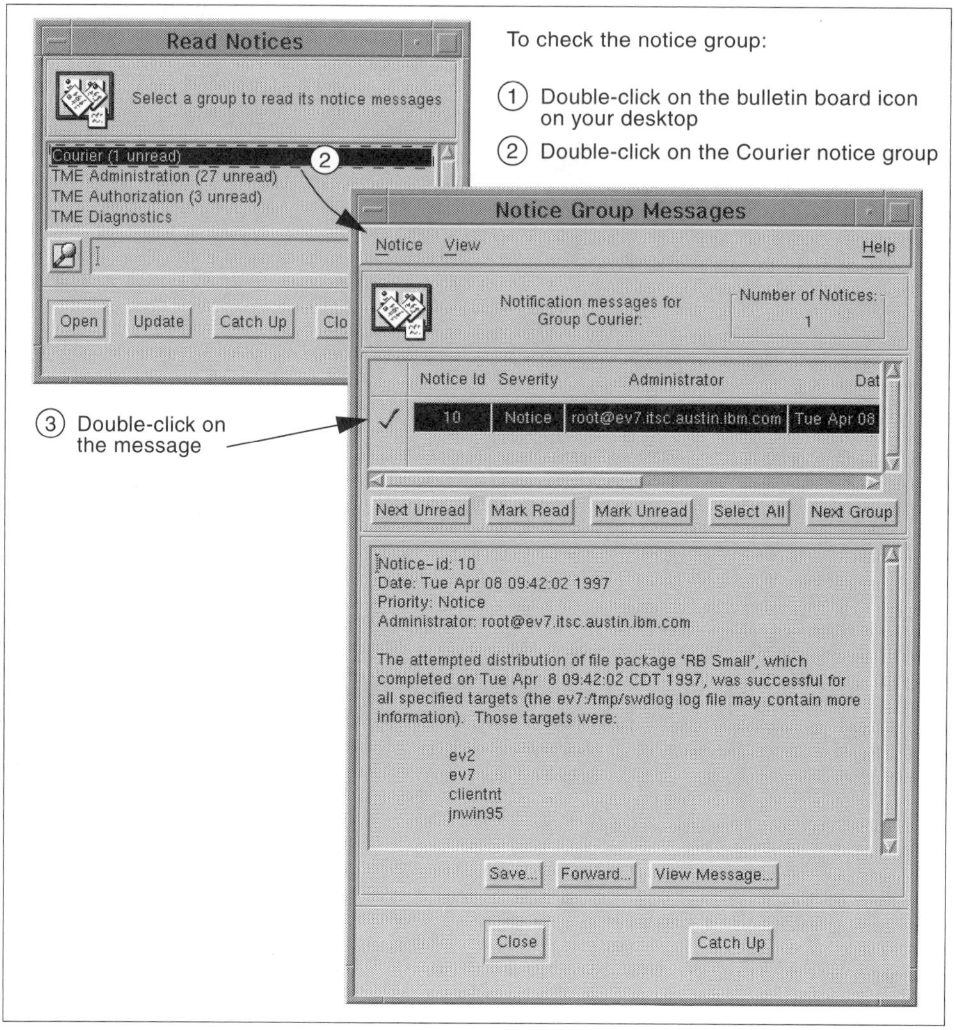

CHAPTER 11

Installing and Using TME 10 Inventory

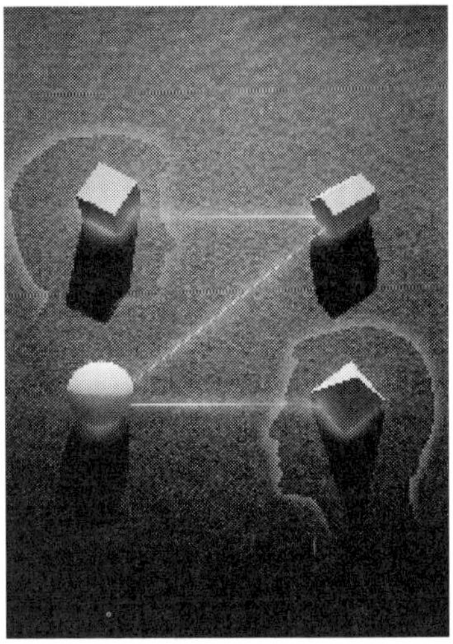

This chapter provides you with step-by-step installation instructions for the TME 10 Inventory product. The first section discusses the TME 10 Inventory installation on the TMR server and on the managed nodes in our TMR. Once the installation is complete, the following sections permit you to exercise the basic functions provided by TME 10 Inventory.

The purpose of this chapter is to make you familiar with the way these functions work and to deepen your understanding of the concepts explained in Chapter 5, "TME 10 Inventory" on page 111. It does not cover every facet and option of this product.

TME 10 Terminology

Please note that the former name of this product was Tivoli/Inventory 3.0. When you follow these steps using the TME 10 Inventory 3.1 or later, some dialogs might show slightly different titles and/or content, particularly in the installation sections. Most dialogs, however, are common to both versions of software.

11.1 TME 10 Inventory Installation

Before installing TME 10 Inventory in the TME 10 environment, you must first have the TME 10 Framework and PC agent installed on the machines you wish to use with TME 10 Inventory. There are instructions for doing this in Chapter 8, "Installing and Using the TME 10 Framework" on page 203. You must also have your Relational Database Management System (RDBMS) installed. We used Oracle on an AIX V4 server in our test environment, and for your convenience, we list the database installation instructions. However, this should not indicate a preference over any other RDBMS system.

11.1.1 Installing the RDBMS System

The RDBMS should be installed before you install TME 10 Inventory. If there is already a supported RDBMS installed that you may use, contact your database administrator for getting and/or setting up the required parameters and tables.

To perform a fresh installation of Oracle, follow these steps:

1. Create a *dba* group:

   ```
   # mkgroup -A dba
   ```

2. Create a user ID named oracle:

   ```
   # mkuser pgrp=dba groups=dba home=/home/oracle oracle
   ```

3. Create an Oracle program directory (ORACLE_HOME), for instance /usr/local/oracle, and set ownership and permissions:

   ```
   # mkdir /usr/local/oracle
   # chown oracle.dba /usr/local/oracle
   # chmod 755 /usr/local/oracle
   ```

   We suggest to create and mount a separate file system to hold the Oracle code. We needed 280 MB of disk space for the Oracle installation.

4. Create an Oracle documentation directory:

   ```
   # mkdir /usr/local/oracle/oracle_doc
   # chown oracle.dba /usr/local/oracle/oracle_doc
   # chmod 755 /usr/local/oracle/oracle_doc
   ```

5. Create the /usr/local/bin directory, if not done yet.

6. Insert and mount the ORACLE installation CD-ROM:

   ```
   # mount /cdrom
   ```

   If you have not created a CD-ROM file system, do the following:

   ```
   # mkdir /cdrom
   # chmod 777 /cdrom
   # mount -rv cdrfs /dev/cd0 /cdrom
   ```

7. Create a local Oracle installation directory that links to the CD-ROM files:

   ```
   # mkdir /usr/local/oracle_link
   # chmod 777 /usr/local/oracle_link
   ```

   This directory needs about 50 MB of disk space.

8. Create a shell script that sets the environment variables for Oracle. For this purpose, we create a /usr/local/bin/db_setup.sh file with the following content:

```
#!/bin/ksh
export ORACLE_OWNER=oracle
export ORACLE_HOME=/usr/local/oracle
export ORACLE_DOC=/usr/local/oracle_doc
export PATH=$ORACLE_HOME/bin:/usr/local/bin:$PATH
export ORACLE_SID=sid1
export ORACLE_TERM=lft
```

9. Add the new script to user oracle's .profile:

```
# echo ". /usr/local/bin/db_setup.sh" >> /home/oracle/.profile
```

10. Log in as oracle, and create the program links from the UNIX file names to the CD-ROM files (takes about ten minutes to complete):

```
# su - oracle
$ cd /cdrom/orainst
$ ./start.sh
$ exit
```

11. Install the post-wait driver kernel extension (as root):

```
# cd /usr/local/oracle_link/orainst
# ./rootpre.sh
```

Observe the messages. If a previous version of the kernel extensions is found, then you need to reboot the system now, then remount the CR-ROM.

12. Install the Oracle code as user oracle (takes about one hour):

```
# su - oracle
$ umask
022                          <<- Make sure the output is 022
$ id
uid=204(oracle) gid=200(dba)
$ pwd
/usr/local/oracle_link/orainst
$ ./orainst
$ exit
```

During the installation, you need to answer a lot of questions, so stand by. We chose the default values or entered the values we defined beforehand for the Oracle directory (/usr/local/oracle), Oracle owner (oracle), and the database ID (sid1). Select the following components for installation:

- Oracle Data Query
- Oracle Easy*SQL

- Oracle UNIX Installer and Documentation
- ORACLE7 Server (RDBMS)
- SQL*Net V2
- SQL*PLUS
- TCP/IP Protocol Adapter (V2)

13. Run the post-installation task (as root):

```
# . /usr/local/bin/db_setup.sh
# cd $ORACLE_HOME/orainst
# sh ./root.sh
```

Continue if you get a message telling you that ORACLE_HOME is not the same as the home directory for this user.

14. If you want to bring up the system at reboot time:

- Edit the /etc/oratab file and change a line:

```
from: sid1:/usr/local/oracle:N
to:   sid1:/usr/local/oracle:Y
```

- Then add the following lines to the /etc/inittab file:

```
mkitab "oracle:2:wait:/bin/su oracle -c /usr/local/oracle/bin/dbstart"
```

Oracle Installation Problem

In order for TME 10 Inventory to successfully access the RDBMS server, all operating system users must be able to log in to SQL with the database administrator ID. For instance, try the following as user nobody:

```
# su - nobody
$ . /usr/local/bin/db_setup.sh
$ sqlplus sys/oracle
```

If you get a normal `SQL>` prompt and no error messages, TME 10 Inventory should work. In the Oracle release (7.1.4.1.0) that we are using, the `oracle` process is not defined with the correct permission bits. So, we had to perform the following steps (as user oracle):

```
# su - oracle
$ chmod 6751 /usr/local/oracle/bin/oracle
$ dbshut
$ dbstart
```

After these steps, user nobody can successfully log in.

11.1.2 Installing Inventory on TMR Server and UNIX Machines

To install TME 10 Inventory on your TMR server and the UNIX systems in your TME 10 environment, use the following steps:

1. Make sure you have brought up the TME 10 desktop as an administrator with the *install_product* authorization role capability. Make sure you have the TME 10 Inventory CD-ROM mounted.

2. From the TME 10 desktop's *Desktop* menu, choose **Install -> Install Product...** This will pop up the window used to install new products in the TME 10 environment. Click the **Select Media...** button if the media is not set correctly for the location of your TME 10 Inventory software. Once the media has been set correctly, you should see the dialog shown in Figure 153.

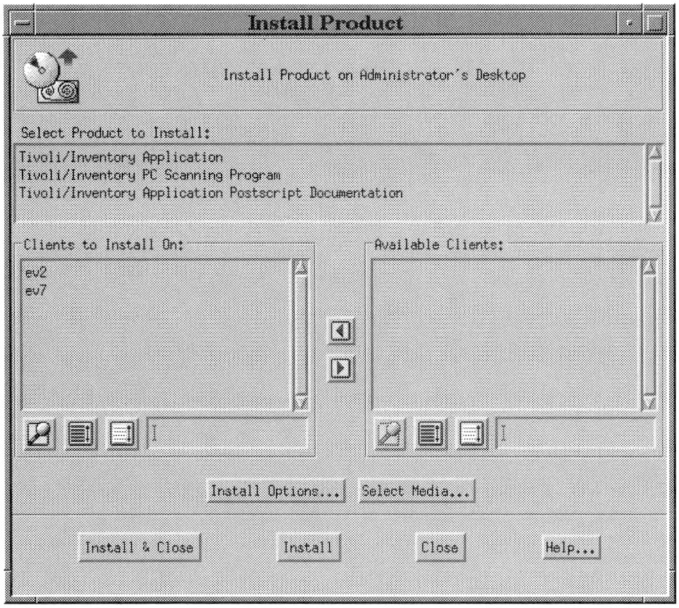

Figure 153. Install Product Dialog with TME 10 Inventory Software Options

As you can see, there are three choices for software installation. You want to install the TME 10 Inventory Application. Select this, and another window will pop up.

3. The *Install Options* window now appears and lets you set the options for connecting the TME 10 Inventory application with the relational database. This window is shown in Figure 154 on page 288. You will have to enter the following information:

   - Database Vendor – Choose either **Sybase** or **Oracle** as the vendor.

- TME RDBMS Access Host – Enter the name of a machine that has SQL*Net access to the relational database server. If it is the TMR server itself, leave the default entry in this field, *ALI_host*.
- Database ID – Enter the name of the database. For Oracle, it is the value of the ORACLE_SID environment variable; for Sybase, it is the name of the database.
- Database Home – Enter the home directory where the database software resides.
- Server ID – Leave empty; we are not using SQL*Net.

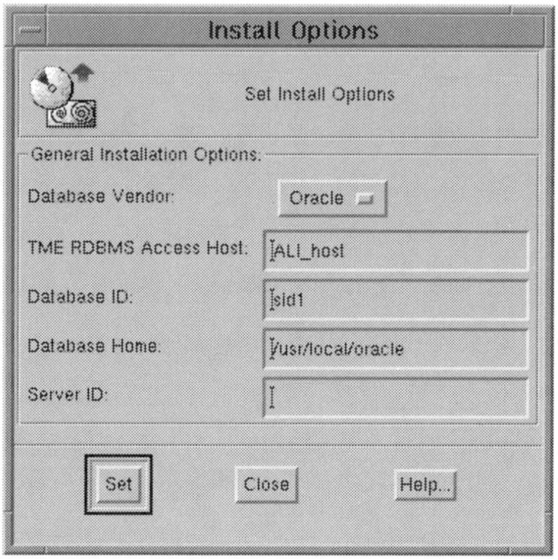

Figure 154. Installation Options for TME 10 Inventory

Once the installation information has been entered, click the **Set** button to continue.

4. You will then see the first window again. Move all of the clients you wish to install to the *Clients to Install On* section of the window. When the clients are set, click the **Install** button to install the software and to also leave the install program window on the screen after the installation is complete.

5. A status dialog will appear showing what is going to be installed. You will be asked to click the **Continue Install** button to continue the installation or the **Cancel** button to cancel. Continue the installation and wait for the `Finished product installation` message to appear so you know that the installation is complete. The status dialog is shown in Figure 155 on page 289.

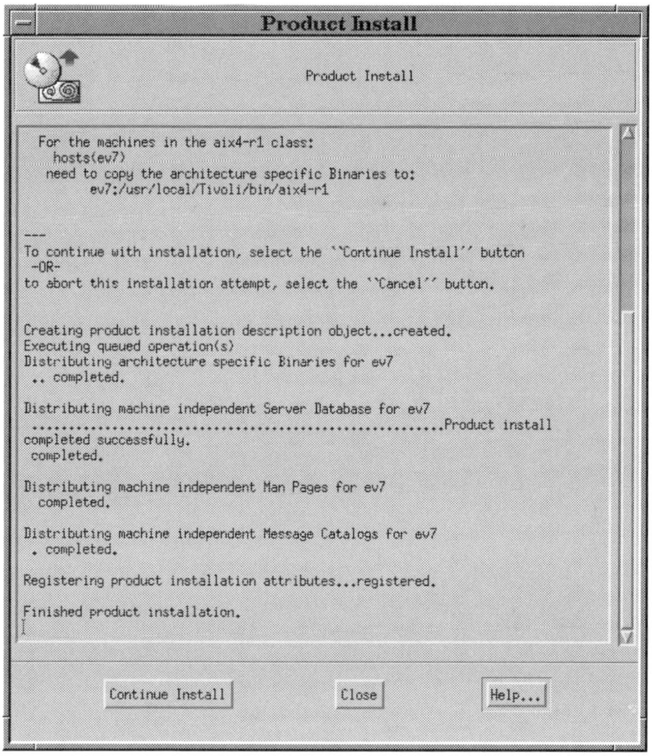

Figure 155. TME 10 Inventory Installation Status Dialog

Click the **Close** button on the status dialog. The installation of TME 10 Inventory is now complete on your server and UNIX machines.

11.1.3 Configuring the Relational Database

Once the software has been installed, you must configure the relational database to work with the TME 10 Inventory product. You must create a database administrator and also create the database tables. Tivoli provides the scripts to perform these functions in the $BINDIR/TAS/RIM/SQL/scripts directory for UNIX machines.

Use the following steps to configure the relational database with an Oracle relational database. For instructions on using Sybase, please refer to the *TME 10 Inventory User's Guide*.

1. As user oracle, change to the $BINDIR/TAS/RIM/SQL/scripts directory:

```
# su - oracle
$ . /etc/Tivoli/setup_env.sh
```

```
$ cd $BINDIR/TAS/RIM/SQL/scripts
```

2. Log in to the relational database server machine as *sys* using the `sqlplus` command (we set the password to *oracle*):

```
$ sqlplus sys/oracle
```

3. Enter the following command:

```
SQL> @tivoli_ora_admin.sql
```

   This will create the database user ID *tivoli*, and also the tablespace required.

4. Log out of the database by entering `quit` at the command line.
5. Log in to the relational database server machine as *tivoli* using the `sqlplus` command.
6. Enter the following command:

```
SQL> @tivoli_ora_schema.sql
```

   This command will create the database schema by adding tables and views required for the TME 10 Inventory database. During the initial running of this script, you will see some errors due to the fact that the script is trying to delete some tables that have not yet been created. This is normal and can be disregarded.

This should complete the relational database setup. You can test this by logging into the database as the user tivoli and running the following command:

```
SQL> select * from INVENTORYDATA;
```

This should return with a message saying that no rows were found. If you receive a message saying that INVENTORYDATA is unknown, there is a problem. The following command lists all tables owned by TIVOLI:

```
SQL> select * from all_catalog where owner='TIVOLI';
```

11.1.4 Installing TME 10 Inventory on PCs

Make sure that your PC Agents are at level 4.005 or higher. The instructions for installing the PC scanning component follow:

1. The install product window should still be on the screen after performing the install process for the server and UNIX platforms. If not, follow steps 1 and 2 in Section 11.1.2, "Installing Inventory on TMR Server and UNIX Machines" on page 286. Choose the *TME 10 Inventory PC Scanning*

Program from the list of products to install by clicking on this selection in the list of products.

2. After you select this, a window will appear that allows you to set the remote directory for the install of this software. By default, the directory is `/TIVOLI`. This will store the software in the `C:\TIVOLI` directory. The window is shown in Figure 156.

Figure 156. Option for PC Scanning Component Installation

Enter the installation directory, and click the **Set** button.

3. You are now returned to the product installation window shown in Figure 153 on page 287. Move the clients you wish to install to the *Clients to Install On* section of the window, and click the **Install & Close** button.

4. A status window will appear showing the status of installation. Wait for the `Finished product installation` message to appear. Once you see this message, you can click the **Close** button. The installation is now complete.

11.2 Practical Examples of Using TME 10 Inventory

We now go through some practical examples of using the TME 10 Inventory product. These examples assume that one is familiar with setting up the TME, creating a policy region, and creating a profile manager. For our example, we have created a profile manager called *Inventory* in the policy region called *ACME PR*. We have subscribed some machines (*ev7* and *jnwin95*) to that profile manager. We have also assigned *InventoryProfile* to be a valid managed resource type for this policy region.

11.2.1 Our Lab Environment

The lab environment to be used for this tutorial is as follows:

TMR Server

- ***ev7*** – RS/6000 running AIX 4.1.4 (TME 10 Framework, TME 10 Inventory installed)

TME 10 Clients

- ***jnwin95*** – PC running Windows 95 (PC agent installed)

11.2.2 Creating an TME 10 Inventory Profile

To create an TME 10 Inventory profile, we first open the profile manager *Inventory* and then choose the *Create* menu's **Profile...** option. This brings up a window that allows us to choose the type of profile to be *InventoryProfile* and to name our profile. In this example, we named the profile *Scan*. We click the **Create & Close** button, and the new profile is added to our profile manager, as shown in Figure 157. The icon for the Inventory profile has a flashlight.

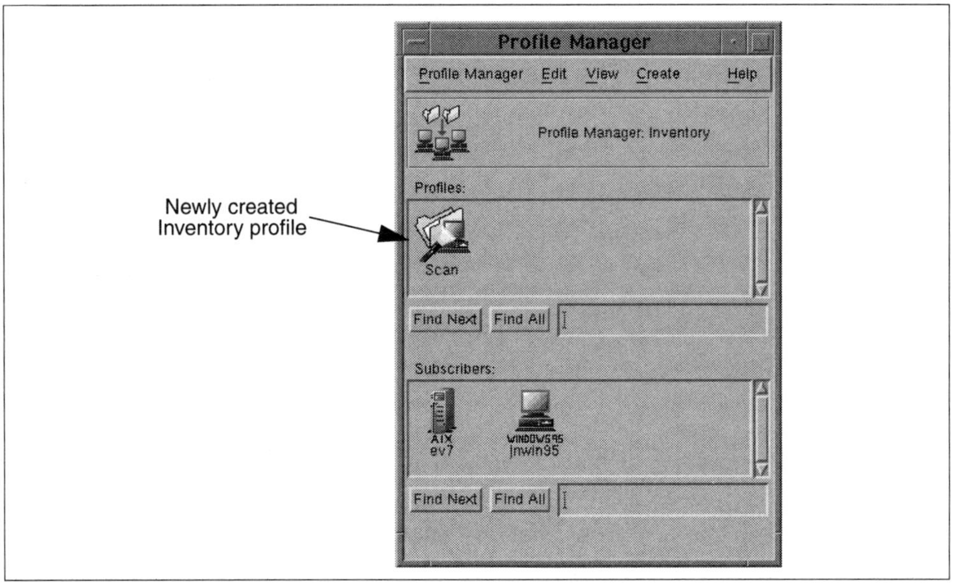

Figure 157. Profile Manager with TME 10 Inventory Profile

11.2.3 Customizing the TME 10 Inventory Profile

Once the profile is created, you can then use the pop-up menu for that icon, and choose the **Customize...** option to customize the inventory scan. This will pop up the window shown in Figure 158 on page 293.

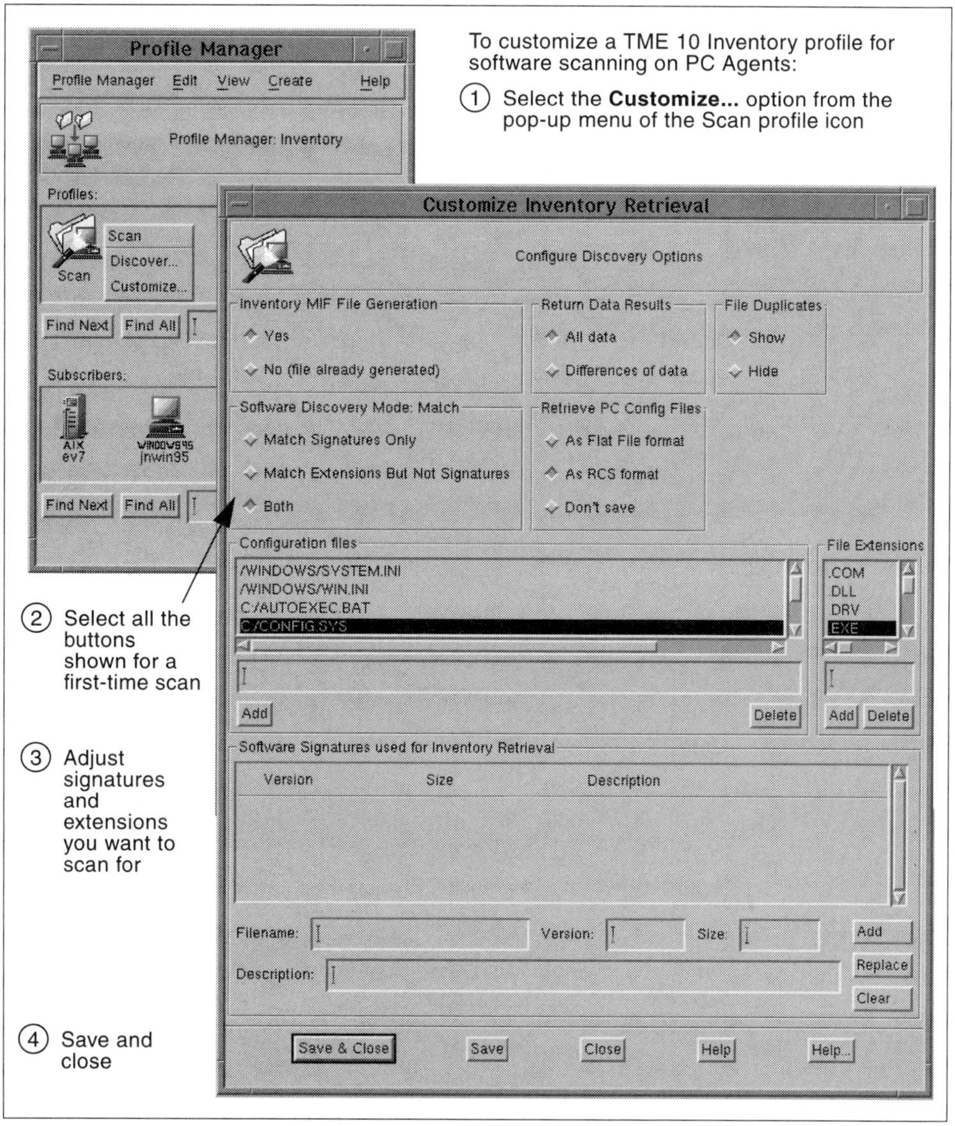

Figure 158. Customizing the TME 10 Inventory Profile

Note that no customization is necessary on UNIX nodes; it would not have any effect. So, on UNIX nodes, you can create the profile and immediately distribute it by dragging the profile icon onto the UNIX node subscriber icon.

11.2.4 Distributing the TME 10 Inventory Profile

When distributing the profile, it scans the hardware configuration of UNIX managed nodes as well as hardware and software configuration of PCs. It takes awhile until the scan is completed. Figure 159 illustrates the steps to perform an inventory scan on a UNIX machine (*ev7*) and a Windows 95 machine (*jnwin95*).

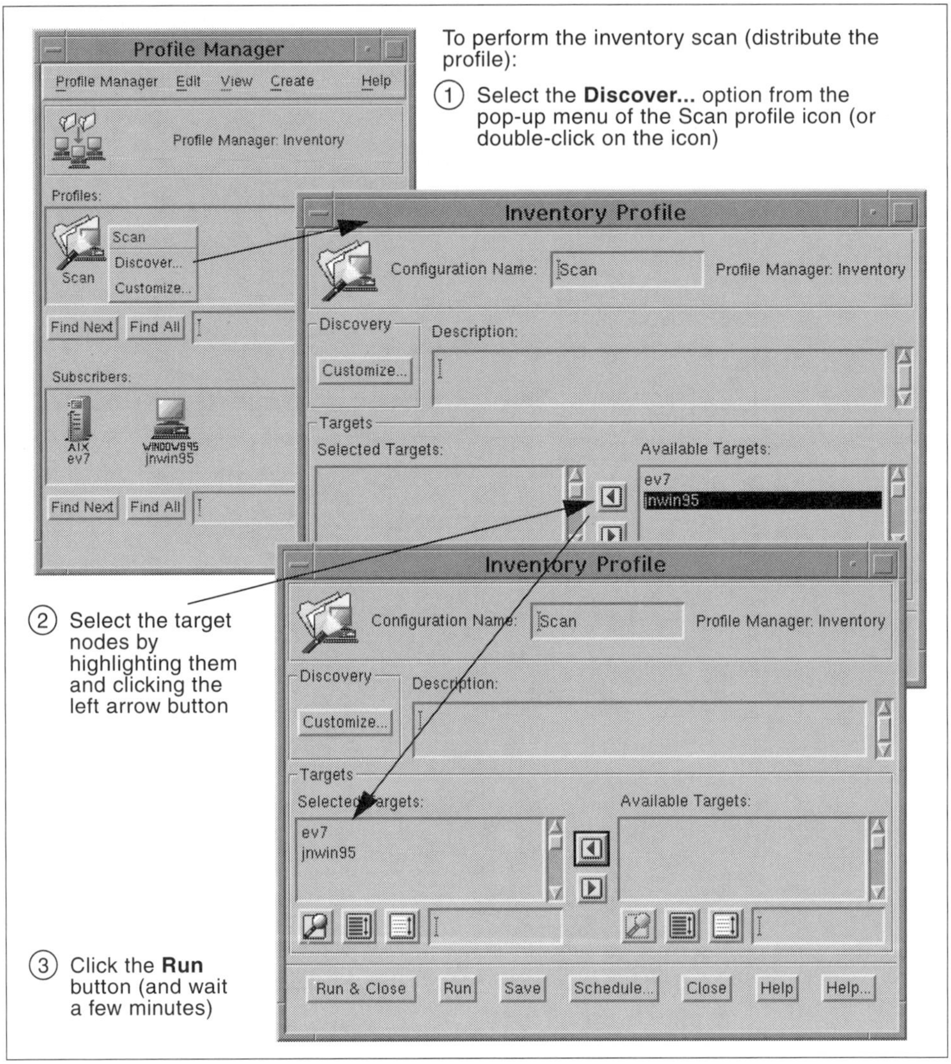

Figure 159. Distributing the TME 10 Inventory Profile

Now check whether the scan was successful by viewing the inventory information.

11.2.5 Viewing Stored Inventory Information

The inventory information can be queried from a node's pop-up menu. Figure 160 shows how to view the hardware inventory for *jnwin95*.

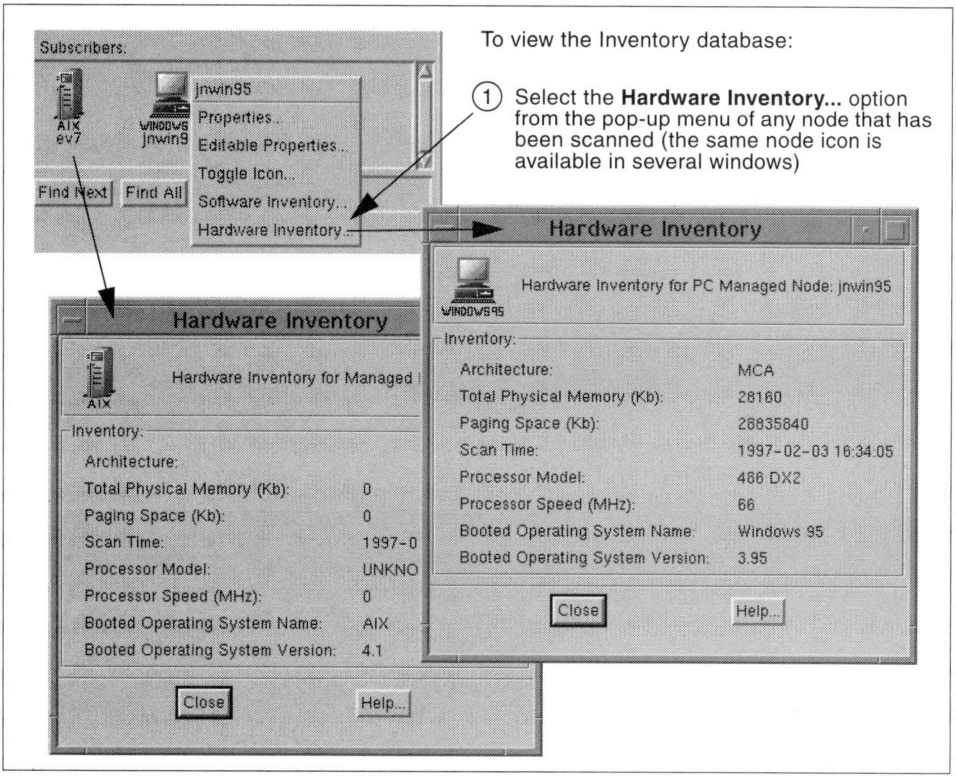

Figure 160. Viewing Hardware Inventory Information

The software inventory information for *jnwin95* is shown in Figure 161 on page 296.

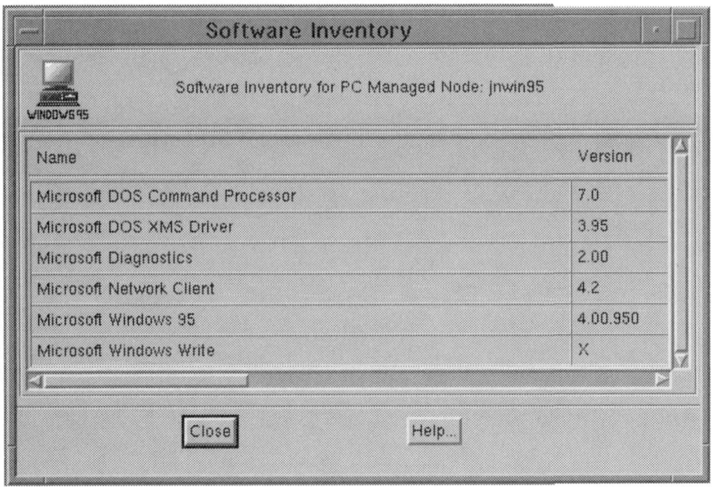

Figure 161. Viewing Software Inventory Information

11.2.6 Creating a Query Library and Query

Queries are resources provided by the TME 10 Framework. They allow you to query the configuration database for nodes whose inventory records meet the search criteria. In the following example, we create a task library and, within it, a query that looks for nodes that run Windows 95 and have less than 32 MB of memory.

The first step is to create a query library. Before **QueryLibrary** appears in the *Create* menu, it must have been added as a managed resource from the *Properties* menu. Figure 162 on page 297 explain show to create a query library.

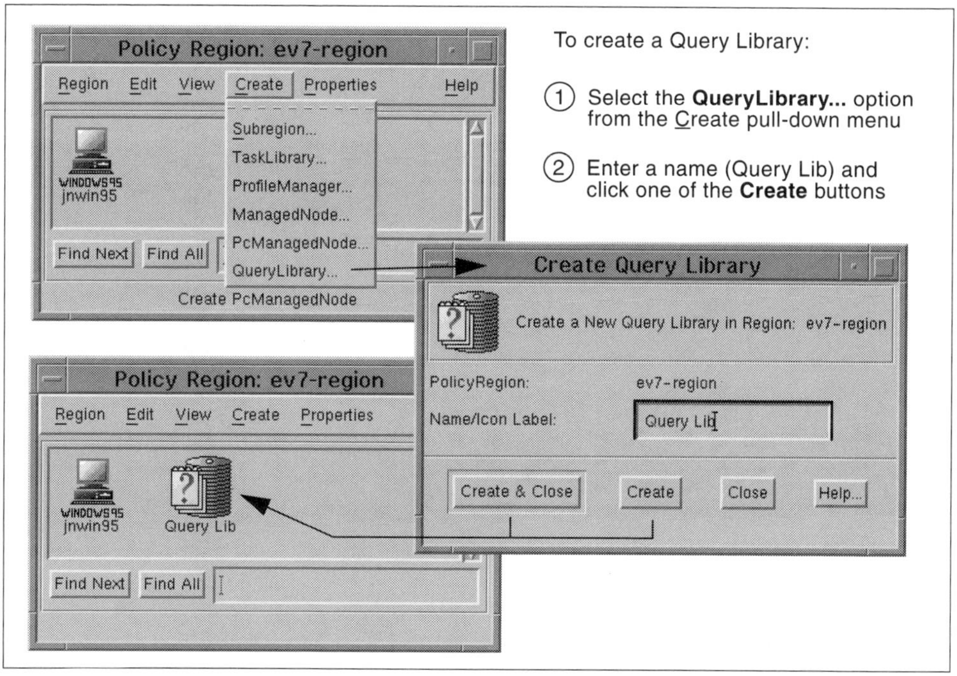

Figure 162. Creating a Query Library

A query can be created from the pop-menu of the *Query Lib* icon or by double-clicking the query library and selecting the **Query...** option from the *Create* pull-down menu within the Query Lib dialog. Figure 163 on page 298 explains how to create a query.

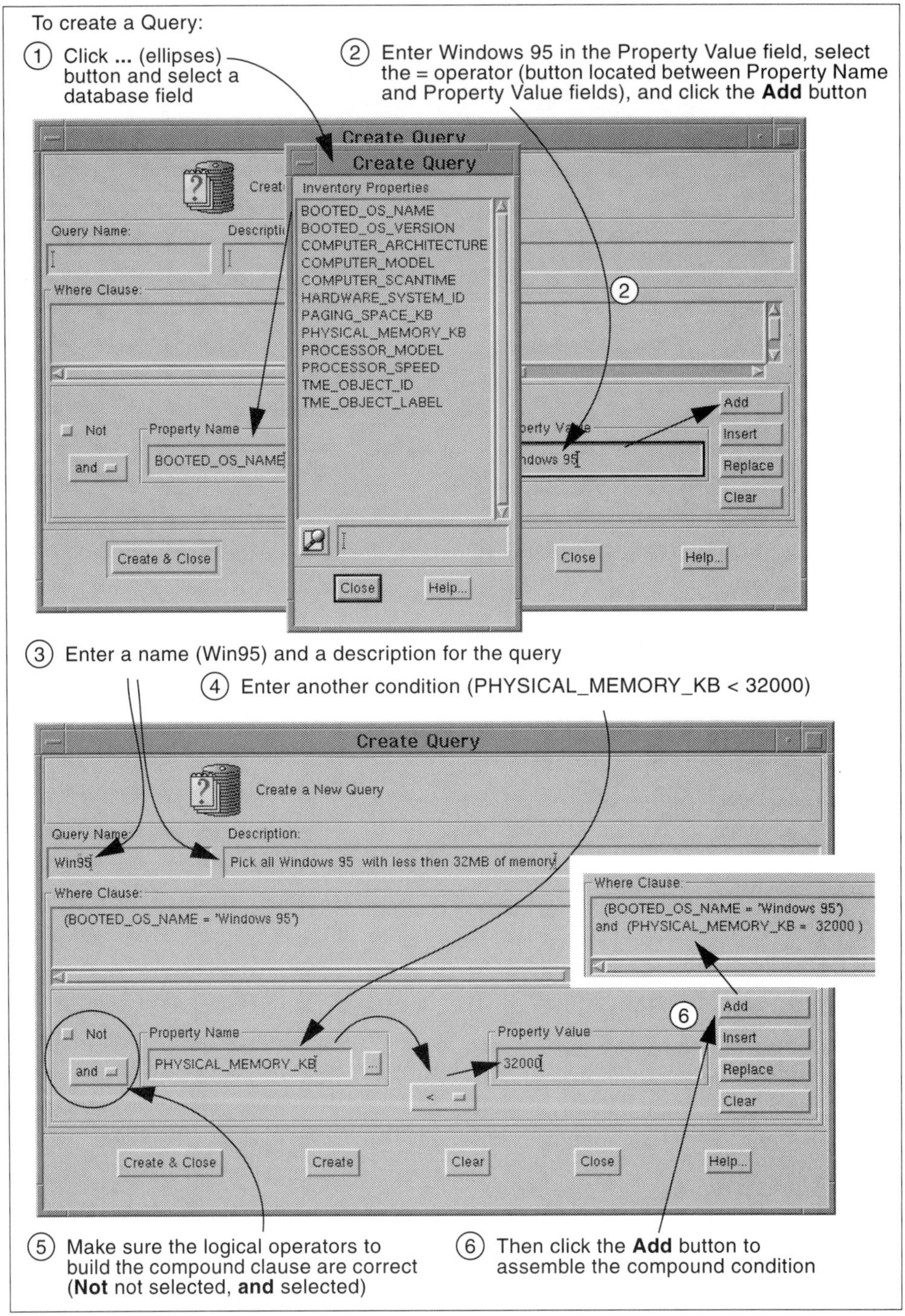

Figure 163. Creating a Query

11.2.7 Using the Query Facility to Choose Subscribers

Queries can be used to select subscribers within a profile manager. In theory you can select endpoints based on TME 10 Inventory information for all kinds profile types. In relation with TME 10 Software Distribution, you can search for machines meeting certain software or hardware conditions. In order to create useful queries, you might have to create new database views that combine the information you need from different database tables. See Section 5.4.2, "Database Tables and Views" on page 122 for more information on this subject.

In order to test the query facility for selecting subscribers, we create a new profile manager, SW Dist, in the ACME PR policy region. See Figure 164 on page 300.

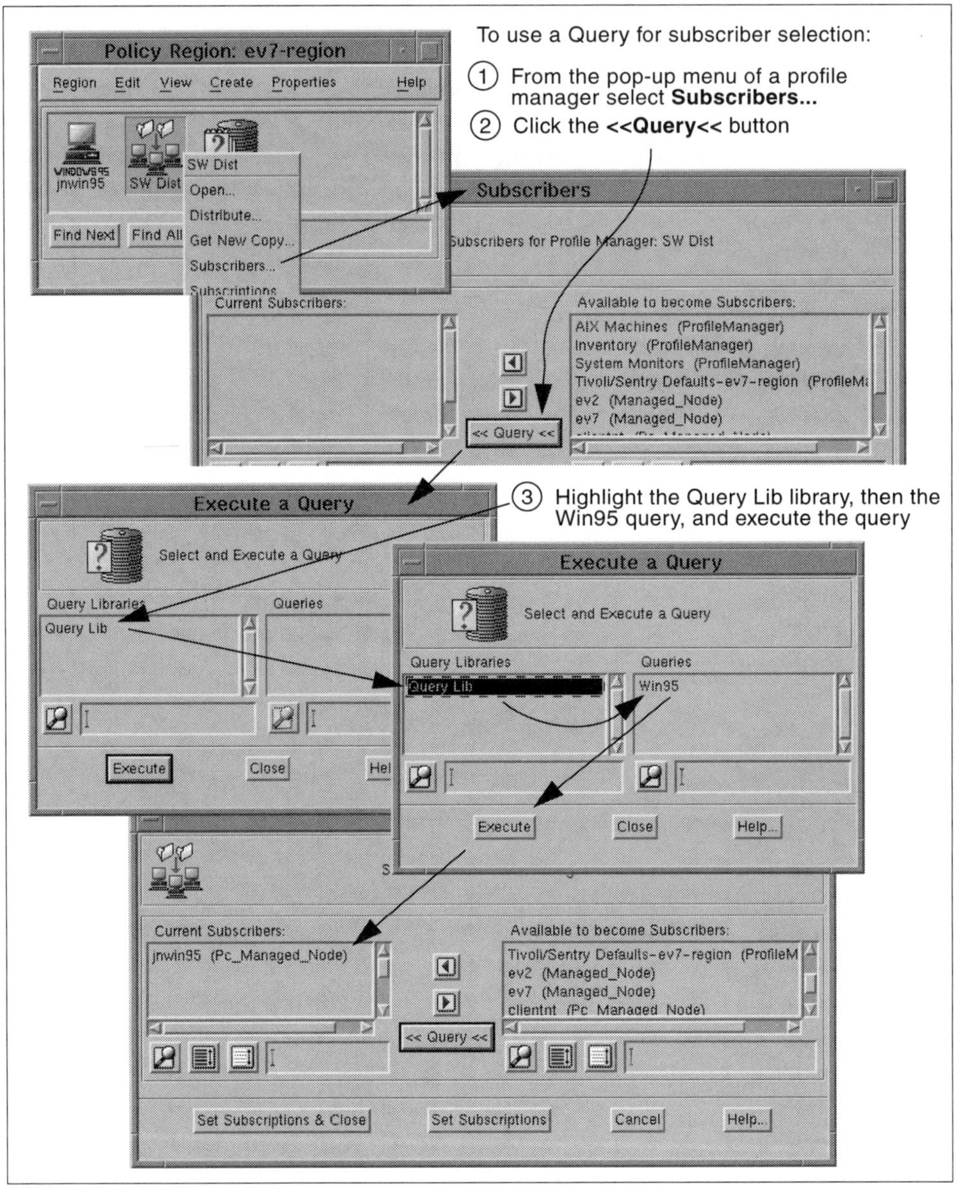

Figure 164. Using a Query to Select Subscribers

jnwin95 is the only Windows 95 machine with less than 32 MB of memory. To check whether the query really works, change its selection criteria.

CHAPTER 12

Installing and Using TME 10 Distributed Monitoring

This chapter provides you with step-by-step installation instructions for the TME 10 Distributed Monitoring product. The first section discusses the TME 10 Distributed Monitoring installation on the TMR server and on the managed nodes in our TMR. Once the installation is complete, the following sections permit you to exercise the basic functions provided by TME 10 Distributed Monitoring.

The purpose of this chapter is to familiarize you with the way these functions work and to deepen your understanding of the concepts explained in Chapter 6, "TME 10 Distributed Monitoring" on page 129. It does not cover every facet and option of this product.

TME 10 Terminology

Please note that the former name of this product was Tivoli/Sentry 3.0. When you follow these steps using the TME 10 Distributed Monitoring 3.1 or later, some dialogs might show slightly different titles and/or content, particularly in the installation sections. Most dialogs, however, are common to both versions of software.

12.1 TME 10 Distributed Monitoring Installation

You must have TME 10 Framework installed and running on the TMR server and the TME 10 clients (managed nodes) on which you want to install the TME 10 Distributed Monitoring application. See the *TME 10 Distributed Monitoring Release Notes* for disk space requirements to install the TME 10 Distributed Monitoring application.

The TME 10 Distributed Monitoring software package contains many components: the TME 10 Distributed Monitoring base product for clients and servers as well as a separate installation object for each monitoring collection provided by TME 10 Distributed Monitoring. The TME 10 Distributed Monitoring base product must be installed on your TMR server first. You may then either install the monitoring collections on the server, or install the base product on your clients (managed nodes).

12.1.1 Installing TME 10 Distributed Monitoring

TME 10 Distributed Monitoring has to be installed on each managed node to which you want to distribute a Distributed Monitoring profile, including managed nodes you add after the initial installation. Install it on the TMR server first.

Use the following steps to install the TME 10 Distributed Monitoring application from the TME 10 desktop:

1. From the TME 10 desktop's *Desktop* pull-down menu, select **Install**, then **Install Product...**
2. You may see an error about the media not being properly set; this is normal and will start the window that allows you to select the location of the TME 10 Distributed Monitoring application.
3. The *Install Product* dialog should then appear as shown in Figure 165. Select **TME 10 Distributed Monitoring** from the *Select Product to Install* scrolling list and the clients on which you wish to install the product.

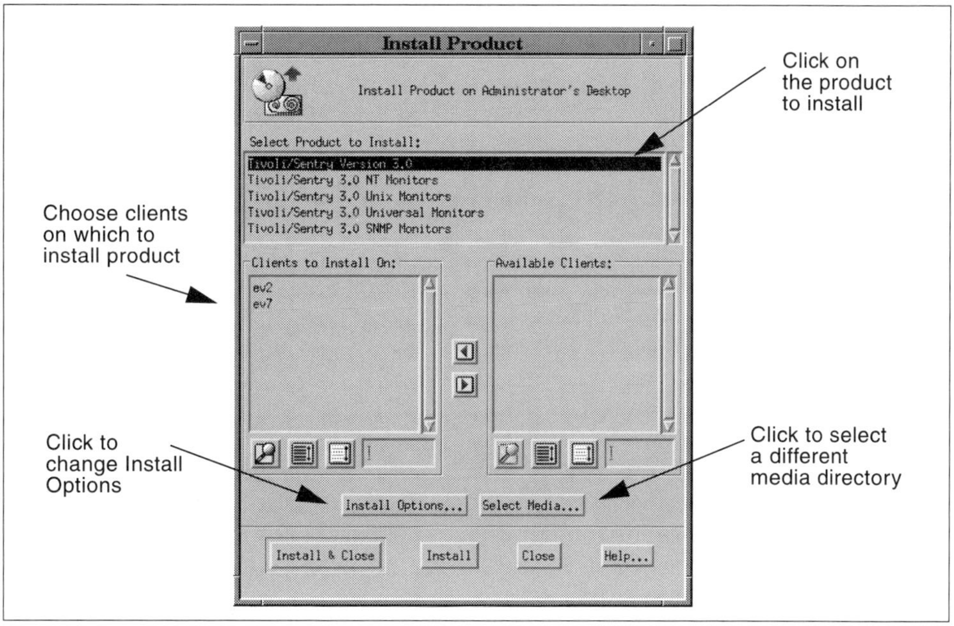

Figure 165. Install Product Dialog

Click the **Install & Close** button to install and close the installation window or the **Install** button to install and keep the installation window open after completion.

4. The *Product Install* dialog should then appear as shown in Figure 166. This window lists all of the software that will be installed. Click the **Continue Install** button to continue or the **Cancel** button to cancel. This is your last chance to cancel the installation of the product.

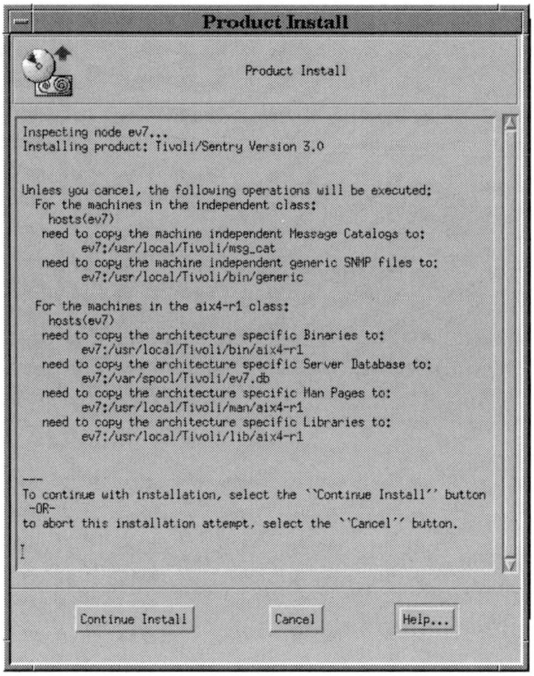

Figure 166. Product Install Dialog

5. The window will then display the status of the product installation. Wait for the `Finished product installation` message to appear. It is then safe to click the **Close** button; the installation is complete.

To install the Monitoring Collections, repeat the steps listed above and select the appropriate Monitoring Collection on the *Install Product* dialog shown in Figure 165 on page 305. For our next examples, we need the *UNIX Monitors* collections. You should install this collection now.

It is important to note that the Monitoring Collections are only installed on the TMR server. In other words, there is no client portion for the monitoring collections. Therefore, you will only need to install each Monitoring Collection once.

12.2 Practical Examples of Using the TME 10 Distributed Monitoring

In this section, we look at some practical uses of the TME 10 Distributed Monitoring application to get a better idea of how it can be used in a real user environment.

12.2.1 Our Lab Environment

The lab environment to be used for this tutorial is as follows:

TMR Server

- ***ev7*** – RS/6000 running AIX 4.1.4 (TME 10 Framework, TME 10 Distributed Monitoring, and the TME 10 Distributed Monitoring UNIX Monitoring Collection installed)

TME 10 Clients

- ***ev2*** – RS/6000 running AIX 4.1.4 (TME 10 Framework and TME 10 Distributed Monitoring installed)

The PC managed nodes are not used in this chapter. TME 10 Distributed Monitoring only runs on managed nodes (UNIX or Windows NT).

12.2.2 Creating a Distributed Monitoring Profile

Distributed Monitoring profiles could be added into an existing profile manager. However, we create a separate profile manager called *System Monitors* within the *ACME PR* policy region. See how this is done in Figure 167 on page 308:

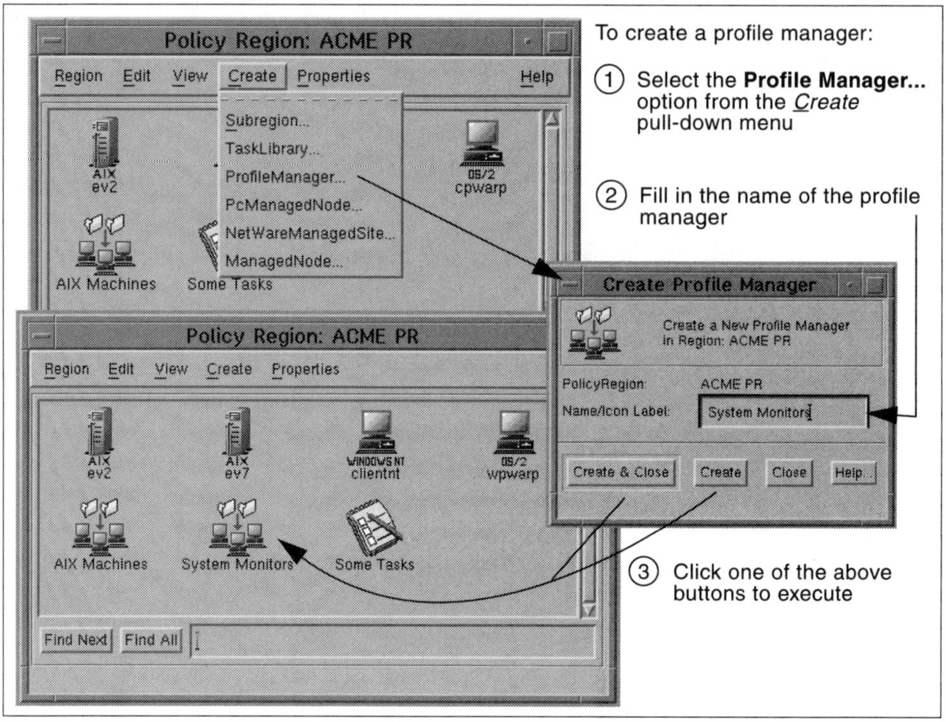

Figure 167. Creating a Profile Manager

Before we can create profiles, we must add their managed resource type to the list of resources that the *ACME PR* policy region can manage. This can be achieved in the *Set Managed Resources* dialog (see Figure 168).

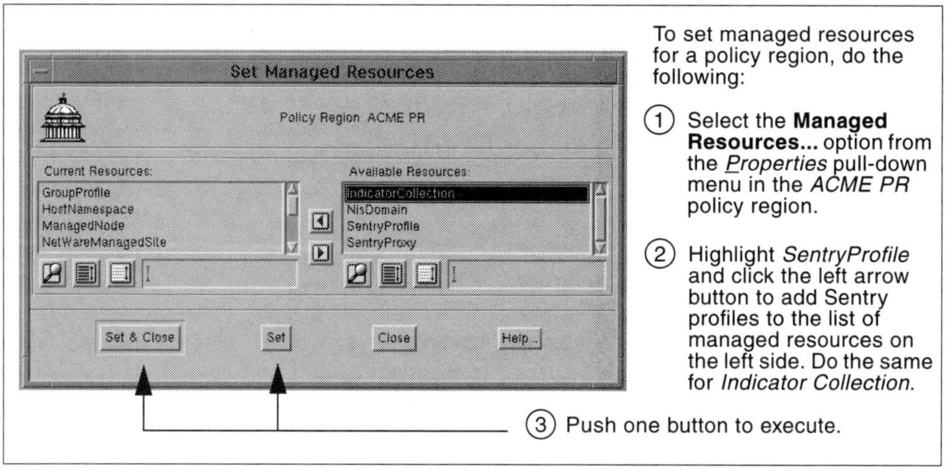

Figure 168. Set Managed Resource Dialog

Now let's create a Distributed Monitoring profile within the *System Monitors* profile manager. The profile should contain monitors that are able to perform functions on all UNIX platforms. See Figure 169 for details.

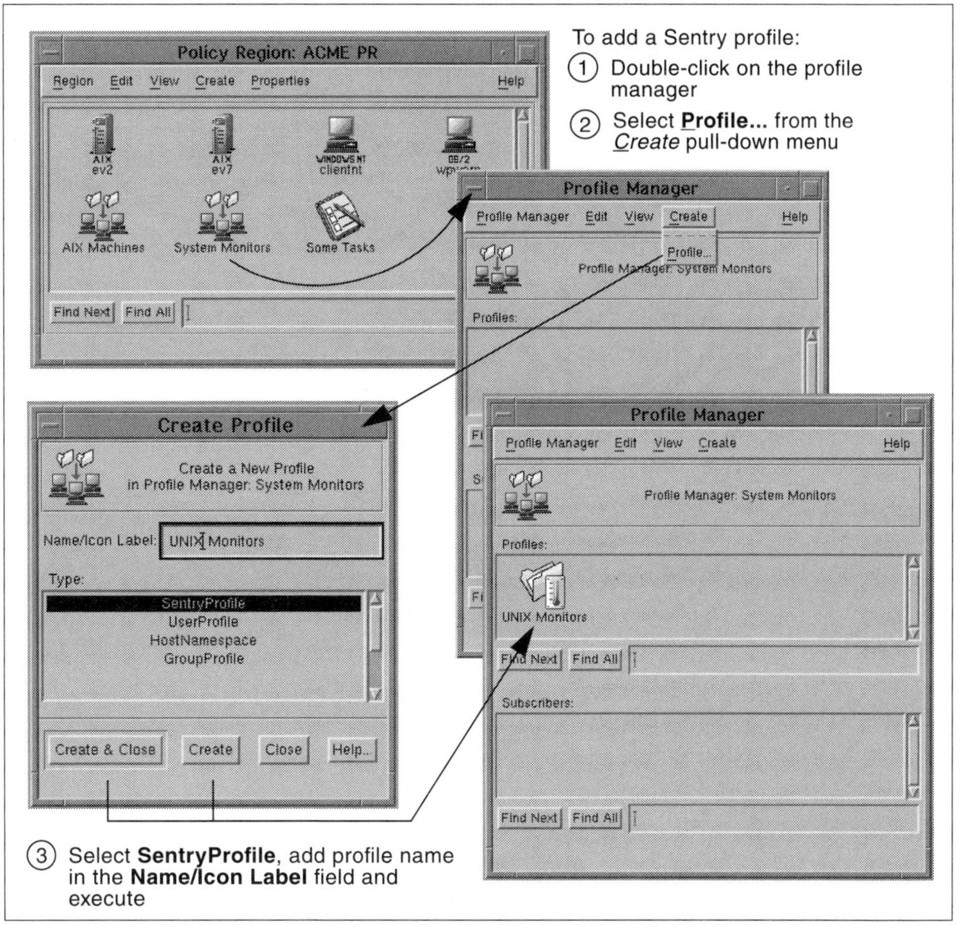

Figure 169. Creating a Distributed Monitoring Profile

12.2.3 Creating Monitors

In this section, we create the following two monitors to show how TME 10 Distributed Monitoring can monitor your host resources:

- The percentage of disk space used on the */tmp* directory
- The available swap space

These monitors will be applied to the *ev2* managed node.

12.2.3.1 Disk Space Usage Monitor

For this exercise, we create the monitor to observe the percentage of disk space used by the */tmp* directory. The default properties for this monitor are shown in Table 17.

Table 17. Default Properties for the Percent Space Used Monitoring Source

Severity	Trigger When ...	Default Actions
critical	Greater than 95%	Send TME 10 notice Pop-up alarm dialog Change icon in the Monitoring Collection
severe	Greater than 90%	Send TME 10 notice Change icon in the Monitoring Collection
warning	Greater than 85%	Change icon in the Monitoring Collection
normal	N/A	none
always	N/A	none

Our monitor must comply with the following conditions:

1. The response levels and the response actions should comply with the default values for this monitor source as shown in Table 17.
2. For the *critical* response level, the monitor should also run the shell script */usr/local/bin/clean.sh* on the managed node. The shell script erases those files from the `/tmp` directory that have not been used in the last 15 days. The shell script can be created as follows:

   ```
   # cat >/usr/local/bin/clean.sh <<EOF
   > #!/bin/ksh
   > find /tmp -atime +15 -exec rm {} \\;
   EOF
   ```

   However, this realistic action would be difficult to test. So, we delete all output files generated by TME 10 instead:

   ```
   # cat >/usr/local/bin/clean.sh <<EOF
   > #!/bin/ksh
   > find /tmp -name "*.output" -exec rm {} \\;
   EOF
   ```

   In order to be able to test multiple times, you would create a tar file with all the files that will be deleted before you distribute the monitor.
3. The monitoring schedule should be once every hour, which is the default.

See Figure 170 on page 311 for instructions on how to define this monitor.

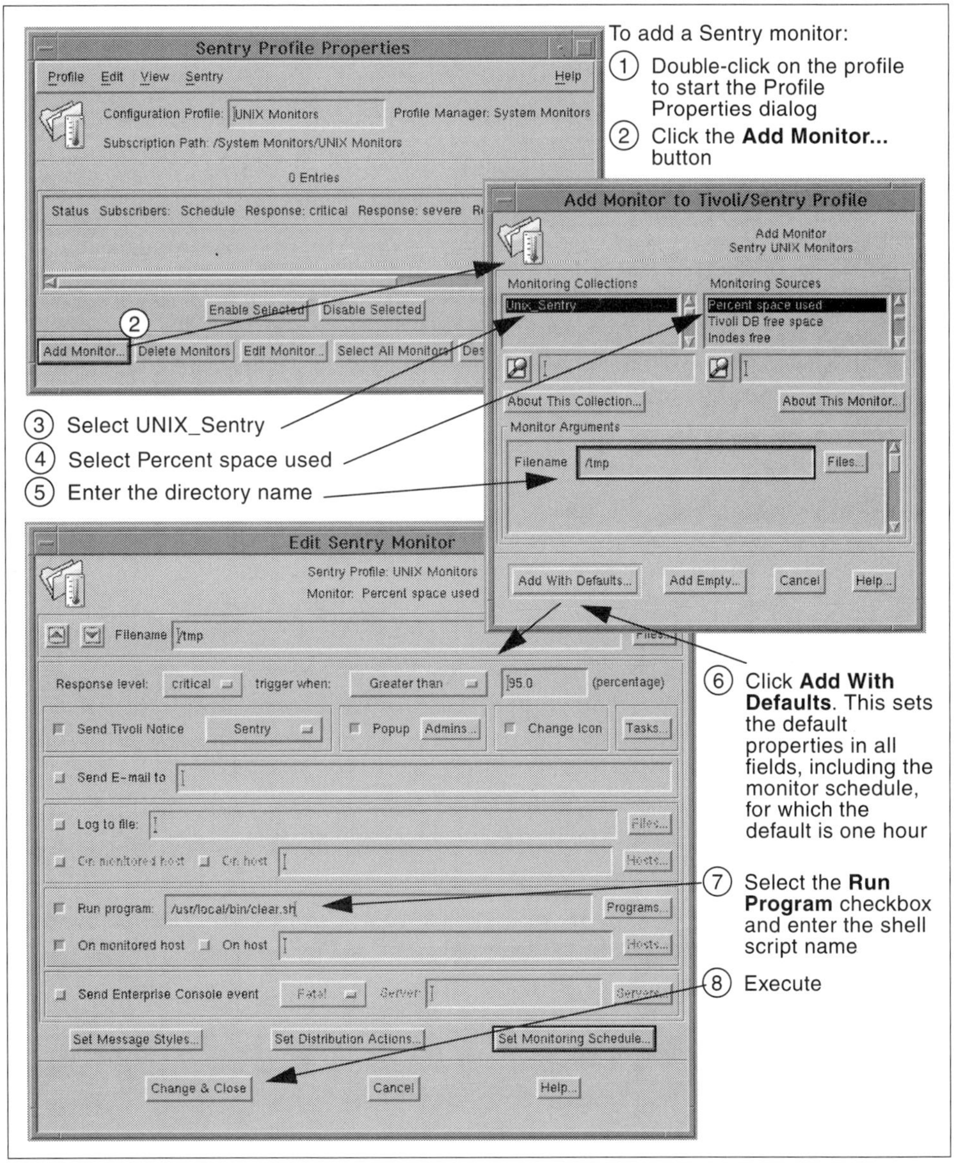

Figure 170. Creating the Percent Space Used Monitor

12.2.3.2 Swap Space Monitor

Now let's create the monitor to observe the available swap space on the UNIX machines. The default properties for this monitor are shown in Table 18.

Table 18. Default Actions for the Swap Space Monitoring Source

Severity	Trigger When ...	Default Actions
critical	Less than 10 MB	Send TME 10 notice Pop-up alarm dialog Change icon in the monitoring collection
severe	Less than 15 MB	Send TME 10 notice Change icon in the monitoring collection
warning	Less than 20 MB	Change icon in the monitoring collection
normal	N/A	none
always	N/A	none

The response levels and the response actions of this monitor should comply with the default values for this source monitor (see Table 18), and it should be run once an hour. Figure 171 on page 313 shows what to select and fill in for this monitor. The steps to add the monitor are the same as for the previous monitor, as shown in Figure 170 on page 311.

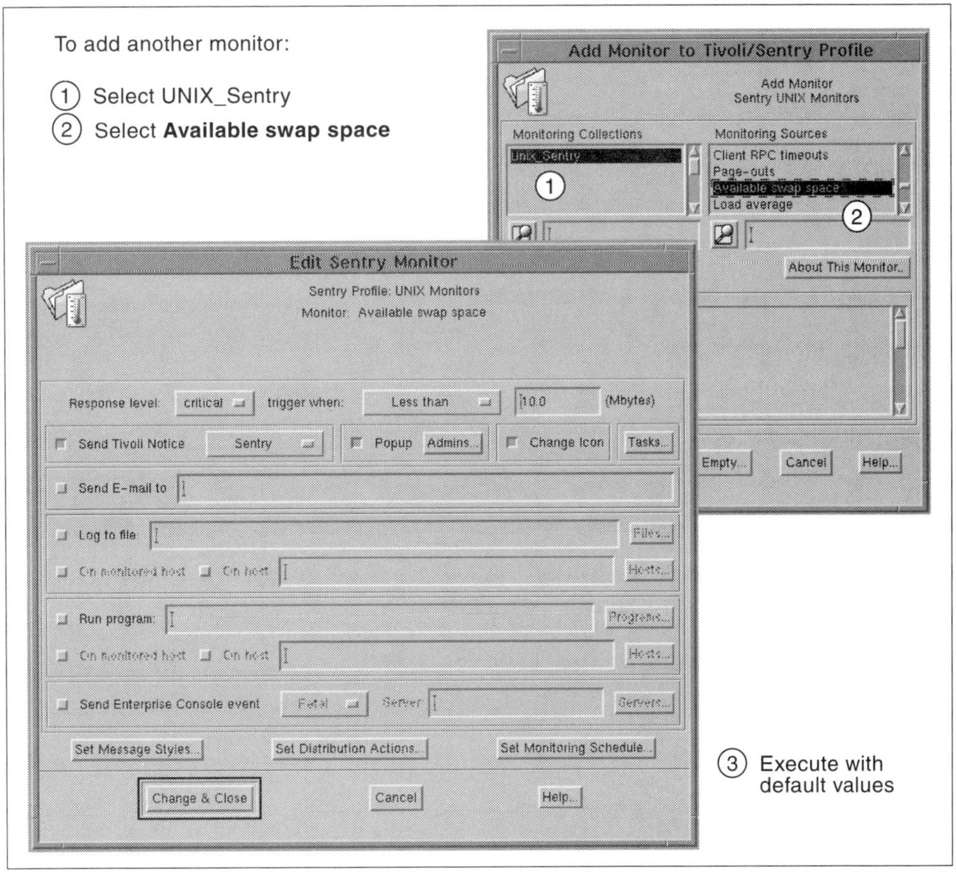

Figure 171. Creating the Available Swap Space Monitor

After creating both monitors, the *Distributed Monitoring Profile Properties* dialog should look like the one shown in Figure 172 on page 314.

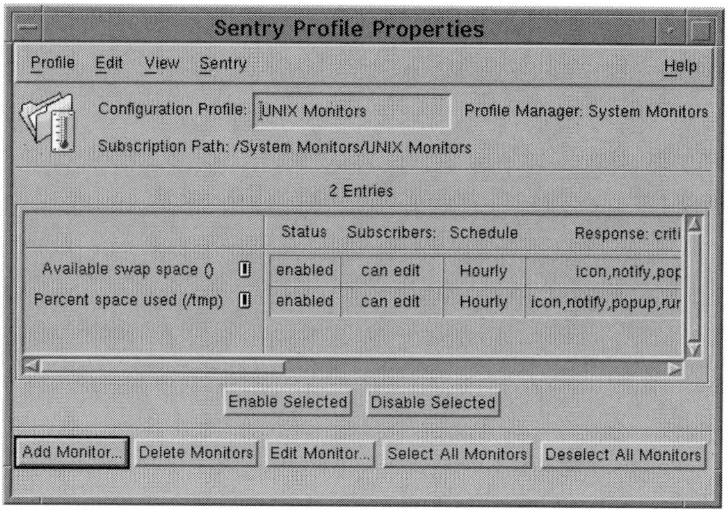

Figure 172. Distributed Monitoring Profile Properties Dialog

Note: You must save the changes made to the profile; otherwise the newly created monitors would be lost. You can do so from the *Profile* pull-down menu.

12.2.4 Creating an Indicator Collection

In order to view the status of our Distributed Monitoring profiles, we create an indicator collection called *Indicators*. Remember that the *IndicatorCollection* managed resource must be in the policy region's managed resources list. That is what we did in Figure 168 on page 308. See Figure 173 for information on how to create the indicator collection.

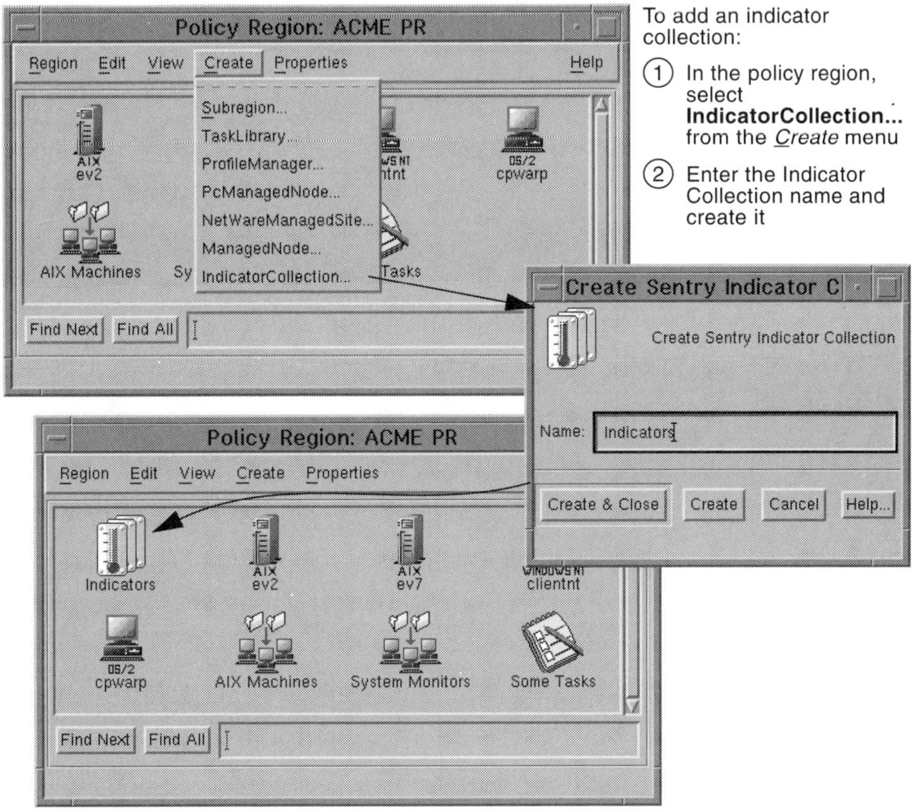

Figure 173. Creating an Indicator Collection

12.2.5 Associating the Profile with an Indicator Collection

Once we have created the indicator collection, we can associate the *UNIX Monitors* profile with the *Indicators* indicator collection, which allows the indicator collection to display the alert status of the monitors belonging to that profile. Figure 174 shows you how to make the association.

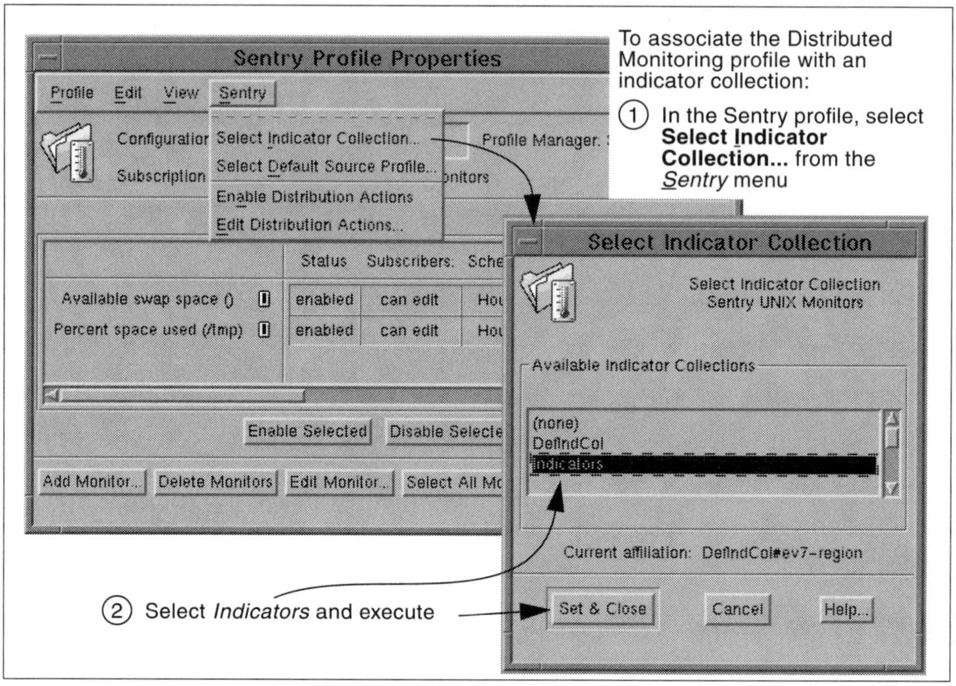

Figure 174. Associating the Profile with an Indicator Collection

12.2.6 Distributing a Distributed Monitoring Profile

After we have created our Distributed Monitoring profile and created monitors in it, we must distribute the profile to the subscribers in order to start the monitoring activity on the target machines.

We subscribe the *AIX Machines* profile to it so that every AIX machine (*ev2* and *ev7*) will be monitored. See Figure 175 for information on how to create the subscription.

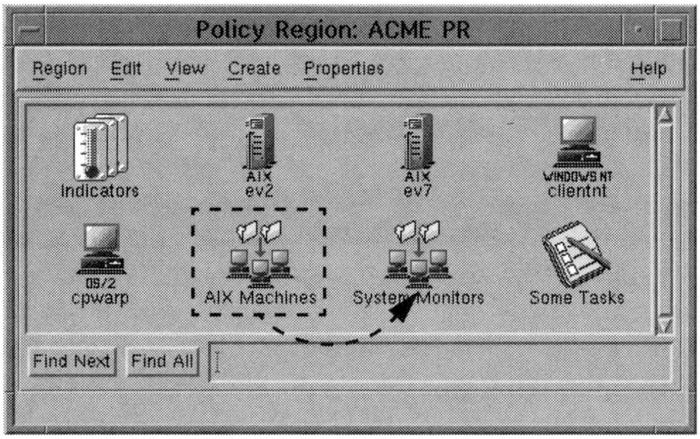

Drag the *AIX Machines* icon and drop it on the *System Monitors* icon to subscribe (use left mouse button)

Figure 175. Drag-and-Drop Distribution

Now we can distribute the *UNIX Monitors* profile to the subscribers. See Figure 176 on page 318 for instructions on how to do this. Note that the profile must be saved after changes in any of the monitors. As long as the profile is not saved, you would not get the **Distribute...** option in the *Profile* pull-down menu.

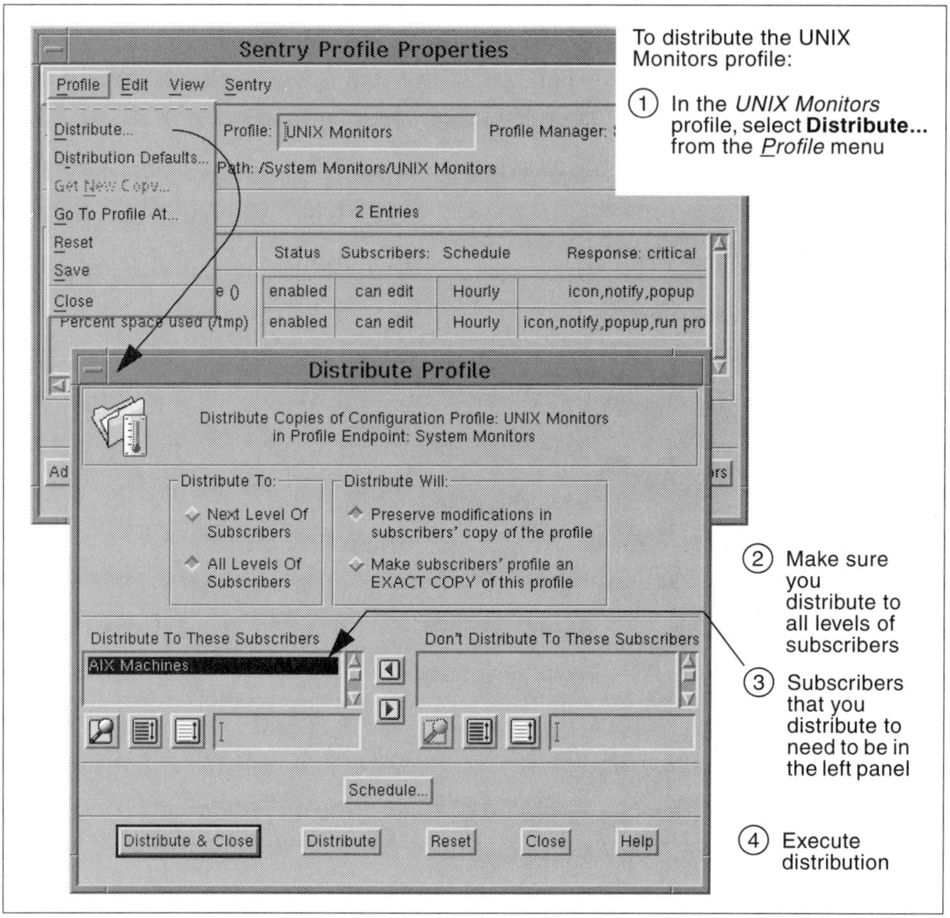

Figure 176. Distributing a Distributed Monitoring Profile

Other ways to distribute profile(s) are:

- In the profile manager window, you can select one or all subscribers and one or all profiles. To select all subscribers or profiles, you use the *Edit* pull-down menu. Then select the **Distribute...** option from the *Profile* pull-down menu. In the upcoming *Distribute Profiles* dialog, you push the **Distribute Now** button. The selected profiles will then be distributed to the selected subscribers, using the *Distribution Defaults* set in the profile(s). You can set these defaults in the *Profile Properties* window by using the **Distribution Defaults...** option from the *Profile* pull-down menu.
- In the profile manager window, you drag a profile and drop it on a subscriber.

12.2.7 Generating Alerts

After the Distributed Monitoring profile has been distributed to the target machines, the monitoring activity starts. If one of the response levels defined in the monitors is reached, the response actions are executed.

We created two monitors that watch over the space used by the */tmp* directory and the available swap space. To see the response actions defined for these two monitors, you need to create some processes that can increase the disk space used by the */tmp* directory and decrease the available swap space.

Our shell script that runs as a response action when the critical level (/tmp 95% full) is reached deletes all files with extension *.output*. So, create some files in /tmp to fill up the file system. Some files should use the file name extension of *.output* so that you can verify the action of removing files.

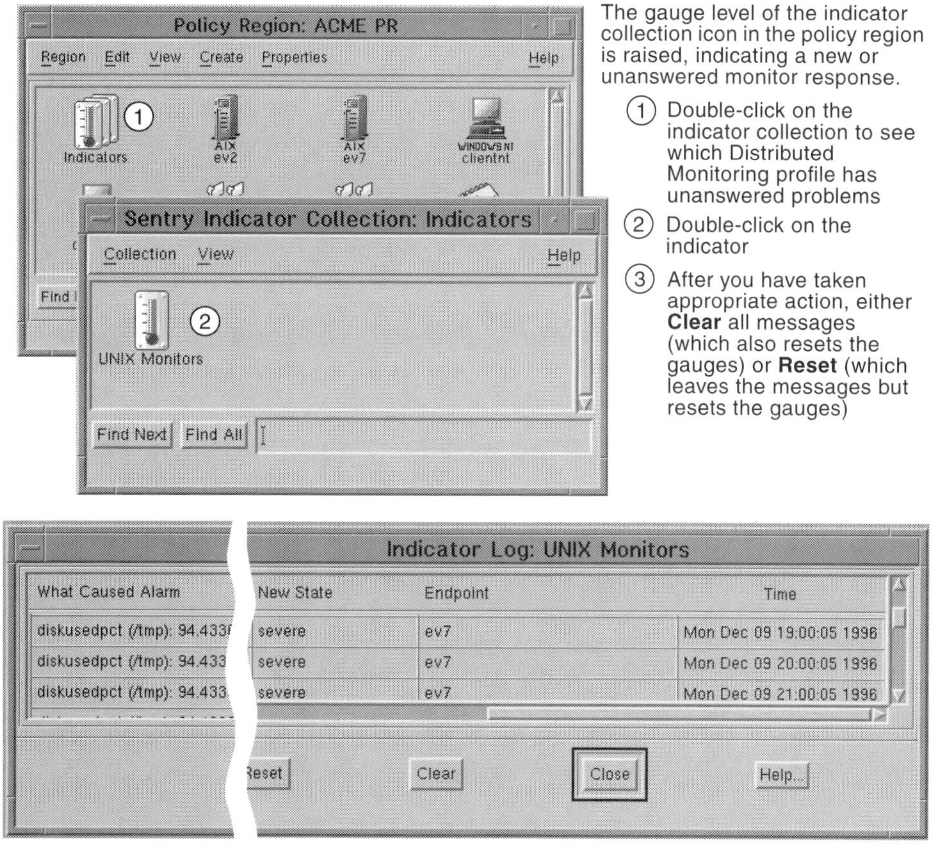

Figure 177. Indicator Collection after Receiving a Severe Status

When a monitor sends a problem record, the indicator collection changes its appearance, as does the indicator representing the *UNIX Monitors* profile in the indicator collection. The indicator contains a list of unanswered alerts. The administrator has to take actions and clear the alerts. Figure 177 on page 319 illustrates this for a status of severe.

When the *critical* response level for the *Percent space used* monitor has been reached, a *Distributed Monitoring Alert* dialog pops up in the administrator's desktop (see Figure 178).

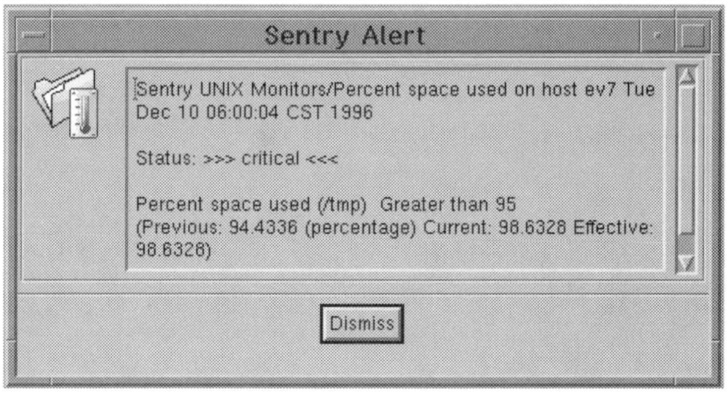

Figure 178. Alert Dialog after Receiving a Critical Status

If the /usr/local/bin/clear.sh shell script that is executed as a response action did not perform what you expected, check the following:

- Check the permissions required to perform the desired actions on the target systems. In other words, find out what permission is required to delete the *.output* files in */tmp*.
- Check the permission under which the monitors run. Choose **Set User & Group ID** option from the *Edit* pull-down menu in the *User Profile Properties* dialog, which is shown in Figure 18 on page 51. Check and/or set the user ID and group ID. By default, it is set to *nobody*, which is not sufficient for most actions.

CHAPTER 13

Installing and Using TME 10 Enterprise Console

This chapter provides you with step-by-step installation instructions for the TME 10 Enterprise Console product. The first section discusses the TME 10 Enterprise Console installation. Once the installation is complete, the following sections permit you to exercise the basic functions provided by TME 10 Enterprise Console.

The purpose of this chapter is to make you familiar with the way these functions work and to deepen your understanding of the concepts explained in Chapter 7, "TME 10 Enterprise Console" on page 163. It does not cover every facet and option of this product.

TME 10 Terminology

Please note that the former name of this product was Tivoli/Enterprise Console 2.6, or T/EC 2.6. When you follow these steps using the TME 10 Enterprise Console 3.1 or later, some dialogs might show slightly different titles and/or content, particularly in the installation sections. Most dialogs, however, are common to both versions of software.

13.1 TME 10 Enterprise Console Installation

When installing TME 10 Enterprise Console in your environment, the Sybase database, event adapters, the Enterprise Console application, which incorporates both the event server and event console support, and the TME 10 Enterprise Console Rule Builder are installed on the machines of your choice. Keep in mind any configuration restrictions. Refer to Section 7.1.3, "Configurations and Machine Roles" on page 166. These products, features, and TME 10 Enterprise Console components take up disk space and system resources, so the initial planning is an important step in performing the TME 10 Enterprise Console installation. After the installation plan is set, the software can be installed using the steps in this chapter.

You must have the TME 10 Framework installed and running on the TMR server before trying to install the TME 10 Enterprise Console application and its supporting products and components.

We will first make any necessary modifications to the operating system kernel, followed by the installation of the Sybase database, the TME 10 Enterprise Console application, the TME 10 Enterprise Console Rule Builder, and finally the Logfile adapter. For the purposes of this installation exercise, we installed all these components on the TMR server.

13.1.1 Installation Considerations

Before installing TME 10 Enterprise Console, be sure to check the TME 10 documentation for current disk space and memory requirements as well as prerequisite hardware and software. The *TME 10 Enterprise Console Release Notes* and *TME 10 Enterprise Console User's Guide, Volume I* provide this detailed information for TME 10 Enterprise Console.

It is assumed that the reader has installed the TME 10 Framework. For the purpose of this exercise, it is not necessary to install TME 10 clients. Just install the TMR server as detailed in Section 8.1.2, "Installing the TMR Server" on page 205, and the patches as outlined in Section 8.1.5, "Installing Patches" on page 219.

13.1.2 Reconfiguring the Operating System Kernel

In preparation for the installation of the Sybase relational database, it may be necessary to configure the kernel of your operating system in order to support the RDBMS. For your convenience, the following information is assembled from the TME 10 documentation.

Note: There are no kernel changes to the AIX operating system nor to HP-UX 10.0.

13.1.2.1 HP-UX 9.0.x Kernel

It is recommended that the steps be performed by someone who is familiar with reconfiguring the kernel on a HP-UX machine.

The SQL Server will not start unless the operating system kernel has enough shared memory available. The operating system's shared memory parameter should always be set to a value larger than the value of the SQL Server's memory parameter.

Adjust the maximum shared memory segment size parameter in the operating system kernel configuration file if these parameters are not already there:

```
shmmax 67108864;
shmmni 100;
shmseg 36;
```

For more information about the kernel, see your operating system documentation.

Build your new kernel, and then reboot the machine for these changes to take effect. See your HP-UX operating system documentation for instructions on this procedure.

If you are running the TME 10 Enterprise Console or a large number of UI Servers from a single HP-UX system, you may see a `file table full` error. If you see this error, you should increase the setting of the `maxusers` parameter to 654, and rebuild the kernel.

13.1.2.2 SunOS Kernel

It is recommended that these steps be performed by someone who is familiar with reconfiguring the kernel on a SunOS machine.

Check that the following two lines appear and are uncommented in your operating system kernel configuration file:

```
options LWP
options ASYNCHIO
```

Without these lines in the kernel configuration file, the SQL Server will fail to boot during installation.

The SQL Server will not start unless the operating system kernel has enough shared memory available. The operating system's shared memory parameter should always be set to a value larger than the value of the SQL Server's memory parameter.

Adjust the maximum shared memory segment size parameter in the operating system kernel configuration file if these parameters are not already there:

```
options "SHMSIZE=0x20000"
options "SEMMNS=640"
```

```
options "SHMMNI=256"
```

For more information about the kernel, see your operating system documentation.

Make sure the following lines are in your operating system kernel reconfiguration file. Add them if they are not already present.

```
# The following options are for various System V
# IPC facilities
# Most standard software does not need them,
# although they are used by SunGKS and some
# third party software.
options IPCMESSAGE
# System V IPC Message Facility
options IPCSEMAPHORE
# System V IPC Semaphore Facility
options IPCSHMEM
# System V IPC Shared Memory Facility
```

Build your new kernel and then reboot the machine for these changes to take effect. See your SunOS operating system manual for instructions on this procedure.

13.1.2.3 Solaris Kernel Reconfiguration

The SQL server will not start unless the operating system kernel has enough shared memory available. The operating system's shared memory parameter should always be set to a value larger than the value of the SQL server's memory parameter.

Adjust the maximum shared memory segment size parameter in the operating system configuration. Add the following line to the end of the operating system file, */etc/system*:

```
set shmsys:shminfo_shmmax=67108864
```

For more information about the kernel, see your operating system documentation.

Reboot your operating system.

13.1.3 Installing the Sybase Database

Use the following steps to install the Sybase database from the TME 10 desktop:

1. From the TME 10 desktop's *Desktop* pull-down menu, select **Install**, then **Install Product...**
2. You may see an error about the media not being properly set, which will start the *File Browser* window. Set the media to be the location of the TME 10 Enterprise Console 2.6 application:
   - Under *Hosts*, highlight the name that has the installation media (disk file or CD-ROM).
   - Under *Path Name*, type in the full path name of the directory that contains the TME 10 Enterprise Console software or where the CD-ROM is mounted.
   - Then click the **Set Media & Close** button.
3. The *Install Product* dialog should then appear as shown in Figure 179. If the TME 10 Enterprise Console applications do not appear in the list of installable products, click the **Select Media...** button to display the *File Browser* dialog (see previous step), and set the correct path to the installation media.

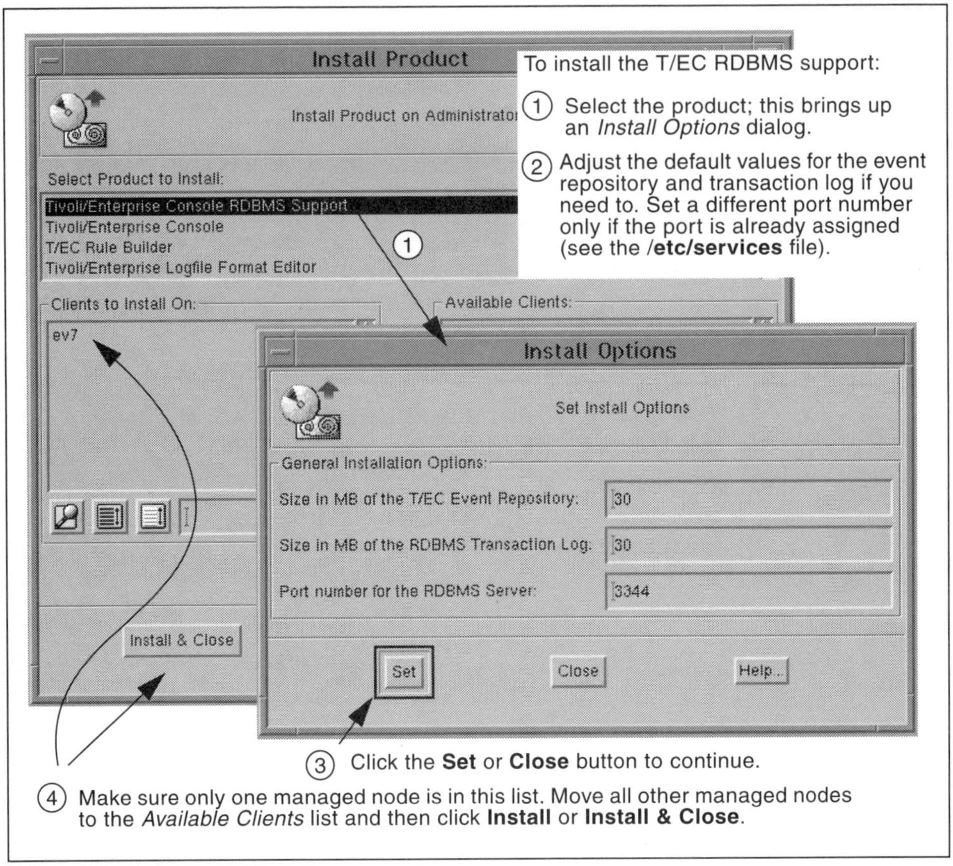

Figure 179. The Install Product Dialog

4. The RDBMS will be installed on the host displayed in the *Clients to Install On* scrolling list.

Note

The RDBMS should only be installed on one host; this must be the same host where the TME 10 Enterprise Console application will be installed.

5. The *Product Install* dialog then appears as shown in Figure 180. This window lists all of the software that will be installed. Watch carefully for error messages. Click the **Cancel** button if you see any error messages, such as a `not enough disk space` message. In this case, increase the disk space and restart the installation. If everything is OK, click the **Continue Install** button to continue.

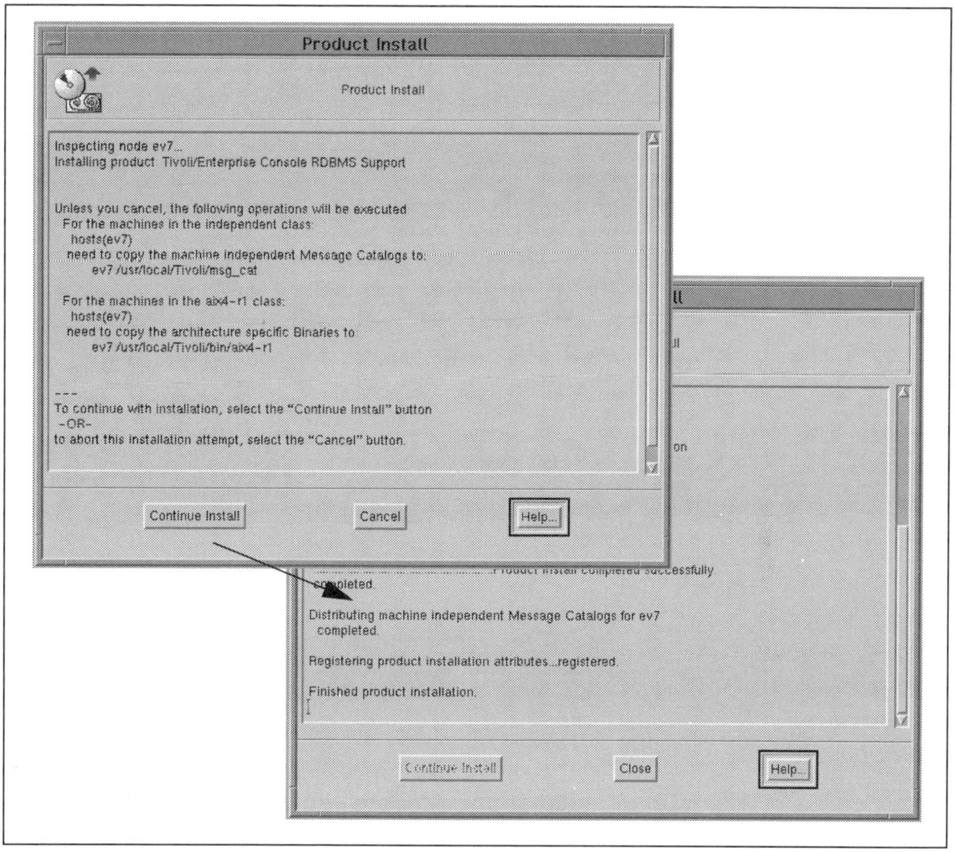

Figure 180. Product Installation Dialogs for Sybase Database

6. Click the **Close** button to close the *Product Install* dialog.

The installation of the Sybase database is complete.

13.1.4 Installing the Enterprise Console Application

Install the TME 10 Enterprise Console application (which includes the event server and event console) after you have installed the RDBMS support. Follow the same basic steps as outlined in Section 13.1.3, "Installing the Sybase Database" on page 326. When you select **TME 10 Enterprise Console** in the *Install Product* window, you will get the *Install Options* window shown in Figure 181 on page 330.

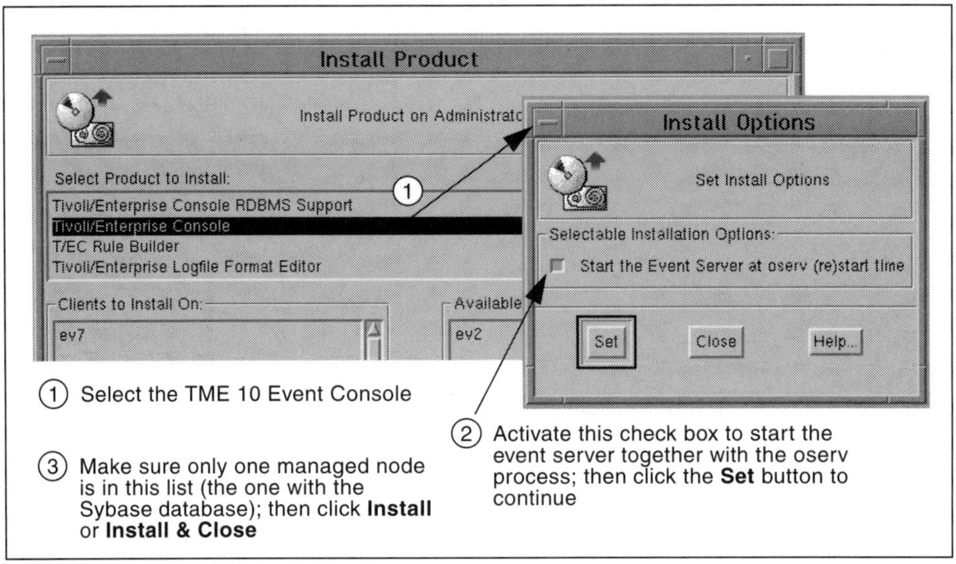

Figure 181. Installing the TME 10 Enterprise Console Application

The event server and event console will be installed on the host displayed in the *Clients to Install On* scrolling list. Make sure you only select the one host where you want the event server to run, which should be the host where you installed the RDBMS support.

The TME 10 installation process then displays the *Product Install* dialog and lists all of the software that will be installed. Watch carefully for error messages. Continue if you don't see any error messages. This dialog returns status information as the installation progresses.

After the enterprise console is installed, two icons will appear on the administrator's TME 10 desktop. Your TME 10 desktop will reflect these changes only after you have closed and then reopened your TME 10 desktop. In order for administrators to handle events, it will be necessary to manually create event console(s). The exercise in Section 13.2.4.1, "Creating an Event Console" on page 335, will lead the reader through the steps to create an administrator's event console on the TME 10 desktop.

The event server is a TME 10 resource. You will need to modify the resource authorization roles for each administrator who is to have access to the event server. For information on Enterprise Console authorization roles, see the *TME 10 Enterprise Console User's Guide, Volume II*. For information on modifying authorization roles, see the *TME 10 Framework User's Guide*. Section 13.2.3, "Setting Resource Roles" on page 334 in this chapter provides an exercise and will lead the reader through the steps to modify the administrator's authorization roles to provide access to the event server and its supported functions.

13.1.5 Installing the TME 10 Enterprise Console Rule Builder

Install the Rule Builder application after you have installed the RDBMS support and TME 10 Enterprise Console. Follow the same basic steps as outlined in Section 13.1.3, "Installing the Sybase Database" on page 326, and select **T/EC Rule Builder**.

When the installation is complete, no icon appears on the TME 10 desktop to represent the TME 10 Enterprise Console Rule Builder. It is accessible from the EventServer icon on the TME 10 desktop.

13.1.6 Installation of an Event Adapter

Install the Logfile adapter after you have installed the Enterprise Console application, the Enterprise Console RDBMS, and the Rule Builder. Follow the same basic steps as outlined in Section 13.1.3, "Installing the Sybase Database" on page 326. When you select **TME 10 Enterprise Console Logfile Adapter** in the Install Product dialog, you will get the *Install Options* window shown in Figure 182.

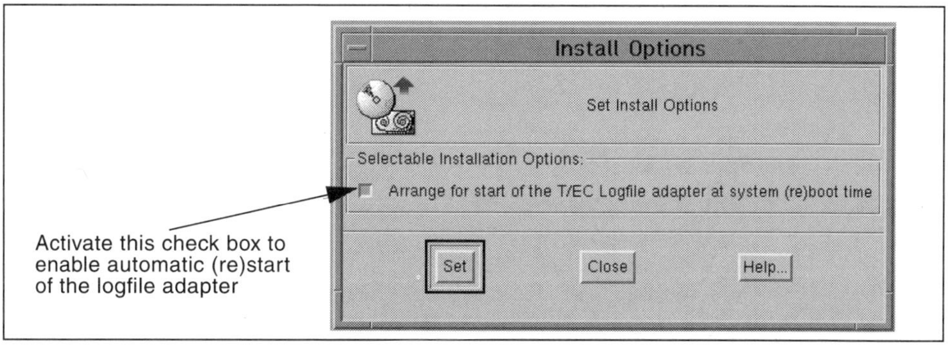

Figure 182. Setting Install Options for the Logfile Adapter Installation

The Logfile adapter receives log messages from the syslogd daemon, reformats them into TME 10 Enterprise Console events, and forwards them to the event server. Thus, the Logfile adapter should be installed on every managed node on which you want to collect events.

For purposes of this exercise, we install the Logfile adapter only on the host where the TME 10 Enterprise Console was installed.

After the installation is complete, exit from the TME 10 desktop.

13.2 Practical Examples Using TME 10 Enterprise Console

In this section, we look at some practical uses of the TME 10 Enterprise Console application.

13.2.1 Our Lab Environment

The lab environment to be used throughout this tutorial is as follows:

TMR Server

- ***ev7*** – RS/6000 running AIX 4.1.4 (TME 10 Framework and TME 10 Enterprise Console installed)

TME 10 Clients

- ***ev2*** – RS/6000 running AIX 4.1.4 (TME 10 Framework installed)
- ***clientnt*** – PC running Windows NT 3.51 (PC agent installed)
- ***cpwarp*** – PC running OS/2 Warp (PC agent installed)
- ***jnwin95*** – PC running Windows 95 (PC agent installed)

All of these machines communicate with each other via the TCP/IP protocol over a token-ring network.

For this tutorial, we show examples from an environment that contains the TME 10 Framework, the TME 10 Enterprise Console software, and its supported products and components. We will not be taking advantage of any of the TME 10 clients.

13.2.2 Logging On to TME 10 and the TME 10 Desktop

From the command line, enter the command `tivoli` to start the TME 10 desktop for your administrator ID. The root ID will have sufficient authorization to perform the exercises listed in the following sections. If you cannot use the *root* ID, then ensure that your administrator ID has the following authorization roles set for your ID: senior, admin, super, and user. Section 8.2.6, "Creating a New Administrator" on page 229, shows how to create a new administrator and assign authorization roles.

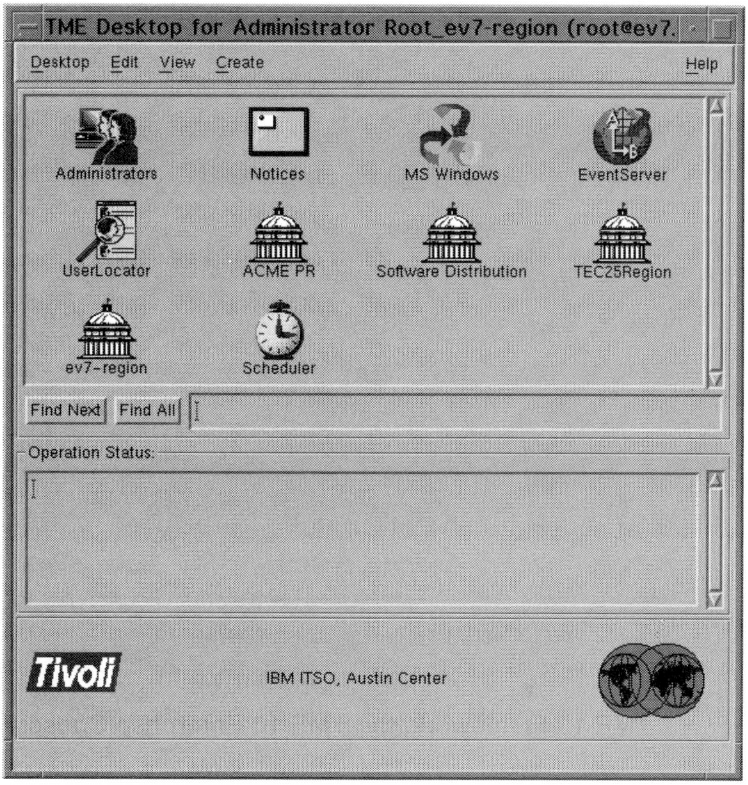

Figure 183. TME 10 Desktop after TME 10 Enterprise Console Installation

The TME 10 desktop now has an additional two icons displayed:

 The EventServer icon represents the event server and all supporting GUI operations for the event server.

 The TEC25 region icon represents a policy region and may be used by the administrator for organizational purposes. It will not be used in any of the following exercises.

13.2.3 Setting Resource Roles

The event server and the TEC25 region are TME 10 resources. In order for the administrator to have access to these resources, administrator roles must be assigned for these new TME 10 resources.

Follow the steps outlined in Figure 184 to give the root administrator the user, admin, senior, and super roles for the EventServer resource.

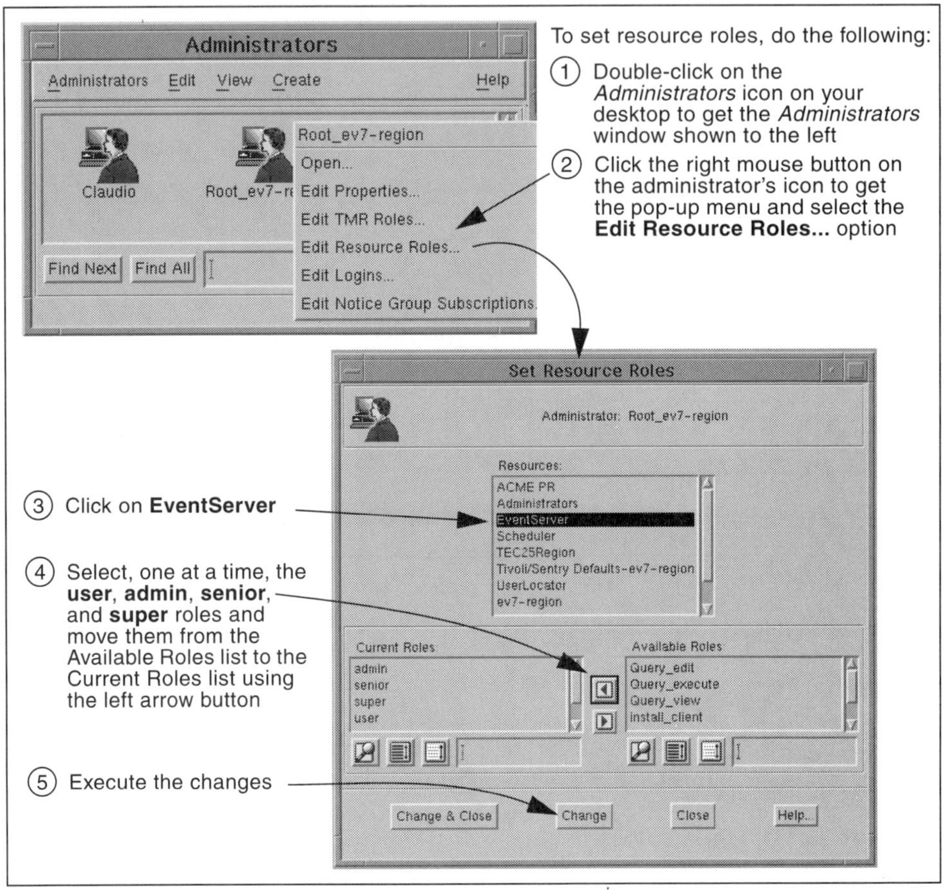

Figure 184. Setting Resource Role

You may get a pop-up window explaining that the changes will not take effect for your administrator ID until you have logged off and logged back into the TME 10 desktop. In this case, select **Dismiss** to dismiss the dialog. We will restart the TME 10 desktop later on.

Perform the same steps for the TEC25Region resource. Now restart the TME 10 desktop. Select **Quit** from the *Desktop* pull-down menu in your TME 10 desktop, and enter the `tivoli` command on the command line, once again, to start the TME 10 desktop.

The changes made now have taken effect for your administrator ID.

13.2.4 Creating and Customizing an Event Console

In order for the administrator to monitor and respond to the events collected by the event server, it is necessary to create an event console on the TME 10 desktop of each administrator responsible for monitoring the computing enterprise. In this exercise, we create the event console for the root administrator ID.

The list of hosts on which the console can execute consists of the TMR server and any TME 10 managed nodes that were installed in earlier chapters.

13.2.4.1 Creating an Event Console

The first step in enabling an administrator to handle events is to create an event console. See Figure 185 on page 336 for instructions on how to create the event console on *ev7* for the root administrator.

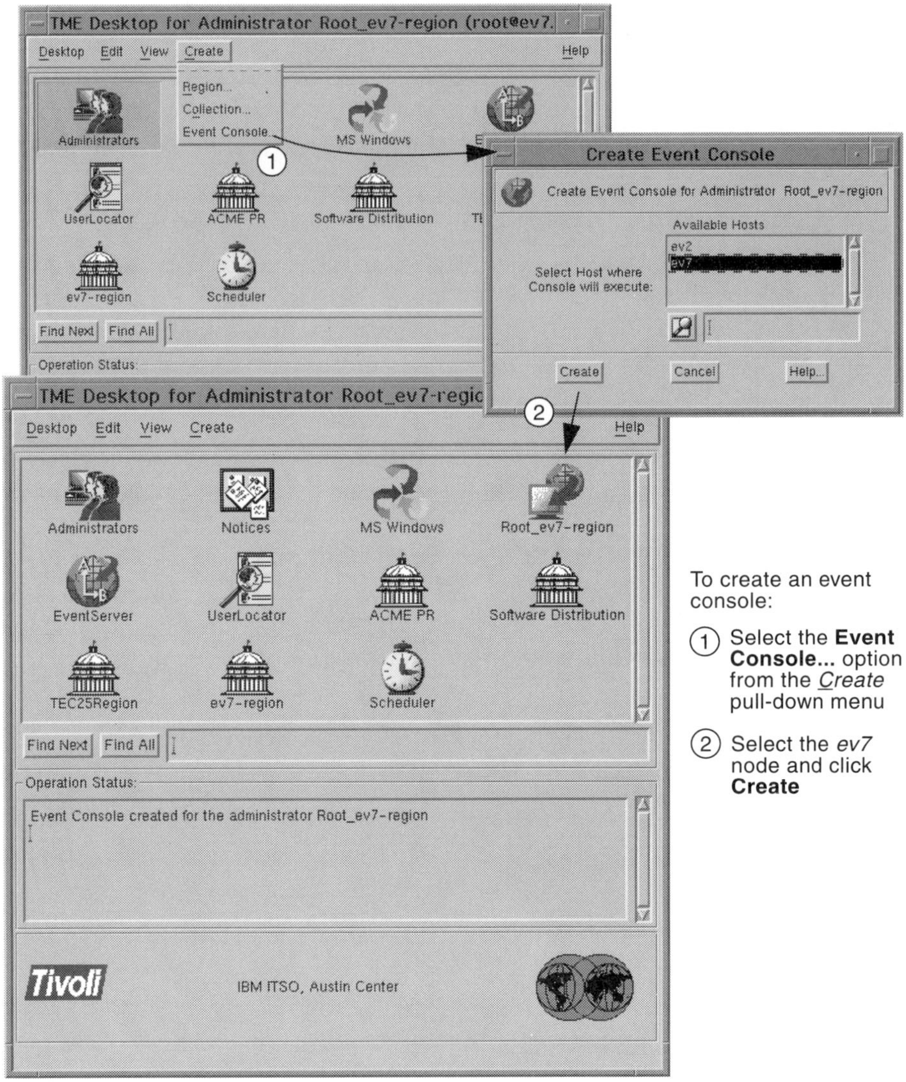

To create an event console:

(1) Select the **Event Console...** option from the *Create* pull-down menu

(2) Select the *ev7* node and click **Create**

Figure 185. Creating an Event Console

 A new icon is added to the TME 10 desktop, which represents the event console for the administrator who owns this desktop. In order to enable other administrators to use an event console, you would have to follow the same steps in the other administrators' desktops. You can access these desktops via the *Administrators* icon on your desktop (see also Figure 184 on page 334).

13.2.4.2 Creating a TME 10 Enterprise Console Source Group

The event console provides two windows to the administrator, a source groups window and an event groups window. The source groups window will present an icon for each event adapter that the administrator needs to monitor. In this exercise, we will add the Logfile adapter to the root administrator's console. Follow the steps outlined in Figure 186.

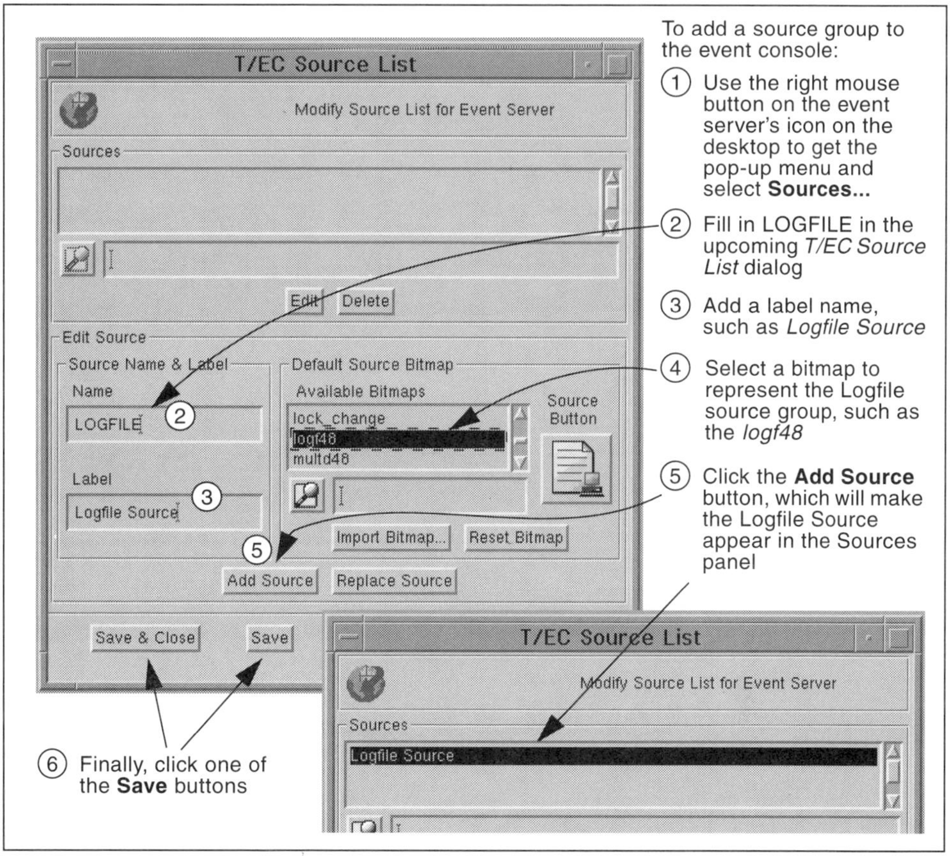

Figure 186. Creating a TME 10 Enterprise Console Event Source

We will not see the effect of these changes until we complete the creation of an event group, start the monitoring operations, and then open the event console.

For more information on the source group, refer to Section 7.7, "Event Console" on page 193.

13.2.4.3 Creating a TME 10 Enterprise Console Event Group

The event groups window, the second window belonging to the event console of an administrator, will present an icon for an arbitrary group of events, possibly from different event adapters. The events may be filtered and grouped for the administrator's convenience in any combination.

In this exercise, we will add the Test Event Group to the root administrator's console. Follow the steps outlined in Figure 187.

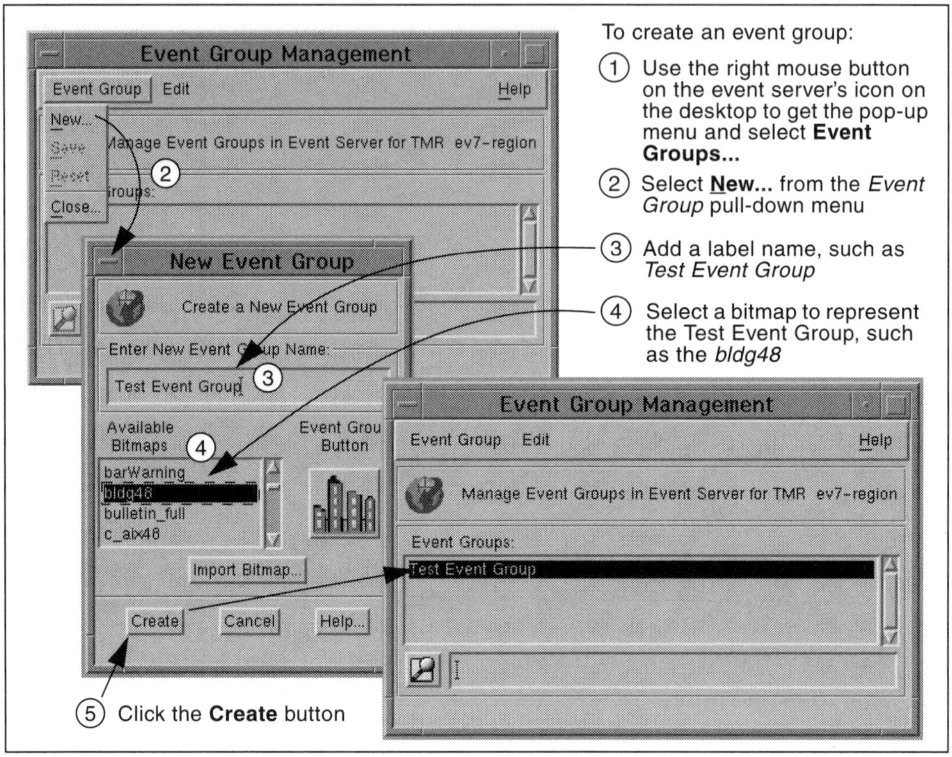

Figure 187. Creating a TME 10 Enterprise Console Event Group

The **Create** button adds the new event group to the list in the *Event Group Management* dialog and immediately sends you to the *Edit Event Group Filters* dialog for this newly created event group, which is discussed in the next section.

For more information on the event group, refer to Section 7.7, "Event Console" on page 193.

13.2.4.4 Creating Filters for the Event Group

Creating an event group automatically takes you to this *Edit Event Group Filters* dialog shown in Figure 188.

We set the filters up such that any incoming event will pass the filters and be displayed on an administrator's event console. In a true production environment, it will be necessary to set several event groups, each having more specific filters. This would permit the administrators to locate the specific problems more easily. A special push button for each filter attribute allows you to select possible filter values from a list that will be displayed. Filter values can encompass a range of values using the wild card character *. For example, you could set a filter criteria to only allow all events incoming from hosts *ev1* through *ev8* to pass the filter. You would then add a value of ev* into the *Origin* field.

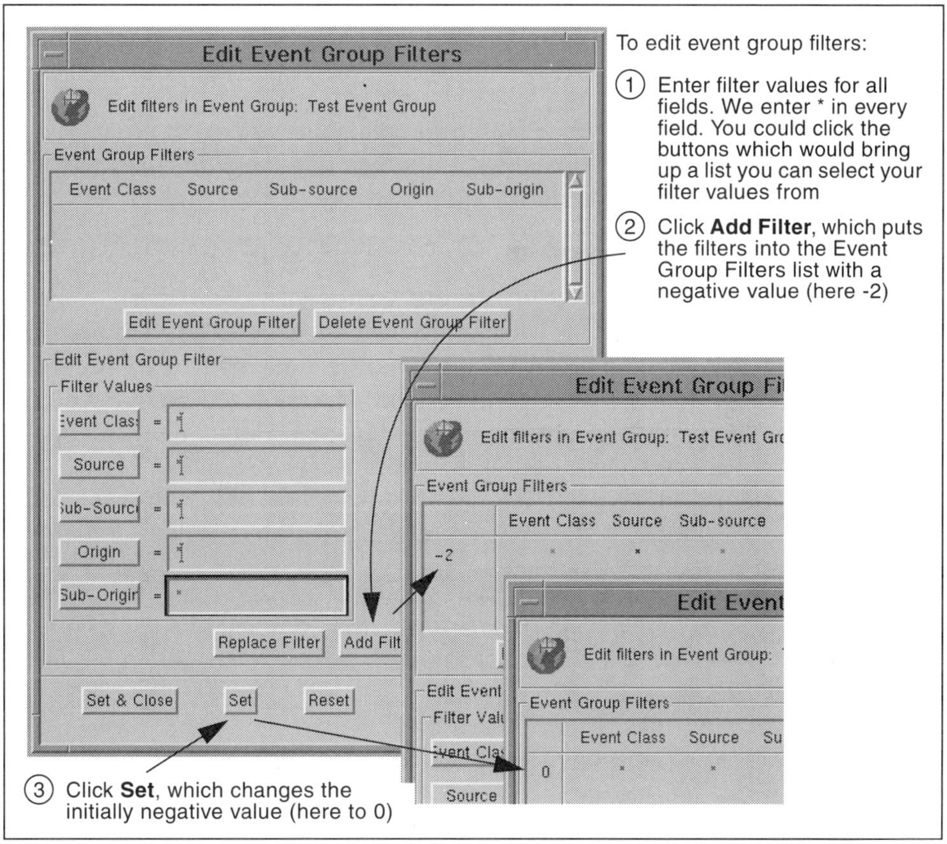

Figure 188. Editing Filters in an Event Group

Select **Close** to close the *Edit Event Group Filters* dialog. You can see the new event group now in the *Event Group Management* dialog shown in Figure 189.

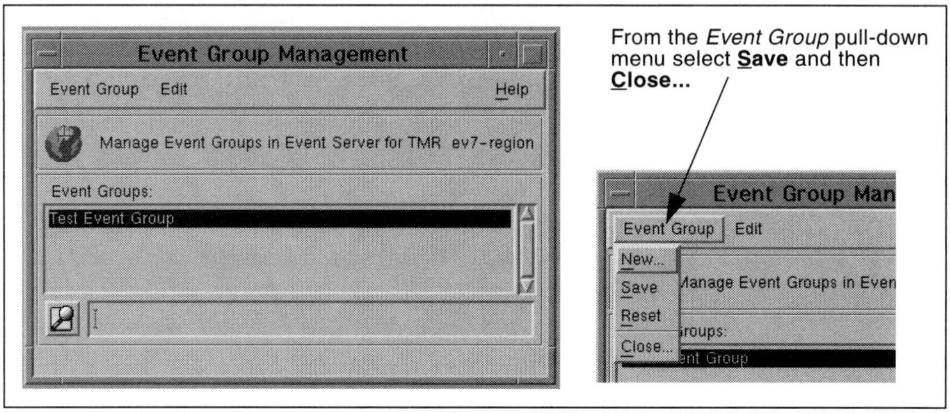

Figure 189. Event Group Management Dialog with a New Event Group

We have explained how you edit filters as part of creating a new event group. In order to edit existing filters, you use the *Edit* pull-down menu in the *Event Group Management* dialog (see Figure 189) and select the **Edit Filters...** option.

13.2.4.5 Assigning Event Groups

It is necessary to assign the event groups to specific administrators and define their authorization roles over the events. In this exercise, we assign the event group to our own administrator ID (root) so that we may monitor events coming from the computing enterprise. Recall that we already defined an event console for our administrator ID in Section 13.2.4.1, "Creating an Event Console" on page 335. For a description of the administrator roles see Section 7.7.1.3, "Events and Administrative Roles" on page 195.

Assigning the event groups is initiated from the event console icon's pop-up menu in the TME 10 desktop of the administrator for whom we want to assign event groups. The necessary steps are illustrated in Figure 190 on page 341.

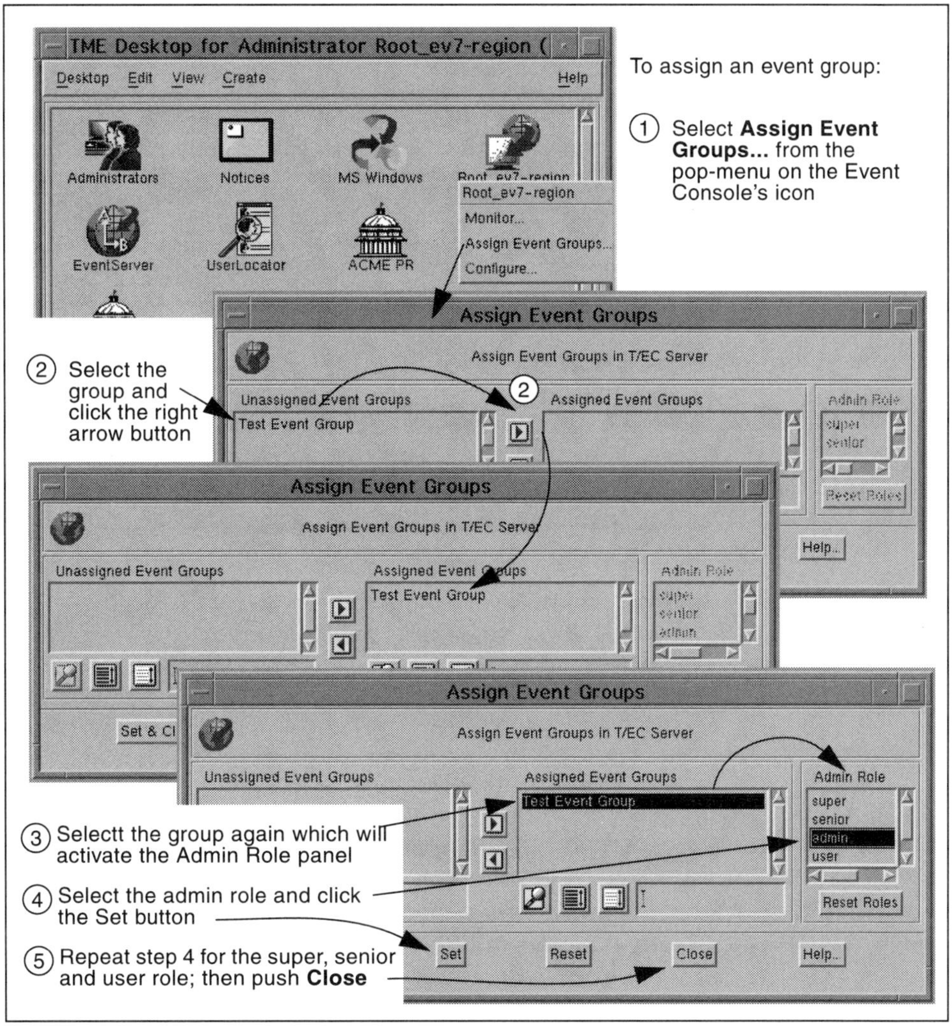

Figure 190. Assigning Event Group Roles to an Administrator

13.2.5 Monitoring and Handling Events

For an administrator to be able to view the events on an event console, the moitoring capability must be activated. Double-clicking on the event console icon will bring up the two windows that constitute the event console shown in Figure 191 on page 342. Another way to initiate the event console is to select the **Monitor...** option from the event console icon's pop-up menu.

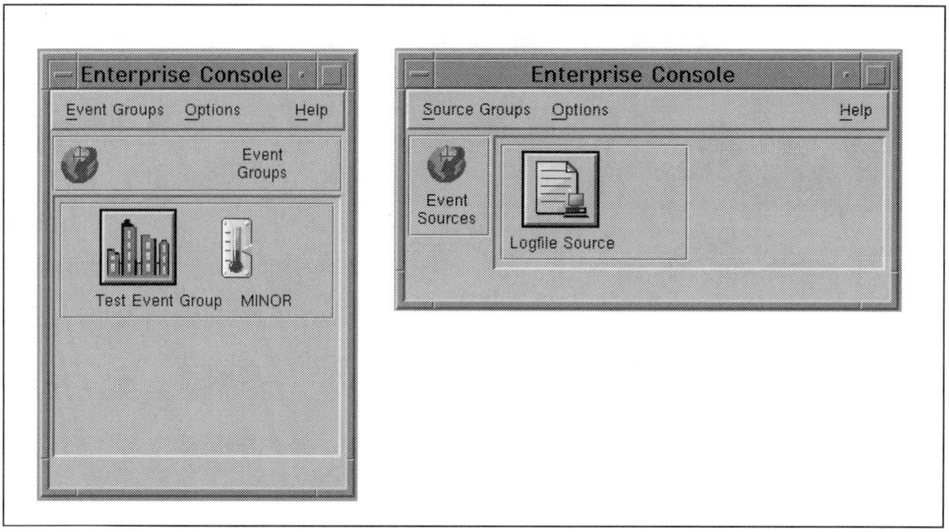

Figure 191. Source Groups and Event Groups

There is already a minor severity event in the event group. As we have not as yet received any events from the Logfile adapter, there are no time stamps, severity indicators, and the like displayed for the sources assigned to this administrator.

13.2.5.1 Viewing the Events

Administrators will need to review the details of the events after they have been received. Click on the **Test Event Group** icon in the *Enterprise Console* window to view the event list.

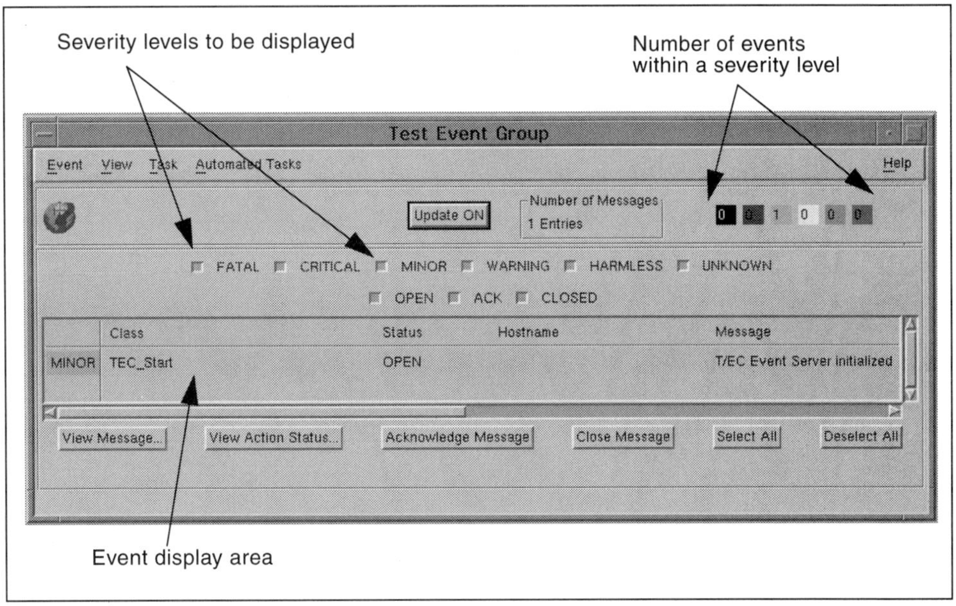

Figure 192. Listing the Test Event Group Events

The window shown in Figure 192 can be customized. Using the *View* pull-down menu, you can specify which of the many attributes are shown and their display order. By selecting the appropriate check boxes, you can also select which status or severity levels should or should not be displayed.

In order to view the details of an event, select the event, and click the **View Message...** button or double-click on the event. This will bring up the *Event Group Message Viewer* dialog shown in Figure 193 on page 344.

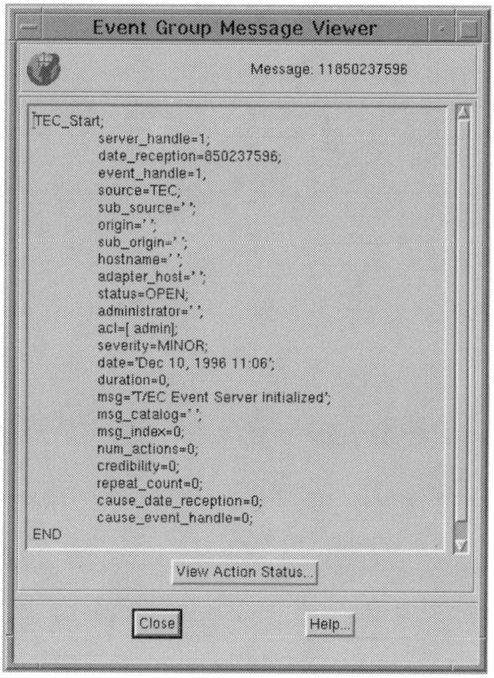

Figure 193. Event Detail

13.2.5.2 Generating Logfile Events

The Logfile adapter installed earlier in this chapter receives messages from the syslogd daemon. The format of the messages that the syslogd daemon receives from the operating system and from applications is not standardized, and therefore the Logfile adapter on every platform may have to be customized to be able to correctly understand and parse the messages coming from the syslogd daemon. If events are not generated as you expect, you might find some useful information in Section 13.2.7, "Tips for Logfile Adapter Handling" on page 361.

Let's first cause an Su_Success event to be created by using the `su` command to switch user accounts from root to claudio:

```
# su claudio
```

As a result of this command, the Logfile adapter sends an event to the event server. You can only see a change in the source groups window because in the event groups window there is still an event with a higher severity. Figure 194 on page 345 shows the resulting event console windows.

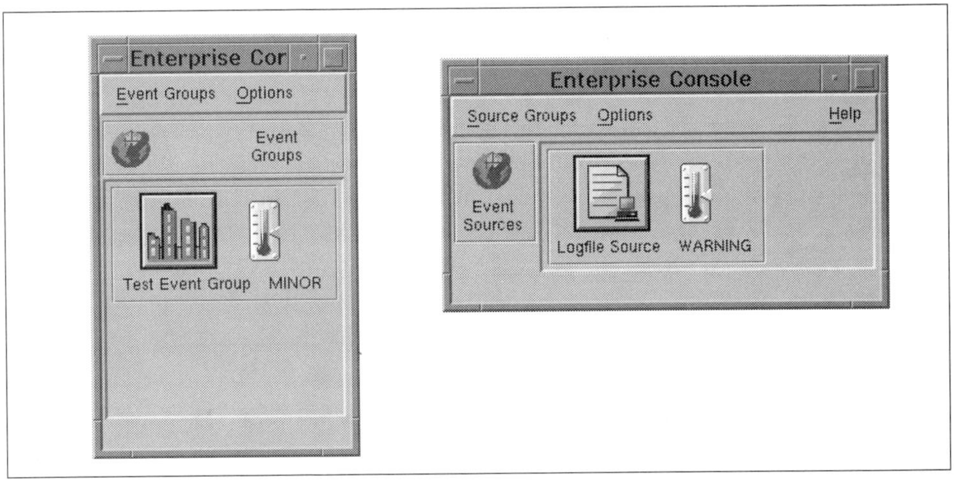

Figure 194. Event Console Windows after an su Command

Next we create some more events using the `wpostemsg` command:

```
# wpostemsg -r WARNING -m "su failure by wpostemsg" Su_Failure LOGFILE
# wpostemsg -r FATAL -m "posted NFS events" NFS_No_Response LOGFILE
```

The result of posting the above two event messages is shown in Figure 195.

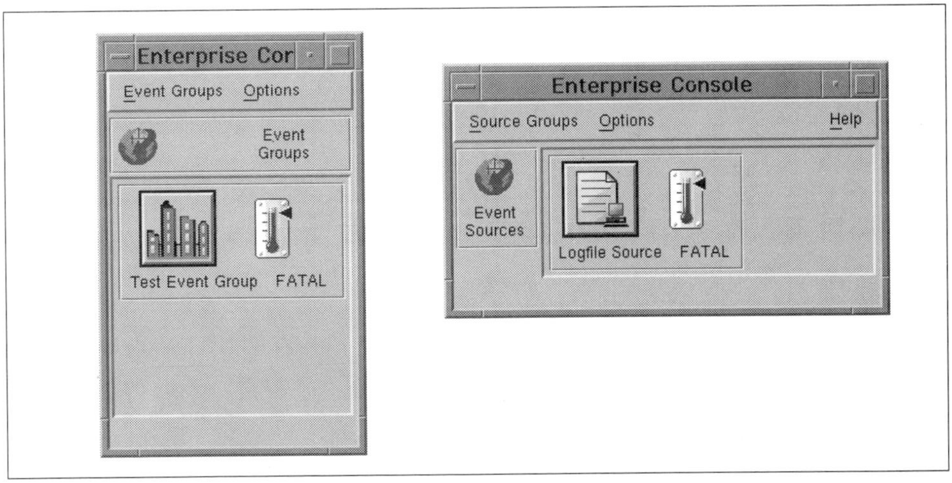

Figure 195. Event Console Windows After Posting Event Messages

13.2.5.3 Customizing the Event Console

Each administrator can customize the personal event console. One option is to change the bitmap or to configure what information is displayed in graphic mode. In Figure 196, you can see how to activate the display of the time stamp of the most recently arrived event with the highest priority.

Note also the **Message Time Limits...** option of the *Options* pull-down menu shown in Figure 196. Here is where you can, for instance, define how long closed events are displayed in your event console. This setting does not affect how long closed events are kept in the database. Other administrators will still see these events as long as they are in the database. In order to define how long closed events are kept in the database, you would set an event server-wide parameter by selecting **Parameters...** from the pop-up menu of the event server icon.

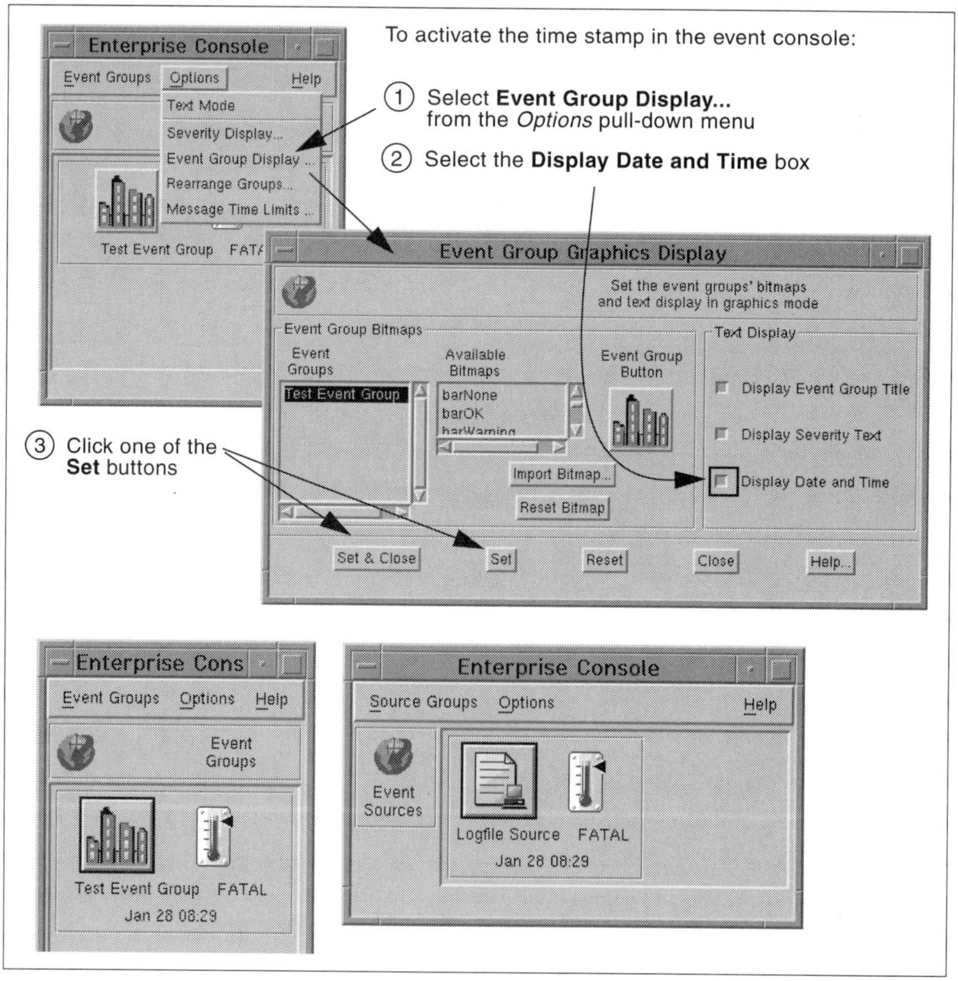

Figure 196. Activating the Time Stamp Display in the Event Console

For all further exercises, we disabled the time stamp again.

13.2.5.4 Acknowledging and Closing an Event

If an administrator has the appropriate permission to change an event, he or she can acknowledge the event(s) and close them later on. In order to do so, select one or more events by highlighting them with the mouse, or select them all by pushing the **Select All** button in the Test Event Group window. Then push either the **Acknowledge Message** or the **Close Message** button.

Events do not have to be acknowledged; they can directly be closed. However, each of these operations is a change request, and the event will go through a new rule processing cycle. Therefore, it might make sense to acknowledge them first, which might trigger some specific, maybe preliminary, actions that are different from the actions upon closing an event.

Figure 197 shows the previously generated events in the OPEN status and, without showing the details of the transaction, in the CLOSED status.

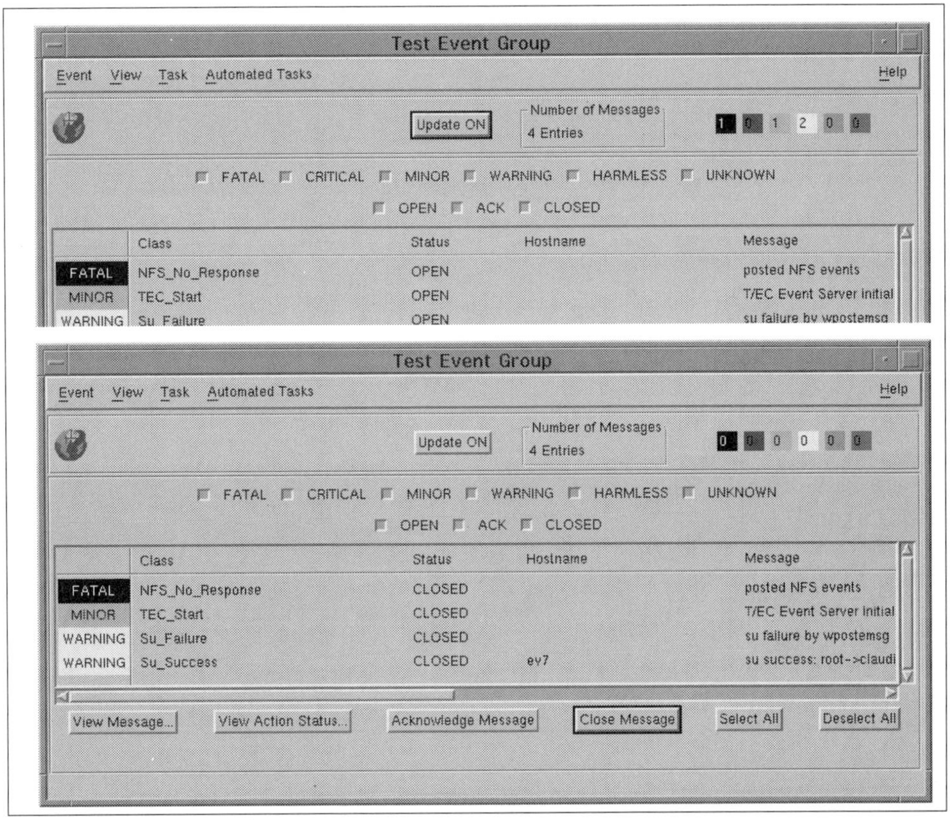

Figure 197. Displaying and Closing the Generated Events

13.2.5.5 Defining Automated Tasks

It is important to make sure that the operators do not get flooded with insignificant events. As we discussed earlier, events can be filtered at the adapter level, in the event server (rules processing), and by event group filters. These filters apply for all operators with access to the same resources. In addition to that, each operator can define tasks that allow them to automate repetitive tasks on specific events.

The *Automated Task* pull-down menu in the Test Event Group window lets the administrator specify conditions and tasks to be run if the event meets the conditions, similar to what can be defined in rules. As an example, if an administrator does not want to be bothered by successful `su` commands, he or she can define a task to close these events automatically.

13.2.6 Customizing Rules

In Section 13.2.5.2, “Generating Logfile Events” on page 344, we created events using the `su` command. Successful and failed `su` commands both generate an event with a severity level of WARNING. We want to relieve all operators from having to close events caused by successful `su` commands. One way to achieve this is to create a rule to downgrade the severity of Su_Success events to HARMLESS and set the status to CLOSED.

13.2.6.1 Listing the Rule Bases

Figure 198 illustrates how you access the rule bases. The *Default* rule base is installed at installation time. It is not modifiable by the TME 10 Enterprise Console Rule Builder. However, it can be used as a basis for development of other rule bases.

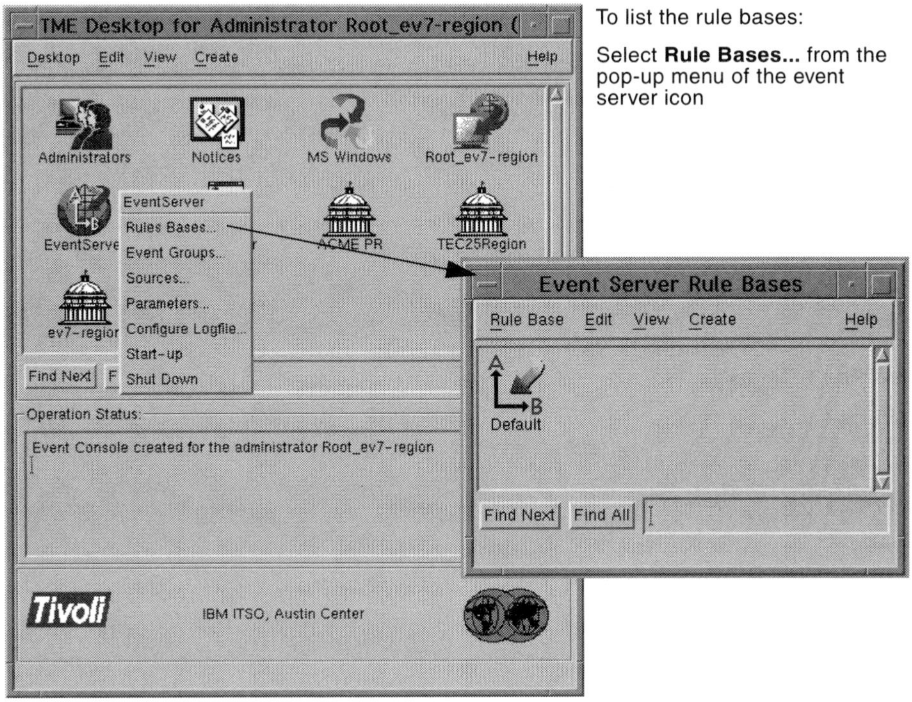

To list the rule bases:

Select **Rule Bases...** from the pop-up menu of the event server icon

Figure 198. Listing the Existing Rule Bases

13.2.6.2 Creating a Rule Base

Let's create a new rule base with the name *Test_Rule_Base.* Follow the steps shown in Figure 199.

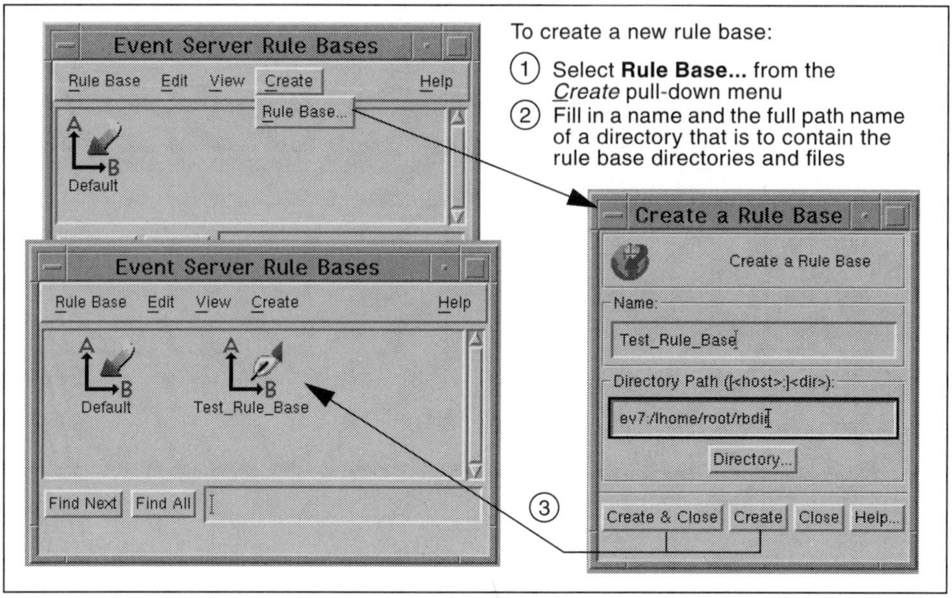

Figure 199. Creating a New Rule Base

In the above example, the *rbdir* directory is created in the */lhome/root* directory on *ev7* and associated with rule base name Test_Rule_Base. Whenever you execute an action against the rule base, such as compiling or loading it, you use the rule base name. TME 10 Enterprise Console internally uses the data structure underneath the *rbdir* directory, which contains the following subdirectories:

```
/lhome/root/rbdir/TEC_CLASSES
/lhome/root/rbdir/TEC_RULES
/lhome/root/rbdir/TEC_TEMPLATES
```

The *Event Server Rule Base* dialog now presents the two rule bases. The icon with the arrow designates the active rule base that has been loaded by the event server.

13.2.6.3 Copying a Rule Base

A new rule base is empty. It is worthwhile to copy an existing rule base to the newly created rule base. The existing rules can be used as a skeleton for further modifications. We copy the content of the default rule base into *Test_Rule_Base* by following the steps shown in Figure 200.

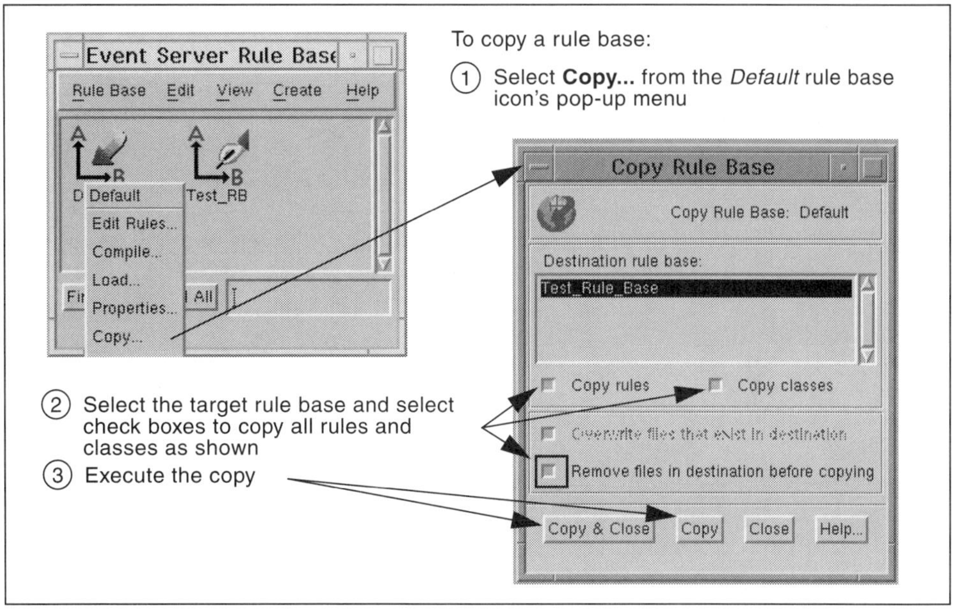

Figure 200. Copying a Rule Base

13.2.6.4 Creating a New Rule Set via the Rule Builder

The pop-up menu of the rule base icon lets you access and use the TME 10 Enterprise Console Rule Builder. In the example shown in Figure 201, we will create a rule set with the Rule Builder.

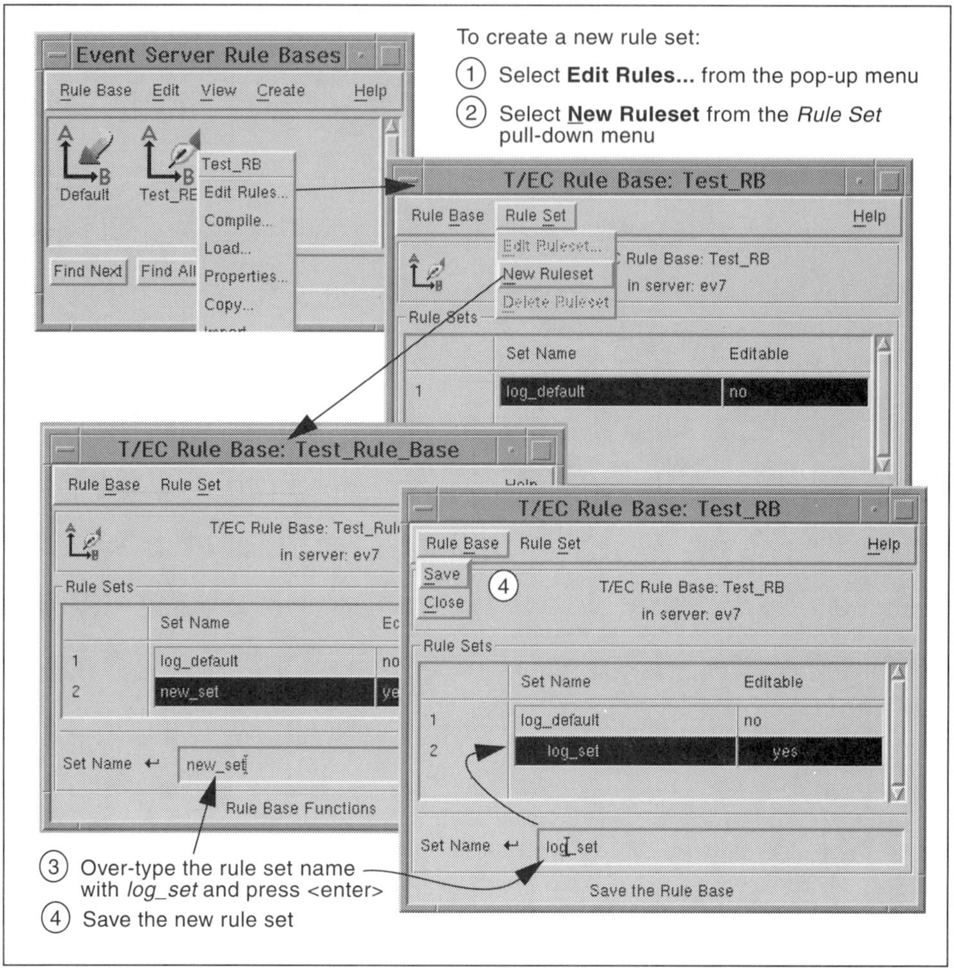

Figure 201. Selecting a Rule Base to Edit

13.2.6.5 Creating a New Rule

Within the new rule set, which is still empty, we are going to create a new simple rule using the Rule Builder. Figure 202 shows you how to create a new rule in the *log_set* rule set.

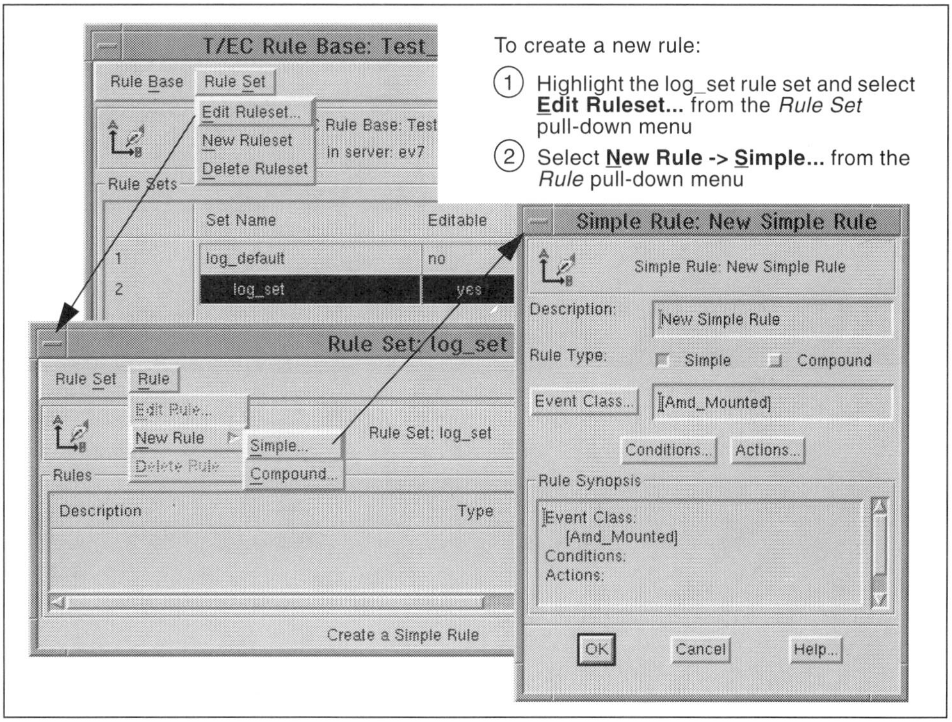

Figure 202. Creating a New Rule within a Rule Set

The new rule then has to be customized. You need to define the event class(es) to which the rule applies, a list of conditions that the event(s) has to meet, and actions that are taken if the event(s) meets the conditions. Figure 203 on page 354 explains how to do this.

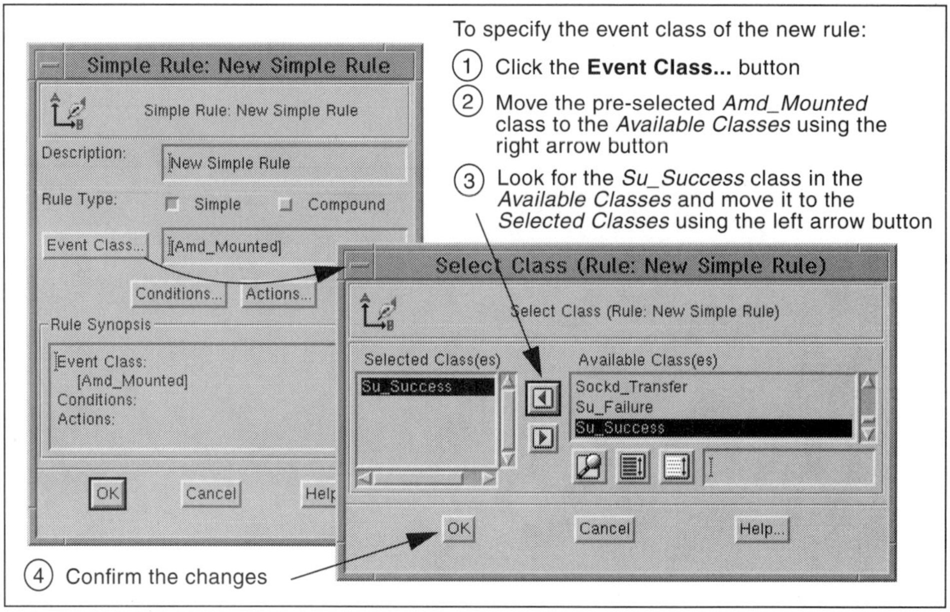

Figure 203. Specifying the Event Class for a New Rule

The next step is to define one or more conditions the event of class Su_Success must meet before any actions are executed. In our example in Figure 204 on page 355, we want to process *Su_Success* events only if they come from a system with hostname *ev7*. We could add more host names to the list, and we could further restrict this condition by adding additional conditions. For example, we could decide to keep these events only if the target user of the `su` command is root.

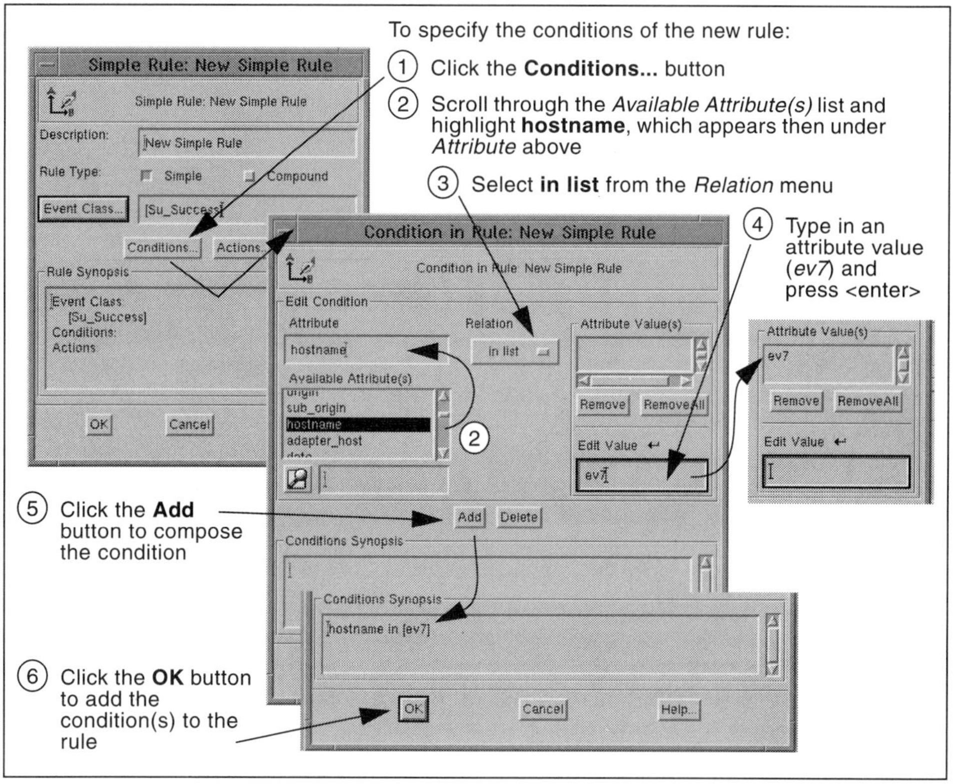

Figure 204. Composing Conditions for a New Rule

Clicking the **OK** button returns you to the *Simple Rule* dialog where we now want to add actions. Note that in Figure 205 on page 356 the *Rule Synopsis* text panel has been updated to reflect our selections made so far.

The default severity of the *Su_Success* event is *WARNING*. We don't want to be bothered by successful `su` commands, so in the following example in Figure 205 on page 356, we will set the severity to *HARMLESS* and the status to *CLOSED*. In this way, the events will be visible for as long as you keep closed messages in your event console. Another option would be to drop the events completely.

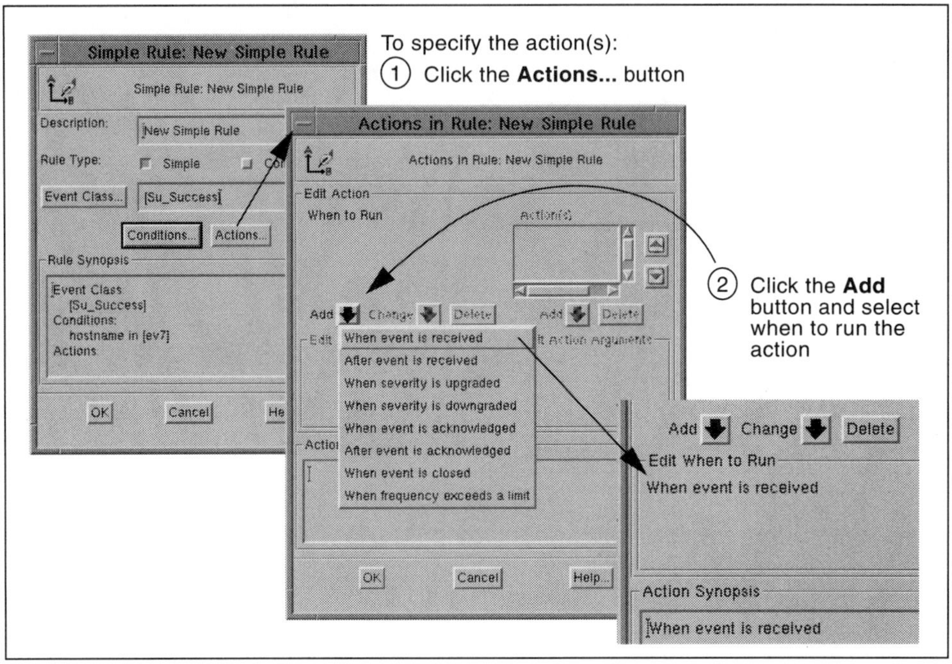

Figure 205. Adding Actions to a New Rule

After defining when the action is executed, we need to define what the action will be. This is depicted in Figure 206 on page 357 and Figure 207 on page 358.

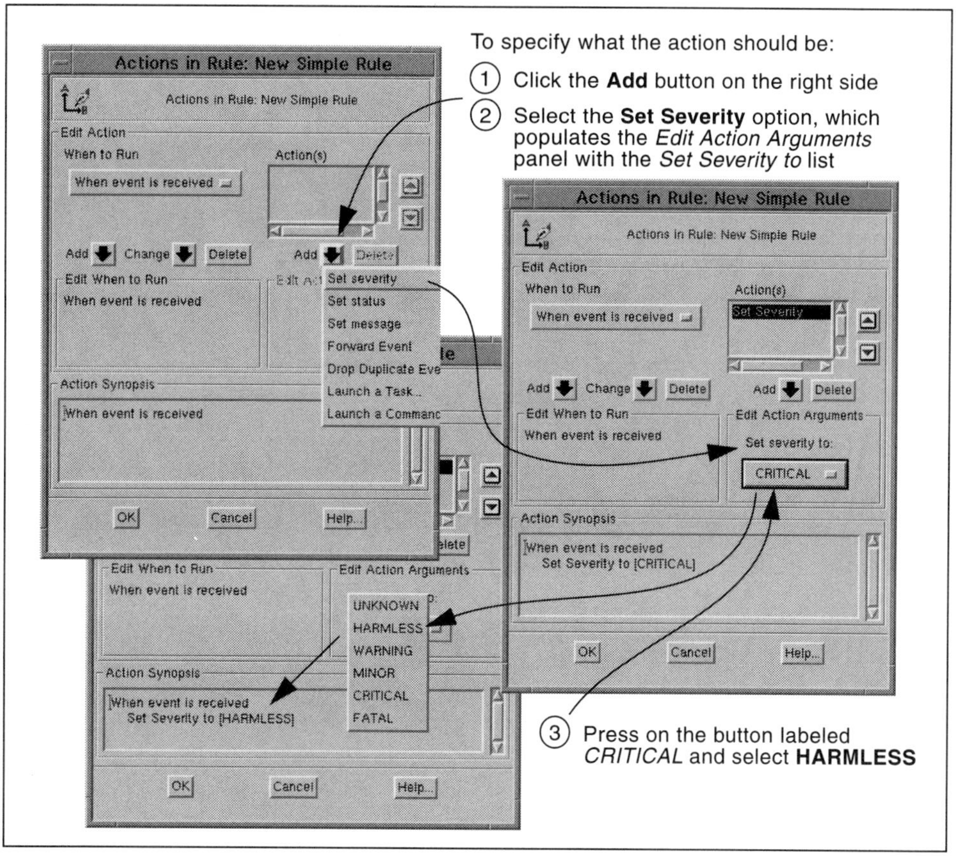

Figure 206. Selecting the Type of Action

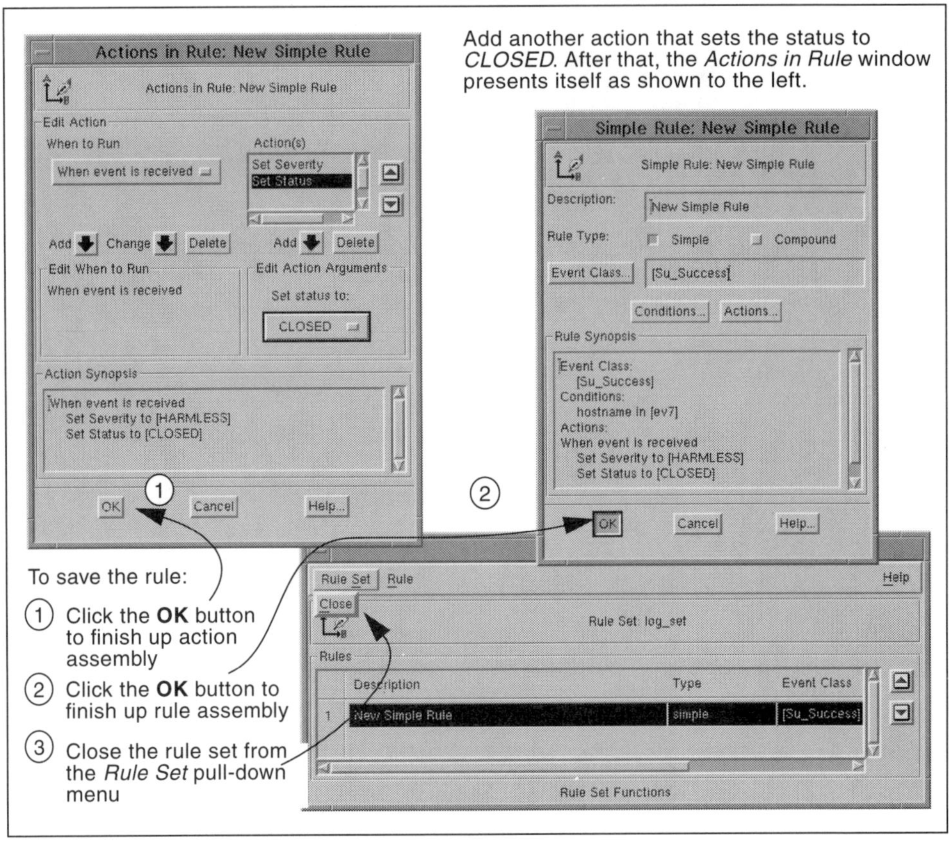

Figure 207. Finishing the New Rule and Closing the Rule Set

The new rule set is not saved until you save the rule base. In other words, if you close the rule base dialog now without saving, the newly added rule set will be gone. Figure 208 on page 359 shows you how to save the rule base.

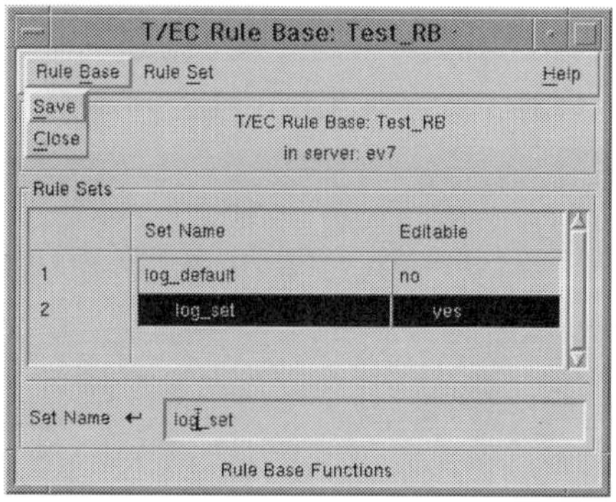

Figure 208. Saving the Rule Base

13.2.6.6 Compiling the New Rule Base

Before the rule base can be activated, it must be compiled. This can be done from the pop-up menu of the Test_RB icon, as shown in Figure 209.

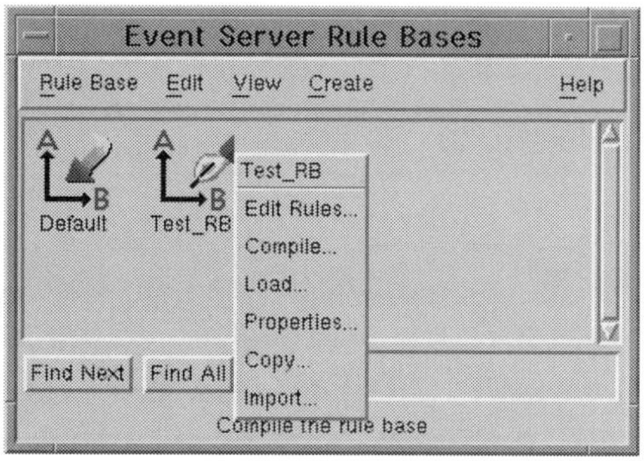

To compile the rule base:

Select **Compile...** from the pop-up menu of the Test_RB icon

Figure 209. Compiling the Rule Base

Temporary Bug in Rule Builder?

In the version of TME 10 Enterprise Console that we were testing, the compilation of the rule base seemed to have completed successfully, but in fact the rule base was not correctly built. In order to make the rule base work, we had to compile it outside of the Rule Builder with the following command:

```
# wcomprules Test_RB
```

This problem might be fixed in the current release of TME 10 Enterprise Console.

13.2.6.7 Loading the New Rule Base

Now, the rule base needs to be activated. By loading the Test_RB rule base, you replace the currently active default rule base. Once loaded, the Test_RB gets the red arrow indicating that it is the active rule base.

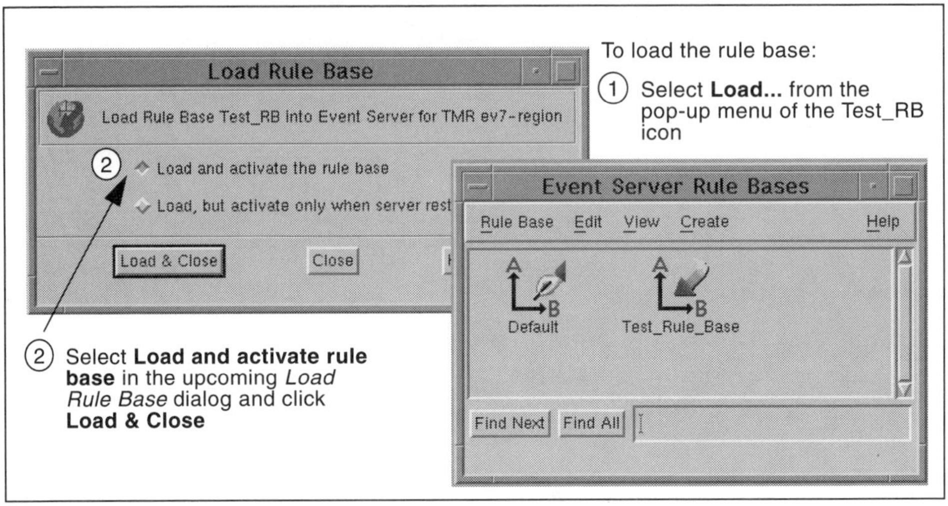

Figure 210. Loading the Rule Base

The event server does not have to be stopped if only rules are changed. If you change class definitions, you need to restart the event server when loading a rule base. The `wloadrb -u Test_RB` command loads a rule base without restarting the event server, which has the same effect as the procedure shown in Figure 210.

13.2.6.8 Stopping and Starting the Event Server

In order to stop and restart the event server, you must have the senior authorization role assigned to your administrator ID. Then simply use the pop-up menu associated with the EventServer icon on the TME 10 desktop, and select **Shut Down** and then **Start-up**.

13.2.6.9 Testing the New Rule Base

In order to test the new rule base, we use the `su` command:

```
# su - claudio
$ su - root
root's Password: WRONG_PW
3004-501 Cannot su to "root" : Authentication is denied.
```

This will generate the event shown in Figure 211. Note that the successful `su` command now generated a harmless event that is already closed.

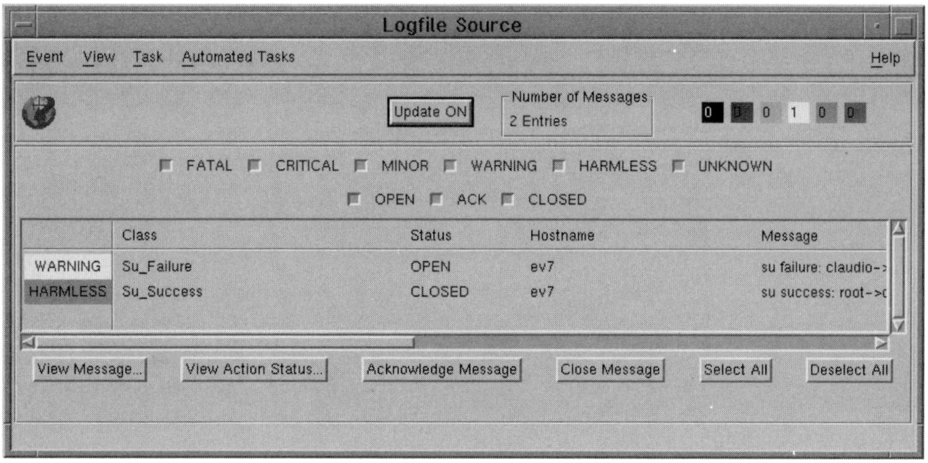

Figure 211. Events after Being Processed by the New Rule

13.2.7 Tips for Logfile Adapter Handling

The following tips may be helpful in finding problems when the Logfile adapter is not sending the events you expect when you perform actions on your system to generate events:

- The Logfile adapter has a configuration file that specifies filters. The configuration file is:

  `/etc/Tivoli/tecad/etc/tecad_logfile.conf`

  The filters specify classes that are *not* forwarded to the event server. The default file contains the following entries:

  ```
  Filter:Class=Logfile_Base
  Filter:Class=Logfile_Sendmail
  Filter:Class=Amd_Unmounted
  Filter:Class=Amd_Mounted
  ```

- The Logfile adapter parses every incoming message from the syslogd and tries to assign a class name and slot values. All classes are derived from the base class, named Logfile_Base. If an event cannot be parsed, it will be assigned the Logfile_Base class and will eventually be filtered out (dropped).

- In order to allow, for instance, Logfile_Base events to pass the filter, comment the line out, and recycle the Logfile adapter by killing and restarting its process. On the event server machine, you can stop and start the event server.

- If an action that you perform in the operating system does not generate the expected event, you can temporarily subscribe a disk file to the syslogd. In order to do so, edit the /etc/syslog.conf file, and add a line like the following:

  ```
  *.emerg;*.alert;*.crit;*.err;*.warning;*.notice;*.info  /tmp/syslog.out
  ```

  Then recycle the syslogd daemon. In AIX you would use the following command rather than signaling or killing the process:

  ```
  # refresh syslogd
  ```

  Use the following command to view the syslogd output:

  ```
  # tail -f /tmp/syslog.out
  ```

  Perform some actions on your system, and see whether and what syslogd is reporting.

  Do not forget to take the line out of the syslog.conf file after you are done debugging, and recycle the syslogd daemon.

- Finally, if syslogd is reporting a system event but the Logfile adapter does not correctly parse it, you can edit the following file:

  ```
  /etc/Tivoli/tecad/etc/tecad_logfile.fmt
  ```

  Editing this file requires some basic C programming skills. In order to activate, you need to restart the Logfile adapter process. You may want to start the adapter in debug mode using:

  ```
  # tecad_logfile -n -d -c /etc/Tivoli/tecad/etc/tecad_logfile.conf
  ```

For more information on the Logfile adapter, see the *TME 10 Enterprise Console Event Adapter Guide - Logile.*

PART 3

Appendices

Appendix A. Special Notices

This publication is intended to help anyone who wonders what the Tivoli TME 10 product family is and what it does to understand the architecture and concepts of the TME 10 core products. It also walks the reader step by step through the installation and some simple examples of the product usage. The information in this publication is not intended as the specification of any programming interfaces that are provided by the TME10 core components at Version Level 3.0. See the PUBLICATIONS section of the IBM Programming Announcement for TME 10 for more information about what publications are considered to be product documentation.

References in this publication to IBM products, programs or services do not imply that IBM intends to make these available in all countries in which IBM operates. Any reference to an IBM product, program, or service is not intended to state or imply that only IBM's product, program, or service may be used. Any functionally equivalent program that does not infringe any of IBM's intellectual property rights may be used instead of the IBM product, program or service.

Information in this book was developed in conjunction with use of the equipment specified and is limited in application to those specific hardware and software products and levels.

IBM may have patents or pending patent applications covering subject matter in this document. The furnishing of this document does not give you any license to these patents. You can send license inquiries, in writing, to the IBM Director of Licensing, IBM Corporation, 500 Columbus Avenue, Thornwood, NY 10594 USA.

Licensees of this program who wish to have information about it for the purpose of enabling: (i) the exchange of information between independently created programs and other programs (including this one) and (ii) the mutual use of the information which has been exchanged, should contact IBM Corporation, Dept. 600A, Mail Drop 1329, Somers, NY 10589 USA.

Such information may be available, subject to appropriate terms and conditions, including in some cases, payment of a fee.

The information contained in this document has not been submitted to any formal IBM test and is distributed AS IS. The information about non-IBM ("vendor") products in this manual has been supplied by the vendor and IBM assumes no responsibility for its accuracy or completeness. The use of this information or the implementation of any of these techniques is a customer responsibility and depends on the customer's ability to evaluate and integrate them into the customer's operational environment. While each item may have been reviewed by IBM for accuracy in a specific situation, there is no guarantee that the same or similar results will be obtained elsewhere. Customers attempting to adapt these techniques to their own environments do so at their own risk.

Reference to PTF numbers that have not been released through the normal distribution process does not imply general availability. The purpose of including these reference numbers is to alert IBM customers to specific information relative to the implementation of the PTF when it becomes available to each customer according to the normal IBM PTF distribution process.

The following terms are trademarks of the International Business Machines Corporation in the United States and/or other countries:.

ADSTAR®	AIX®
AS/400®	BookManager®
HACMP/6000	IBM®
NetView®	OS/2®
RS/6000®	SystemView®

The following terms are trademarks of other companies:

UNIX is a registered trademark in the United States and other countries licensed exclusively through X/Open Company Limited.

Microsoft, Windows, and the Windows 95 logo are trademarks or registered trademarks of Microsoft Corporation.

Other company, product, and service names may be trademarks or service marks of others.

Appendix B. Related Publications

The publications listed in this section are considered particularly suitable for a more detailed discussion of the topics covered in this redbook.

B.1 International Technical Support Organization Publications

For information on ordering these ITSO publications see "How To Get ITSO Redbooks" on page 369.

- *Setting Up a TME 3.0 NT Environment,* SG24-4819
- *TME 3.0 NT - Automated Processes*, SG24-4793
- *TME 10 Cookbook for AIX Systems Management and Networking*, SG24-4867
- *Migrating NetView DM/6000 Release 1.2 to TME 10 Software Distribution*, SG24-4621
- *An Introduction to TME 10 Performance Monitoring*, SG24-4644
- *TME 10 Software Distribution - Mobile Clients*, SG24-4854
- *Examples of Using TME 10 NetView for Windows NT*, SG24-4898

B.2 Redbooks on CD-ROMs

Redbooks are also available on CD-ROMs. **Order a subscription** and receive updates 2-4 times a year at significant savings.

B.3 Other Publications with IBM Form Numbers

These publications are also relevant as further information sources (although they use old product names, they contain the latest documentation):

- *Tivoli Management Platform Documentation Kit*, SK2T-6058
- *Tivoli/Admin Documentation Kit*, SK2T-6055
- *Tivoli/Courier Documentation Kit*, SK2T-6046
- *Tivoli/Sentry Documentation Kit*, SK2T-6052
- *Tivoli/Enterprise Console Documentation Kit*, SK2T-6050
- *Event Integration Facility User's Guide*, GC31-8337

B.4 TME 10 Information on the World Wide Web (WWW)

A great deal of information on TME 10 is available via the Web. To access it, start with the following URL:

```
http://www.tivoli.com
```

How To Get ITSO Redbooks

This section explains how both customers and IBM employees can find out about ITSO redbooks, CD-ROMs, workshops, and residencies. A form for ordering books and CD-ROMs is also provided.

This information was current at the time of publication, but is continually subject to change. The latest information may be found at URL http://www.redbooks.ibm.com.

How IBM Employees Can Get ITSO Redbooks

Employees may request ITSO deliverables (redbooks, BookManager® BOOKs, and CD-ROMs) and information about redbooks, workshops, and residencies in the following ways:

- **PUBORDER** – to order hardcopies in United States
- **GOPHER link to the Internet** – type GOPHER WTSCPOK.ITSO.IBM.COM
- **Tools disks**

  To get LIST3820s of redbooks, type one of the following commands:

  ```
  TOOLS SENDTO EHONE4 TOOLS2 REDPRINT GET SG24xxxx PACKAGE
  TOOLS SENDTO CANVM2 TOOLS REDPRINT GET SG24xxxx PACKAGE (Canadian users only)
  ```

  To get lists of redbooks:

  ```
  TOOLS SENDTO USDIST MKTTOOLS MKTTOOLS GET ITSOCAT TXT
  TOOLS SENDTO USDIST MKTTOOLS MKTTOOLS GET LISTSERV PACKAGE
  ```

  To register for information on workshops, residencies, and redbooks:

  ```
  TOOLS SENDTO WTSCPOK TOOLS ZDISK GET ITSOREGI 1996
  ```

  For a list of product area specialists in the ITSO:

  ```
  TOOLS SENDTO WTSCPOK TOOLS ZDISK GET ORGCARD PACKAGE
  ```

- **Redbooks Home Page on the World Wide Web**

  http://w3.itso.ibm.com/redbooks

- **IBM Direct Publications Catalog on the World Wide Web**

  http://www.elink.ibmlink.ibm.com/pbl/pbl

  IBM employees may obtain LIST3820s of redbooks from this page.

- **REDBOOKS category on INEWS**
- **Online** – send orders to: USIB6FPL at IBMMAIL or DKIBMBSH at IBMMAIL
- **Internet Listserver**

  With an Internet e-mail address, anyone can subscribe to an IBM Announcement Listserver. To initiate the service, send an e-mail note to announce@webster.ibmlink.ibm.com with the keyword subscribe in the body of the note (leave the subject line blank). A category form and detailed instructions will be sent to you.

How Customers Can Get ITSO Redbooks

Customers may request ITSO deliverables (redbooks, BookManager BOOKs, and CD-ROMs) and information about redbooks, workshops, and residencies in the following ways:

- **Online Orders** (Do not send credit card information over the Internet) – send orders to:

	IBMMAIL	**Internet**
In United States	usib6fpl at ibmmail	usib6fpl@ibmmail.com
In Canada	caibmbkz at ibmmail	lmannix@vnet.ibm.com
Outside North America	dkibmbsh at ibmmail	bookshop@dk.ibm.com

- **Telephone orders**

United States (toll free)	1-800-879-2755
Canada (toll free)	1-800-IBM-4YOU
Outside North America	(long distance charges apply)
(+45) 4810-1320 - Danish	(+45) 4810-1020 - German
(+45) 4810-1420 - Dutch	(+45) 4810-1620 - Italian
(+45) 4810-1540 - English	(+45) 4810-1270 - Norwegian
(+45) 4810-1670 - Finnish	(+45) 4810-1120 - Spanish
(+45) 4810-1220 - French	(+45) 4810-1170 - Swedish

- **Mail Orders** – send orders to:

IBM Publications	IBM Publications	IBM Direct Services
Publications Customer Support	144-4th Avenue, S.W.	Sortemosevej 21
P.O. Box 29570	Calgary, Alberta T2P 3N5	DK-3450 Allerød
Raleigh, NC 27626-0570	Canada	Denmark
USA		

- **Fax** – send orders to:

United States (toll free)	1-800-445-9269
Canada	1-800-267-4455
Outside North America	(+45) 48 14 2207 (long distance charge)

- **1-800-IBM-4FAX (United States)** or **(+1) 408 256 5422 (Outside USA)** – ask for:

  Index # 4421 Abstracts of new redbooks
  Index # 4422 IBM redbooks
  Index # 4420 Redbooks for last six months

- **Direct Services** – send note to softwareshop@vnet.ibm.com

- **On the World Wide Web**

Redbooks Home Page	http://www.redbooks.ibm.com
IBM Direct Publications Catalog	http://www.elink.ibmlink.ibm.com/pbl/pbl

- **Internet Listserver**

  With an Internet e-mail address, anyone can subscribe to an IBM Announcement Listserver. To initiate the service, send an e-mail note to announce@webster.ibmlink.ibm.com with the keyword subscribe in the body of the note (leave the subject line blank).

IBM Redbook Order Form

Please send me the following:

Title	Order Number	Quantity

First name | Last name

Company

Address

City | Postal code | Country

Telephone number | Telefax number | VAT number

☐ Invoice to customer number

☐ Credit card number

Credit card expiration date | Card issued to | Signature

We accept American Express, Diners, Eurocard, Master Card, and Visa. Payment by credit card not available in all countries. Signature mandatory for credit card payment.

DO NOT SEND CREDIT CARD INFORMATION OVER THE INTERNET.

List of Abbreviations

ADE	Advanced Developer's Environment
AEF	Application Extension Facility
ARS	Action Request System
BAROC	Basic Recorder of Objects in C
CLI	Command Line Interface
CORBA	Common Object Request Broker Architecture
DHCP	Dynamic Host Configuration Protocol
DSM	Distributed Systems Management
EIF	Event Integration Facility
GEM	Global Enterprise Manager
GUI	Graphical User Interface
IBM	International Business Machines Corporation
IP	Internet Protocol
IPX/SPX	Internet Packet eXchange / Sequenced Packet eXchange
ITSO	International Technical Support Organization
LCF	Light Client Framework old: Logfile Configuration Facility
LFE	Logfile Format Editor
MIF	Mangement Information Format
MDist	Multiplexed Distribution
MOTD	Message of the Day
MVS	Multiple Virtual Storage
NCF	NetWare Command Files
NDS	NetWare Directory Services
NFS	Network File System
NIS	Network Information System
NLM	NetWare Loadable Modules
NWMS	NetWare Managed Site
OMG	Object Management Group
PROFS	Professional Office System
RCS	Revision Control System
RDBMS	Relational Database Management System
RIM	RDBMS Interface Module
Remedy/ARS	Remedy Action Request System
SPX	Sequenced Packet eXchange
TME	Tivoli Management Environment
TMP	Tivoli Management Platform
TMR	Tivoli Management Region
TNWR	TME NetWare Repeater
TRIP	TME Remote Execution Service

Index

D

J

K

L

M

Q

R

S